John Ford's
Westerns

John Ford's Westerns

A Thematic Analysis, with a Filmography

by WILLIAM DARBY

McFarland & Company, Inc., Publishers
Jefferson, North Carolina, and London

British Library Cataloguing-in-Publication data are available

Library of Congress Cataloguing-in-Publication Data

Darby, William, 1942–
    John Ford's westerns : a thematic analysis, with a filmography /
by William Darby.
        p.   cm.
    Filmography: p.
    Includes bibliographical references and index.   ∞
    ISBN 0-7864-0080-3 (lib. bdg. : 50# alk. paper)
    1. Ford, John 1894–1973 — Criticism and interpretation.   I. Title.
PN1998.3.F65D37   1996
791.43'0233'092 — dc20   96-4041
                                                                     CIP

Manufactured in the United States of America

*McFarland & Company, Inc., Publishers
    Box 611, Jefferson, North Carolina 28640*

To my father, William L. Darby

Table of Contents

Acknowledgments   ix

Introduction   1

1 Ford and the Filming of the West   5
2 *Straight Shooting, The Iron Horse,* and *Three Bad Men*   16
3 Thematic and Narrative Continuities: *Drums Along
       the Mohawk* and *How the West Was Won*   22
4 *The Horse Soldiers*   38
5 Ford's Western Literary Sources and Their Adaptations   56
6 *Fort Apache* and *Rio Grande*   82
7 *She Wore a Yellow Ribbon* and *Sergeant Rutledge*   118
8 *My Darling Clementine* and *The Man Who Shot
       Liberty Valance*   147
9 *Wagonmaster* and *Two Rode Together*   185
10 *Three Godfathers* and *The Searchers*   216
11 *Stagecoach* and *Cheyenne Autumn*   249

Conclusion   279
Notes   283
Bibliography   287
Filmography: Ford's Westerns   289
Index   298

Acknowledgments

My principal intellectual debts are owed to many of the writers on Ford and westerns, who are cited in the bibliography.

In addition, I would like to thank Professor Eric Lunde, of the American Thought and Language Department of Michigan State University, and Professor Frank Beaver, of the Communications Department of the University of Michigan, for encouraging me very early in this project in ways that they have undoubtedly forgotten by now.

Claire Brandt, of Eddie Brandt's Saturday Matinee, went far beyond the usual call of duty in finding still photos for this book, and I am again in her debt.

My good friend Bernie Cohan not only listened patiently to many of these ideas but also improved them through our conversations. I thank him for his criticisms and, of course, exonerate him from any blame for the finished product.

Finally, there is my beloved wife, Carolyn, who has always supplied a most welcome "anchor to windward" for my writing endeavors.

Introduction

John Ford completed his last western, *Cheyenne Autumn*, in 1964. Since that time his position as one of the leading directors in American and world cinema has been established and enhanced by numerous biographical and critical studies.[1] In what follows, I have taken Ford's exalted status, which was extended to him by contemporary as well as later observers, as a given. My aim is not to place him inside any theory of cinematic authorship or to filter his work through some current ideological sieve but rather to demonstrate the high degrees of thematic and artistic coherence in his western films. Like any director, Ford must be judged by the abilities of his works to augment themes through narrative structure, technical finish, dramatic actions, and sophisticated characterizations. When viewed for such qualities, Ford's westerns can be appreciated as both entertainments and serious works.

Anyone writing about Ford, like anyone writing about William Shakespeare, might be moved to apologize for daring to think that anything new, let alone original, can be said about a recognized master. Such objections as "Why Ford?" and, even more pressingly, "Why just his westerns?" have to be addressed, since they reflect much popular thinking about any work of film criticism not immediately focused on what is currently being shown on theater screens.

The simplest answer to these questions is, of course, the one most likely to arouse distrust. Ford is a protean artist whose meanings no single critical approach is ever likely to exhaust. His films clearly enjoy an ongoing life, so that they have come to mean, and will continue to mean, new things to new generations. Indeed, the very fact that we discover new delights in re-viewing Ford's films raises the central critical issue of why one filmmaker stands above his contemporaries. Why do we never tire of Ford's films and always entertain the thought that we must and will have to see them again? Why do we feel, conversely, that the films of other directors are either time fillers to be seen once and forgotten or pleasures we would want to reindulge in only at much longer intervals? Thus, those writing on Ford, again like those writing on Shakespeare, are justified on the ground that their interpretations may shed new light on an old master.

There are other clearer and less impressionistic reasons why Ford's films compel our interest. Perhaps foremost are his characters, who rarely fail to arouse an audience's sympathies. In Ford's films we consistently find figures who seem to possess "ongoing" lives because of the rounded personalities and elaborated pasts that they are nearly always provided. In this regard, Frank Nugent's comments about working with Ford on *Fort Apache* (1948) are highly instructive.[2] According to the screenwriter, Ford insisted that Nugent supply background details for all the characters before the actual film narrative began. These "pre-lives" were Nugent's real preparation for doing the screenplay to *Fort Apache*; and Ford's insistence on such a procedure offers an obvious clue to the depths of characterization that so often distinguish his films. This method also suggests the extent to which Ford planned his films, a trait that belies his oft-described improvisations on sets and locations during filming.

Ford's thematic evolution, in which more resigned views of human society and individual capacities replace an earlier optimism, can best be seen in his westerns, since this genre is based on easily recognized elements and, especially, since the director utilized it so many times. No serious understanding or appreciation of Ford is possible without considering his westerns, for in them, thematic questionings and the frequently dialectical cast of his thinking can be readily discerned against the traditionalized features of the most apparent American film genre. Ford's perceptions of the possibilities for man in society can be more quickly grasped by considering *Stagecoach* (1939) and *The Man Who Shot Liberty Valance* (1962), in which the generic données are constant, then by looking at *The Grapes of Wrath* (1940) and *The Quiet Man* (1952), in which such thematic concerns must be established (and ascertained) against much less immediately familiar generic terrains.

Ford's westerns also demonstrate the great staying power normally attributed to a significant artist in any field. There is, finally, simply too much artistic coherence in too many films to attribute Ford's westerns to accident or to a lot of talented people all having good days together. Indeed, Ford's artistry lies ultimately in the ways he uses certain character types, plot situations, camera setups, and musical allusions to enrich thematic concerns. Thus, his westerns, precisely because of their generic similarities, offer the clearest expressions of Ford's creative genius. In any listing of his best works, at least six and as many as eight of his westerns are likely to be included. Even those that are generally omitted (*Three Godfathers*, 1948; *Sergeant Rutledge*, 1960; *Two Rode Together*, 1961; and *Cheyenne Autumn*, 1964) are usually valued above most other western films.

Ford's westerns clearly demonstrate their creator's artistic coherence — a quality that is, of course, relatively rare in a medium as commercial as Hollywood filmmaking, despite the often ingenious arguments of the most extreme

Opposite: John Wayne and John Ford on location.

advocates of auteurism. In the chapters that follow, I will be concerned with showing how Ford broadens characterizations and thematic concerns to unify his films around recurring interests or values. Great dramatic art resonates in that all of its individual stylistic features point toward, or are imbued with, its author's thematic concerns; and Ford's westerns embody just such an all-encompassing coherence. Unlike so many other enthusiasms from our viewing pasts, Ford's westerns do not fade but actually gain in intensity when seen through the more rational perspectives of later life.

Various continuities in pre-production, actual production, and post-production offer striking arguments for Ford's multilayered thematic vision. We begin with an examination of how he and his collaborators functioned during the silent era; then we consider how *Drums Along the Mohawk* (1939) and the brief middle section of *How the West Was Won* (1962) anticipate or utilize themes and techniques that are more fully elaborated in Ford's other sound westerns. A discussion of what was done to transform *The Horse Soldiers* (1959) from a novel into a shooting script reveals that this production embodies the three principal plot motifs — the meaningful institution of the cavalry, the bonding of male heroes, and the journey into wisdom about one's self — around which Ford's other westerns are organized. An examination of how the director and his screenwriters handled the specific literary sources for these other westerns, a process that saw notable additions, alterations, and deletions in line with Ford's larger abiding themes, follows.

The six subsequent chapters, which are devoted to twelve sound westerns, match these works in pairs designed to illustrate their primary thematic emphases, which emerge as dialectical problem-solution and initial vision-reconsidered vision in the director's artistic evolution. Thus, *Fort Apache* (1948) and *Rio Grande* (1950) represent meditations on the nature of command within the larger structure of the benevolent military institution. *She Wore a Yellow Ribbon* (1949) and *Sergeant Rutledge* (1960) use this same background to explore the relationship between embattled individuals and the larger entity in which such characters had previously found their personal identities. *My Darling Clementine* (1946) and *Liberty Valance* (1962) utilize male bonding to demonstrate the necessity for, as well as the costs of, civilization imposing itself on a frontier in the form of nascent urban society. *Wagonmaster* (1950) and *Two Rode Together* (1961) place such a male relationship in a wilderness to show some of the ambiguities in civilized attitudes toward individuals who fall outside the pale of society. *Three Godfathers* (1948) and *The Searchers* (1956) utilize the journey motif to show how their characters travel within themselves, as well as within the surrounding environments, in order to return to society. Finally, *Stagecoach* (1939) and *Cheyenne Autumn* (1964) are more highly contrasted in their views of the effects that such travel has on individual characters; an optimistic sense of justice emerges at the end of the earlier film, whereas only a muted resignation remains at the conclusion of the later work.

Chapter 1

Ford and the Filming of the West

Western movies were a staple feature of the American cinema from its inception until the mid–1960s.[1] Edwin S. Porter's *The Great Train Robbery* (1903) is often cited as the first American film that told a story in recognizable narrative steps; and such early luminaries as Thomas Ince and D. W. Griffith were active in making feature-length westerns by the mid–1910s. Ford served a brief apprenticeship under his brother Francis, Griffith, and others; in 1917, Universal studio head Carl Laemmle gave Ford his start as a director of westerns. During the following decade, Ford turned out 37 silent westerns (all but three of which have disappeared) and worked extensively with such western stars as Harry Carey, Buck Jones, Hoot Gibson, and Tom Mix.[2] In the 1920s, following the commercial success of James Cruze's *The Covered Wagon* (Paramount, 1923), Ford directed *The Iron Horse* (Fox, 1924), a work that has often been cited as a truly epic western. He followed that film with *Three Bad Men* (Fox, 1926), whose plot loosely resembles that of his later *Three Godfathers*; however, this was Ford's last western until 1939 and *Stagecoach*.

In the interim, sound movies replaced the silents, and a period of adjustment and experimentation ensued during which camera and sound-recording techniques had to be remastered. Notable early sound westerns included Raoul Walsh's *In Old Arizona* (Fox, 1929), which was the first serious talking feature, Victor Fleming's *The Virginian* (Paramount, 1929), and Wesley Ruggles's *Cimarron* (RKO, 1930). These early sound efforts are perhaps best epitomized by John Wayne's first starring feature, *The Big Trail* (Fox, 1930), whose visual splendors were vitiated by its overritualized acting and sparse music.

If techniques had improved noticeably by the middle of the 1930s, Cecil B. DeMille's ham-fisted direction added little to such films as *The Plainsman* (Paramount, 1936) and *Union Pacific* (Paramount, 1939); indeed, if anything, DeMille's penchants for epic production gloss and overdone histrionics played against the western genre. While scores of B westerns featuring Ken Maynard, Tex Ritter, Bob Steele, Gene Autry, John Wayne, and (the proverbial) many others poured out of the Hollywood studios during the 1930s, there was

5

a lack of serious ("A") features until 1939. In that seminal year, in addition to Ford's return with *Stagecoach*, such admired works as Henry King's *Jesse James* (20th Century–Fox), Michael Curtiz's *Dodge City* (Warner Bros.), and George Marshall's *Destry Rides Again* (Universal) were released. With the commercial success of these films, the production of westerns surged and continued throughout the 1940s, despite the conditions imposed by wartime.

Westerns not only became bigger but also began to incorporate newer social and film fashions. In *The Outlaw* (Howard Hughes, 1943) and *Duel in the Sun* (Selznick, 1946), sex became a major force in the movie West; and although these films' lovers seem odd or overwrought by our standards, their often irrational passions laid the groundwork for a greater psychological complexity in later works. The more equivocal atmosphere of film noir appeared in Walsh's *Pursued* (Warner Bros., 1947) and the lesser-known *Coroner Creek* (Columbia, 1948), while more emotionally divided characters, such as Glenn Ford's Colonel Owen Devereaux in *The Man from Colorado* (Columbia, 1948), were widely introduced.

The 1950s witnessed a continuing proliferation of A westerns at the same time that the B feature faded away, largely due to the emergence of television. The distinctive styles of Anthony Mann and Budd Boetticher were augmented during this period by some of the most popularly and critically acclaimed westerns ever made. Elia Kazan's *Viva Zapata!* (20th Century–Fox, 1952) and Fred Zinneman's *High Noon* (United Artists, 1952) raised serious political and social questions about their own times by means of the conventionalized world of the western. Nicholas Ray's revisionistic *Johnny Guitar* (Republic, 1954) and Arthur Penn's *The Left-Handed Gun* (Warner Bros., 1958) continued these trends as, first, women assumed male roles and, then, an angst-driven juvenile delinquent fell victim to the society in which he unwittingly found himself. Much of that same psychological ambience attaches to the stylistically ambivalent *One-Eyed Jacks* (Paramount, 1961), in which the Billy the Kid story was reworked to accord with star-director Marlon Brando's screen persona. While the 1960s saw the emergence of distinctive directorial styles in the westerns of Sam Peckinpah and Sergio Leone, the decade was also marked by such familiar and unchallenging fare as *McClintock!* (United Artists, 1963), *The Professionals* (Columbia, 1966), and the grossly overrated *Butch Cassidy and the Sundance Kid* (20th Century–Fox, 1969).

Nostalgia and revisionism have been the leading trends in western films since 1970 as the genre has itself fallen on lean times. The dying off and aging of longtime leading men (John Wayne, Randolph Scott, William Holden, Burt Lancaster, Kirk Douglas, Robert Mitchum) and the increasing public skepticism over the possibilities of individual heroism and benevolent political

Opposite: George Bancroft, John Wayne, and Louise Platt in *Stagecoach* (Walter Wanger–United Artists, 1939).

leadership undoubtedly contributed to the demise of the genre. At the same time, the retirements or deaths of such directors as Ford, Mann, Walsh, Hathaway, and Peckinpah accelerated this trend. Ironically, Hollywood's new emphases undermined and eventually bankrupted the genre that had been so essential earlier to its very survival. Films like Ralph Nelson's *Soldier Blue* (Avco Embassy, 1970), Robert Altman's *McCabe and Mrs. Miller* (Warner Bros., 1971), and Arthur Penn's *Little Big Man* (National General, 1971) and *The Missouri Breaks* (United Artists, 1976) presented a West controlled by racism, xenophobia, repression, and greed. Gradually filmmakers were asserting the position that there was little, if anything, for a western protagonist to fight or die for. At the same time, films such as Mark Rydell's *The Cowboys* (Warner Bros., 1972) and Don Siegel's *The Shootist* (Paramount, 1976), in chronicling the dying of legendary western archetypes — the independent rancher and the gunfighter (both played by John Wayne, who himself died in 1979) — further symbolized a fading world.

Beginning in the 1980s, the revival of the western was proclaimed several times: one heralded film would bring Hollywood back to the halcyon days when it frequently released more than a hundred westerns in a year.[3] Michael Cimino's colossal box-office failure *Heaven's Gate* (United Artists, 1980), with its inane plotting and casting and all-but-frozen pacing, undoubtedly did much to undercut the return of the western as a viable commercial genre. Lawrence Kasdan's *Silverado* (Columbia, 1985) emerged as merely a pastiche of many older westerns, heading ultimately to a predictable showdown; as a film made in terms of other films, *Silverado* was too coy for a serious western. The virtues of Walter Hill's *The Long Riders* (United Artists, 1980) and Christopher Cain's *Young Guns* (20th Century–Fox, 1988) — casting real-life brothers for outlaw brothers and young men for young men — were undone by their revisionism and their uneven pacing. Kevin Costner's *Dances with Wolves*, despite its revival of the visual beauties of the western film, is mired in a politically correct ideology that reduces its characters to the moral certainties and posturings of melodrama. None of these films, however historically "accurate" they may be, were likely to spur a notable upsurge in the production of westerns.

In terms of consistent quality, Ford's work surpasses that of every other western director; only a handful of filmmakers can be significantly compared to him. Although numerous celebrated directors have tried their hands at westerns, none from Ford's own generation of filmmakers can match him. William Wyler's *The Westerner* (1940) and *The Big Country* (1958), while pleasant enough, are too leisurely to compare with Ford's films. The tall-tale nature of the first film palls, whereas the excessive plotting and the straining for epic

Opposite: **Harry Carey, Jr., John Wayne, and Hank Worden in *The Searchers* (Warner Bros., 1956).**

effects in the latter become tiresome during repeated viewings. George Stevens's *Shane* (1953) is as fatiguing in its photographic finish and its less-than-enthralling playing of Alan Ladd. Stevens's pondered film, along with his equally slow-moving *Giant* (1956), resembles what David Lean might have done had he ever directed a western. John Huston's critical reputation would be considerably lessened if *The Unforgiven* (1960) and *The Life and Times of Judge Roy Bean* (1972) were listed as the major efforts in his canon. The first film suffers markedly in comparison with Ford's *The Searchers*, which is also based on an Alan LeMay novel; and the story in the second work becomes too elaborate for its own good.

Howard Hawks has often been lauded as a superior director of westerns, but this claim is difficult to sustain when we consider that *El Dorado* (1967) and *Rio Lobo* (1970) are among his efforts in the genre. The familiar Hawksian emphases on male camaraderie, tough females who will pursue their men, and screwball comedy mar *Red River* (1948), *The Big Sky* (1952), and *Rio Bravo* (1959). Typically, we are never sure whether Hawks wants to be serious or funny, so that *Red River*, with its visual resemblance to Ford and its numerous Fordian players (Wayne, Hank Worden), ultimately flounders into bathos at its end when the principals are reunited by a garrulous heroine. All the tension that is built up around Dunston's (John Wayne) need for revenge on his stepson (Montgomery Clift) is simply thrown away in Hawks's ridiculous ending. If the same structural weakness is not as apparent in *Rio Bravo*, the comic and romantic elements override its more serious themes. Hawks's shortcomings as a western director are also signalled by Dimitri Tiomkin's excessive musical scores, which augment these three films. Such scores exhibit the composer's habit of providing too much music too prominently orchestrated; that a supposed master craftsman like Hawks chose such accompaniment suggests that even he may have realized that many of the scenes in his films needed to be saved (or at least compromised) by music. It is all but impossible to believe that Ford would have agreed to such obviously histrionic musical accompaniments being heard in any of his films.

King Vidor's reputation as a western director rests on *Billy the Kid* (1930) and *Man Without a Star* (1955); however, his collaboration on *Duel in the Sun* (1946) is a significant offset to those earlier films. Certainly Vidor does little or nothing to puncture or least rein in the excesses of David O. Selznick's screenplay. Such emotional excess also undoes Fritz Lang in *Rancho Notorious* (1952), which undercuts his earlier *Return of Frank James* (1940) and his visual and thematic tour de force *Western Union* (1941), with its stunning death of Randolph Scott in the last reel. Michael Curtiz, although blessed with the full production panache and gloss of Warner Bros. for *Dodge City, Virginia City* (1940), and *Santa Fe Trail* (1940), does little to raise these westerns above the ordinary; indeed, their characters, with the possible exception of Raymond Massey's John Brown in the last film, are clichés who never act out of the ordinary and come to represent veritable plot turns whenever and wherever they appear.

Henry King was more fortunate in that 20th Century–Fox provided him with better scripts in *Jesse James* (1939), *The Gunfighter* (1950), and *The Bravados* (1958). Although the first film relies on patent melodramatics and gets bogged down in the title character's domestic life, King's other westerns are careful examinations of serious thematic concerns. In many ways *The Gunfighter* equals or surpasses *High Noon* in terms of structure and production while, at the same time, it raises the question of what future there could ever be for its central character, Jimmy Ringo (Gregory Peck). *The Bravados* questions the willingness of its protagonist (Peck once more), or indeed of any traditional western hero, to seek revenge. Although the film has perhaps too much of a religious cast from its inception, King nicely suggests the irony of Jim Douglas's pursuit and killing of three men who really did not harm him.

Raoul Walsh's career as a Hollywood director was as long as Ford's, and he directed more sound westerns. His output was seemingly controlled by the scripts that he was given, so that, while he could adapt himself to various studio styles (Republic, Warner Bros., Universal), his films always exhibit a headlong pace that works well in crime and action dramas. When confronted with unpromising material such as *Cheyenne* (1947), *Silver River* (1948), or *Saskatchewan* (1952), Walsh could do little to raise it above the cliché. Ford, on such occasions, left us with either rounded characters (as in *Mogambo*) or with characterizations that transform old-fashioned materials into more relevant tales (as in *Seven Women*). We can admire Walsh's western successes like *Dark Command* (1940), *They Died with Their Boots On* (1942), *Pursued*, and *Colorado Territory* (1948); however, we do not return to any of them (let alone his numerous lesser efforts) to seek out additional subtleties of characterization or theme. Henry Hathaway also enjoyed a lengthy Hollywood career, starting with a series of Zane Grey–based westerns featuring Randolph Scott in 1932–34 and then moving on to *Garden of Evil* (1954), *From Hell to Texas* (1958), and *True Grit* (1969). Like Walsh, he is a stylistic chameleon, and we find such extremes as *Brigham Young* (1940) and *Five Card Stud* (1967) in his output. William Wellman's *The Ox-Bow Incident* (1943) is surely one of the most thoughtful and "adult" westerns ever made; however *Buffalo Bill* (1944) is as maudlin as the director claimed it was.

Andre de Toth directed many Randolph Scott vehicles in the 1950s, running a gamut from the competent (*Carson City*, [1951]) to the ludicrous (the 3-D inspired *The Stranger Wore a Gun* [1953]). De Toth rises above such standard fare in *The Indian Fighter* (1955), whose protagonist resembles the male lead in *Broken Arrow* (1950) in wanting to bring peace to the frontier. Delmer Daves, who came into western direction with *Broken Arrow* and its revisionist view of the Indians, also supplied notable films in *3:10 to Yuma* (1957) and *Cowboy* (1958), the former a reworking of *High Noon* and the latter an unvarnished look at a cattle drive. Daves unfortunately also turned out such unenthralling westerns as *Drum Beat* (1954), the excessively literary *Jubal* (1956), and *The Badlanders* (1958). A more esteemed but far less substantial western director is John Sturges, whose *Gunfight at the O.K. Corral* (1957) and *The Magnificent Seven* (1960) again feature music scores that often substitute for (or disguise) slow pacing. While Sturges's *Hour of the Gun* (1967) is initially intriguing because it reexplores the situation set forth in *Gunfight at the O.K. Corral*, it quickly palls by turning everything in the earlier film into its diametric opposite. Sturges's reputation becomes even more questionable in the light of *The Last Train from Gun Hill* (1959), *Sergeants 3* (1962), and *The Hallelujah Trail* (1965).

Samuel Fuller's idiosyncratic view of the West can be seen in *I Shot Jesse James* (1949), *The Baron of Arizona* (1950), *Run of the Arrow* (1957) and *Forty Guns* (1957). Fuller's work is wildly uneven; thus, while we can applaud his having Bob Ford (John Ireland) suffer pangs of guilt when reenacting his famous shooting of Jesse James on stage, we quickly become dismayed by the romantic plot involving Preston Foster and the over-the-top scene in which Jesse (Reed Hadley) insists that Ford scrub his back. Nicholas Ray's revisionism is more consistent, if perhaps not quite as likeable, in *Johnny Guitar*, with its emphases on role reversals leading to psychological reversals, and *The True Story of Jesse James* (1957), which turns the outlaw's saga into something close to *Rebel Without a Cause*. A stronger, more sober revisionist from this period is Robert Aldrich, whose *Apache* (1954) and *Ulzana's Raid* (1972) remain fresh and harrowing experiences. His *Vera Cruz* is also a polished effort, but he fails to match Ford's consistency when he turns out such works as the overly psychologized *Last Sunset* (1961) and the mediocre *Four for Texas* (1964).

In the 1950s two Hollywood directors created remarkable western series that struck out on paths quite different from what Ford was doing. Budd Boetticher, after some undistinguished features at Universal (with the possible exception of *The Man from the Alamo* [1953]), teamed up with producer Harry Joe Brown and star Randolph Scott to deliver such small-scale masterpieces as *Seven Men from Now* and *The Tall T* (both 1956), *Ride Lonesome* (1959), and *Comanche Station* (1960). These outdoor westerns pit Scott, who increasingly resembles the taciturn silent film star William S. Hart, against various bands of outlaws whom he is either seeking for revenge or trying to outsmart. Boetticher's emotionally charged protagonists inevitably triumph because of their greater wisdom and experience, as Ben Brigade does so notably over his adversaries in *Ride Lonesome*. Boetticher gets onto shakier ground in the other three films of this series—*Decision at Sundown* (1957), *Buchanan Rides Alone* (1958) and *Westbound* (1958). These films, with their town locations, do not supply the kind of mythical setting that we see in the other films. The most successful of these three works, *Decision at Sundown*, carries far too much exposition about the town of Sundown and its denizens before revealing that the reason for Scott's presence (a wish to avenge his wife's seduction by a town bigshot) is foolish. *Buchanan Rides Alone* simply degenerates into too much comedy, whereas *Westbound* fails to tie its plot together in as consistent a fashion as Boetticher's other Ranown films do. Although Ford allows for revenge as a legitimate motive (as in *Stagecoach* and *My Darling Clementine*), he would not be interested in the kinds of reversals we see in *Decision at Sundown* or in the extended drawing of attractive villains, such as Usher (Richard Boone) in *The Tall T*.

Such dichotomous characters would, of course, fit very nicely into Anthony Mann's western films, with their uneasy suggestions of the common values shared by hero and villain. While Mann's westerns exhibit some partial failures — as in *The Furies* (1950), with its uneasy mix of oater and soap opera, *The Last Frontier* (1955), with its tacked-on happy ending, and the remake of *Cimarron* (1960), with its unconvincing lurches between vibrant outdoor locations and obvious studio sets — yet they are nearly all as integrated as Ford's. Indeed, *The Tin Star* (1957) is based on a script by Dudley Nichols, and *Devil's Doorway* (1950) touches on many of the same racial concerns that we see in *The Searchers* and *Two Rode Together*. But it is Mann's westerns starring James Stewart that establish him as a major genre director. The first of these collaborations, *Winchester '73* (1950), while the most episodic, introduces the more psychologically complex world that we find in Mann's films. Lin McAdam is as kill-crazy as his villainous brother (Stephen McNally); and we see his desperate need for vengeance erupt into all-but-uncontrollable violence in the way he manhandles the villainous Waco Johnny Dean (Dan Duryea). That outlaw is a much more vibrant character than the evil McAdam, so that we lament his being shot down, as Mann seemingly wants us to. The final battle between the brothers takes place among rocks and emphasizes Mann's use of landscape in his westerns. Their terrain is far different from what we see in Ford's films, for Mann's characters frequently have to battle with natural elements, as in *The Naked Spur* (1953) and *The Far Country* (1955). Mann also often chooses to put his action in "un-western" locations, such as dense forests or snow-covered passes, and takes delight in angled shots that emphasize the difficulties of moving through such locations.

The symbiotic relation of hero and villain becomes the central focus in *The Naked Spur* as Ben Vandergroot (Robert Ryan) instinctively knows how to get under the skin of Howie Kemp (Stewart), as well as the others who have come to capture him. In *Bend of the River* (1952) Glyn McLyntock (Stewart) rescues Emerson Cole (Arthur Kennedy) from a lynching party, only to learn that the man he has saved not only is an outlaw but also knows about his own shady past. The symbolic link between them is later emphasized when McLyntock reveals a rope burn on his own neck; and Mann stages a climactic fight between them in a river to suggest that the hero, at last, purifies himself by killing his antagonist. *The Man from Laramie* (1955) and *The Far*

Country begin to ameliorate the central character's need for cathartic physical violence. While Will Lockhart (Stewart) suffers mightily in the former
film, his character finally resists killing Vic Hansbro (Arthur Kennedy), the
man who has been running guns to the Indians and whom the protagonist has
come seeking. In *The Far Country*, Jeff Webster (Stewart) must cleanse the
town of Judge Gannon (John McIntyre) and his cohorts, but in the process
the protagonist must also learn his own need for human community.

Mann's greatest accomplishment, *Man of the West* (1958), finds Link Jones
(Gary Cooper) thrown back into his outlaw past and having to destroy the
gang/family with which he used to ride. In killing his cousin Claude (John
Dehner) and the villainous patriarch, Dock Tobin (Lee J. Cobb), Link not
only saves Billie (Julie London) but also exorcises the demons of his own past.
Mann's extended portrait of this outlaw brood and his suggestions that the
protagonist is just like them, supply character relationships and thematic implications that would be anathema to Ford. Indeed, the closest Ford comes to
Mann is in *Two Rode Together* when McCabe (James Stewart) threatens to
kill Gary (Richard Widmark) as they return from the Indian camp.

A filmmaker with whom Ford shared even fewer sympathies was Sam
Peckinpah, who celebrates the end of the West in his heavily violent films.
Ride the High Country (1962) pursues this notion almost elegiacally in chronicling the last time that Steve Judd (Joel McCrea) and Gil Westrum (Randolph Scott) ride together. Judd's determination to die an honest man (to
enter "his house justified" as he eloquently puts it) eventually dissuades his old
sidekick Westrum from stealing the gold they have been sent to escort and,
in one last blaze of glory, to fight the semicivilized villains. *Major Dundee*
(1965) resembles Ford's *She Wore a Yellow Ribbon* in being about a cavalry mission; *The Searchers* in centering on the rescue of kidnapped children (for a
time); and *Fort Apache* in the central figure's pursuit of seemingly idle military glory. The combined Union and Confederate force that Dundee (Charlton Heston) commands represents a microcosm of American society; and there
is finally no battlefield reconciliation between these different elements, as there
is in *She Wore a Yellow Ribbon* when Trooper Smith is laid to rest. Peckinpah's
next western, *The Wild Bunch* (1969), became a cause célèbre because of its
highly graphic violence. That element would never have appeared in a Ford
film, and the type of characters shown and the bases of their loyalty would have
been of even less interest to the veteran director. Peckinpah's *Wild Bunch* and
Pat Garrett and Billy the Kid (1974) are nihilistic in comparison to Ford's films:
there is no nurturing or benevolent society, so that the very notion of a social
contract has been abandoned. Men fight and kill because it is in their nature
or because it is the wish of those richer or more powerful than themselves.

Equally violent and fatalistic milieus can be seen in the westerns of Sergio
Leone and his most famous star, Clint Eastwood, who has gone on to be a
formidable director himself. *A Fistful of Dollars* (1964), *For a Few Dollars More*

(1965), and *The Good, The Bad, and the Ugly* (1966) all find Eastwood as the Man with No Name whose unruffled approach to violence turns him into an abstraction rather than a character. *Once Upon a Time in the West* (1968) reveals Leone at his most characteristic as his figures move through a world of unspoken motivations and seemingly suspended time in a ballet of death that ultimately reveals the anachronistic nature of both the villain Frank (Henry Fonda, cast decidedly and chillingly against his normal persona) and the hero Harmonica (Charles Bronson). The two must die or disappear, just as must the symbolically crippled railroad owner and the outlaw Cheyenne (Jason Robards, Jr.), so that a newer civilization, one controlled by the railroad and served by the ex-prostitute Jill (Claudia Cardinale), can emerge. Leone's almost operatic pacing is aptly supported by a vibrant Ennio Morricone score that further signals the difference between this film and almost any other western. Leone's western world is totally devoid of the kinds of sacrifices that we see in Ford, all the way from Hatfield (John Carradine) in *Stagecoach* to Tom Doniphon in *The Man Who Shot Liberty Valance*.

Clint Eastwood's westerns fall into two distinct stages. *Hang 'Em High* (1967) and *Two Mules for Sister Sarah* (1970) are attempts to redo Leone and Peckinpah in style and location. It is in the westerns that Eastwood directs — *High Plains Drifter* (1972), *The Outlaw Josey Wales* (1976), *Pale Rider* (1986), *Unforgiven* (1992) — that we see a gentler character gradually emerge from beneath the impervious exterior of the Man with No Name. Indeed, while the protagonists of *High Plains Drifter* and *Pale Rider* both appear, like the mystical Shane, to rescue downtrodden civilian communities, the protagonist in Eastwood's earlier film emerges out of a glaring haze and eventually demands that the town he has been sent to save be renamed Hell, whereas the second rescuer wears a clerical collar and descends into a valley to answer a young girl's prayers. Josey Wales, Eastwood's most arresting central creation, forms an integrated community around himself as he flees from the aftermath of a Civil War that has consistently victimized and brutalized him. Josey's destruction of Red Leg (Bill McKinney) and the decision of his former commander (John Vernon) to stop hunting him create the only safe haven that an Eastwood protagonist ever finds. The outlaw-turned-farmer protagonist of *Unforgiven* fights against much more equivocal enemies before reverting and becoming the same kind of revenging angel that we have seen elsewhere in Eastwood's westerns. It is, finally, the excessive violence of these works that distinguishes them from Ford's; indeed, these contemporary works celebrate the mechanics of killing at the expense of the mystery of death, whereas Ford's films are more rewarding precisely because they reverse that equation. In Peckinpah's, Leone's, and Eastwood's films, there is always another enemy to be killed, with little thought being given to what such killing means; in Ford's movies, killing is always undertaken reluctantly, for some perceived good that is larger than individual survival.

Chapter 2

Straight Shooting, The Iron Horse, and Three Bad Men

John Ford arrived in Hollywood in 1914 and immediately went to work for his brother Francis as a stunt man and jack-of-all-trades. In 1917 Ford became a director at Universal, where studio head Carl Laemmle had been impressed by his organizational abilities. Over the next dozen years Ford would direct sixty-five silent films, varying in length from modest two-reelers to epics. Unhappily, because of studio storage practices and the rapid decomposition of nitrate film stocks, only 11 of Ford's silent films survive today. Thirty-seven of these silent assignments were westerns; of these, only three can still be seen in their entirety. While such a condition may well be lamented, Ford's career in films did continue until 1965, so that nearly three-quarters of his working life occurred during the sound era. Having all of his silent westerns would be welcome, but it hardly seems likely that they would substantially alter overall evaluations of Ford's later accomplishments. Indeed, in what we can examine, it seems apparent that Ford was learning his craft and implementing his sense of character and theme throughout the silent era.

Ford began with a pair of two-reelers (*The Trail of Hate* [1917] and *The Scrapper* [1917]), which he wrote and starred in as well as directed. These modest productions found the Ford protagonist caught in love triangles that took him to the Philippines and into a town brothel, respectively, to save the heroines. Ford's third assignment, *The Soul Herder* (1917), paired him with veteran cowboy actor Harry Carey (1878–1947); and the two men went on to create a memorable series of films in which Carey emerged as the laconic Cheyenne Harry. From 1917 to 1920, Carey was the star and Ford the director in 24 films. In addition, Ford and Carey were generally responsible for the story lines that were used; the director later insisted that the actor had taught him the movie business.[1] *The Soul Herder*, in which Carey gives up his outlaw ways to become a minister, was followed in 1917 by another two-reeler, *Cheyenne's Pal*, in which Harry was driven by the love of his horse.

With *Straight Shooting* (1917) Ford and Carey extended the scope of what they were doing into a five-reel production that focused on a range war whose

John Ford in the 1930s.

action scenes were noteworthy for their day. Cheyenne Harry (Carey) initially hires on as a gun hand ("regulator") for the ranchers but joins the homesteaders when he sees the suffering of Joan Sims (Molly Malone) and her family over the murder of Tom Sims (Ted Brooks). Harry then kills his former cohort Placer Fremont (Vester Pegg) in a classic street shootout before riding to the rescue of the besieged Sims family. After dispatching the villains, Harry decides he must travel on, despite his love for Joan, whom he leaves to the care of an ardent suitor, Sam Turner (Hoot Gibson). However, this classic resolution is compromised by a final scene in which Harry and Joan embrace; critics and commentators are uncertain whether this scene was added for a rerelease of *Straight Shooting*.[2] In either case, one can readily see that *Straight Shooting*, like so much of Ford's later work, is character driven, as the outcast hero, Harry, moves from unthinking badman to good badman.

This film also exhibits some other features that distinguish Ford's subsequent westerns. At one point a location that reappears in *Stagecoach*—a narrow pass, in which a man is stopped and held at gunpoint, reprised in the later film when the final Indian attack begins—is photographed from a similar angle. Joan Sims's table-setting scene, in which she distractedly lays out a plate for her dead brother and then, on thinking, idly caresses it, is reminiscent of the later scenes in *The Searchers* in which Martha (Dorothy Jordan) fusses over and with brother-in-law Ethan's (John Wayne) jacket. Ford also uses doorframes to establish shots in *Straight Shooting*, and the funeral of Tom

Sims is, again, reminiscent of *The Searchers* and its hilltop service for the dead Edwards family members. The static quality of Ford's compositions in *Straight Shooting* and the often mechanical ways in which scenes begin and end reinforce the verdict of Judith Kass: "So many early Ford films have been lost, that it is difficult to ascertain where this one stands in his overall opus."[3]

Ford and Carey followed *Straight Shooting* in 1917 with *The Secret Man*, in which Harry rescues a girl, *A Marked Man*, in which he is an accused outlaw, and *Bucking Broadway*, in which he goes to New York to save a girl he loves.

In 1918 Ford and Carey produced seven films, five of which have Cheyenne Harry as their protagonist. *The Phantom Riders* deals with a range war; *Wild Women* has Harry dreaming of adventure in the South Seas; *Thieves' Gold* pits Harry against a duplicitous friend; *Hell Bent* finds him as a saloon bouncer in love with a singer; and *Three Mounted Men* is a prison-escape story. In *The Scarlet Drop*, Carey plays "Kaintuck Cass," a poor man who endears himself to some southern aristocrats. The plot includes a stage holdup and some machinations arising from blackmail based on miscegenation. *A Woman's Fool* is based on an Owen Wister novel. After being rejected by a worthless woman, Lin McLean (Carey) finds romance with another and adopts the son of his former love.

Ford directed fifteen westerns in 1919. His efforts were divided between six two-reelers starring Pete Morrison and Ed Jones and nine longer works with Harry Carey. In *The Fighting Brothers*, *By Indian Post*, *The Rustlers*, and *Gun Law*, Pete Morrison is featured as a sheriff who arrests and then helps his own brother to escape; as the butt of a romantic joke; as the infiltrator of a rustlers' band; and as a lawman who discovers a mistaken mail-robbery plot. In *The Gun Packer*, Ed Jones is caught in a range war; more interesting, he reappears as the aged cowboy coming home from prison to encounter the often disconcerting ways of the modern world in *The Last Outlaw*.[4]

Harry Carey's nine films with Ford in 1919 take up more complicated plots and themes. Carey reprises Cheyenne Harry in seven of these works, beginning with *Roped*, in which he again travels to the modern-day East. *A Fight for Love* finds Harry as an escaped outlaw who flees to Canada and becomes involved with Mounties and Indians. *Bare Fists*, in which Harry is the son of a murdered sheriff who swears not to use his guns, foreshadows such later films as George Marshall's *Destry Rides Again* (Universal, 1939) and Ford's own *The Man Who Shot Liberty Valance* (Paramount, 1962). *Riders of Vengeance* finds Harry out for revenge after his bride and her parents are murdered on his wedding day. Harry's later softening foreshadows the plot development of Henry King's *The Bravados* (20th Century–Fox, 1958). *The Age of the Saddle*, in which Carey is a rancher caught in a range war, and *A Gun Fightin' Gentleman*, in which he is an outlaw, were standard items. However, *Marked Men*, in which Carey was joined by J. Farrell MacDonald and Joe Harris, is noteworthy for being based on Peter Kyne's novel *The Three Godfathers*. In this version, Carey has the role that John Wayne plays in Ford's later reworking (MGM, 1948); MacDonald and Harris die trying to preserve the infant's life just as Pedro Armendariz and Harry Carey, Jr., do in the remake.

In *The Outcasts of Poker Flat*, Carey portrays Harry Lanyon, a man beset by romantic angst who turns to the Bret Harte tale for advice so that the film can flash back to this narrative, in which Carey appears as John Oakhurst, a similar figure. From Oakhurst's story, Lanyon realizes that he must sacrifice his happiness for the girl he loves; however, Ford's film then switches gears by having the girl in the framing story tell Lanyon that she loves him truly. The last collaboration of 1919, *The Rider of the Law*, finds Carey as Texas Ranger Jim Kyneton in search of thieves. Two later films, released in 1920, find Carey portraying, in the first, a successful Alaskan gold miner who saves a young couple and gives up any romantic thoughts about the heroine in order to act his age (*The Wallop*) and, in the second, a man, Bert Carson, who goes to jail to protect the woman he loves (*Desperate Trails*). Harry Carey continued to work in movies until his death in 1947, but he appeared in only one other Ford film, *The Prisoner of Shark Island* (20th Century–Fox, 1936), in which he was the stern but compassionate commander of the prisoner fortress to which Doctor Mudd (Warner Baxter) is sent.

Ford also directed Buck Jones in *Just Pals* (1920) for his new studio, Fox. In this film Jones is a town bum who thwarts a robbery and marries the (proverbial) schoolteacher in a plot that is reminiscent of Dorothy Johnson's original story "The Man Who Shot Liberty Valance." *Action* and *Sure Fire* (both 1920) launched the career of Hoot Gibson at Universal. In these films he is a wandering cowhand who ultimately saves or wins damsels in distress, rescuing them from outlaws who would take their mines or steal their money. Gibson would later have a small role in Ford's *The Horse Soldiers* (United Artists, 1959).

North of Hudson Bay and *Three Jumps Ahead* (both 1923) coupled Ford with the celebrated cowboy star Tom Mix. In the former film, Mix battles wolves, waterfalls, and outlaws to clear his name and win the girl in northern Canada; in the latter (written by Ford), he struggles against outlaws in a hidden mountain cave.

Ford's major western from the silent era was *The Iron Horse* (Fox, 1924), which was produced to take advantage of the new interest in epic westerns, an interest generated by James Cruze's *The Covered Wagon* (Paramount, 1923). Ford's film, marked by its location shooting and large numbers of extras, deals with the building of the transcontinental railroad and interweaves this historical epic with the private story of a young man's need for revenge. In a prelude we are introduced to Davy (George O'Brien) and Miriam (Madge Bellamy) as childhood sweethearts listening to the advice of Abraham Lincoln about the necessity for a rail link between East and West. Shortly thereafter, Davy witnesses the murder of his father by Indians and a three-fingered white man. We then move forward ten years to find Davy as a pony express rider who reenters Miriam's life, only to find that she is enamored of an eastern railroad engineer, Jesson (Cyril Chadwick). Jesson is secretly working for Deroux (Fred Kohler), who wants to sell the railroad more expensive land for its passage. Davy battles with Jesson and kills Deroux (who turns out to be his father's killer) in a large Indian battle. Miriam then rejects Davy, so the hero heads west and joins the Central Pacific railroad. The young people are finally reconciled, and Jesson is dispatched just in time for the meeting of the railroads at Promontory Point, Utah.

Ford's staging of this final scene reflects his interest in creating an exciting tableau, for he literally copies contemporary photographs of the ceremony. At the same time, by having the lovers reconcile and walk away to end this film, Ford manages to link the historical and the private stories in a most convincing fashion. Indeed, it is such moments and the presentation of character types that redeem *The Iron Horse* from its all-too-familiar B-movie plot. Corporal Casey (J. Farrell MacDonald) emerges as the first of Ford's lovable western drunks — a stock figure that will be reprised by Thomas Mitchell, Francis Ford, Judson Pratt, and most notably, Victor MacLaglen in the sound westerns. Judge Haller's traveling saloon also presents another familiar feature of Ford's later work; indeed, MacDonald will reappear as the barman in *My Darling Clementine* even more celebrated saloon. George O'Brien would later appear for Ford as Captain Collingwood in *Fort Apache*, as Major Mack Allshard in *She Wore a Yellow Ribbon*, and as Major Braden in *Cheyenne Autumn*. Produced at a then astronomical cost of $280,000 on location in Nevada, and replete with such additional western elements as a cattle drive, Wild Bill Hickok, and Buffalo Bill, *The Iron Horse* returned more than $2 million domestically, made "Ford internationally famous and put a Fox film on Broadway for the first time."[5] Unfortunately, since surviving copies of *The Iron Horse* do not include its original rousing musical score by Erno Rapee, some of the film's initial effects have been permanently lost.

George O'Brien also stars in *Three Bad Men* (1926), Ford's final silent western and his last work in the genre until *Stagecoach* in 1939. Set against the Dakota gold rush of 1877, *Three Bad Men* begins with the heroine, Lee Carlton (Olive Borden), and her father going to Dakota. They are helped by Dan O'Malley (O'Brien), but the villainous Sheriff Layne Hunter (Louis Tellegen) subsequently kills Lee's father anyway. At this point the three outlaws, Mike (J. Farrell MacDonald), Spade (Frank Campeau), and Bull (Tom Santschi), approach Lee, ostensibly to rob her; however, like Cheyenne Harry in *Straight Shooting*, they are converted into helping her because they see how she is suffering. Dan soon joins them and Lee, and the outlaws actively promote the romance between the young people. In the meantime, the nefarious Hunter has made Bull's sister into his mistress and then killed her in a fire — a bit of plotting that adds to the film's climax. In the final battle the three outlaws lay down their lives to protect Dan and Lee; appropriately enough, the last one to die, Bull, kills Hunter. The lovers then have a child, whose name uses each of the outlaws' names in a symbolic pattern that is repeated in *Three Godfathers* and *Fort Apache*.

The additional strengths of *Three Bad Men* include its location shooting (in Wyoming), its staging of the land rush, and its themes about westward expansion and heroes who sacrifice themselves for a greater social good. The three outlaws of Ford's film (who were originally to have been played by Tom Mix, Buck Jones, and O'Brien) clearly hearken back to his earlier *Marked Men*, a version of the Peter Kyne *Three Godfathers*. This oft-filmed tale (there were additional versions in 1916 and 1936 as well as Ford's 1948 effort) stresses the need for its protagonists to lay down their compromised and evil lives to ensure a happier and better future for weaker but purer characters. Such figures are present not only in Ford's *Three Bad Men* and *Three Godfathers* but also, and perhaps more notably, in *The Searchers*, with Ethan Edwards, and *The Man Who Shot Liberty Valance*, with Tom Doniphon. Indeed, the sacrifices of such men are one of the keys to understanding Ford's cinematic West.

The director's sense of personal drama is perhaps best displayed in the sequence during the land rush when some anxious parents leave their infant in the path of oncoming horsemen. The threatened child appears in the foreground as we see riders approaching from the distance; the director's sense of timing then takes over as a single hand appears to lift the child out of harm. Another Fordian touch can be seen in the villainous Hunter, who carries a whip and brandishes it in the style of Pa Clanton (Walter Brennan) in *My Darling Clementine* and Liberty Valance (Lee Marvin) in *The Man Who Shot Liberty Valance*. Unhappily, *Three Bad Men*, although a superior film, did not enjoy the box office success of *The Iron Horse*; indeed, after its initial release, the film was severely cut, so that existing prints generally do not contain many of the location shots that were in Ford's original version.

While characteristic themes, characters, and devices can be seen in *The Iron Horse* and *Three Bad Men*, Ford's films with Harry Carey often appear to have been hastily assembled and rapidly plotted. Like the later films of Gene Autry and Roy Rogers, the Cheyenne Harry films often place the hero in the modern world in what might be termed "post Westerns." Although such liberties suggest the easy ambiance of the B western and can be accepted or dismissed with that proviso, it is more important to realize that Ford's silent films do not ensure him any serious place in film history. Andrew Sarris is certainly right when he claims: "If Ford's career had ended in 1929, he would deserve at most a footnote in film history, and it is doubtful that scholars would even bother excavating too many of his Twenties works from the Fox vaults."[6]

Thematic and Narrative Continuities: *Drums Along the Mohawk* and *How the West Was Won*

John Ford's entire cinematic output is marked by obvious technical and narrative continuities. Indeed, the persistent visual and thematic emphases found in nearly every Ford film, whether made under the auspices of RKO, 20th Century–Fox, Columbia, MGM, or another studio, are what mark the works as distinctly his. Various personality types and traits are perhaps most immediately apparent in Ford's films, whether westerns or nonwesterns. The religious zealot Saunders (Boris Karloff) in *The Lost Patrol* foreshadows the excesses of Mrs. McCandless (Jeanette Nolan) in *Two Rode Together*. This association of religion with madness or malevolence casts further light on the hypocrisies of Uncle Shiloh (Charles Kemper) in *Wagonmaster*. Pride carried to excess can be seen in *Judge Priest* when Caroline (Brenda Fowler) takes far too much delight in her station. Like the smug society ladies of *Stagecoach*, *Sergeant Rutledge*, and *Two Rode Together*, the Judge's sister fails to exhibit even the benefit of a doubt toward those less exalted than herself. While her moral myopia is symbolized in her treatment of her son (Tom Brown) and the déclassé Ellie May (Anita Louise), Caroline's pride is corrected through the union of these young people. No such comic redemption ultimately transforms Owen Thursday's (Henry Fonda) dislike for Mickey O'Rourke's (John Agar) attentions to Philadelphia (Shirley Temple) in *Fort Apache*. The colonel's petty concerns are finally overc   nly by the larger forces of time, society, and his own death.

Doctor Mudd (Warner Baxter) and his wife (Gloria Stuart) in *The Prisoner of Shark Island* represent the marital devotion we see so prominently in Ford's cavalry films. Shattered by the travesty of justice that sends the doctor to prison, the Mudds emotionally support each other in a fashion that foreshadows the elder O'Rourkes (Ward Bond and Irene Rich) in *Fort Apache* and

Ford directing Jane Chang (Miss Ling) in his last film, *7 Women* (MGM, 1965).

the Collingwoods (George O'Brien and Anna Lee) in *Fort Apache* and the All-shards (George O'Brien and Mildred Natwick) in *She Wore a Yellow Ribbon*. In the earlier prison film we also see various mobs running out of control, a situation Ford reprises in *Two Rode Together* when Lieutenant Gary (Richard Widmark) proves incapable of restraining such an outbreak. The injuries the Mudds endure at the hands of an unresponsive governmental bureaucracy also foreshadow the similar sufferings of the Cheyennes in *Cheyenne Autumn*.

In *The Prisoner of Shark Island*, when Mudd goes to the barricaded black soldiers and pleads for their help, and in *Mogambo*, when Vic (Clark Gable) allows the natives to test his courage, we encounter situations that are reminiscent of the parleys between Captain York (John Wayne) and Cochise (Miguel Inclan) in *Fort Apache* and between Captain Brittles (John Wayne) and Pony-That-Walks (Chief Big Tree) in *She Wore a Yellow Ribbon*. The Fordian hero's ability to negotiate under such stress is manifest in each instance. The military hierarchy also figures prominently in *Wee Willie Winkie*, in which rank and its privileges form a veritable subtext as Colonel Williams (C. Aubrey Smith) continuously asserts his status as commander and as Sergeant MacDuff (Victor McLaglen) makes a proper trooper out of the title character. If Priscilla (Shirley Temple) quickly becomes attired like a soldier, she proves to be the real thing when she forces Khoda Khan (Cesar Romero) and her grandfather to make peace as a tribute to her love for the fallen MacDuff.

situation, that of the relation between apprentice ... e in *Wee Willie Winkie* when the heroine is trained ... *Glory* when Quirt (Dan Dailey) exercises the troops ... and in *The Last Hurrah* when Skeffington (Spencer ... acy to Adam Caulfield (Jeffrey Hunter), who, like ... Carey, Jr.) in *She Wore a Yellow Ribbon*, ends up ... ciple of the older leader. *Mogambo* further echoes ... in the failed trek (or mission) that Vic and the others undertake, ... that even features their being accompanied by an unwanted female, Kelly (Ava Gardner), for whom they try, unsuccessfully, to supply transportation — as Brittles does for Mrs. Allshard and Olivia (Joanne Dru). The journeys in these films lead to the realization of true love, with romantic triangles being dissolved as a result.

An even more noticeably repeated feature is the often weary and frustrated return to a base or an original starting point, a situation that figures prominently in *She Wore a Yellow Ribbon* and *Rio Grande*. A beleaguered patrol's reappearance in *Wee Willie Winkie*, accompanied by the dying MacDuff, and the return of Rusty Ryan (John Wayne) to the PT boat base in *They Were Expendable* (1945) both create the same feeling of loss and weariness seen in the opening credits, in which troops trudge through the mud, in *What Price Glory*. The romantic possibilities in such returns are perhaps best dramatized in *The Hurricane*, where returning to Manakoora represents getting back to love and life itself both for the beleaguered Tarangi (Jon Hall) and eventually for the martinet DeLaage (Raymond Massey).

Familiar themes also abound in Ford's nonwestern films. In *Judge Priest*, the comically exaggerated wartime recollections of the old Confederates raise the same issue that colors the end of *Fort Apache*. These garrulous oldsters are rearranging the past to suit their memories of it: Captain York, in defending the memory of Colonel Thursday, is supplying a similarly usable past for (presumably) an entire nation. Ford's keen awareness of the eroding power of time, which makes human memories create versions of the past that diminish its ravages, is also conspicuous in *How Green Was My Valley* (1941), with its narrator's insistence that there is a "living truth" in memory. Such redemptive nostalgia finds its opposite expression in *The Last Hurrah*, in which the electoral defeat of Skeffington is equated with the loss of an entire way of life. Not only are the mayor's cronies displaced people but so is Caulfield, who has come to see how his uncle's more honest and honorable ways have been replaced by television commercials and plastic candidates.

The psychology of racism that so colors *The Searchers* and *Two Rode Together* is further elaborated in *Donovan's Reef*, where it serves as an unsettling element in an ostensible comedy. In this film, Amelia Dedham (Elizabeth Allen), represents a spiritual sister to Clementine Carter in *My Darling Clementine* in being a novice in a new society. Amelia brings her own personality and values to bear on the situation, and her acute reactions to the duplicities practiced on her ultimately restore communal health. From this angle, *Donovan's Reef* is potentially as dark in mood as the late westerns, since it is the dominant society that decrees that the half-breed children of Doctor Dedham (Jack Warden) be passed off as belonging to Donovan (John Wayne) so that presumed "outsider" delicacy will not be insulted. That Doctor Dedham himself goes along with such an arrangement finally supplies as sinister an undertone as does Laurie Jorgenson's (Vera Miles) urging Martin that Debbie (Natalie Wood) should be killed in *The Searchers*; indeed in *Donavan's Reef*, only Amelia's good sense saves all these people from their own worst selves.

Many Ford films take up the ideas of what home means and how societies have to function. The necessity for support from outside one's family arises in *The Long Voyage Home* (1940), in which the merchant seamen, much like members of Ford's cavalry, take care of each other whether in death (Dris [Thomas Mitchell] tenderly overseeing the demise of Yank [Ward Bond]) or life (the crew rescuing Ole [John Wayne] from being shanghaied). It is the erosion of such larger protective institutions and mores that marks both *The Grapes of Wrath* (1940) and *How Green Was My Valley*; indeed, it is only in the rate at which sustaining community values disappear that these films differ markedly. The need for a social contract, a binding spiritual and ethical consensus that assures disparate individuals that their lives and aims are respected and protected by the community at large, can also be seen in such diverse films as *They Were Expendable*, in which wartime exigencies dictate the need for sacrifice; *The Last Hurrah*, in which political bonds are used to assuage personal grievances; and *Donovan's Reef*, in which love can prosper only after deceptions have been abandoned.

Small pieces of dialogue from Ford's other works also recur in the westerns. Thus, Judge Priest admonishes one of his colleagues that the latter has breath "like a mince pie," a line that Captain Brittles uses fifteen years later to describe Sergeant Quincannon's (Victor McLaglen) state of sobriety in *She Wore a Yellow Ribbon*. The name Quincannon appears as early as *The Lost Patrol*, where it is the name of one of the soldiers (J. M. Kerrigan), and it reappears frequently as a good Irish-sounding moniker. In *The Informer* (1935), the line "Shut your gob!" figures prominently in the scene at Mrs. Betty's (May Boley) all-night party; it is hardly surprising when Sergeant Quincannon, in a moment of exasperation, urges Olivia Dandridge to do the same in *She Wore a Yellow Ribbon*.

When Mrs. Clay (Alice Brady) details the death of her husband in *Young Mr. Lincoln*, we are reminded of two of the westerns. His death at the hands of a drunken Indian immediately suggests the antics of Indian Charlie (Charles Stevens), the figure Wyatt must expel from Tombstone to get a shave in *My Darling Clementine*. At the same time, Mrs. Clay's emphasis on sunset foreshadows the eerie atmosphere during the assault on the Edwards' ranch in *The*

Searchers. The figure of Carrie Sue (Doris Bowdon) in *Young Mr. Lincoln*, who impulsively kisses the hero as the restored Clay family sets out for its farm, might well stand for the unseen Cory Sue, the beloved of James Earp (Don Garner) in *My Darling Clementine*, of whom Wyatt speaks. Certainly in her spontaneity of feeling, Carrie Sue represents the ideal young woman any Fordian hero would want to have at home.

Similar settings abound in Ford's films. The desert in *The Lost Patrol* is every bit as hostile as it appears to be in *Three Godfathers*. Courtrooms in *Judge Priest* and *Young Mr. Lincoln* resemble those in *Three Godfathers* and *Sergeant Rutledge* in their seating arrangements and easy judicial familiarities. The train station in *Wee Willie Winkie* resembles similar locations in *Three Godfathers*, *Sergeant Rutledge*, and most notably, *The Man Who Shot Liberty Valance*; and the carriage that MacDuff brings for the ladies in *Wee Willie Winkie* resembles a similar vehicle that takes Colonel Thursday and Philadelphia to Fort Apache. Koda Khan's rescue from jail by his tribesmen in *Wee Willie Winkie* also foreshadows a later western. The yanking away of the bars in his cell window is all but duplicated visually when the Apaches rescue their leader in *Rio Grande*. Ann Rutledge's gravesite in *Young Mr. Lincoln* and the pictures of the dead wives in *Judge Priest* and *The Last Hurrah* represent icons dedicated to the past and clearly resemble similar props in *My Darling Clementine* and *She Wore a Yellow Ribbon*. Just as Wyatt Earp and Nathan Brittles talk to their beloved dead, so do Judge Priest, the young Lincoln, and the elder Skeffington, remember the women they loved.

Fights in *Young Mr. Lincoln* and *Donovan's Reef* recur stylistically in the westerns. If anything, the close-quarter tussle between the Clay brothers (Richard Cromwell and Eddie Quillan) and Scrub White (Fred Kohler, Jr.) gives way to broader and stagier effects when Donovan and Gilhooley (Lee Marvin) go at it in *Donovan's Reef*. The comic tone of this latter kind of movie fisticuffs is caught up in the extended brawl between Sergeant Quincannon and those sent to arrest him in *She Wore a Yellow Ribbon*. The more serious grappling of *Young Mr. Lincoln* is reprised in *Wagonmaster* when Sandy (Harry Carey, Jr.) fights with Sam Jenkins (Don Summers) and Elder Wiggs (Ward Bond) must break it up. Ford's staging of the arrival of the Mormons at a creek in *Wagonmaster* is similar to the Joads' going swimming on their arrival in California in *The Grapes of Wrath*. In *Mogambo*, the staging of interiors, with a constant visual emphasis on the constraints of such spaces, recalls the scene in *Rio Grande* in which Jeff Yorke (Claude Jarman, Jr.) and his father (John Wayne) awkwardly talk inside the latter's tent.

The setting for the battle between the strikers and the security police in *The Grapes of Wrath*, a creek bottom with mist rising from it, is brought back in *The Searchers*. The wreckage of war in *They Were Expendable* is caught in a devastated camp and dynamited bridge that strikingly foreshadow settings in *She Wore a Yellow Ribbon* and *The Horse Soldiers*. Saloons figure prominently in *They Were Expendable, What Price Glory*, and *Donovan's Reef*; in these films such settings are where older professionals can be themselves and indulge in the nostalgic remembrances that make the saloons into viable communities. If the bar in New Jerusalem in *Three Godfathers* has some of that same quality, such locations in *Stagecoach, My Darling Clementine*, and *The Man Who Shot Liberty Valance* are more equivocal in their meanings; indeed, these barrooms become arenas in which the forces of good and evil struggle for ascendancy as gamblers, physicians, politicians, and cowboys try to assert their individual dominance.

The significance of meals, generally used by Ford as situations for courtship or community, can be seen in *The Hurricane, They Were Expendable*, and *Mogambo*. In the first film, such moments extend the intellectual and thematic struggle between DeLaage and the islanders he wants to control. The elaborate dinner for Sandy Davis (Donna Reed) in *They Were Expendable* is, of course, a full-scale rehearsal for the formal meals over which Kathleen Yorke (Maureen O'Hara) and Hanna Hunter (Constance Towers) preside in *Rio Grande* and *The Horse Soldiers*. The dinner party in *Mogambo* offers Kelly an opportunity to sing, a pattern already familiar from *Rio Grande* when the regimental singers' performance allows the married lovers' genuine feelings to surface.

Parades are prominent in *Judge Priest, Wee Willie Winkie, The Sun Shines Bright*, and *The Last Hurrah*. They function as reaffirmations of the community's commitments to military or political causes; and the ultimately redemptive or healing function of such episodes, best seen in *Judge Priest* and *The Sun Shines Bright*, clearly attaches to the final parades in *She Wore a Yellow Ribbon* and *Rio Grande*. In *The Last Hurrah*, Skeffington's walking away from his victorious opponent's parade signifies the emergence of a new order; the defeated mayor, like Tom Doniphon in *The Man Who Shot Liberty Valance*, has become an anachronism and must now exit from the "stage" of society. If concluding parades often allow for a kind of curtain call for Ford's performers, they also implicitly resolve the conflicts that have been at work in the films.

Two more notable plot situations that Ford consistently uses are funerals and dances. The solemnity of death, an occasion on which attention has to be shown for even the least worthy of a community's members, can be seen as early as *The Lost Patrol*; indeed, the zealous Saunders is cut short by the Sergeant (Victor McLaglen) in a scene that foreshadows Ethan Edwards's (John Wayne) stalking away from Martha's gravesite in *The Searchers*. The military funeral of MacDuff in *Wee Willie Winkie*, the sea burial of Yank in *The Long Voyage Home*, the interment of the grandfather (Charley Grapewin) in *The Grapes of Wrath*, and Rusty's eulogy for his fallen comrades in *They Were Expendable* all exhibit a pointed solemnity in the treatment of death. It comes as no surprise that similar rituals of respect occur in *She Wore a Yellow Ribbon*, when Captain Brittles salutes the fallen Trooper Smith (Rudy Bowman), and in *The Searchers*, when the protagonist's antisocial actions set in motion a host of far darker implications.

Church socials and dance settings are exploited in *Judge Priest, Mary of Scotland, Wee Willie Winkie, Young Mr. Lincoln*, and *They Were Expendable*. In nearly all these cases, romantic interests predominate, with the dance representing an acceptable occasion for the would-be lovers to be together. Although the outside world can intrude into such idyllic situations, as when Colonel Williams comes into the soirée in *Wee Willie Winkie* or Commander Brickley (Robert Montgomery) arrives to disengage Rusty from Sandy in *They Were Expendable*, romantic bonding largely controls these sequences. Only in the ornate and formal dance at Elizabeth's (Florence Eldridge) court in *Mary of Scotland* do we see a reversal of these associations, since that occasion serves as a prelude to additional political conniving on the part of the English Queen. The musical formality of this dance underlines its sinister nature; some of the same uneasiness carries over into the military dances in *Fort Apache* and *Two Rode Together*.

In Ford's films, the hero's drinking is generally a sign of spiritual fatigue or ethical weakness. In *Arrowsmith* (1931) the protagonist (Ronald Colman) imbibes heavily to soothe his spirit after he has lost his beloved wife (Helen Hayes); a similar pattern emerges in *They Were Expendable* when Rusty and the others drink to solace their grief over lost comrades and lovers. These associations make Colonel Marlowe's (John Wayne) angry drinking in *The Horse Soldiers* more suggestive, especially when we recall that the Union commander has lost his wife because of what he believes were doctors' errors. In *The Informer*, the poster of Frankie McPhillip (Wallace Ford), which clings to the leg of Gypo Nolan (Victor McLaglen), finds a reprise in *Wee Willie Winkie* when the wind blows away a message, and in the dust bowl that surrounds the Okies at the beginning of *The Grapes of Wrath*; such sequences make us much more aware of the meaning of the scenes that Ford chooses to surround with dust in *Fort Apache*. Religiosity heavily colors the end of *Mary of Scotland* and, of course, is dominant throughout *The Informer* and *The Fugitive*; it is little wonder that a biblical parable such as *Three Godfathers* should have interested Ford.

Among many symbolic objects that appear in Ford's films are the binoculars through which DeLaage spies Tarangi's escape in *The Hurricane* and that, finally, link the French governor with redemption and forgiveness — traits that Captain Brittles consistently shows to his subordinates in *She Wore a Yellow Ribbon*. The youthful Lincoln's excitement when he learns that the Clays have some books in their wagon at the beginning of *Young Mr. Lincoln* establishes the connection between reading and civilization, so that a similar emphasis in *The Man Who Shot Liberty Valance* comes as no surprise. Lincoln's sprawling postures in the earlier film, when he reads a law book or settles a dispute between two local farmers (Charles Halton and Russell Simpson), foreshadow Wyatt Earp athletically sitting in front of the hotel in *My Darling Clementine*. Ford's use of a newspaper headline to announce the death of Dris in *The Long Voyage Home* anticipates a similar device in *The Man Who Shot Liberty Valance* when Dutton Peabody (Edmond O'Brien) reads his own headline before being attacked by the outlaws. Finally, pictures abound as mementos of personal and historical pasts; indeed, the portrait of the deceased Polynesian mother in *Donovan's Reef* is simply part of a gallery that also includes Secretary Schurz's (Edward G. Robinson) portrait of Lincoln in *Cheyenne Autumn*.

Repeated camera setups also contribute heavily to the coherence of Ford's films. Long, dark corridors figure prominently in *Arrowsmith*, where we see the dying wife, Leora, physically receding into the darkness, and in *Judge Priest*, where the protagonist is framed in a doorway after he has stepped down from his beloved judicial bench. Such setups also abound in *Young Mr. Lincoln*, in which the hero is continuously framed in doorways to signify his emerging status; in *They Were Expendable*, in which the emergency hospital as well as the military headquarters are presented against this kind of visual emphasis; and in *Mogambo*, in which the lovers are seen noticeably in a doorway. Such visual framing also figures prominently in *Stagecoach* and *The Man Who Shot Liberty Valance*, in which romantic decisions, whether positive or negative, take place against such backdrops. Another celebrated Ford visual trademark, that of a mounted column moving against the horizon, works its way into *The Lost Patrol*; and similar assemblages figure in *The Grapes of Wrath*, *What Price Glory*, and *Mogambo*. We even see buglers, so noticeable in the credits to *Fort Apache* and *She Wore a Yellow Ribbon*, outlined against the horizon in *The Lost Patrol* and *Wee Willie Winkie*.

The impressionistic use of shadows in *The Informer* has been widely noted; *Mary of Scotland*, another RKO release from the same period, also exhibits intricate lighting patterns designed by Joseph August.[1] Although westerns do not usually lend themselves to such conspicuously artistic effects, *My Darling Clementine* abounds in such atmospheres, with Holliday's face being repeatedly seen in shadow to suggest his eventual fate. The gauzy photographic effects in *Rio Grande*, when Kathleen searches through Kirby's quarters for plates and silverware, are also present in *The Prisoner of Shark Island*, when the assassination of Lincoln takes place against such a pattern, as if to suggest the historical distance between the film audience and the time of the story. The juxtaposed closeups by which Ford introduces the villains in *My Darling Clementine* and *Wagonmaster* can be seen earlier in *The Informer* when the soldiers of the I.R.A. are shown contemplating Gypo before his trial. In *The Prisoner of Shark Island*, with its many visual suggestions of the drudgery of prison life, shots of feet foreshadow similar moments in *Wagonmaster*, which evokes a comparable atmosphere of endurance in the face of great odds. The sprightly riding scene involving the young lovers in *Fort Apache* reprises earlier moments in *Mary of Scotland* when the protagonist (Katharine Hepburn) and Bothwell (Fredric March) gallop away after he has freed her from the lairds, and in *Wee Willie Winkie* when Priscilla's mother (June Lang) and "Coppy" (Michael Whalen) ride away for an afternoon.

The pining, waiting woman appears regularly in Ford's films. The sequence in which Bothwell leaves the queen in *Mary of Scotland* typically ends with the heroine framed photographically to suggest the loss and loneliness descending upon her. Such a pattern can also be found at the end of *My Darling Clementine* as the heroine watches Wyatt become a speck in the distance, and in *Fort Apache* when the cavalry column sets off to pursue Colonel Thursday's foolish dreams. Lovers on balconies, so prominent in *Fort Apache* and, in a slightly more comic rendition, in *Two Rode Together*, can be seen in *Young Mr. Lincoln*, where the past intrudes to make Ann Rutledge (Pauline Moore) a more treasured memory to the hero than the living Mary Todd (Marjorie Weaver), with whom he is sharing his present.

Gestures also recur with great regularity. We see a character finding a whiskey bottle in a pail in *Arrowsmith* just as Sergeant Quincannon does in *She Wore a Yellow Ribbon*. Spitting in order to cut through pomposity is featured noticeably in *Judge Priest* and *Young Mr. Lincoln*, in which the same actor (Francis Ford), playing town drunks, consistently punctures the pomposity of the court proceedings; the same actor reprises this behavior in *Fort Apache*, at the waystation where his ringing assaults on a spittoon diminish Colonel Thursday's pompous outrage. The accusing finger, used so markedly by Captain Shattuck (Carleton Young) in *Sergeant Rutledge*, figures in both *The Informer* and *How Green Was My Valley* when characters try to either deflect or to establish guilt by this means. Male discomfort at waiting for children to be born is experienced by Hightower (John Wayne) in *Three Godfathers* and crops up as early as *The Prisoner of Shark Island*. Comic shouting, designed to embarrass rather than inform, finds its way into *Wee Willie Winkie* and *What Price Glory*, films whose military ethos accords well with that of *She Wore a Yellow Ribbon*, in which the same device is used.

We find a spooked horse and a distraught rider photographed in a similar fashion in both *Wee Willie Winkie* and *Wagonmaster*. Mulie (John Qualen) lets the earth slip through his fingers in *The Grapes of Wrath* to symbolize his loss of station, while Cochise defiantly throws dust to the ground to start the assault on the cavalry in *Fort Apache*. Water is poured into a bathtub in the same fashion in *How Green Was My Valley* and *The Searchers*. A gesture of respect for death is enacted in both *They Were Expendable* and *Three Godfathers* when a fallen comrade is comforted by one of his mates holding a hat over him to block out the sun and allow for some kind of demise in tranquility.

Larger narrative formulas and devices can also be seen in both Ford's westerns and his other films. *The Lost Patrol* embodies the same kind of initiation journey that is found in *She Wore a Yellow Ribbon. Judge Priest* and *The Grapes of Wrath* both have flashbacks handled in a style similar to what occurs in *The Searchers, Sergeant Rutledge,* and *The Man Who Shot Liberty Valance*; indeed, the increasing use of this narrative tactic in these later films implicitly suggests Ford's disenchantment with the more classic plot structures of his earlier westerns. It is as if such elaborate narrative structuring suggests the filmmaker's own growing self-consciousness about the very myths and values he has been presenting.

Dr. Kersaint's position as the narrator-rememberer of *The Hurricane* resembles that of Ransom Stoddard in *The Man Who Shot Liberty Valance.* Events draw the senator into a recollection of his past, and a shipboard conversation triggers a similar reverie for the French physician. The narrator in *How Green Was My Valley* supplies a complexity to the film by suggesting Huw (Roddy McDowall) as an adult looking back on these events; the same process is evident in *She Wore a Yellow Ribbon,* in which the narrator places the tale in a definite historical context in order to make the events of the past more coherent and meaningful. Finally, the use of monologues in *Drums Along the Mohawk*—Gil lamenting over the pain he has caused Lana in childbirth, or Father Rosenkrantz (Arthur Shields) combining religion, business, and social gossip in his sermon—prepares us for Hightower's lengthy oration about the woman and the busted well in *Three Godfathers.*

Drums Along the Mohawk (20th Century–Fox, 1939) is generally considered a western by commentators and critics, even though it takes place during the American Revolution and centers more on the domestic activities of female protagonist than on its male leading character. As a kind of "pre-western," *Drums Along the Mohawk* foreshadows many of the thematic and narrative concerns found in Ford's later efforts in the genre; however, its strongest claims to be a western are its frontier setting and Indian antagonists rather than its time, place, or characters. Ford's film is controlled by abrupt contrasts between the settled domesticity symbolized by Lana Martin (Claudette Colbert) and the nightmare world of marauding "savages" whose principal joy seems to be the burning of the settlers' homes. Indeed, the use of fire by the female protagonist and by the Indian raiders clearly dramatizes the two opposed worlds of these characters. By eschewing numerous opportunities for battle scenes and action sequences, Ford creates audience sympathy for Lana, who comes to embody the film's major themes. In operating from the woman's point of view, *Drums Along the Mohawk* serves as a commentary on all the other waiting and suffering wives and sweethearts in Ford's westerns.

Walter Edmonds's novel, which serves as the basis of Ford's film, is not only more diffuse in its plot but also quite different in key thematic emphases. Edmonds insists that the colonists in the Mohawk Valley had to protect themselves from the Tories and their Indian allies. Indeed, these settlers "suffered the paralysis of abject dependence on a central government totally unfit to comprehend a local problem."[2] Thus, throughout Edmond's novel, the colonists have to fight without any help from either the Continental Congress or the Revolutionary Army. In contrast, Ford's film, which was scripted by Lamar Trotti, Sonya Levien, and an uncredited William Faulkner, places a heavy emphasis on how much help the Mohawk Valley gets from General Washington. Also, in the interests of film narrative, the movie compresses campaigns and battle actions into a much shorter period than the novel does, with its narrative from 1776 to 1781.

To whittle Edmonds's book down even further, the screenwriters dropped such characters as John Woolf, a Tory sympathizer who is wrongly imprisoned and whose escape makes up a large part of the novel. The figures of Nancy Schuyler and her retarded brother, Hon Yost, were also jettisoned. Nancy's sexual escapades, her illegitimate child, and her final choosing of an Indian husband were features of her character that would, undoubtedly, not have played well with the Hays Office (Motion Picture Producers and Distributors of America) in 1939. In addition, many of Edmonds's Tory commanders either were not in the film or were amalgamated into the single character of Caldwell (John Carradine). The peacock feather that Lana so admires is retained for the movie, as are the characters of Pastor Rosenkrantz and Mrs. McKlennar (Edna May Oliver). These two characters even give speeches that are lifted from Edmonds's work; however, the screenwriters and Ford contrive to make these figures more dramatically rounded in the film. Thus, the churchman not only delivers a sermon in which he mentions a merchant's sale but also announces the invasion of the Mohawk Valley. Mrs. McKlennar gives a speech about her late husband's love for war; however, in Ford's version she moves much more to the center of the community than she does in the novel. Characteristically, Ford has Mrs. McKlennar die, dramatically, from an Indian arrow, whereas Edmonds merely records her death in a final chapter and, ironically, points out that the bequest of her property to Gil and Lana was contested and overruled by the local government, which wanted back taxes from her estate.[3]

The film imposes a host of additional changes: Lana's parents are wealthy residents of Albany rather than struggling lower-class farmers who get massacred; the property and homes of the Tories are not raided by the colonists; Blue Back (Chief Big Tree) is consistently loyal to his American friends rather than wandering the forests and warning his Indian allies of an impending colonial raid; John Weaver (Robert Lowery) is only wounded and not killed at the end of the story. Joe Boleo (Francis Ford), who functions as a scout throughout the novel, dies dramatically in Ford's film when the besieging Indians capture him and attempt to burn him in front of the fort. While Edmonds mentions a similar incident (in which the Indians wisely stayed out of rifle range), Ford's treatment turns this episode into a visually and thematically arresting sequence in which the austere Rosenkrantz must finally commit murder in the interests of mercy. General Herkimer's (Roger Imhof) death is turned into a nighttime operation inside Mrs. McKlennar's house, in order to stress the tragic aftermath of war. In the novel the commander is wounded in the knee and dies after some time as an invalid at home. Gil Martin's return from war shows him as primarily fatigued and taciturn in the novel; Ford's film alters this return into another dramatic high point in which Lana finds her wounded husband in the road and then nurses him as he recounts the battle (which is presented directly by Edmonds). In this long monologue, which is intercut with a scene of Herkimer talking with the military doctor, Ford again emphasizes the lack of glamour or glory in warfare.

That theme is combined with the personal growth of Lana Martin in the wilderness to give *Drums Along the Mohawk* its intellectual spine. Initially horrified at her rugged surroundings, a reaction brought on by the entry of Blue Back, Lana becomes a resilient frontier woman, symbolized when she shoots an Indian at the fort in the final battle scene. Her transformation is signaled when the Martins lose their first farm to marauding Indians and she urges that it's like "losing part of ourselves." Ford combines this loss with Lana's miscarriage to heighten the change in his protagonist, for when she and a now-despondent Gil visit the burned-out ruins of their cabin, it is Lana who insists that they can rebuild. Her insistence that they go to work for Mrs. McKlennar and her subsequent successful pregnancy further show how Lana changes; indeed, after the hoedown wedding of John Weaver, she spies Gil with their son and prays that their life will go on "forever" just as it is. During the siege at the fort, Lana does not allow Gil to see her fears about his going for help; instead, she faints only after she hears that he has gotten away. Ford then reverses the earlier sequence, in which Lana found Gil in the road, by having the husband discover his exhausted wife and crying child after the battle has been won.

Ford's themes in *Drums Along the Mohawk* are ably abetted by Alfred Newman's musical score, which uses both original and derived melodies. A stately minuet underscores the marriage of Gil and Lana in her parents' house, and we hear this theme on Lana's first evening in her new cabin home. Newman reprises this music in slightly discordant and somber renditions to suggest the sense of loss that Lana is feeling. When she picks up a broken teapot in her burned home, we hear a more recessed version of this minuet, in keeping with how Lana has begun to put her old life behind her. Newman's score also features a love theme, which significantly drowns out his minuet when Gil consoles Lana after Blue Back's first appearance, and a traveling theme, which underlines their initial trek into the wilderness. In addition, the composer supplies agitated figures and "Indian" music to signal Lana's distress on meeting Blue Back and the assault of Caldwell's Indians on the Martins' farm. Such musical figures are also prominent when Gil outruns three Indian pursuers during the celebrated chase sequence. While Adam Helmer (renamed

Hartmann and played by Ward Bond in the film) performs this feat in Edmonds's novel, Newman's music offers extended support to a lengthy sequence that is without dialogue.

Newman works in "Yankee Doodle" through Gil's run to imply that the colonist is winning, for that theme has been prominent during the militia drill and the earlier appearance of Washington's regulars. When we see the locals marching to impress their women, we hear a slightly skewed version of this familiar music; with the American regulars, we get a more prominent rendition. During Gil's race with the savages, "Yankee Doodle" simply assumes greater prominence as he pulls away from them. Newman's other notable musical borrowing is "My Country 'Tis of Thee," which dominates the final scene. Since Ford's film has consistently presented the colonists as united behind the larger government, in contrast to Edmonds's book, it is only natural that his *Drums Along the Mohawk* ends with Adam getting an American flag to decorate the highest spire in the fort and with Gil, Lana, and the others staring affectionately at the new symbol of their nation. Such overt patriotism may, again, have been more expected in 1939 than today; however, this melody and Ford's camera shots are intended to close the film on a high note for any audience.

Ford's sense of composition, aided by cameramen Bert Glennon and Ray Rennahan, is also striking in *Drums Along the Mohawk*, which was his first technicolor film. The title credits feature designs that represent homelike crocheted scenes to suggest the domestic emphasis of the film. Lana's initial dismay at her new home finds her seated forlornly before a fire with her back to the camera. Gil moves to the fire and then smiles at her, as if to indicate that he is still the dominant partner. However, when the protagonists are later shown their new home by Mrs. McKlennar, Ford has both of them sit facing a fireplace, presumably to suggest how Gil and Lana have become equals. One other striking camera shot occurs when two drunken Indians burn Mrs. McKlennar's house and Gil, out in the fields, reacts to the disaster. In a long shot, we see Martin threshing as smoke billows from the house; then Gil turns and reacts, which leads to another long shot in which we see him riding headlong toward the trouble. Mrs. McKlennar's confrontation with the two Indians once again shows the often violent contrasts of Ford's plot and, at the same time, is infused with humor, as the widow dominates her two would-be assailants and inveigles them into taking her and her bed downstairs.

Other comic touches are not quite as deft. Rosenkrantz tells what is no doubt an inside joke during his sermon when he mentions how "nothing good" can be said about any man from Massachusetts (Ford was born in Maine). The lengthy birth sequence, in which Gil becomes the center of attention amid a group of supportive if drunken men, uses clichés that are a little difficult to find amusing. Martin is so upset that he must run out and vomit, and comic remarks are elicited from Blue Back about a "woman's place" during childbirth —

both of which seem heavy-handed at best today. The comic antics of Christian Reall (Eddie Collins), who gets angry and then apologetic when no one answers to his repeated shouting of his own name during the militia roll call, also pall very quickly. Reall's penchant for alcohol throws him into conflict with Rosenkrantz, but his being so drunk that he believes Gil's new son is his child simply comes across as excess. The final joke in *Drums Along the Mohawk* finds Blue Back answering the angry Captain Morgan (Tom Tyler), who wants to know what has become of the Tory leader Caldwell. Ford's Indian rises in a pulpit to show that he is now wearing Caldwell's distinctive eye patch. Although dialogue has been subordinated to editing here, the presence of an overreacting Reall makes the effect simply too obvious.

Moments in *Drums Along the Mohawk* that foreshadow Ford's other sound films are more notable. Blue Back's cutting of a stick for Gil to beat Lana with anticipates the moment when one of the locals gives Sean Thornton (John Wayne) a stick to "beat the lovely lady [Maureen O'Hara as Mary Kate] with" in *The Quiet Man*. The appearances of such actors as Francis Ford, Ward Bond, and Jack Pennick also supply *Drums Along the Mohawk* with the familiar aura that many have come to refer to as the Ford "stock company." Digging up a tree stump to clear Gil's meadow is an undertaking that later westerns have copied; indeed, we see a variation of this action in *Shane* (Paramount, 1953) when the protagonist (Alan Ladd) and Joe Starrett (Van Heflin) dig up a seemingly immovable stump and, again, in *Pale Rider* (Warner Bros., 1985) when the mysterious "Preacher" (Clint Eastwood) helps the miners break a large stone. Gil is lowered from the fort to outrun the Indians, an act that is visually reprised in *The Searchers* when Martin Pauley (Jeffrey Hunter) is lowered from a cliff into Chief Scar's camp. When Gil pauses in the woods to note that Caldwell has renewed the assault, he is interrupted by an arrow that nearly hits him and alerts him to the presence of his Indian pursuers. A similar moment occurs in *She Wore a Yellow Ribbon* when Sergeant Tyree (Ben Johnson), looking at a hat he has found on the trail, is stopped by an arrow that flies past him, alerting him to a nearby enemy.

Drums Along the Mohawk also features two scenes in which tired troops return from a mission. In the first, Gil and the others come back sullenly after chasing Caldwell for "eight miles," and the overall effect is subordinate to Martin's wanting to find out about Lana's miscarriage. In the second sequence, the bedraggled remains of Herkimer's command trudge through the rain, and the wounded are taken into Mrs. McKlennar's house. This sequence — with its emphasis on sheer survival, its ominous notes in Morgan's warning that no one behind him has been left alive, and Lana's going forward to find the fallen and exhausted Gil — anticipates the somber returns we see in *She Wore a Yellow Ribbon* and *Rio Grande*. The overall horror of war that we see in *How the West Was Won* is also suggested more subtly by this earlier sequence.

The most visually striking moments in *Drums Along the Mohawk* occur when Gil leaves on the second mission. Ford's camera cuts between Gil, marching, and Lana, following, but Lana gradually becomes the dominant focus of interest. She runs parallel to the marching column to keep Gil in view, and then, after a cut to Mrs. McKlennar talking to her servant, we are returned to a long shot in which Lana stands on a rise and the soldiers trek toward the horizon down a narrow trail. As the troops march away, Lana falls to the ground on one arm to symbolize her sense of loss. This discreet long-shot treatment will be reworked in the same situation at the end of *My Darling Clementine,* while painful romantic partings will be featured in *Rio Grande* and *The Searchers.*

How the West Was Won (MGM, 1962) contains a twenty-five-minute middle section directed by Ford in seemingly offhand fashion. This nearly three-hour epic — designed to lure audiences to something they could not see on television — is, at best, overblown and uneven. Since the bulk of the film was directed by George Marshall and Henry Hathaway, and since the emphasis throughout is on stars and costly effects, *How the West Was Won* could hardly have been an inviting project for the aging John Ford. Despite all these reservations, we can clearly recognize his stamp on the Civil War section that he directed; indeed, characteristic touches are probably more noticeable in a threadbare effort such as this one than in Ford's more developed westerns.

This section of *How the West Was Won* tells of the initiation of Zeb Rawlings (George Peppard) into the brutal realities of war. The younger Rawlings is eager to leave home and go to battle despite the efforts of his mother (Carroll Baker) to send him west to California and safety. Zeb's enthusiasm is initially abetted by a corporal (Andy Devine) who insists there is no glory in pushing a plow and that the Civil War will be a short one. When Ford cuts to the aftermath of the battle of Shiloh, Zeb now notes, to a newfound Confederate friend (Russ Tamblyn), that war "ain't quite what I expected." The hellishness of combat is carried even further when Zeb must bayonet the Confederate to prevent the latter from shooting General Grant (Harry Morgan). After he has killed the southern deserter, Zeb holds the lifeless body and cries, "Why did you make me do that?" Ford has reinforced this theme earlier by showing the death of Zeb's father, Linus (James Stewart), whose corpse is placed on an operating table only to be dismissed by a harried physician (Willis Bouchey). At the same time, in the aftermath of battle, we see Union soldiers digging and then filling a mass grave for their dead comrades. When Zeb returns home triumphant some years later, he belatedly learns of his mother's death when he sees a stone for her in the family plot; his brother reinforces the horrors-of-war theme by remarking that their father's corpse is, of course, not really under the headstone next to their mother's. Zeb now decides that he will reenlist and head west, thus setting up the movie's final section.

Once again, Alfred Newman is the featured composer, and he begins this section of *How the West Was Won* by quoting one of his leading melodies for Ford's *Young Mr. Lincoln*. This theme, which is used to invoke the heroic image of the future president in that earlier film, is used here to underscore a silent scene in which we see Lincoln (Raymond Massey) writing, with narration by Spencer Tracy. When Zeb insists that he will go to war, his mother's dismay is caught by Newman's somber rendition of his main theme; later, when we see Mrs. Rawlings collapse by the fence around the family plot, the scene is accompanied by "When Johnny Comes Marching Home," suggesting how unthinking Zeb must be. That familiar melody reappears when young Rawlings comes home and lands at a wharf, but then Newman underscores Zeb's learning of his mother's death with a somber version of his otherwise quite inspiring main theme to *How the West Was Won*. Throughout this section of the film, music has consistently been used to demarcate loss and sorrow, for even the jaunty lyrics to "When Johnny Comes Marching Home" quickly become pointless in the face of the slaughter of Shiloh.

Ford also managed to imbue his part of *How the West Was Won* with such characteristic devices as Lincoln as an American icon. Indeed, the Great Emancipator is invoked in the same reverent way in which he is treated in *The Prisoner of Shark Island*, at the end of *Young Mr. Lincoln*, and in *Cheyenne Autumn*. The sacrifices of mothers are also underscored by the photographic and dramatic treatment of Eve Rawlings. When she is thwarted by her son, she retreats to the family graveyard and talks to her dead father in a scene that automatically recalls moments in *My Darling Clementine* and *She Wore a Yellow Ribbon* as well as similar scenes from *Judge Priest* and *The Last Hurrah*. Communication with the dead suggests the ongoing social community of past and present in which all of Ford's good characters have to choose or learn to live. Sitting on the ground by a conspicuously crossed section of wooden fence, Eve resembles a suffering Madonna at the foot of a cross — an artistic suggestion that is not altogether amiss when we realize that she has sacrificed her life to the men in it and when we learn that she dies largely because she loses the will to live after she hears of her husband's death at Shiloh. Perhaps Ford's most obvious signature feature that we can see in his section of *How the West Was Won* occurs when Grant and Sherman (John Wayne) talk while Zeb and the Confederate deserter eavesdrop. This sequence, despite its almost schoolbook-sounding dialogue between the two generals, again shows how Ford combines the public (historical) narrative with the private lives of ordinary (i.e., nonhistorical) figures.

Indeed, the private story, in which Zeb must kill his friend, stands for the larger, public story, of the Civil War, in which Americans killed Americans. However, what Ford quickly suggests in *How the West Was Won* is worked out in much richer detail in *The Horse Soldiers*, a film that offers a narrative key to the rest of Ford's sound westerns.

Chapter 4

The Horse Soldiers

Hardly any commentators rate *The Horse Soldiers* (1959) among John Ford's better films.[1] Yet this work exhibits the plot motifs, character types, and dramatic situations that distinguish his westerns. Ford's characteristic methods of dealing with a text, the omissions and additions that arose between an original source and a finished movie, can be clearly discerned in *The Horse Soldiers*. Notably, the three major plot motifs around which his remaining sound westerns are organized — the cavalry, the double heroes, the journey — are all utilized in this film. For anyone wanting to examine a typical Ford work that catches his blemishes as well as his beauty spots, *The Horse Soldiers* will serve well. In its pictoral emphases, its manipulations of historical facts, and its adherence to recurrent settings, *The Horse Soldiers* functions as a prime example of what the director did and how he did it.

By examining the specific changes that take place between Harold Sinclair's novel and the completed film, we can see how Ford created narratives that reflected his own commercial sense and thematic interests. Saying that a director should possess the latter quality is, of course, not quite the same thing as saying that he possesses it; the number of truly inspired films produced in any single year, let alone by a single filmmaker over his career, is never likely to be large. Since Ford is one of the very few directors who offer subtle thematic works, an examination of his methods in even a less celebrated work shows the artistic consistencies that mark his entire output.

The most immediately striking feature of *The Horse Soldiers* is its sense of photographic composition. Long shots of mounted riders are veritable icons in Ford westerns, and he satisfies here with shots of the Union column as it leaves La Grange in a manner highly reminiscent of Captain Brittles's (John Wayne) departure for his last patrol in *She Wore a Yellow Ribbon*. We are, indeed, brought into the narrative of *The Horse Soldiers* by shots of a moving cavalry column in the opening credits, shots that juxtapose these mounted men to railroad tracks to foreshadow the key elements of the plot. An early scene at La Grange finds Matthew Brady posing the principals for one of his compositions, in a sequence that Ford uses to call attention to the personalities of Colonel Marlowe (John Wayne) and Colonel Secord (Willis Bouchey).

Johnny Miles (Carleton Young) leads the Confederate troops at the end of their symbolically futile charge down the main street of Newton Station in *The Horse Soldiers* (United Artists, 1959).

Later, on the mission, shots of Confederate horsemen on a distant riverbank reprise those of the Union column. The entire sequence at Newton Station, replete with the destruction of railroad ties, rails, and train cars, as well as the heroic, futile, and foolhardy charge of the Confederate forces down the town's main street, continues this visual assault, as does the splendidly athletic rendering of the later attack of the military school cadets on Marlowe's weary troopers. *The Horse Soldiers* also exhibits a photographic mastery during the last battle between Marlowe's troopers charging over the bridge and the Confederate batteries commanding the opposite side of the river. The final moments between Doctor Kendall (William Holden) and Hannah Hunter (Constance Towers) also underline Ford's superb visual sense, for his juxtaposition of these two individuals with the incoming Confederate cavalry column nicely makes the point that Marlowe has gone and that a different social order has been restored in his wake.

The Horse Soldiers presents some patent falsifications that are designed to create artistic truths at the expense of historical veracity. As a maker of westerns, Ford clearly recognized their fictional nature. A critic of *Stagecoach* faulted the chase across the flats, urging that, in reality, the Apaches would have killed some of the horses and brought the whole affair to a quick end.[2] The director rather sagely responded that if that had happened, he would not have had a movie. While such freewheeling with historical realities may upset some viewers, Ford's awareness of the need to entertain an audience was perfectly in keeping with Hollywood filmmaking being a notoriously uneasy mixture of art and commerce. Throughout his career, Ford remained cognizant of the disparities that arise between the ways things were and the ways humans wish they had been or choose to remember them as having been. Indeed, some of his most powerful westerns, *Fort Apache* and *The Man Who Shot Liberty Valance* especially, consciously examine this often troublesome and troubling relationship.

The Confederate characters who appear in Sinclair's novel are not particularly noteworthy, since they are driven by short-range, personal, and immediate motives, just as real people might actually be as they experience the larger "historical" circumstances in which they are living. Thus, we find a local merchant who protests the burning of cotton at Newton Station on the grounds of financial loss, and a railroad official who can think only about getting a cashbox out of a building the Yankee troops are about to destroy. Sinclair's Captain Bryce encounters a southern matron, whom he treats with great deference, but her mental weakness is never given any serious symbolic weight; and the appearance of her daughter, who has lost a husband in the war, does not notably add any thematic density to this essentially chance encounter. Sinclair's portrayal of such unfortunate characters is rather consistently subordinated to his awareness of historical accuracy, an allegiance he maintains by using the proper names of those who actually pursued Grierson in his 1863 raid. These brief references in the novel to commanders who essentially lack any luck do not, finally, make the Confederates appear as fools. Indeed, since so much of Sinclair's novel illustrates the vagaries that attend any military operation, the misfortunes of the Confederate pursuers simply demonstrate that chance as well as skill may be essential to military success.

Among a host of chronological and factual liberties, John Lee Mahin and Martin Rackin's film script for *The Horse Soldiers* refers to Andersonville and so ignores the fact that this particular prison was not in existence when Grierson's raid actually took place (April 1863). Naturally, such references can be dismissed as merely a shorthand way of calling up the horror of being incarcerated in a South in which there was hardly enough food to feed citizens, let alone prisoners. An even more glaring change (albeit another one that can be rationalized on the grounds that any fictional historical reconstruction can take liberties when it presents conversations that were never recorded verbatim) takes place at the very beginning of the film when Marlowe is called in to confer with Generals Grant (Stan Jones) and Sherman (Richard Cutting). Whereas he meets with only General Hurlbut in the novel, the protagonist's meeting with these more prestigious figures is probably consistent with the assumption that most movie audiences would be more likely to "recognize" these more celebrated historical figures. However, when the two Union commanders argue that they stand to lose the entire war because of the protracted siege of Vicksburg, they increase the importance of Grierson/Marlowe's raid about tenfold. If anything, after the battle of Shiloh in 1862 (which is mentioned by Sinclair but never alluded to by any character in the film), Grant moved rather consistently through his Confederate opposition.

While Ford and his writers may well have felt that a little exaggeration wouldn't hurt, at the same time the director manages to use this foundation to build a notable subtext about the Civil War and its outcome. Since Marlowe's expedition carries such an important status within the film, the encounter with the Confederates at Newton Station also comes to have a greater symbolic weight. In effect, the mechanical and rational means that Marlowe uses to defeat his more courageous and foolhardy opponents becomes a microcosmic enactment of the entire war, with Union efficiency and technology eventually wearing down Confederate bravery. Indeed, unless Ford is operating with such a thematic intention, it is very difficult to make any sense of the Confederates' precipitate behavior at Newton Station.

Ford's film also softens and extends its portrayals of Confederate characters by presenting them in more idealized conditions. Hannah, whose plantation is ostensibly suffering from the effects of Union pressure, is still able to provide three capons for the officers' dinner she presents, even though she must apologize that the price of sugar makes offering any sort of dessert impossible. Her devotion to the southern cause, which leads her to spy on Marlowe's conference about going to Baton Rouge, puts Hannah's conduct above that of the novel's greedy stationmasters and eccentric old ladies. Johnny Miles (Carleton Young), another character found only in the film, symbolizes the doggedness that Ford associates with the Confederacy at its best. Certainly Miles resembles such stalwarts as Sergeant Tyree and Trooper Smith in *She Wore a Yellow Ribbon*. The elderly Sheriff Goodboy (Russell Simpson) naturally tries to round up the deserting "trash," Virgil (Strother Martin) and Jagger Jo (Denver Pyle), even though he appears far too frail for such a task and has been made a prisoner by these rascals. Hannah's devoted black servant, Lukey (Althea Gibson), gladly accompanies her mistress when Marlowe insists that he cannot leave them behind because of their knowledge of his plans, and this faithful woman is ultimately mystified when she is accidentally killed by a Confederate sniper near a black church.

The crucial issue of slavery is, in fact, raised only once, when Kendall notes, to a petulant Hannah, that Southerners have grown accustomed to being waited on. For the most part, slavery is reduced to jokes about "contraband" (with even Lukey noting at one point that this is what she must be), and so the South takes on a much gentler air because of the film's comic downplaying of the "peculiar institution." The grandfatherly head of the military academy (Basil Ruysdael), who walks into battle calmly like a biblical prophet, further embodies the film's idealized perception of southerners, as does the anonymous cavalry commander whose first remark to Kendall, after Marlowe has escaped and destroyed the only bridge by which his force could have been pursued, is to chivalrously ask if his company physician might be of any assistance. Naturally, in keeping with the transformation of *The Horse Soldiers* from a realistic historical novel to a viable commercial film, the Confederacy must also contain such comic "trash" as Virgil and Jagger Jo. And, even more consistently in line with conventional cinematic heroics, Marlowe not only returns these reprobates to southern justice but also takes delight in knocking them both out before doing so.

Ford's film also embodies numerous plot lines and camera setups that can be found in his other works. Hannah Hunter clearly resembles Kathleen Yorke (Maureen O'Hara) in *Rio Grande*. Like that character, Hannah has her southern home invaded by Yankee soldiers in time of war; however, Marlowe's troops do not destroy Greenbriar, whereas Kirby Yorke's soldiers do destroy Bridesdale in the earlier film. Kirby (John Wayne) and Kathleen were already married when he burned her plantation because of orders, and this incident, which precipitates their marital estrangement, is never shown but only referred to when their son Jeff (Claude Jarman, Jr.) and his mother arrive at Yorke's western military encampment. *The Horse Soldiers,* which conspicuously grafts the romantic relationship of Marlowe and Hannah onto its original source, reverses Ford's earlier film by having the hero's arrival at the heroine's plantation lead to love between them despite the later destruction of Newton Station. In effect, Hannah Hunter achieves a romantic rapprochement with her Yankee beloved in a matter of days, whereas Kathleen Yorke takes years to arrive at a similar point in *Rio Grande*.

When Marlowe's troops encounter the young cadets in yet another instance in which Ford's film takes liberties with history, the Union commander foils Sergeant Kirby (Judson Pratt) in his attempt to fire on the advancing youngsters. Marlowe drives Kirby's rifle into the ground so that it discharges harmlessly in a gesture that duplicates the action of the Reverend/Captain Clayton (Ward Bond) and Ethan Edwards (John Wayne) at the river battle in *The Searchers.* Just as Clayton wants to prevent the killing of wounded Indians, Marlowe strives to prevent his men from becoming child killers. Given the more comic tone of *The Horse Soldiers* at this point (one trooper is knocked off a log by the cadets' rifle fire and get up immediately to scurry away), Marlowe's conduct is not resented by Kirby. After all, in a pell-mell retreat, in which a headstrong Confederate drummer boy manages to evade his careworn mother (Anna Lee) only to end up being spanked by one of Marlowe's troopers, such haste is everything.

Ford also uses a tent for the initial confrontation between Marlowe and Kendall, when the physician finally insists that his commander "get off" his back. Shots in which tents are photographed to emphasize the equal status of those inside figure prominently in *Rio Grande*, when Jeff and his father speak about the boy's unexpected arrival; in *Two Rode Together*, when McCabe (James Stewart) and Gary (Richard Widmark) argue after the former has accepted the offer of Henry Wringle (Willis Bouchey) to bring back any Indian boy who will fit his new wife's description of her lost son; and in *Cheyenne Autumn*, when such crowded quarters highlight the growing anger of Captain Archer (Richard Widmark) over the dawdling congressional party and the increasing dismay of Sergeant Wichowsky (Mike Mazurki) over his role in pursuing the Indians. In each case, Ford uses this setting to highlight conflicts while, at the same time, reasserting the military ethos in which such disputes take place.

Comedy also attaches to such settings because Captain Yorke measures Jeff's height after the boy has left his tent in *Rio Grande*, and McCabe stands uncomfortably at attention, mocking army ceremony, with his head against the top of the tent in *Two Rode Together*. The primary emphasis in each of these scenes is initially on the character who challenges established authority before he moves out of the enclosure. However, in the more somber *Two Rode Together* and *Cheyenne Autumn*, characters leave such settings to exit into the nightmare worlds of the searchers' camp or the blistering sun baking the patient and supplicant Indians. Major Kendall in *The Horse Soldiers* and Jeff Yorke in *Rio Grande* go out into safer worlds than do McCabe or Captain Archer, who inhabit narratives in which there are far fewer possibilities for heroic acts.

Ford also uses shadows to indicate impending influences, and we can see this device when Marlowe returns to say goodbye to Hannah before blowing up the bridge. His shadow's emergence across her figure subtly suggests how he has become the center of her life, and once again, Ford varies a recurrent visual image. A more sinister employment of the same technique occurs in *The Searchers* during the massacre at the Edwards' ranch: Debbie's (Lana Wood) escape to supposed safety in the family graveyard is quickly cut short when the shadow of Chief Scar (Henry Brandon) falls across her kneeling figure. A more benign instance of this device finds Olivia Dandridge (Joanne Dru) intruding on Captain Brittles's nightly report to his dead wife in *She Wore a Yellow Ribbon*; she first appears as a shadow that comes across the headstone by which the aged Captain Brittles is sitting.

Still another device that Ford uses in *The Horse Soldiers* and then reprises elsewhere occurs when Kendall finishes operating on Marlowe's leg wound and douses his operating table with water to wash away the blood. Since we have already seen an orderly literally pouring a bucket of blood into the street outside Newton Station's emergency hospital, such imagery stands prominently for the butchery that accompanied the Civil War. In the later, brief section of *How the West Was Won* directed by Ford, we see another operating table in the aftermath of the battle of Shiloh in which such dousing symbolizes the death of Linus Rawlings in *How the West Was Won*. Since these episodes dramatize one of Ford's more pressing observations about the Civil War — showing friends who have to kill each other so that the nation might survive — this visual association of washing and primal loss fits into his larger thematic concerns. In *The Horse Soldiers*, Kendall's action occurs only after he has exacted professional revenge on Marlowe by causing the latter to wince while having a bullet removed.

A far larger repetitive visual pattern is seen when Hannah momentarily looks after Marlowe's departing image in a romantic farewell. This scene appears most conspicuously in *Drums Along the Mohawk*, when the marching column that contains Gil (Henry Fonda) goes off as Lana (Claudette Cobert) collapses on a rise that overlooks their path. We see similar moments in *My Darling Clementine* when Clementine Carter (Cathy Downs) stands at the top of another rise and looks down on the winding trail on which Wyatt (Henry Fonda) and Morgan Earp (Ward Bond) ride off to the west; in *Three Godfathers* when Ruby Latham (Dorothy Ford) waves goodbye to the repentant Bob Hightower (John Wayne), now on his way to prison; and in *The Searchers* when Martha Edwards (Dorothy Jordan) waves farewell to Ethan (John Wayne) as he rides away looking for Lars Jorgenson's (John Qualen) stolen cattle. Such departures, in which the woman is always portrayed as the waiting half of the relationship, reach an apogee in *Fort Apache* when the wives and lovers (Irene Rich, Anna Lee, Shirley Temple) stand on a parapet as the troop sets out on its final, disastrous mission under Colonel Thursday (Henry Fonda). In *The Horse Soldiers*, Hannah's pensive stance, as she stares through the smoke of the burned bridge, places her solidly in this line of thematic imagery; and Kendall's emergence to guide her back into the cabin hospital reasserts the notion that love must be subordinated to duty, a prominent theme in Ford's cavalry films.

Such emotional decorum is surely in keeping with Ford's treatment of romance and marriage throughout his films. Men and women can be passionately attracted and can act on such feelings (as in *The Quiet Man* in the graveyard when it rains on the "runaway" Sean Thornton [John Wayne] and Mary Kate [Maureen O'Hara]), but such emotions are better expressed in private than in public moments. Ford's lovers invariably inhabit middle-class environments, so that restraint rather than appetite is a much more reliable guide for their behavior. There is, finally, no clinging female like Josefa (Jean Peters) who must be kicked away by her husband (Marlon Brando) in *Viva Zapata!* when she intuits that he is riding into a death trap. The ideal Ford woman is like Mrs. Collingwood (Anna Lee) in *Fort Apache*: she places her mate's (George O'Brien) social role above her feelings and their romantic commitment.

Since Sinclair's novel utilizes the historical record of Grierson's Raid for its basic plot, military maneuvers dictate how the story unfolds. The novelist adds considerable chunks of conversation and individual motivation by means of his third-person point of view; Mahin and Rackin's plot, while it offers far more improbabilities, coheres much better simply in terms of an initial event leading to its successor and so on. Sinclair concentrates on how mud, rain, hunger, stumbling and broken horses, fatigue, distance, confusion over directions, and hurry beset his principal characters. Military leadership consists of taking advantage of every opportunity thrown into one's path and, at the same time, of always knowing just how far to drive one's subordinates. Thus, Captain Bryce emerges as the ideal commander during a diversionary raid he undertakes at Marlowe's order. The captain knows when to rest his men and realizes that such necessities as food and sleep are more essential than glory. Bryce's letter written home, which brings Sinclair's novel to its end, establishes the character's respect for Marlowe by offering a fitting verdict on the protagonist.

Only two significant conflicts between the officers occur in the novel: when Marlowe places Keller, one of two physicians assigned to the raid, under arrest because he has aided a pregnant Confederate woman when Union troops were hurting; and later when Captain Gray becomes angry at what he perceives as cutting behavior by his commanding officer. Since this second instance arises from a tactical mistake that Gray makes and that costs the entire column valuable time, it is not without foundation — a perception that Sinclair augments by showing that, after Gray's error has come to light, Marlowe thinks about promoting Bryce over Gray. Gray's subsequent suicidal behavior — charging an entrenched Confederate position and promptly getting killed — brings this potential source of irritation to an end. Keller's willingness to stay behind with the wounded, and so become a prisoner, effectively mutes his earlier disagreement with Marlowe. Sinclair's novel also devotes lengthy sections to the actions of subordinates such as Bryce and Blaney, who is sent back to La Grange, according to a preconceived plan, to draw the Confederates' attention.

Ford's film adds numerous details to the plot of Sinclair's novel. The quarrel between Marlowe and Kendall, which culminates with the physician's being reprimanded and placed (briefly) under arrest after he delivers a black baby, starts from the moment the doctor appears at the initial strategy session with the rest of the general staff. Their rivalry is exacerbated by Kendall's insistence that he has taken a higher oath — to practice healing whenever and wherever he finds a need for it. Ford's film also uses the physician's nobility to motivate the delay that Marlowe's command later experiences in the novel. At Newton Station, Kendall insists that he will be operating for up to five hours, and Marlowe fumes in a nearby bar as a result.

At the same time, the film places these two characters on a nearly equal footing, since each man is adept in war and compassionate toward the injured. Kendall uncovers Hannah's duplicity and brings it to Marlowe's attention at Greenbriar, while the tough commander gently comforts a dying trooper in the makeshift hospital at Newton Station and states how "proud" he is of the young man's sacrifice. The death of Sergeant Dunker (Bing Russell), who foolishly refuses the prescription that Kendall gives him, leads to the brief fistfight between the principals; in keeping with their equal status, neither conspicuously bests the other. When Marlowe is wounded at the bridge, Kendall is able to get even for some of the insults he has had to swallow, but the physician's respect emerges uppermost when he shakes hands with his erstwhile tormentor. In keeping with the status the film accords to his character, Kendall also functions to bring Hannah and Marlowe together; to make the southern girl aware of how capable and humane the northern leader really is, Kendall points the colonel's paradoxical treatment of the two Confederate deserters.

The film also adds more encounters with Confederate forces than can be found in the novel. The sniper fire that greets Marlowe's point riders when his column first enters southern territory, the passage of the large Confederate patrol on the opposite side of the river (and the hiding of Marlowe's force among the trees), and the battles at Newton Station and before the Jefferson Military Academy, as well as the final struggle to cross the last river, are all added to the movie. Indeed, in the novel, Marlowe's forces fight only one extended engagement, in which various groups from both sides characteristically get intertwined. Such confusion ultimately makes quick work of the struggle and reinforces Sinclair's emphasis on the chaos of actual combat.

The hospital scenes at Newton Station and during the last battle are also not in the novel. Sinclair does show a field hospital, which Marlowe enters to discover that Keller has left to attend the pregnant southern woman; however, in the film this sequence finds Kendall delivering a black baby, and Marlowe's harshness is dissipated. Whereas Keller is kept under guard from this point on in the novel, Kendall is never burdened with any such escort, although the film does have two inept soldiers guard Hannah instead. The amputation of Dunker's leg, while visually reminiscent of earlier operation sequences in *Drums Along the Mohawk* and *My Darling Clementine*, brings the conflict between the principals to its height; after the sergeant's death, Kendall becomes enraged when Marlowe questions his integrity. The sequence in which the colonel's leg wound is treated by Kendall is, of course, absent from the novel, in which Marlowe gets shot off his horse only to discover that a prize watch has taken the bullet's impact, so that he is more shocked than wounded. Finally, the beautifully uniformed cadets of the Jefferson Academy provide still another visual opportunity for the film that is missing in the book.

The most significant character addition to the film is, of course, Hannah, obviously brought in because the lack of any love interest in the novel was deemed inadvisable. Her plantation, the dinner she prepares, and her spying are all added to Ford's version; the extended trip she makes with the Union column, her attempts to escape, and the subsequent indignities she suffers all make the love affair between her and Marlowe more probable and symbolic. After the death of Lukey, Hannah's position as a prisoner alters slightly. By now she has become a favorite of the soldiers, who, as exemplars of the chivalry that Ford's troopers nearly always show to ladies, bring her small gifts to cheer her up. Hannah clashes with Marlowe over Kendall's "calling," even though she herself cannot function as a nurse within the hospital at Newton Station. In her squeamishness, Hannah resembles a lesser version of Scarlett O'Hara encountering the corpses and wounded in Atlanta in *Gone with the Wind*; however, Ford's southern belle recovers to damn Marlowe for his blind hatred of the medical profession.

Hannah represents one-half of a symbolic equation that American filmmakers have long been fond of making between the opposing sides of the Civil War. In Hollywood, whether in *Birth of a Nation* (1915) or in such later, far less prominent fare as *Virginia City* (1940), lovers from opposing sides get together to symbolize the "binding up of the nation's wounds." Ford elaborates this notion in *Young Mr. Lincoln* when the hero (Henry Fonda) plays a jew's-harp version of "Dixie," many years before that tune was actually written, and in *Rio Grande* when the reconciliation of Kirby and Kathleen is underlined by the same tune being played on a parade ground.

Ford's *The Horse Soldiers* significantly alters other details of the novel to sharpen conflicts. Sinclair mentions that Marlowe's wife has died of frailty; however, in the film the protagonist gives an extended description of her death, which accounts for his hatred of doctors. While the Marlowe of the novel did what he could to save his wife, and ended up mildly wealthy as a result of assets he liquidated to ensure her comfort, the movie's colonel was a poor section hand on the railroad with hardly enough money to support himself or his misdiagnosed wife. The medical error that caused her death, as well as his own complicity in that event, caused Marlowe to hate the medical profession. He believes that doctors are simply experimenters who delight in appearing to be wiser than they have any right to think they are; it takes the love of Hannah and the stubbornness of Kendall to bring enlightenment to Marlowe.

In the novel, Colonel Marlowe orders his physicians to remove any potentially sick trooper from the duty roster because of the arduous task in front of them. Only after he has been approached by an eager young soldier, who was his neighbor in prewar days and who has been found to be unfit, does the commander challenge his physicians' judgment. All of this maneuvering is done through official channels and leads, ironically, to the death of the young trooper who so much wanted to be a part of the raid. In the film, a similar order leads to a confrontation inside Kendall's hospital as Marlowe storms in after having learned that Sergeant Major Mitchell (Jack Pennick) is not going on the mission. Marlowe all but pulls Mitchell out of a sickbed with the argument that his aide has been suffering fevers for years, only to be checkmated by Doctor Kendall's equal physical resolve. At the same time, the physician's orderly, the fastidious Hoppy (O. Z. Whitehead), disconcerts Marlowe by insisting that a hospital is not subject to the same rules of military decorum found elsewhere. This comic tone extends to a moment when Kendall cuts off a boil on a trooper's backside in a sequence that visually harkens back to the Reverend/Captain Clayton's medical treatment at the end of *The Searchers*.

At the same time, in keeping with standard practices in movie adaptation, Ford's film omits numerous plot details from Sinclair's book. The familiar axiom that a novel usually contains more material than a film can portray guides such deletions. The exploits of Blaney, who manages to fight his way back to La Grange against very heavy odds, find no place in the film; in addition, Bryce's diversionary tactics are never shown, and his character is not even mentioned in the movie. Sinclair's account of the Newton Station raid is far less extended than Ford's cinematic treatment, for the novel's soldiers must concentrate on destroying as much as they can within a tight time schedule. One of their major problems is the destruction of an engine that has come into the terminal moments before they captured the town. In this section of the book, Private Murphy, who claims to be an old railroad hand, volunteers to drive the engine to a point where it can be blown up. In doing so, however, Murphy miscalculates and gets burned to death, an event that the movie ignores. As it is, Ford's film supplies many visually striking scenes during the wrecking of Newton Station after the street battle.

Ford's film also adds major and minor characters to further emphasize the romantic and historical predilections of its director. General Hurlbut appears in both narratives as a somewhat obsequious figure. In the novel, Hurlbut reluctantly issues orders only after Marlowe and General Smith patiently explain the raid to him. Thus, Hurlbut's primary aim seems to be maintaining his own position. In the film, Hurlbut accompanies the protagonist into the meeting with Grant and Sherman and then is shown at La Grange at the staff meeting. While Marlowe criticizes his commander for saddling the raid with a doctor (a protest the novel's protagonist never made), such remarks take a backseat to Hurlbut's concern with being photographed for posterity by Brady. Hurlbut thus resembles Secord, and the two of them chat about their careers during the photographic session.

Secord comes off much better in Sinclair's novel, where he functions as the second-in-command and as a sounding board for Marlowe; in the film, he offers a never-ending string of stupid objections to virtually every tactical proposal the protagonist makes or acts on. The film's Secord, personified by Willis Bouchey, an actor never cast in a warm light by Ford, emerges as merely a hypocrite. Secord talks incessantly about his political ambitions, and as the raid proves successful, his aims rise from "governor" to "vice-president." Naturally, such egotism is checked by Marlowe's more pragmatic temperament. Captain Gray, the singular failure in the novel, becomes an ex-actor in the film and is given excessive gallantries to perform when Marlowe's staff dines with Hannah. Gray's thespian flourishes mark him as something of a fool; he is left behind with the badly wounded after the battle at the bridge, further softening Sinclair's treatment of the character. Nonetheless, Gray is a better man than Secord in the film version because of his sincere devotion to the Yankee cause, signaled when, though wounded, he looks with satisfaction at the

Union flag that has just replaced the Confederate one. Gray's death in the novel is reprised by a stuntman in the film who is shot off his horse and into the water as he charges across the final bridge.

Sergeant Bullen, the primary point rider in Sinclair's book, has been replaced by Sergeant Dunker in the film. Once again, however, the movie adds considerable supporting details in line with Ford's thematic emphases. Dunker is first seen when Kendall asks him where the staff meeting is taking place. This early meeting foreshadows their later dealings, which are Dunker's most important moments in the film. When Kendall tells the sergeant that his infected leg will have to be amputated, Dunker delivers a lengthy speech on what such surgery will mean. His prognosis that he will end up in Andersonville, and his obvious revulsion at having to depend on the charity of others, offer the performer a choice screen moment. This temporary elevation to center stage of a minor character can be seen throughout Ford's films, perhaps nowhere more strikingly than in *The Grapes of Wrath* when Leroy Mason, as a distraught father, outlines the perils of California to the Joads. The grisly removal of Dunker's leg, after he had neglected to follow Kendall's treatment, serves as yet another ironic juxtaposition to Marlowe's intransigence toward the entire medical profession; and the colonel's being wounded in the same leg surely represents a calculated design.

The Confederate "trash," Virgil and Jagger Jo, replace the single character picked up by Marlowe's column in the novel. Whereas that figure stays with the Union force until the protagonist feels safe about releasing him, Ford's twosome appears as comic relief and an opportunity for Marlowe to increase his standing with Hannah. The noblesse oblige implied to the Union commander's treatment of Virgil and Jagger Jo (and in Hannah's reaction) is ironically caught up in Kendall's comments as these deserters are pumped for information and then returned to Sheriff Goodboy in a manner reflecting how any gentleman would act toward such reprobates. Marlowe may be hell-bent on the destruction of as much Confederate property as possible, but he does not stoop to dealing with rabble any longer than is necessary. Indeed, in knocking out these deserters and in recognizing Goodboy's authority over them, the protagonist once again foreshadows the eventual settlement between the warring sides. Just as Hannah and he will unite after the war in a symbolic personal rapprochement, so Marlowe's gentlemanly conduct here implies a reunion at the national level.

Kendall (Keller in the novel) is considerably enlarged in Ford's plot. Keller irritates Marlowe in the novel, utters that medicine is "where you find it," and sacrifices his personal freedom to care for his patients at the end of the journey (and so falls into Confederate hands). But in the film Kendall challenges Marlowe earlier and more avidly, starting at La Grange and culminating with their fistfight in the woods before the Jefferson Cadets attack. Kendall also functions far more efficiently as a military officer, especially when he catches Hannah spying and when he becomes uneasy, at Newton Station, about Johnny Miles's seeming passivity, which alerts Marlowe to the incoming Rebel train.

Kendall also functions as a symbolic midwife to the love between Hannah and Marlowe. While he apparently sees through the southern woman's hypocrisy at their first meeting, when he declines her invitation to dinner because he is under "officer's arrest," Kendall allows Hannah to condemn herself before he pounces. His subsequent treatment of the southern belle, as he consistently jibes about Marlowe's peculiarly just ways, helps the girl to realize her deeper feelings. Kendall's final moments with Hannah and Marlowe, when he urges them to part and resume their tryst when the war is over, reflect both the practical and the sentimental sides of his character. Kendall manages to get Marlowe away and, at the same time, to ensure that Hannah will survive in her old world. The doctor's impatience with the lovers resembles that of Captain Brittles in *She Wore a Yellow Ribbon* when Flint and Olivia (John Agar and Joanne Dru) embrace at the river crossing only after the aged commander has shouted his "permission." In standing for duty before pleasure, Kendall personifies the ideal cavalryman and asserts one of Ford's major themes in *Fort Apache, She Wore a Yellow Ribbon, Rio Grande,* and *Sergeant Rutledge.*

Marlowe more thoroughly dominates the action in the film for two reasons. On the one hand, the film character cannot suggest the mental processes his fictional counterpart experiences (a common difference between virtually any movie and a novel on which it is based). Sinclair's protagonist is beset by numerous doubts and quandries that appear as internal moments; however, given the nature of the film, such sequences are all but impossible to render visually, so that personal agitation must either be shown as outward action or be forgotten. Since illustrating every one of Marlowe's problems would, naturally, lead to an agonizingly long film that could hardly justify itself as entertainment or art, the protagonist's dilemmas have been telescoped into his overriding quarrel with medicine in general and Major Kendall in particular. The film's plot, by cutting out any sections of the novel that do not include him, as well as adding many occasions in which his personal leadership is demonstrated, keeps Marlowe uppermost in the audience's perceptions and ensures a more easily followed narrative.

In the film, the colonel's lengthy recollection of his wife's death resembles the speech Hightower delivers in *Three Godfathers* when the expectant mother is discovered. In *The Horse Soldiers,* Hannah's reaction to this outburst moves the plot along thematically because of her insistence that medicine is noble and the protagonist mistaken. At the same time, the film provides Marlowe with a lower-class background to suggest his self-made nature: he has risen from section hand to railroad engineer. After Hannah starts chattering about how nice it must be to be able to drive a train, Marlowe corrects her, explaining that he built railroads, and an additional irony becomes apparent.

Marlowe has been sent to destroy the very thing he has learned to build, and some of his subsequent anger at Newton Station reflects his personal sense of the ultimate waste of warfare. The protagonist's capacity for self-learning has seemingly fitted him for military command as well, a situation that again transforms the novel, in which Marlowe discovered his talent for leadership after a life spent in relatively easy middle-class circumstances. Ford's central figure is designed to reinforce the popular American notion of equality of opportunity for anyone willing to work for it (i.e., the Horatio Alger notion of the self-made success story). Marlowe's romance with Hannah also runs contrary to Sinclair's novel in that the novel's commanding officer more nearly resembles a perennial bachelor like Nathan Brittles in *She Wore a Yellow Ribbon*, especially in his fond recollections of the wife he has lost.

Ford's film also adds numerous Union soldiers, whose personalities are more in keeping with the actors playing these parts than with similar minor figures in the novel. Grant and Sherman remain remote figures up the chain of command in Sinclair's book, whereas they emerge as a convenient means to summarize a historical situation in the film. In essence, the two Union commanders take the place of a title card that, in an older film, would have explained the situation; they would reappear for Ford in the middle section of *How the West Was Won* in which Grant (Harry Morgan) despairs after the battle of Shiloh only to be rallied by Sherman (John Wayne). In the movie Wilkie, a point rider, displays the same hayseed accent and musical proclivities that Ken Curtis supplied for a similar enlisted man in *Rio Grande* and as Charlie McCorry in *The Searchers*. Wilkie is associated with a religiously addled figure, the Deacon (played by Hank Worden, who portrays a similar figure in Mose Harper of *The Searchers*), when he calls Marlowe's attention to the fact that his colleague knows a secret path through the swamps. This deus ex machina device, by which the aged soldier has fortuitously spent earlier days "preaching the gospel" and helping runaway slaves all through "these parts," saves the Union column and, of course, adds yet another visual opportunity (the ride into the whirling waters of the swamp) that is missing from the novel.

Hoppy, who serves as Kendall's principal orderly, and Sergeant Kirby, who replaces Sergeant Mitchell as the "top soldier," are film additions intended as comic relief. Hoppy is a martinet who does not back down when Marlowe storms into the field hospital at La Grange to question why Mitchell has been put to bed. Later, wounded troops are taken back to the Union lines by Hoppy; in the novel, a junior officer has this duty. The final conversation between Hoppy and Kendall only reaffirms the affection that the enlisted man has for the doctor; and when Kendall urges him to "finish" his medical degree, Hoppy eagerly agrees. Kirby reprises the familiar, hard-drinking sergeants embodied by Victor McLaglen in *Fort Apache*, *She Wore a Yellow Ribbon*, and *Rio Grande*. His fondness for liquor is seen when he first reports to Marlowe, who destroys an incriminating bottle after ordering Kirby to get sober in three hours. Later the sergeant must "test" the brandy that Lukey is taking to Kendall, and at Newton Station, Marlowe breaks yet another bottle concealed in Kirby's pants.

Most of the film's additions occur on the Confederate side. While Sinclair mentions the actual southern commanders and their lack of success in pursuing Grierson (a notion that the film reduces to a single battery commander who persuades the aged head of the Jefferson Military Academy to allow his cadets to attack Marlowe's encampment), the movie's cast includes several figures who embody the nobility of the "Lost Cause." Commander Jefferson, the head of the military prep school, and Sheriff Goodboy, the frail magistrate into whose hands Marlowe consigns the deserters, represent the extent to which the Confederacy must sacrifice to fight the war. The attempts by these aged men to fulfill functions that younger men should be performing symbolize the Yankee pressure that is winning the war. Their nobility is matched by Lukey, who never questions her place by Hannah's side, in a reprise of the kind of slave loyalty found in *Gone with the Wind*. Mrs. Buford, who refuses to let her youngest son march with the other cadets because she has already lost a husband and a son, offers a momentary vision of southern womanhood that sharply contrasts with the mob of women who throw dust at Marlowe's troops when they enter Newton Station. Mrs. Buford's wish is comically granted and reinforced when her drummer-son escapes from home, only to end up being spanked by the retreating Union soldiers.

Johnny Miles (Carleton Young), the one-armed Confederate officer, plays a more complex role, for he not only manages to outsmart the Yankees and send for reinforcements but also personally leads the charge down the main street of Newton Station. In this highly symbolic fight, one that finds a reluctant Marlowe stating that he "never wanted it" after he has set up an ambush of epic proportions, Miles's blind courage represents all the Confederacy can throw into the scales against the better-armed Yankees. His doggedness continues even after the battle and his rescue by Kendall, for we last see Miles plotting which way Marlowe has gone and getting the information to his superiors.

Hannah Hunter illustrates the grace of the South, its other redeeming feature; as a pure invention of the film, she also embodies the suggestive role of the potential military bride, the woman who must learn the importance of her would-be husband's calling and accede to its demands. Hannah, by falling in love with Marlowe in spite of the travails she experiences, emerges as a proper army wife. Her evolution is similar to those of Philadelphia Thursday in *Fort Apache*, Olivia Dandridge in *She Wore a Yellow Ribbon*, Kathleen Yorke in *Rio Grande*, Mary Beecher in *Sergeant Rutledge*, and Marty Purcell in *Two Rode Together*. At the same time, by virtue of her temper and her beliefs, Hannah represents the ideal Fordian romantic female, whose own sense of herself ultimately attracts the hero (e.g., Mary Kate in *The Quiet Man*).

The music score to *The Horse Soldiers* is also typical for a Ford film. While it embodies many of the standard features of such accompaniments, traditional tunes rather than original cues add most to the thematics of the film. David Buttolph, a longtime Hollywood composer who specialized in westerns, supplies the bulk of the original music for *The Horse Soldiers*.[3] His cues briefly suggest the duplicity of Hannah Hunter at Greenbriar when comic orchestral colorings augment her behavior before Kendall discovers that she has been spying on Marlowe and his staff. Typically furious chase music accompanies the sequence in which Hannah tries to escape from the column and is captured after falling off her horse in a swamp. The fight between the male leads finds musical accents being invoked to mimic such actions as their throwing aside their hats, in what is yet another staple feature of Hollywood scoring. Buttolph's most extended theme accompanies the love scenes between Hannah and Marlowe; as a foreshadowing of the feelings that will develop between these characters, its expansive melody is introduced when the Union column first arrives at Greenbriar. It resurfaces during Marlowe's apology to Hannah over the death of Lukey and again when the Union commander's shadow falls across the kneeling heroine and when she stares longingly at the bridge over which her lover has fled.

The prominence of certain musical instruments in a Civil War adventure film such as *The Horse Soldiers* is also to be expected. Guitars and banjos are strummed at various camp sites, while a melancholy solo harmonica underscores the scene in the Newton Station hospital when Marlowe comforts the dying young trooper. Drums and fifes serve as natural accompaniment to the appearance of the Jefferson Academy cadets as they march toward the Union forces. Even more predictably, bugle calls are woven into numerous scenes as obvious source music; at one point Marlowe asks a youthful bugler if he is nervous before a battle — in an exchange that resembles a similar moment in *Wagonmaster* when Elder Wiggs (Ward Bond) asks Travis (Ben Johnson) and Sandy (Harry Carey, Jr.) if they are afraid of the outlaws. Such familiar bugle calls as "Assembly," "Recall," and, of course, "Charge" are featured in *The Horse Soldiers*.

A more obvious musical pattern centers on tunes, both original and traditional, in the film. Stan Jones's "I Left My Love" is featured during the opening credits and is subsequently both sung and played. Jones, whose tunes are also featured in *Wagonmaster* and *The Searchers*, supplies appropriate lyrics that center on having to leave a loved one behind so that the horse soldiers can "ride to hell and back ... for Ulysses Simpson Grant!" Buttolph then arranges Jones's tune to fit such moments as the departure of Marlowe's column from La Grange, when the music gradually diminishes, in keeping with the slowing of the command to a walk, and the resumption of the mission after the dinner at Hannah's. This sprightly tune is last heard on the drunken lips of Dunker just before he learns he must lose his leg. A traditional tune that is also consistently used for the Union troops is "When Johnny Comes Marching Home," which is heard before the Newton Station battle but assumes greater importance only after that setting has been reached. In a clever bit of musical juxtaposition, Buttolph intermixes this tune, redolent of the eventual Yankee triumph in the Civil War, with a more sinister-sounding ostinato in the Newton Station sequence to suggest the madness of all armed struggle. In such a way, the musical score manages to underline the ambiguities in Marlowe, who, as commanding officer, must order the destruction that brings on the very "insanity" he believes war to be. This character conflict is also nicely set off in the film's opening scenes when a railroad bell sounds briefly as Marlowe and Hurlbut enter to confer with Grant and Sherman.

Other traditional tunes are arranged to underscore the Confederate forces in *The Horse Soldiers*. "The Bonnie Blue Flag," the actual anthem of the Confederacy, is given a choral rendition when Marlowe and his force must hide from a Rebel cavalry column passing on the other side of a river. A much less obvious working of this same tune accompanies the heroic and futile charge of the Confederates up the main street of Newton Station; appropriately enough, this theme gets quickly submerged by the harsher cues that reinforce what we see — the firepower of Marlowe's troops destroying the gallant but foolish southerners. The Jefferson Academy cadets' parade also features this tune as these boys proceed through the local town, arrive at the battlefield, and serve up volleys of rifle fire that precipitate the headlong Yankee retreat.

The success of the cadets in routing their adult opponents, while contingent on Marlowe's refusal to fight against boys, is further augmented by the playing of "Dixie." The Union cavalrymen make a hasty comic withdrawal, emphasized by their being knocked off logs and by Marlowe's sweeping of his command before him just out of range of the charging cadets; the highly familiar "Dixie" is broadly rendered to underline the fun. At one point the same tune serves to emphasize the difficulty that one small cadet is experiencing as he goes through a hollow tree stump and then scrambles to his feet. The use of this tune elsewhere in Ford's films — most notably when Lincoln asks to hear it in *The Prisoner of Shark Island*, when the same (here youthful) character plays it on a jew's harp in *Young Mr. Lincoln*, and when Kathleen and Kirby Yorke flirt to its strains at the end of *Rio Grande*— clearly establishes it as music of reconciliation. Its appearance at this particular point in *The Horse Soldiers* deftly augments the nation's symbolic reconciliation, already implicit in the love of Hannah and Marlowe.

The Horse Soldiers incorporates the three principal plot motifs that we find in Ford's westerns. First, the larger life of the cavalry, the institution that functions as a family to veritably guide its members throughout their lives, serves as a groundwork against which the plot takes place. Kendall resembles Nathan Brittles of *She Wore a Yellow Ribbon* and Braxton Rutledge (Woody Strode) of *Sergeant Rutledge* in that he must prove that he properly belongs within the cavalry world. Marlowe embodies the notion of the ideal commander as the man who, like Captain York in *Fort Apache* and Colonel Yorke in *Rio Grande*, sees the necessity for subordinating a romantic life to the demands of the larger institution.

The second motif concerns the central relationship between Kendall and Marlowe; this dual heroism resembles that embodied by Wyatt Earp (Henry Fonda) and Doc Holliday (Victor Mature) in *My Darling Clementine*, Travis Blue (Ben Johnson) and Sandy Owens (Harry Carey, Jr.) in *Wagonmaster*, Guthrie McCabe (James Stewart) and Jim Gary (Richard Widmark) in *Two Rode Together*, and finally, Ransom Stoddard (James Stewart) and Tom Doniphon (John Wayne) in *The Man Who Shot Liberty Valance*. The twosome in *Wagonmaster* represents the least complex of these pairings, since Travis and Sandy have clear motives and neither man dies. Such male partnerships in *My Darling Clementine* and *Two Rode Together* are far more equivocal: the individuals either die or are forced to separate. The dual heroes in *The Man Who Shot Liberty Valance* ultimately illustrate the often harsh choices imposed by creating a civilization. Marlowe and Kendall separate in *The Horse Soldiers* but not before they have become conscious of their mutual abilities, so that they resemble the twosomes of *Wagonmaster* and *My Darling Clementine* rather than the more bitter and resigned male pairings we see in *Two Rode Together* and *The Man Who Shot Liberty Valance*.

The major narrative underpinning in *The Horse Soldiers*, the journey-raid, offers the third obvious plot motif, one through which the central characters can experience personal change and growth as a result of adventures along the way. In this regard, *The Horse Soldiers* strongly resembles *Stagecoach*, *Three Godfathers*, *The Searchers*, and *Cheyenne Autumn*, all of which depend on traveling to bring about important thematic and personal changes. The sweetly melancholy mood when Marlowe must leave Hannah in *The Horse Soldiers* lies halfway between such optimistic conclusions as the flight of Dallas and Ringo in *Stagecoach* and Hightower's minimum sentence in *Three Godfathers* and the more difficult final moments in which Ethan Edwards realizes he has no abiding home in *The Searchers* and Deborah Wright (Carroll Baker) surrenders her Cheyenne pupil to the restored tribal world in *Cheyenne Autumn*.

Despite its relatively minor reputation, *The Horse Soldiers* embodies many of the same interests that distinguish Ford's more celebrated films. Certainly this late work is typically Fordian in its methods of adaptation, its character types, and its interplay of techniques and themes. Indeed, *The Horse Soldiers* so often recalls other Ford films that it comes to resemble a veritable cell in a larger organic body. The director's cohesive artistic powers set *The Horse Soldiers* above nearly all other Civil War films to the same extent that his westerns are superior to most others of that genre. Even a less celebrated Ford film is, finally, so artistically distinct and thematically intriguing that we end up preferring it to more lauded fare by other directors.

Chapter 5

Ford's Western Literary Sources and Their Adaptations

Ten of John Ford's sound westerns are derived from various literary sources. *Stagecoach* uses Ernest Haycox's "Stage to Lordsburg"; *Fort Apache* ("Massacre"), *She Wore a Yellow Ribbon* ("War Party"), and *Rio Grande* ("Mission with No Record") are based on short stories by James Warner Bellah; and *The Man Who Shot Liberty Valance* is derived from the short story with that title by Dorothy Johnson. *Three Godfathers*, which was filmed previously, is based on the novel by Peter B. Kyne; *The Searchers* is drawn from the novel by Alan Le May; *Two Rode Together* is derived from Will Cook's *Comanche Captives*; and *Cheyenne Autumn* uses the novel by Mari Sandoz. *My Darling Clementine* utilizes Stuart Lake's biography *Wyatt Earp: Frontier Marshal*, along with some borrowings from the Sam Hellman script to *Frontier Marshal* (TCF, 1939). The screenplays based on these various literary works were written by Dudley Nichols (*Stagecoach*), Winston Miller (*My Darling Clementine*), Frank S. Nugent (*Fort Apache, Three Godfathers, She Wore a Yellow Ribbon, The Searchers, Two Rode Together*), James Kevin McGuinness (*Rio Grande*), Willis Goldbeck and James Warner Bellah (*The Man Who Shot Liberty Valance*), and James R. Webb (*Cheyenne Autumn*).

Ford's writers formed something of a "stock company"; many of them worked on other Ford films in addition to their western assignments. Thus, Dudley Nichols, perhaps the director's most celebrated literary collaborator, was also associated with Ford's *Men Without Women* (1930), *Born Reckless* (1930), *Seas Beneath* (1931), *Pilgrimage* (1933), *The Lost Patrol* (1934), *Judge Priest* (1934), *The Informer* (1935), *Steamboat Round the Bend* (1935), *Mary of Scotland* (1936), *The Plough and the Stars* (1936), *The Hurricane* (1937), *The Long Voyage Home* (1940), and *The Fugitive* (1947). Nichols was also the only writer honored with an Oscar for a Ford film (for *The Informer*), though he refused to accept the award. Frank Nugent also collaborated on what has come to be regarded as Ford's most beloved film, *The Quiet Man* (1952), as well as *The Rising of the Moon* (1957), *The Last Hurrah* (1958), and *Donovan's Reef* (1963). James Kevin McGuinness scripted Ford's first two sound films, *The Black Watch*

Ford adjusting Richard Widmark's costume on the set of *Two Rode Together* (Columbia, 1961).

and *Salute* (both 1929); and Laurence Stallings, who cowrote *Three Godfathers* and *She Wore a Yellow Ribbon*, turned out the screenplay for what Ford himself often claimed was his favorite work, *The Sun Shines Bright* (1953).

The literary sources of Ford's westerns experience alterations and omissions that consistently emphasize visual moments at the expense of characters' interior lives. In line with standard Hollywood practice, these adaptations consistently eschew what cannot be filmed convincingly (states of mind) for what can be shown (physical action) while simultaneously increasing the thematic density and plot pace of the originals. At the same time, throughout the period in which Ford's sound westerns appeared, Hollywood still adhered to a fairly stringent production code about what could and could not be shown. Although most of Ford's films did not seriously challenge such strictures (and the director's own moral temperament was generally in line with the precepts of the Hays office), his westerns also had to adhere to such provisions. Thus, certain plot deletions and character shadings become more readily understandable as simply modifications dictated by Hollywood's censorship system. In addition, to add heightened conflicts to the plots, to refer to "real" people as characters as a shorthand means of establishing temporal settings or emotional colorings, and to make conflicts and situations more immediately

Martha Edwards (Dorothy Jordan) welcomes Ethan Edwards (John Wayne) home at the opening of *The Searchers* (Warner Bros., 1956). The repressed feelings between the characters are rendered by their expressions and body language.

dramatic and thus better reflect the director's overriding themes, Ford's westerns continuously present historical inaccuracies and distortions.

Ford's literary sources are often either too realistic or "downbeat" (as in Bellah's cavalry stories) or too redolent of the literary tradition of the tall tale (as in "The Man Who Shot Liberty Valance"). Thus, the director and his screenwriters add or omit characters and details to transform original works that lack romance or are too stylized. Ford's own themes and values determine much of this process, so that, in essence, these literary sources are changed into cinematic narratives that are unmistakably closer to his vision of the West than they are to their originators'. In this regard Ford is clearly different from a filmmaker like John Huston, who could (and did) remain highly faithful to the printed sources he treated.[1]

Ford's westerns nearly always extend or add romantic complications, with the augmented love scenes between Dallas and Ringo in *Stagecoach* and the addition of the courtship of Captain Archer and Deborah Wright in *Cheyenne Autumn* representing extreme cases. Individual roles are often enlarged or changed in keeping with the performers who are to play them; thus, a whole host of Ford's western characters, perhaps most obviously Victor McLaglen's cavalry sergeants, become more prominent than in the literary originals. Finally, Ford's major plot motifs are often grafted onto the existing literary materials. Thus, the institutional benevolence of cavalry life looms larger in *She Wore a Yellow Ribbon* than in the James Warner Bellah short story from which it derives; the relationships of the male leads in *My Darling Clementine* and *Two Rode Together* are much more complicated than in their respective literary sources; and the journeys are far clearer and more elaborate in *Stagecoach* and *Cheyenne Autumn* than they are in their fictional renderings.

The script and the plot of Ford's *Stagecoach* differ significantly from Ernest Haycox's "Stage to Lordsburg" which appeared in 1937. The plot skeleton of a stagecoach traversing hostile country and being attacked by Apaches is retained while significant characters and motivations are added. A traditional western movie motive of revenge bred by family honor is also incorporated, as are characters who travel for much more pressing reasons than those motivating them in the short story.

In the Haycox version, no one wants to chase anyone out of Tonto; indeed, the stage has not been running for forty-five days, so all its passengers are consciously traveling at their own risk. Since the stage itself has three rows of seats, it never becomes as crowded (or as convivial) as it does in Ford's film. At one point Haycox's stagecoach even overturns—a moment suggested cinematically by its precarious passage up some rough terrain with the help of Lieutenant Blanchard (Tim Holt) and his cavalrymen. Haycox's soldiers stay with the stage for only three hours and simply escort it to a certain point, with no animosity being expressed by them or toward them by any of the passengers. The subsequent journey, replete with stops at waystations, adds the male lead, who simply boards as an ordinary passenger.

Haycox's driver, Happy Stuart, becomes Buck (Andy Devine) in the film, while his shotgun guard, John Strang, is transformed into the sheriff of Tonto, Curly Wilcox (George Bancroft). Strang dies during the Indian assault and is not greatly mourned when the coach arrives in Lordsburg. In the film Curly serves as a plot anchor for the pursuit of the Ringo Kid (John Wayne), and it is this amiable lawman's final task to release the young hero after the latter's climactic fight with the Plummer boys. Miss Robertson of the story becomes Lucy Mallory (Louise Platt) in the film. Like her cinematic equivalent, Miss Robertson is traveling to rejoin her army lover — although she is only engaged (not married) to this officer. She is thus not pregnant, though during the trip she does hear that her intended has been wounded and, later, that he is all right. Both these bits of information are passed on to her by soldiers, rather than stationkeepers or civilians as in the film. Miss Robertson is taken aback by her traveling companion Henriette, although she does not apologize in a left-handed way once they have safely arrived in Lordsburg. The film's Lucy Mallory uses some of Miss Robertson's language when she tries to reconcile with Dallas (Claire Trevor).

Haycox's whisky drummer remains nameless and dies (apparently from the heat) very soon after the story begins. His death provides Henriette a chance to show compassion; she cradles his head in her lap — an activity the film transforms into Dallas's more suggestive and symbolic concern for Lucy and her baby. There is also a gambler in the story (again unnamed), who is killed after he provides guns for both Miss Robertson and Henriette as a way for them to avoid rape and death at the hands of the Apaches. Ford's film provides much richer characters in Peacock (Donald Meek) and Hatfield (John Carradine). The little salesman, Peacock, serves both as a foil to Doc Boone (Thomas Mitchell) and as an embodiment of the increasing compassion that nearly all the "proper" characters must learn to show toward Ringo and Dallas. The headstrong southern gambler, Hatfield, reflects Ford's abiding interest in the "Lost Cause"; he prefigures several later characters in the director's other westerns, with Sergeant Tyree of *She Wore a Yellow Ribbon* and Ethan Edwards of *The Searchers* being the most notable.

Haycox's cast also includes two characters who are omitted from the film. An Englishman, who has come west for sport, blazes away with a hunting rifle at the Apaches but otherwise remains in the background. A cattleman, who makes off-color remarks to Henriette and then gets beaten up (offstage), is included to dramatize the essential purity of the male protagonist's feelings for the frontier prostitute. Malpas Bill is, of course, the fictional source for the Ringo Kid; he also falls in love with the "fallen" woman of the story, but this character is both older and more legitimate than his movie counterpart. Haycox's protagonist-hero still needs to shoot it out in Lordsburg against (presumably) ancient enemies (here named Plummer and Shanley), and he does ascend to the coach roof to fight off the attacking Indians.

It is, however, the openness with which Malpas Bill approaches Henriette that sets him apart from the more chivalrous Ringo of the film. Henriette is impressed by Bill from the time of his arrival; however, she quite casually tells him that she runs a "house" in Lordsburg so that there is never any confusion or guilt about her profession. Since such an unrepentant admission would have been anathema under Hays Code provisions, Ford transforms the easily accepting ways of Malpas Bill into the idealism of Ringo who, because he is a genuine innocent, has no qualms once he finds out that Dallas lives in the "bad" part of Lordsburg. At one point Henriette speaks about the deaths of her parents because of an Indian raid in the neighborhood of "Superstition Mountain," dialogue that is lifted for the film. If Henriette is both older and more embroiled in prostitution in the story, her patient waiting for Malpas Bill leads to the same general conclusion of united lovers as found in the film.

Ford's two major character additions to the Haycox plot are the absconding and cowardly banker Gatewood (Berton Churchill) and the drunken but capable Doc Boone. The former's flight from Tonto reemphasizes the stern and repressive moral tone of that town, since it seems clear that the banker cannot endure the prospect of another meal with his wife and the ladies of the "Law and Order League." Gatewood ultimately supplies a character against whom the others can all emerge as better people; indeed, against the background of the Great Depression, such a figure might well be meant to symbolize the kind of bureaucratized and legalistic villainy that many a common man felt had precipitated the economic crisis.[2]

Doc Boone is more central to Ford's narrative; he functions as a veritable conscience and prophet to the others, whether he is chiding Gatewood (who obviously would not have come on the trip had the Indian threat been as clear as it is in the story) or advising Dallas. Boone's demeanor is ultimately belied by his good heart when he prevails on Hank Plummer (Tom Tyler) not to go out into the streets of Lordsburg armed with a shotgun. In this respect, Doc foreshadows the more contemporary and less amenable but finally friendly Doctor Kendall (William Holden) in *The Horse Soldiers*. At the same time, Ford emphasizes his ongoing interest in the medical profession as one from which he will draw a gallery of competent professionals who can function under stress. These figures range from the hastily drafted Doc Holliday (Victor Mature) in *My Darling Clementine*, to the noble physicians who attend the cavalry in *Fort Apache*, *She Wore a Yellow Ribbon*, and *Rio Grande*, and to the doctor (Sean McClory) who restores himself in *Cheyenne Autumn*. This character type, prefigured by Nichols's Doctor Kersaint (Thomas Mitchell once again) in *The Hurricane*, becomes a prophetic spokesman, as epitomized by the angry physicians in *Sergeant Rutledge* and *The Man Who Shot Liberty Valance*, who rage against what they see as villainy. Doc Boone's ability to come out of his alcoholic haze and deliver Lucy's baby is matched by the ability of Doc Willoughby (Ken Murray) to function when his friend Peabody (Edmond O'Brien) is beaten and needs serious attention in *The Man Who Shot Liberty Valance*.

"Massacre" (1947), the first of three stories by James Warner Bellah that would become Ford westerns, provides the basis for *Fort Apache*. Once again, Ford and his writers add considerable detail to flesh out a narrative that is, by its very nature, too truncated to sustain a feature-length film. The most notable

additions are female characters who not only introduce romance but also supply a larger social canvas that adds considerable thematic weight and depth
to Bellah's plot. The foolish pride of Colonel Thursday (Henry Fonda) and
his Custer-like bravado in the field come across much more tellingly when we
see an entire community suffering and recovering from the damage that the
character causes. While Bellah's story is about a failure, Ford strives to show
that Thursday's death has served a larger purpose. Indeed, the communities
in his western films, whether transient (as in *Stagecoach*) or more prominent
(as in *My Darling Clementine* and the cavalry films) can prosper only after
some individuals have sacrificed themselves for the greater good. Thursday's
foolhardiness is thus transformed, by those who remain, into a usable heroism and a basis for building a present and a future; in doing so, the remaining characters reveal how Ford's vision of society calls for communal bonds
based in a shared mythology.

Bellah's story has Flint Cohill, a character who will surface in Ford's *She
Wore a Yellow Ribbon*, as its protagonist, who argues with Thursday over both
the mission and the abilities of their Apache foes. Cohill is the son of a general, and we initially see him recalling a day on which his father hailed the
resignation of U.S. Grant from the service in 1854. Now, twenty years later,
Cohill finds himself musing over his own dim prospects of ever becoming a
general remotely comparable to either Grant or his own father. The arrival of
the unaccompanied Thursday introduces a character who has known glory
and lost it. "Brevet Major General Thursday of Clarke's Corps — Thursday of
Cumberland Station and of Sudler's Mountain, at twenty-six. Now, a major
of cavalry at thirty-eight, back in the slow Army runway again, with the flame
of glory burning low on his horizon ... for it is far worse to go up and come
back than it ever is to go up at all."[3] Thursday ignores his subordinates and
their advice from the first, preferring instead to surge forward on a punitive
raid against the Indians.

Major Thursday is dismayed by the appearance his new troopers make in
the field, calling them "scratch farmers on market day" (in a phrase that recurs
in the film); however, there is a scandal in the major's past, one that Cohill
remembers hearing about years before, at a time when the "good of the service" imposed silence on all. The conference between Thursday and the Indian
leader Stone Buffalo takes place at the behest of the sanctimonious trader
Meachem, who is more of a religious hypocrite than the villain (Grant Withers) we see in Ford's film. Thursday impulsively destroys any chance of negotiation, though his subordinates argue that the Indian leader is simply stalling
for time to enjoy a possible greater military advantage.

Cohill is assigned to the rear when the final battle starts, but he is not
sent there because of any insubordination. He quickly perceives the disaster,
has his troops dig in for an expected onslaught, and sends a rider back for
reinforcements. Thursday's emergence from the struggle leads to a confrontation

in which Cohill urges his commander to remain on the ridge with him. Cohill refuses to consider Thursday's order that they fight their way out of an impossible situation, and he even offers his pistol to his commander as a sign of being under arrest for disobeying an order. Cohill's defiance makes Thursday realize that his proper place is with those he has so foolishly led to their deaths. However, Cohill assures his superior that he will report what has happened for "the good of the service" rather than tell the "truth."

Thursday then rides back to his death (by suicide). Afterward Cohill, so that no disgrace will come to the cavalry, deliberately throws away the pistol he loaned his commanding officer and sets out to cover the sordid events of this day with a legendary patina. Bellah's main theme emerges only at the very end of his story, when an aged Cohill critically asks other officers what they mean by "the good of the service"; we realize the strain caused by his allegiance to the myths that celebrate Thursday.

Ford's film transforms Bellah's story by softening its conclusion and by, typically, introducing other characters. We see Thursday die with the officers and men he has rejoined because of the assault Cochise finally mounts against their weak position. But the Apache chief has no thought of slaughtering the remaining soldiers under the command of Captain York (John Wayne). Cochise is simply answering Thursday's insults delivered during their conference, and, once the offender has been punished, the Indian chief's desire for revenge is sated. At the same time, we see Thursday's talent as a tactician when he sends out a decoy party so that he can defeat the Apaches earlier.

The film retains some of Thursday's dialogue, particularly his insistence on being addressed as a major rather than as the general he once was; however, while some of the actions of the story's lesser characters are retained, Ford's cast is quite different than Bellah's. Meachem remains self-serving and much more conspicuously hypocritical and villainous, and the device of returning a rider for aid is also retained. But this latter figure is transformed from an irritating noncom in the story to Mickey O'Rourke (John Agar), whose being sent for help symbolizes the notion that those who live in the present must sacrifice to ensure the future.

The film also adds such notable characters as the Collingwoods (Anna Lee and George O'Brien), who represent the ideal military marriage in which duty must supersede romance; Doctor Wilkens (Guy Kibbee), whose penchant for wine conceals a sentimental heart worthy of Doc Boone in *Stagecoach*; and the elder O'Rourkes (Irene Rich and Ward Bond) who provide the means by which all ranks within the garrison are made into a veritable family. The joyful arrival of their son, Mickey, from West Point and the father's receipt of the Medal of Honor place the O'Rourkes in sharp contrast with Thursday and his social arrogance disguised as noblesse oblige. Ford emphasizes the mores by which a "real" army family lives, both by knowing their places within the hierarchy and by insisting on their privileges within that status. The love of the O'Rourkes offers one more example of a fidelity to duty that produces domestic harmony, just as the sergeant major's military past deftly counterpoints his commanding officer's pride and dismay at being assigned to the western outpost. Mickey's romance with Philadelphia Thursday (Shirley Temple), a figure who serves to humanize and further soften Bellah's story, dramatizes how such characters can forge a viable future for themselves inside the institution they serve.

In Bellah's story, that process is embodied by Cohill, who, like Tom Doniphon (John Wayne) in *The Man Who Shot Liberty Valance*, becomes a grim witness to the past; in *Fort Apache*, however, the entire community is involved in the process. This thematic interest accounts not only for the title of the film but also for such additional characters as the four sergeants, who function as Mickey's symbolic godfathers and guardians, and Captain York, the man Thursday immediately displaces from command upon his arrival. In the film, York fulfills Cohill's public adherence in the story to the myth of the fallen Thursday ("No man died more bravely"); however, his interview scene with the eastern journalists stresses the mystical unit that the larger military community has become because of the willingness of its members to follow the fallen leader. By reassuming command, York, who now dresses like the dead Thursday, dramatizes the group's capacity to assimilate defeat and turn it into the basis for continuing existence. Thus, *Fort Apache* uses the more sober plot of Bellah's "Massacre" as the basis for a meditation on how men shape their pasts to influence the present and the future. Ford's ambition here, in a film that he needed to be commercially successful to retrieve the faltering finances of his Argosy production company, leads to one of his richest thematic efforts, a work certainly comparable to *The Hurricane, Young Mr. Lincoln, They Were Expendable*, or *The Searchers*.[4]

Ford returned to James Warner Bellah with *She Wore a Yellow Ribbon*, which is based on the short story "War Party" (1948). Once again, Ford and his writers soften Bellah's characters and extend the narrative to include a larger temporal and social setting. At the same time, Ford also supplies a much happier ending, drawing on what is only hoped for in the story and turning it into a reality. In essence, Bellah's tale of the aged Nathan Brittles, who defuses an Indian war by disobeying the exact letter of his orders on his final day in the cavalry, works itself out within a masculine military world. Ford's film incorporates romantic and social complications not only to make the property a more salable commodity but also to augment his own thematic and historical visions.

In Bellah's story, Captain Brittles awakens, receives a gift from his troopers, and then moves out quickly after being told by his superior (Allshard) that there is no continuing life in the service for him. Brittles wants to head west, after going back to Massachusetts, but when he notices the gravestones of his wife and son, he has no desire to visit them, for he lacks that "kind of sentiment." Brittles took their loss hard and became an alcoholic, a past mis-step that apparently makes him suspect in the eyes of those higher up (and which is momentarily alluded to in the film). Flint Cohill has already been besieged by the Apaches when Bellah's story begins; indeed, his small force is all that stands between the garrison and these marauding Indians. Thus, Brittle's assumption of command in the field represents military sagaciousness rather than any attempt to rectify a situation for which the protagonist feels personally responsible. Bellah has Brittles give Cohill a note that will, hope-fully, exonerate the younger man at any future court-martial, and the Indians are then defeated when their ponies are stampeded. The older man then rides off, and Cohill and Lieutenant Pennell are left to receive the news of Brit-tles's long-awaited commission. It remains for Cohill to dispatch a rider to catch Brittles: "And tell him ... that by the date on that order, he's been absent without leave for forty-eight hours! But tell him I said 'Don't ever apologize; it's a mark of weakness!'"[5]

Ford's film is different from its very outset: to place the local story into a larger historical context, a narrator intones about the seriousness of Custer's defeat. Much of this opening speech is factually inaccurate or exaggerated (especially its anachronistic reference to the pony express, which had disap-peared years before the Little Big Horn massacre, and its insistence that west-ward advancement would stop at a time when pioneers had infiltrated nearly the entire continental United States), yet Ford's rapid movement from a larger canvas to the smaller one at Fort Stark adds a considerable symbolic weight to the story. In the film, Brittles (John Wayne) awakens to many additional days in the service and the necessity of conducting a last routine patrol. Sergeant Quincannon (Victor McLaglen), the loyal aide who not only dotes on Brittles but also adores the whiskey he has hidden in his commander's quarters, supplies comic relief. The aide in Bellah's tale, Tyree, becomes even more symbolic in the film, since he (Ben Johnson) represents a heroic mili-tary ideal as well as the nobility of the Confederacy's "Lost Cause."

Brittles's position in the film is further enhanced by his intervention in the love affairs of the post's younger people — Cohill and Pennell, who are rivals for Olivia Dandridge (Joanne Dru), added to the film for love interest. Brit-tles also berates his commander's wife (Mildred Natwick) when he is forced to take her along on his last mission. The affection that these two women bear for the aged protagonist is, of course, manifest when he returns to the fort and sets out on his own supposed westward trek. Mrs. Allshard is mentioned in Bellah's story, but she becomes a major force in the film, since she exhibits the best spirit of the cavalry while helping with the wounded trooper who must have an operation. Indeed, she is a conspicuous model to the more headstrong and immature Olivia, who, like Philadelphia Thursday in *Fort Apache*, must learn how a proper army wife acts so as to be a proper helpmate.

Pennell (Harry Carey, Jr.) and Hockbauer (Michael Dugan) are fleshed out in the film to add further significance to Brittles's leave-taking. The younger lieutenant, who learns that Olivia is not in love with him despite the symbolic ribbon she wears on the patrol, must also realize that he belongs in the military life. In this process he is aided by Cohill's jibes and, more significantly, by Brittles's inclusion of him when they oversee the killing of the treacherous sutler Rynders, who has run guns to the Indians just as Meachem did in *Fort Apache*. The less noticeable Hockbauer, an aide to Major Allshard, is present to hear Brittles's complaint about the women going on his last mission. In addition, Hockbauer is also mentioned as having contributed to the gift that the grateful company presents to Brittles on his (supposed) last day before Pennell is to lead them back into battle.

Ford has also created a more developed Indian group to enhance the struggle between them and the cavalry. The nefarious Red Shirt (Noble Johnson), who never speaks, represents the mindless and nightmarish savagery that critics have so often deplored in westerns, while Pony-That-Walks (Chief Big Tree) shows the same resignation to the world that Brittles embodies. It is, of course, the defeat of Red Shirt by Brittles's strategy that ultimately symbolizes the triumph of civilization over barbarism in *She Wore a Yellow Ribbon*. This theme is further developed by the narrator's final comments about life in the cavalry and the mystical force that drove on these "fifty-cents a day" soldiers to create the very American society they were serving.

The nostalgic mood of Ford's film is what distinguishes it most strikingly from its literary source. Bellah's short story occurs within a pragmatic world dominated by the need for action within the present. *She Wore a Yellow Ribbon*, on the other hand, clearly looks more to the past by emphasizing Tyree's sense of historical loss and Brittles's devotion to his departed family. The graveyard scenes, in which the protagonist speaks to his dead wife about the losses he experiences both as a member of the larger society and as an individual, show Ford's captain to be a much more nostalgic figure than Bellah's.

Tyree's role as the veritable hero of the film is underscored by his having been a highly efficient cavalry officer for the Confederacy; indeed, his rank then was equal to Brittles's now, and the skill Tyree exhibits while going to the beleaguered Sudro's Wells far surpasses anything that Cohill or Pennell ever do. Naturally, Brittles relies on Tyree as a scout and takes him along when he goes into the hostile Indian camp to try and negotiate a peace settlement with Pony-That-Walks. The film script also adds Tyree's devotion to Trooper Smith, who was his Civil War commander, to make plausible the way in which the sergeant retires at romantic or nostalgic moments into his own seemingly impenetrable world. Through such character drawing, Ford's film shows that history is always a matter of loss as well as gain and that such losses are not always smoothed over by the supposedly healing powers of time.

This thematic interest is reversed in *Rio Grande*, which is again based on a Bellah story, "Mission with No Record" (1949). The story's tone is once more dominated by the male quality of cavalry life and the austere existence actually led by men who risk their lives in combat. General Sheridan arrives with the recruits to issue his order that there is no official order, and the protagonist's son is among these arrivals after failing at West Point. Colonel Massarene, Bellah's main character, then delivers a verbal browbeating in which he informs his son that nothing will come easy to him by virtue of their relationship. The colonel speaks of having shot a deserter at Chapultepec, the son of a U.S. senator, in order to emphasize the necessity for the severest discipline in the service; Ford's film incorporates this dialogue into the tent scene between Colonel Kirby Yorke (John Wayne) and his son Jeff (Claude Jarman Jr.).

The subsequent raid that Massarene leads after being given General Sheridan's implicit permission to proceed involves the burning of seven Indian villages, a process that sounds much more historically accurate than what we encounter in Ford's film. The younger and elder Massarenes reconcile at the end of Bellah's story when, although they are both wounded, they recognize each other's military skills. Throughout this expedition, and in general as a leader, Colonel Massarene keeps his troops distant and angry with him so as to get the best out of them. While certain characters reappear from earlier Bellah stories, most notably Cohill and Pennell, the observer-narrator of "Mission with No Record," Topliff, is another officer, and the action predates that covered in "Massacre."

Ford's film considerable augments Bellah's story along predictably romantic and social lines. The expansion of various characters, who are merely suggested in the story, is necessitated by the additional complication of the family reconciliation enacted by the Yorkes. Ford also adds predictably comic and heroic figures in Sergeant Quincannon (Victor McLaglen) and Trooper Tyree (Ben Johnson). The latter character joins the cavalry with his pal Sandy Boone (Harry Carey, Jr.), a figure who serves as a foil to both Quincannon and Tyree.

Rio Grande also includes an elaborate series of plot developments to provide time and space for its romantic/historic conflict to be brought into focus. Kathleen Yorke (Maureen O'Hara) must arrive, demonstrate her feelings for Kirby against her wishes for Jeff, and then learn what it means to be the proverbial army wife. Jeff must come to understand the purposes behind his father's severity in the maelstrom of combat with an Apache foe who kidnaps children and murders women. Kirby must find within himself the patience to allow his wife and his son to appreciate his expertise in the military life and, finally, must realize how much he needs them in order to have a full life in the future.

Communal life is also celebrated much more elaborately in this film (and in *Fort Apache* and *She Wore a Yellow Ribbon*) than it ever is in Bellah. While women are slightly less prominent here than they were in Ford's two earlier cavalry films, they do play significant roles as mothers, both individually and as a group. Kathleen's concern for Jeff is mirrored by the women who pensively wait on a hillside after the Indians have kidnapped their children. This emphasis on the future generation is further caught up in the comic byplay between Quincannon and the little girl who refers to him as "Uncle Timmy." Children may have been present in the earlier cavalry films, but romantic and professional relationships were more prominent to suggest that adjustments would be needed before any offspring (or future) could emerge.

The professional and romantic problems in *Rio Grande* occur within an older family whose individual members have been driven apart by history. Thus, the Yorkes embody the post–Civil War sectionalism that was more muted in *Fort Apache* and *She Wore a Yellow Ribbon*. Kathleen has to abandon her injured pride over the destruction of her family home in Virginia and come to understand that, for Kirby, duty has to supersede any other consideration. To remain within the family she hopes to perpetuate, she must finally acquiesce to the military life that both the men in her life want to pursue. In essence, in her western journey Kathleen experiences a conversion in which she discovers that life apart from Kirby, even with her rebuilt plantation, is no life at all. At the same time, Kathleen must discover that military ruthlessness is essential against enemies who do not fight fair — the Indian kidnappers. These thematic "lessons" are more easily conveyed to an audience through a character such as Kathleen, who not only supplies a love interest in *Rio Grande* but also stands in closer initial proximity to modern-day values about the efficacy of violence.

Ford augments *Rio Grande* with additional characters who represent types within his western worlds. Thus, we encounter the wise Doctor Wilkins (Chill Wills), whose common sense is symbolized by his whittling, as well as a more humane General Sheridan (J. Carroll Naish), who orders Yorke out only after the Apaches have provoked him beyond all measure. The general also shows his sensitivity when he selects musical fare ("Dixie") designed to please Kathleen and to symbolize the reunion of the principals on the parade ground. Trooper Tyree's expertise enables him to tutor Jeff in the ways of the military, a process that culminates when he chooses Kirby's son as a companion on the nighttime infiltration to rescue the children from the Indian camp.

The benevolent nature of Ford's cavalry, which accords so well with his personal idealism about military life, is brought forward in the solicitude shown by Wilkins, Quincannon, and even Colonel Yorke toward Tyree in his various flights from the intrusive lawman (Grant Withers) who has been sent to extradite him to Texas. Another crucial alteration in the film is that the cavalry attacks only one Indian stronghold, instead of several villages as in the story. Ford's troopers ride against only equally armed foes and never against women and children (at least not until *The Searchers*). Such chivalry extends the decorum with which a woman like Kathleen is treated by everyone in uniform. Given such nobility, it is only natural that she and Jeff must come to see how they need to fit their lives into Kirby's.

Dorothy Johnson's short story "The Man Who Shot Liberty Valance" (1951) is distinguished by its almost O. Henry–like tone of restrained comedy and ironic sentimentality. Ransome Foster, who has suffered at the hands of the leading outlaw of the territory, lives solely for revenge throughout much of the story; he is saved from death only by the intervention of Bert Barracune, who guns down Valance from afar to save the protagonist for the smitten Hallie. Johnson's story utilizes the same framing device that is seen in the film by having Ransome and Hallie return for Barracune's funeral. The latter figure's nobility is further underscored by the way in which he gives up Hallie when he realizes that Ransome has won her heart.

In the story, Ransome and Bert are brought together only by their love for Hallie, love that continues throughout their adult lives as Bert consistently presses Ransome to rise in the world. The two men hardly stand apart in any other way except that Barracune's prowess with a gun exceeds Foster's as well as Valance's. Indeed, for much of the story, Ransome is a vagabond who works only to stay alive for the day he will call out Valance. His path has already crossed Barracune's when the latter finds Ransome, friendless, in the desert, where he has been roaming for several months.

While Barracune speaks briefly about the gun as the basis of western law, that phrase is never used in the threatening way that it is in the film. The character of Valance (Lee Marvin) is considerably elaborated by Ford's screenplay, for in the story the outlaw remains a (very) distant presence. There is also an absence of supporting characters in Johnson's tale, so that Barricune notifies Foster of Valance's arrival in town before their gunfight. After that event, Foster is left with a useless arm, and Barricune quickly tells his romantic rival of his intercession to keep the protagonist bound to a life of duty and obligation. Ransome does start a school in Twotrees and he does feel sorry for the illiterate Hallie, but his political career comes about years later and is never promoted or enhanced by his encounter with Valance.

Foster's calculating nature, by which he contrives to appear more humble than he ever truly feels, also stands in stark contrast to the film's idealized and idealistic Ransom Stoddard (James Stewart). In a somewhat comic fashion, Foster is browbeaten into marriage by Barricune, who truly wants only what is best for Hallie. Indeed, when Bert announces earlier that Hallie is "his girl," Ransome is more than content to go along with that arrangement. Johnson's irony thus builds throughout her story, albeit without the symbolic weight that these characters assume in the film. Foster is driven into a career — domesticated as it were, with a vengeance — while Hallie, in a final touch, confesses that she has placed flowers on Barricune's casket.

This short story seemingly illustrates the pressures of conscience that drive nearly all men, even one as basically irresponsible as Ransome Foster at the beginning of the tale. Johnson is hardly concerned with the taming of the West; indeed her narrative is ultimately about the taming of Ransome Foster, who can be seen as embodying a characteristically American male shiftlessness toward the duties and obligations of civilized (feminine) society. The darker force of Valance, who carries a whip and is accompanied by two henchmen, hardly surfaces in this essentially domestic comedy in which the final revelation of Hallie's feelings for Barricune represent an O. Henry kind of reversal.

The rest of Johnson's cast includes a town marshal, who remains unnamed and exhibits none of the timidity or comic relief supplied by the film's Link Appleyard (Andy Devine), and Handy Strong, who as the "first teacher west of the Rosy Buttes" does not at all resemble the calculating politician of that name in the film (Robert F. Simon). Such significant figures as Pompey (Woody Strode), Lars and Nora Ericson (John Qualen and Jeanette Nolan) and Dutton Peabody (Edmond O'Brien) are missing from the short story; others, such as Valance's cohorts (Strother Martin and Lee Van Cleef), the denizens of the town, and the politicians of the state convention, are considerably fleshed out from meager suggestions in the story. One other important variation is that Ransome and Hallie depart not on a train (which places them closer to the world of the "Wild West") but on a plane (which puts them more solidly in modern times).

Ford and his screenwriters expand Johnson's tale into a narrative that symbolizes the settling of the West. In reinvoking the ambience of *My Darling Clementine*, the film becomes an epic presentation of the civilizing of a town. By the removal of those elemental forces that threaten its preservation and growth, Ford's film ultimately turns on the paradox of the classical cowboy hero who, like Jack Schaeffer's Shane, renders himself useless through his own heroism and his association with violent means that civilized society cannot long tolerate. In essence, the community for which the hero risks his life can no longer contain such an anachronistic, potentially independent, and dangerous figure once the threat of the villain has been removed. The very expertise and temperament that set Tom Doniphon (John Wayne) apart from his fellow citizens in Shinbone eventually render the hero a threat to the new order that is going to replace the way of the gun.

Ford's film poignantly illustrates this paradoxical conflict by expanding Johnson's principal characters into the more symbolic figures of Doniphon, whose allegiance to gunplay and individual bravado marks him as a veritable alter ego to Liberty Valance, and Stoddard, whose allegiance to the institutional ways of the law and politics marks him as the corporate man of the future. It is, of course, the struggle between these central figures that marks *The Man Who Shot Liberty Valance* as more than just another shootout western; and it is the figure of Hallie who moves between them, that ultimately points up the costs of progress, which are only slightly suggested in Johnson's story.

Ford has contrived, in *The Man Who Shot Liberty Valance*, to extend the customary western movie mythology in which the hero-savior rides away to an unknown destiny (à la Shane) or on to another town badly in need of taming (with or without his lady love). Doniphon must stay and watch the success of the man he has saved and ironically "created"; unlike Barricune, who could displace his pain with his higher love for Hallie, Doniphon has finally only his anger and loneliness. In essence, this western hero has died long before his funeral, which opens the film; indeed, Doniphon has become such a forgotten figure that the newspapermen of Shinbone have apparently never heard of him.

This bitter irony is, of course, underscored by the film's main section, in which Doniphon is the most popular man in the town — a point that is emphasized when he turns down the political nomination in the saloon because of his desire to marry Hallie. Thus, Ford's version attains a broader thematic range by distorting some of the elements of Johnson's plot; although such variations may seem questionable to some literal-minded viewers, the story's artistry is markedly increased. Just as Tolstoy could illustrate the forces of history in the romantic and emotional vicissitudes of his characters in *War and Peace*, so does Ford interweave the social, the mythical, and the personal in *The Man Who Shot Liberty Valance*. The staginess of the film has often been seen as its marked weakness, but for those who can see that a western might well embody serious historical and political themes, *The Man Who Shot Liberty Valance* is one of Ford's most thoughtful masterpieces.

The filming of *Three Godfathers* presented some of the same problems of adaptation as did *My Darling Clementine*. Once again, Ford was confronted with an oft-filmed tale, for there had been at least four earlier versions of the Peter Kyne novella. One of them, *Marked Men*, Ford had directed for Universal in 1919, and the most recent version (*Three Godfathers*, 1936) had been made by the same studio (MGM) that would release Ford's remake. While Kyne's novella offers some of the same gritty realism that we see in Bellah's tales of the cavalry, Ford's film again softens, sentimentalizes, and changes character relationships by adding a much larger cast to provide a veritable society against which the actions of his leading figures can gain broader thematic significance. Minor figures, such as an incompetent deputy (Hank Worden) and a long-suffering conductor (Jack Pennick), whose train is habitually late, are introduced to add comic relief.

Sheriff "Buck" Sweet (Ward Bond) and the society of the town of Welcome add the larger communal dimension that constantly colors Ford's reworking of Kyne. The compassionate lawman, who comes to admire Bob Hightower (John Wayne) because of the tactics the outlaw uses to evade capture, appropriately ends up being the infant child's uncle and as concerned with the baby's welfare as the outlaw protagonist comes to be. In this arrangement we see the sense of individual commitment to the future that also marks *Fort Apache* and *The Searchers*. The town banker's daughter, Miss Ruby Latham (Dorothy

Ford), also symbolizes that future because her flirtation with the captured Hightower suggests he will return to become a fruitful member of the community. Thus, Welcome lives up to its name by embodying the ideal society; the law court, the bank, and the jail, which differentiate it from the squalid town that Pete (Pedro Armendariz) remembers visiting, are but the outward signs of its having become civilized.

The three principal characters' ages are also altered; Kyne's badmen are distinctly older in two instances, and their actions are reassigned so that Hightower, who corresponds to the "worst bad man" in the novella, becomes the means by which the infant is saved. Indeed, Ford's film has Hightower and Kyne's "youngest bad man" change roles when the latter character carries the baby until the man dies. In the novella we see the "worst bad man" all but running across the salt flats as the younger character saves his energy for the final leg of the trip. After Kyne's three outlaws find the infant, they consciously plan to save it.

The third outlaw, wounded and close to death, serenades the child in the novel, whereas this task falls to the younger Abilene Kid (Harry Carey, Jr.) in the film. This latter character also reads from the Bible. Kyne's oldest outlaw remains skeptical about the holy book and gets no opportunity to redeem himself, as Hightower does during the extended trek with the infant in Ford's film. However, in the novella, for a brief moment at his death, Kyne's oldest outlaw uses his hat as a parasol for the child and seemingly gains God's grace through this gesture. The film transforms this situation into the Abilene Kid's death scene — when Hightower shields his hallucinating comrade from the sun — to create a subtly different impression. Ford's religiosity, so conspicuous in *The Informer* and *The Fugitive*, is carried even further when Hightower comes upon a donkey, which carries him and the special child into New Jerusalem. In the novella the more prosaic killing of the animal provides food for the youngest outlaw and the infant so that they can survive long enough to get to the next town.

Hightower's lengthy monologue when he discovers the pregnant mother and the deserted wagon is lifted almost verbatim from Kyne's book; as a result, one of the most histrionic bits of Ford's film can be traced back to that source. In Kyne, this "worst bad man" (whose name is Tom Gibbons) suggests that the inexperienced husband, who by now is undoubtedly dead, has brought ruin on them and the future by blowing up the water tanks.

> He just put Terrapin Tanks out o' business forever — cracked the granite floor o' that sump-hole an' busted down the sides an' the water's run out into the sand an' the tanks run dry. They'll stay dry. We can have cloud-bursts in this country from now until I get religion, but them tanks'll never hold another drop o' water. That fool tenderfoot's dead, I guess; but he's goin' to keep right on killin' people just the same.[6]

Kyne's linking of this character with religion receives a more consistent and extended treatment in Ford's film, for Hightower may be right about the well, but he is clearly wrong about his own need for faith.

While Kyne has the oldest outlaw die repentant, Ford dramatizes Hightower's conversion, so as to extend that individual process into the larger human community his film has established. The novella's truncated ending has the benumbed youngest outlaw (Bob Sangster) find his way into a town, where a women relieves him of the infant. Ford's epilogue finds Hightower as an honored guest in Buck's jail; he wins a light prison sentence from a lenient judge (Guy Kibbee) who is moved by the protagonist's refusal to give up the child he has rescued from the wilderness. The judge realizes that Hightower wants to become a part of the community of Welcome, and he arranges, like a veritable fairy godfather, to turn that possibility into a reality. This prospect is then celebrated by the townspeople, who see Hightower off while singing hymns of praise that might well have been heard from Ford's Mormons on their arrival at the promised land in *Wagonmaster*.

Alan LeMay's *The Searchers* (1954) provides the fictional source for what many consider to be Ford's finest western, if not his finest film. LeMay, who directed a western (*High Lonesome*) for Eagle-Lion in 1950 and wrote works on which others were based (most notably *The Unforgiven*, which was directed by John Huston for United Artists in 1960), supplied a narrative that required cutting, as most novels do when they are transformed into films. The film's screenplay compresses some of LeMay's details and amalgamates disparate characters into single figures to achieve rapidity and coherence. In addition, Ford's film suppresses or transforms much of the harshness of the novel by having certain characters live instead of die, while others do not indulge some of the appetites that they exhibit in LeMay's novel.

By transforming the protagonist from the younger Martin Pauley (Jeffrey Hunter) to the older Ethan Edwards (John Wayne), Ford changes *The Searchers* from a comparatively simple revenge story into a more sophisticated exploration of racial and sexual feelings among family members. At the same time, the director opted for an ending that dramatizes a spiritual growth on the part of his main character, a possibility that is clearly not presented by LeMay. Once again, Ford alters not only to accommodate the sexual mores of his audience and industry but also to accentuate thematic issues that fascinated him throughout his career.

While the tone of the novel and that of the film remain fairly similar, there are some minor alterations. Henry Edwards, the husband of Martha and a younger man than his vengeful brother, becomes Aaron (Walter Coy) in the film; his wife and daughters reappear in the film, but his two sons in the novel, who are nineteen and fourteen, are reduced in the film to one boy who acts considerably younger than either of them. Laurie Mathiesen is the Edwards' next door neighbor and is, in fact, romantically smitten with Martin, but Charlie McCorry very early in the novel emerges as a serious suitor. In

LeMay's book, old Mose Harper is a rancher with sons, and we see him arguing rationally about how to proceed in tracking the raiding Comanches as well as about what to do when those in the original party realize that they have been lured away from their ranches by a ruse. Mose later scolds his oldest son after the battle at the river crossing because the latter has not fought well; thus, LeMay's character embodies traits that get reassigned to Reverend/Captain Clayton (Ward Bond) and to the simpler-minded Mose Harper (Hank Worden) in the film.

Another rancher, Ed Newby, argues against directly raiding into the Comanche camp because of the possible deaths of the Edwards' girls; in doing so, he exhibits another quality that gets assigned to Clayton in the film. Newby, who is wounded on the trail, eventually commits suicide in the novel; in the film he is also injured at the river battle, but he then reappears as a minor character at the abortive "wedding," in keeping with Hollywood censorship standards that proscribed showing suicide. Lije Powers, a strong-willed eccentric in LeMay's novel, comes closest to Mose Harper in Ford's film; indeed, this headstrong character, who abandons the initial search party because he disagrees with how they are "reading sign" (i.e., the marks left by those they are pursuing), manages to find Debbie and brings that knowledge to Amos and Martin. Sol Clinton, a Texas Ranger but not a minister, appears during the last third of LeMay's novel and threatens to arrest the leading characters for their involvement in the death of the trader Futterman. In addition, Clinton delivers the speech ("I'm the hard case you're up against out here") that Clayton makes to young Lieutenant Greenhill (Patrick Wayne) in the film.

LeMay's Amos Edwards has his name changed to Ethan and assumes a much larger status in the film. Amos Edwards has loved Martha for years, and he never deviates from his quest for revenge once he embarks on it. There is no redeeming love for anyone or anything else in LeMay's character, who, appropriately, dies seeking Indian scalps during the climactic battle at Scar's camp. Amos's maniacal need for vengeance is best seen when, despite being seriously wounded, he refuses to be left behind. By transforming Amos into Ethan, and then casting talismanic actor John Wayne to play the role, Ford ensured that the character would have to be more central and, ultimately, more sympathetic. The search for Debbie becomes an obsession to Ethan, and we are even led to think that he will kill her; but the final scenes show his transformation, brought on by the heat of battle and remembrance, qualities that Ford establishes through cinematic and mimetic devices rather than verbally. That Ethan does not die but remains to be a searcher-wanderer for the rest of his life, as indicated by his symbolic inability to enter the Jorgenson home at the end, makes the character a much more tragic one than LeMay's frontier roughneck.

In elevating Ethan, Ford has to reduce the importance of Martin Pauley, who becomes much more of an apprentice than he is in the book. The recurrent dream that haunts LeMay's Martin, in which he envisions part of the massacre of his parents from years earlier, is finally resolved when he and Amos visit the place where the Pauley ranch stood. This cathartic experience does not cause Martin to give up looking for Debbie, however; and, despite his romantic rivalry with Charlie McCorry for Laurie, he ends up seeking the younger girl after both Scar and Amos have died. LeMay's Laurie is dominated by a hatred for frontier life and a compulsion not to end up an old maid. While both of these traits are present in the film's Laurie Jorgenson (Vera Miles), her overt sexuality in the book is considerably diminished in Ford's film. She urges that Debbie should be killed because of being "tainted" by the Comanches, but she never offers to bed down with Martin, as she does in the novel. Her marriage to Charlie McCorry in LeMay's book seems especially appropriate in light of later events, which show Martin, after finding Debbie on his last search, discovering and indulging his deeper feelings for his half-sister by ending up with her under a buffalo hide on the snowbound prairie. LeMay's sexual and romantic implications are apparent; but Ford, ever a gallant romantic in his portrayals of women, naturally altered this ending for his more idealized conclusion — in which Martin returns to Laurie, and Debbie comes home (presumably) to the blessings of civilization.

If the film retains many of the novel's incidents, it often changes emphases to augment its altered characters. There is a funeral scene for Martha and her family in LeMay's novel, but Amos does not interrupt it to get on with the pursuit, as Ethan does so conspicuously in Ford's film. Many dead Indians are found buried on the trail, but again, unlike Ethan, Amos does not mutilate a corpse. Amos delivers a speech, about the inevitability of catching the Comanches, since he and Martin "will be coming on" like the seasons, and this speech is closely followed in the film. The entire sequence with Futterman also occurs in a similar fashion, albeit without the film's narrative device of the letter that Laurie reads.

Look is also inadvertently purchased by Martin in the novel, but she is fairly attractive and flees from the white men only when she is rescued by her Indian lover. This grain of realism is then abetted by the burning villages that Amos and Martin come upon — a process that Ford heightens into a pointed visual criticism of the very cavalry he has celebrated elsewhere. Amos does write his will, and Martin refuses to be his beneficiary, but this development occurs later in the novel than in the film. The fight between Charlie and Martin over Laurie ends up in a clear-cut victory for Martin; however, Laurie ends up married to the ranger, and when Charlie and Martin next meet, there are no hard feelings between them.

LeMay stresses the necessity for endurance on the frontier under trying conditions. While Henry Edwards has managed to get rich as a rancher, he has been able to stick out the difficult times only because Martha has constantly pushed him. The need for such ongoing sacrifice is, of course, symbolically

suggested by the entire narrative with its emphasis on driving out the uncivilized forces that beset the frontier community and thus creating a world that
can be inhabited by settlers. Brad Jorgenson's headlong death in pursuit of those
who have killed Lucy appears as a mad act in both the novel and the film;
however, Ford's choice to have the dead boy's mother make a speech about
the necessity for personal sacrifice to tame the wilderness softens this catastrophe considerably. That Amos gives this speech in the novel only confirms
the physically harsher and psychologically simpler world that LeMay is delineating. Amos Edwards is, at last, only capable of burying his niece in an old
blanket without speaking of his act, whereas Ethan Edwards may be equally
reticent but can offer a much more symbolic shroud in his old Confederate
jacket. In this way, Ford represents one of his most recurrent and profound
themes — the emergence of the past into the present with the suggestion that
no individual ever walks away from his own history.

The director's transformations for *Two Rode Together*, which is based on
Will Cook's *Comanche Captives* (1958), are also similar to what happens with
The Searchers; once again needs for reduction and propriety supersede problems of elaboration. At the same time, Ford's film introduces alterations that
take away much of the physical harshness and sexual explicitness of the novel.
Thus, Guthrie McCabe's amorous evening with a rancher's wife is dropped
in favor of the more elaborate comic triangle between the marshal (James
Stewart), the sinister and cynical Belle Aragon (Annelle Hayes), and the simple deputy Ward Corby (Chet Douglas). McCabe and Belle's sexual life, which
becomes apparent in the film's lengthy riverside conversation between him and
Lieutenant Gary (Richard Widmark), is tainted by the lawman's fear of marriage. Ward's emergence in McCabe's place supplies political comedy ("I didn't
even get a chance to vote for myself!") totally absent from the novel. Belle's
desire to control McCabe, a desire that initially seems motivated only by sheer
bitchiness, becomes far more sinister in the film's concluding scenes. If the
transformation of Ward represents a political necessity for Belle, her desire to
incorporate Elena (Linda Cristal) into bordello life underscores the racism so
prominent at the fort.

Cook's Jane Donovan, who becomes Marty Purcell (Shirley Jones) in the
film, is much more matter-of-fact and far less romantic or naive than Ford's
character. When she shows McCabe a picture of her lost brother, there are
no major emotional outbursts from either her or the sheriff-scout. Indeed,
McCabe's impassioned warning to the girl in the film emphasizes the racist
theme that Ford pursues throughout, in distinct contrast to Cook, who focuses
more on the relationship between McCabe and Gary. Ford's romantic idealism, which has men and women ultimately joining so that society's future can
be ensured, supplies mates for both male leads.

If the elaborate courtship of Marty and Lieutenant Gary fits well into the
ceremonial world of Ford's cavalry, the abrupt transformation of McCabe's

feelings toward Elena suggests other possibilities. Ford's romantic ending — in which the sheriff rides away with Elena to the comments of Gary and the bemused Belle — is, of course, far different from Cook's. In the novel, such a resolution is lacking in large measure because Stone Calf's wife turns out not to be the Hispanic Elena but rather the white Janice Tremain, who quickly goes back to eastern society, never suffers any insults in doing so, and shows no romantic feelings for anyone.

Cook's more downbeat tenor is also caught as Janice becomes quickly resigned to the fact that her former fiance has married another (in contrast to Ford's Elena, who never even considers that any man would have waited for her). Miss Tremain, who can easily bathe naked with McCabe in order to plan her escape from her Indian husband, simply wants to resume her "normal" white life. Elena, on the other hand, is reluctant to leave the Comanches, since she rightly fears the racism of "civilized" white society. It is only the grim realities of life with Stone Calf, expounded on by the enraged McCabe at the army dance, that finally cause her to ride out with Gary and the lawman. While Ford transforms Elena into a symbolic victim of racist hypocrisy, as well as the means by which McCabe accepts the larger social role a hero must play, Cook portrays Janice as simply the victim of a more difficult style of life, from which she gladly escapes.

The greatest difference between the novel and the film is that Cook supplies a harrowing section in which McCabe becomes a prisoner of the Comanches after he has taken some captives back to white society. Gary wants to return to Iron Hand's camp to explain what has happened, and McCabe, in an uncharacteristically charitable moment, rides in Gary's place after urging that Jane Donovan marry the lieutenant. McCabe subsequently suffers the privations of an Indian slave — a section that would, of course, have significantly darkened, if not entirely obviated, the moral scheme of Ford's film. While the director's Indians remain hostile and alien figures inhabiting a kind of nightmare landscape of the mind, especially when Stone Calf (Woody Strode) emerges from the shadows to die at McCabe's hands, any extended portrayal of the sufferings of their captives could vitiate the moral outrage exemplified by the principal male characters on their return to Fort Grant.

In Cook's novel, it is Gary who, significantly, kills the pursuing Indian chief and then squelches Janice Tremain's ritual incantation over the corpse. McCabe, ever the opportunist in the novel, has ridden ahead with the boy he plans to sell to the highest bidder among the settlers seeking their long-lost relatives. Gary then escorts Janice to the army ball, where she delivers a very brief defense of her life with Stone Calf; however, her rhetoric underlines the novel's more equivocal horrors, in which characters are beset by brutalities, physical or psychological, no matter which side they join.

While the demented Mrs. McCandless (Jeanette Nolan) also appears in the novel and dies at the hands of the Indian boy, Cook's Henry J. Wringle is far more idealistic than Ford's scheming merchant (Willis Bouchey). Indeed, Cook's Wringle laments over the returned savage boy and then decides to stay and become a real settler — a decision that ultimately costs him his life. In the film, Ford displaces that part of Wringle's temperament onto Ole Knudsen (John Qualen) to make his theme about racist hypocrisy more obvious. The reprehensible Clegg family is another film addition designed to suggest the seething animosity within white society. Not surprisingly, the comic fight between Ortho (Harry Carey, Jr.) and Greeley Clegg (Ken Curtis) and Gary is modeled on a much more somber passage from the novel in which the lieutenant is beaten by Jane Donovan's father and brother, who resent his attentions to the girl.

Cook's novel also includes a therapeutic brawl between McCabe and Gary after the former has been rescued from his Indian captivity. This conflict is given greater symbolic weight in the film; McCabe's admonitions to Gary ("Don't buck me, Jim!") finally erupt in a ferocious showdown on the way back from the Comanche camp. At this point McCabe reveals that he is capable of killing Gary, in a scene that echoes the harsher and often hysterical psychology so often found in Anthony Mann; however, this unsettling moment is defused when McCabe sends Gary off with the Comanche boy and stays behind with Elena to kill Stone Calf.

Ford's romanticized ending is also, of course, decidedly different from the end of Cook's novel, which has McCabe learning that his longtime lover (the rancher's wife) has fled, leaving both him and her husband behind. In a further ironic touch, McCabe, who earlier had to be knocked out to prevent his riding back for sexual sport, also learns that, despite suffering for months among the Indians, he is going to be paid for only three weeks' work and that he has been unceremoniously dumped as town marshal. All of these indignities lead to a night of drunken revelry with Gary, and both of them get jailed. The novel ends with Jane Donovan wistfully realizing that her married life with the lieutenant will be interesting, as McCabe characteristically starts thinking about how to restore his position in society.

The adaptation of *Cheyenne Autumn* is not quite as successful, despite the considerable and all but predictable alterations and additions that once again are worked on its literary original. While Mari Sandoz's book enjoyed a belated popularity in the civil rights–conscious 1960s, this 1953 account of the flight of the Cheyennes from their reservation in Oklahoma hardly represents promising movie material. Sandoz sets out to celebrate the mores and folkways of the beleaguered Indians as they make their way home. In doing so, she utilizes a kind of Native American vernacular to re-create the thought patterns of her characters, as well as offering lengthy extracts from various contemporary (white) historical sources to provide an aura of accuracy.

Occasional chapters take up the tactics of the pursuing cavalry and the ineptness of their leaders — points that are made much more effectively in the film. Sandoz does use Little Wolf and Dull Knife; and the former does, indeed, kill another Cheyenne brave after the tribe has arrived at its destination, causing him to become an outcast from his people. There is also a ravine battle between the Cheyennes and their cavalry pursuers, and later, Dull Knife's half of the tribe is incarcerated in the Fort Robinson barracks, where they are tormented by Captain Wessels. There is even a reaction in Dodge City to the fleeing Indians, but it is only briefly mentioned and then done ironically to indicate that the Cheyennes have hardly carved a path through their white antagonists.

Ford's film expands on Sandoz's psychohistorical material by adding a romance between Captain Archer (Richard Widmark) and the Quaker idealist Deborah Wright (Carroll Baker), a figure who enables Ford to more plausibly present the Indian flight in a sympathetic way. The cavalrymen who accompany Archer are also more individualized, in keeping with the familiar Ford formulas, so that such iconic figures as Ben Johnson and Harry Carey Jr., who appear as comic relief in unbilled roles, and Sergeant Wichowsky (Mike Mazurki) hold up the exemplary notions of the service seen previously.

The lengthy burlesque in Dodge City plunges us into revisionism, seemingly in keeping with making *Cheyenne Autumn* commercially acceptable to a 1960s audience. It is, however, this revisionist tone that sits badly on Ford's final western; indeed, the decision to cut out the Wyatt Earp–Doc Holiday shenanigans in many later release prints of *Cheyenne Autumn* seems quite understandable. Ford, of course, renders much that is inert in Sandoz's book into fairly moving drama by compressing complex historical passages into significant individual acts; thus, Secretary Schurz (Edward G. Robinson), who is mentioned in the novel, comes to stand for enlightened white opinion in ways that the film can visualize. To say that Ford improves significantly on Sandoz's novel would be a serious overstatement; the epic scale of *Cheyenne Autumn*, coupled with Ford's age and his health problems, renders the film a somewhat less than satisfying coda for this most notable of western film directors.

Ford's *Cheyenne Autumn* is, finally, undercut by its lack of character conflict on the order of that in *Fort Apache* or *The Man Who Shot Liberty Valance*. Despite his serious revision of its literary source, Ford seems to be too often parodying his earlier works; Sandoz's Indians are unrealized, and the central conflict of her book is melodramatic. We miss the moral ambiguities that surround such figures as Colonel Thursday, Ethan Edwards, Ransom Stoddard, or Tom Doniphon, in this saga where length, alas, largely substitutes for thematic subtlety. A moral monster like Captain Wessels (Karl Malden), however appealing to a 1960s audience that could see him as a crypto-Nazi, proclaims the thematic poverty of *Cheyenne Autumn*; even the potentially intriguing conflict between Indian generations gets largely subsumed by the larger epic of flight and pursuit. There is a vicious irony when Little Wolf

(Ricardo Montalban) chooses to cut himself off from the people he has led, but there is so little substance to his antagonist (Sal Mineo) that their rivalry barely suggests the depths of the opposing forces in Ford's earlier westerns. From any other director, *Cheyenne Autumn* might well be hailed as a major effort; from John Ford, it emerges as overly long and thematically simplistic. *Cheyenne Autumn* shows Ford turning out an adaptation that is mostly Ford-like and only rarely Fordian: his customary thematic additions and character alterations could not be made to fit the requirements of epic scale or to disguise the ideological biases and narrative weaknesses of the original source.

My *Darling Clementine* is even further removed from its immediate literary source, Stuart Lake's all-but-hagiographic biography *Wyatt Earp: Frontier Marshal* (1931). Ford's film also draws on Alan Dwan's *Frontier Marshal* (20th Century–Fox, 1939) for the incident when the hero dunks the saloon girl in a horse trough; however, that earlier version of the O.K. Corral shootout finds Doc Holliday (Cesar Romero) being killed, precipitating Wyatt's (Randolph Scott) actions against the villains. Ford centers his principal character's movitvations once more around concerns for family and civilization; just as the Ringo Kid had to settle a debt owed to family honor in *Stagecoach*, so Wyatt must respond to the Clantons' murders of his two brothers. Ford's plot also moves at a brisker pace than Dwan's film or Lake's book in order to present characteristic thematic concerns.

Turning to Lake's biography, we can readily see the necessity for the adaptation undertaken by the screenwriters of both the 1939 Dwan version (Sam Hellman) and the 1946 Ford film (Winston Miller, Samuel Engel). Lake's book recounts Earp's entire career, from his youthful beginnings as the son of emigrant farmers who settled in California (a note that may be reflected in having *My Darling Clementine's* protagonist initially, and finally, heading to rejoin his father there). Lake also chronicles Earp's various jobs as a teamster, a surveyor, and a buffalo hunter, as well as his friendship with Wild Bill Hickok in Kansas City, and his subsequent confrontations with frontier badmen in various Kansas towns. Leon Uris's script for *Gunfight at O.K. Corral* (Paramount, 1957) adheres much more closely to Lake in terms of names and places and in having Wyatt travel to Tombstone at the behest of his brother. Lake shows Holliday as a deputy in Dodge City, where Wyatt brings order through the establishment of a "dead line" across which no armed man could pass. The hero's career in Tombstone finds him continuously falling afoul of Sheriff Behan, who supported the Clantons or at least stood in opposition to what later commentators have seen as Earp's less-than-noble motives.

Ford's film reduces the historical grayness of Lake's fulsome biography to a more black-and-white conception of both hero and place. Whereas the historical Wyatt was looking for opportunity, and Tombstone was composed of various types of lawmen and business opportunities, Ford presents the character as a pure soul defending family honor and consciously trying to build a

West in which civilization can prosper. At the same time, Tombstone is the archetypal wild western town of the movies, badly in need of law and order so that its ordinary (i.e., unarmed) citizens can enjoy a stable (i.e., profitable) communal life. While such a generic situation demands the removal of such spontaneous and anachronistic figures as the Clantons or Holliday, Ford's film transforms Doc into a figure who redeems himself from the drunken malaise into which he has fallen and, by his death, provides the kind of individual sacrifice essential to creating civilization out of wilderness. Chihuahua (Linda Darnell) and Clementine Carter (Cathy Downs) are, of course, cinematic additions; and although the former character is present in Dwan's film, the eastern nurse, with all the echoes of Holliday's past that she verbalizes, is a new development.

There are also some notable omissions between the original screenplay and the shooting script, ones that — characteristically for Ford — shorten the narrative and, thus, add to the pace of his film.[7] Thus, an entire sequence, in which the drunken actor Thorndyke (Alan Mowbray) arrives by stage, has been omitted, and some significant dialogue between Billy Clanton (John Ireland) and Chihuahua, as well as between Doc and Clementine, has been dropped. In the screenplay, the prefatory remarks of John Simpson (Russell Simpson) before the church social and dance are considerably longer, and Pa Clanton (Walter Brennan) even appears during this same sequence when we see Wyatt gracing the boards with his "lady fair."

In essence, both *Frontier Marshal* and *My Darling Clementine* use Lake's biography as a starting point while focusing on only a small part of its narrative. Ford's film predictably goes much further in the direction of romance by transforming nearly all the characters into ideal types so that he can present the settling of the West within his own, admittedly mythically toned, conception of that process. Thus, like nearly all of Ford's other sound westerns, *My Darling Clementine* attains the kind of character drawing we associate with poetry and melodrama — literary and psychological perspectives that do not always accord with current or popular thinking about either westerns or commercial films. In adding romantic complications to heighten the symbolic weight of various thematic conflicts in his sound westerns, Ford goes beyond the limits of realism and revisionism; indeed, his screenplays are ultimately executed as films whose artistry exhibits the kinds of thematic and aesthetic coherence that we associate with great literature.

Chapter 6

Fort Apache and *Rio Grande*

Fort Apache (1948) and *Rio Grande* (1950) are the most obviously linked of Ford's westerns. These films have visual, thematic, and plot similarities that almost immediately mark them as companion pieces. Despite their numerous affinities, the two films actually stand in sharp contrast, for the world of *Fort Apache* emerges as thoughtfully unsettling, whereas that of *Rio Grande* is melodramatically reassuring. *Fort Apache* raises issues and paradoxes that make it a richer and more complex film. In a very real sense, it is "open ended" because its plot and character resolutions pale beside the deeper thematic issues it raises. *Rio Grande* is sunnier; its conflicts are resolvable (and resolved) within its plot. Given its more economical structure and treatment, *Rio Grande* portrays a "closed world" with no loose ends. In both films, the need to impose peace and order on a frontier wilderness, and thus provide the basis for an emergent urban civilization, is coupled with an emphasis on the physical and emotional adjustments of individual characters. While Ford's soldiers must strive to keep the peace with the Apaches, his women strive to bring a more civilized life to Fort Apache and Fort Stark by creating domesticity; this quest for settled family life is further emphasized by the romantic conflicts in both films. Mickey O'Rourke (John Agar) and Philadelphia Thursday (Shirley Temple) in *Fort Apache*, and Kirby (John Wayne) and Kathleen Yorke (Maureen O'Hara) in *Rio Grande* must reconcile their individual feelings with the demands imposed both by their society and their own consciences.

While numerous conflicts (man against man, man against environment, man against himself) represent standard plot fare, *Fort Apache* and *Rio Grande* also comment on thematic issues through comparison and juxtaposition. Both films illustrate the necessity for adjustment and accommodation by the individual. Ford consistently places newcomers—whether neophytes from afar, natives returning from lengthy absences, or more experienced figures merely passing through—in situations that either alter or destroy them. The most obvious examples of such figures in *Fort Apache* and *Rio Grande* are the raw recruits who come into the cavalry; however, the relative ease with which they are assimilated into army life and the often comic ways in which they achieve such adjustments diminish their symbolic weight.

82

Ford's more interesting newcomers must learn, through painful experience, what it means to be both a westerner and "army," roles that Philadelphia Thursday and Kathleen Yorke come to embody in *Fort Apache* and *Rio Grande*. The traveler returning from an extended absence from his native land is embodied by Mickey O'Rourke; his reintegration into the social ethos represents a major thematic development in *Fort Apache*. Colonel Owen Thursday (Henry Fonda) represents a transient figure in the same film, a man who is significantly measured by his many failures to accept frontier life. In the generic landscape of these cavalry films, which posit the struggle between white and Indian styles of life as a given condition of existence, these newcomers must both adapt to and modify the ways they encounter, even if the balance between their ways and those of the natives is decidedly in the latter's favor. Indeed, given Ford's personal feelings about military life, one can expect the life-style of the cavalry to prove of more worth than the eastern or effete ways of these newcomers.

These two films also touch on a contemporary issue that reflects the post–World War period in which they were made. Thomas Heggen's *Mister Roberts* (1946), which was adapted into a huge theatrical success on Broadway (and which would emerge in a film version codirected by Ford in 1955), and films such as *Command Decision* and *Twelve O'Clock High* (both 1949) suggest that commanders can be shortsighted or war-weary. Norman Mailer in *The Naked and the Dead* (1948), Herman Wouk in *The Caine Mutiny* (1951), and James Jones in *From Here to Eternity* (1951), in different ways and for different reasons, showed that such leaders could be egomaniacs, madmen, or incompetents. In *Fort Apache* and *Rio Grande*, Ford offers a conservative response by illustrating the personal and professional qualities that mark inspired military leadership. The two westerns establish and illuminate these ideal martial and character traits through figures who change during their narratives. It is a measure of the seriousness of Ford's intentions that flat (one-note) characters are avoided in presenting this issue: even Colonel Thursday has noble and necessary traits that redeem him.

Ford uses numerous visual and verbal techniques in both *Fort Apache* and *Rio Grande*. Comedy, whether verbal or physical, frequently emphasizes larger, thematic meanings. Thus, in *Fort Apache* the four sergeants (Mulcahy [Victor McLaglen], Beaufort [Pedro Armendariz], Shattuck [Jack Pennick], and Quincannon [Dick Foran]) spank Mickey O'Rourke, a motif that is continued by his father (Ward Bond) and Captain York (John Wayne) with playful swipes at his midsection, in order to establish their proprietary interests in the young man. Through these scenes Ford establishes not only the regard that each of these older characters has for Mickey but also the moral universe of the cavalry (in which the veterans must teach the rookies) that they share. Because these individuals can indulge in such seeming horseplay, they also stand in the sharpest juxtaposition to the austere Thursday, a rigidly controlled

figure who disdains any kind of frivolity. Kirby York becomes a surrogate father to Mickey O'Rourke when he disobeys Thursday's command and takes the young man (and not his father) with him and the supply train at the scene of the massacre. When Captain York subsequently sends Mickey for help, we see another thematic point much stressed in *Fort Apache* and elsewhere in Ford's westerns: the need for people to sacrifice (their happiness or lives, if need be) to ensure a better future for an oncoming generation (whether already present or implicitly to come).

The sequence in which Mulcahy, Beaufort, Shattuck, and Quincannon decide they must dispose of the sutler Meacham's (Grant Withers) whiskey by drinking it — and then suffer being put in the guardhouse, being broken in rank, and being forced to work on the post's manure pile — offers another example of Ford's often knockabout sense of comedy. Captain York's emphasis of the phrase "silver salver," a term he introduces to ease Mickey's dismay at having to formally call on Philadelphia and leave his card, demonstrates a standard kind of Fordian verbal play while, again, underlining York's role as a kind of fairy godfather to the young lovers. The relationship between them is further served verbally at the Collingwoods' when the disappointed Philadelphia bursts in to lament that her father has been unable to have dinner with her on their first night at the post. In a bit of polite badinage, Captain York asks Philadelphia how she got her name; after a series of explanations that do not ultimately enlighten, Captain Collingwood (George O'Brien) attempts to change the subject. However, in a slightly befuddled way, he mispronounces Philadelphia's name, offering a sharp contrast to his commanding officer's penchant for making such errors. Whereas Thursday consistently mispronounces Mickey's last name to illustrate his disdain for others as well as his disapproval of any romance between his daughter and the son of an Irish sergeant major, Collingwood's error with Philadelphia carries the opposite connotation, for he quickly corrects himself to underline the very warmth with which the girl is surrounded in his home.

The arrival of the recruits at Fort Stark in *Rio Grande* and the various ways in which they answer Sergeant Quincannon's (Victor McLaglen) roll call establish the comic relationship between Sandy Boone (Harry Carey, Jr.) and the sergeant when the recruit must be admonished to say "Yo!" (a phrase he seems to utter at every opportunity thereafter). In another scene Sandy dispels Quincannon's bravado by asking for the name of the tribe after the sergeant boasts about jumping a horse and carrying an Indian under each arm; he also naively asks what the phrase "chowder-headed Mick sergeant" means, mentioning that this is how Trooper Heinze (Fred Kennedy) has referred to

Opposite: Cochise (Miguel Inclan) and his warriors contemplate the foolhardy approach of Thursday's command in *Fort Apache* (Argosy-RKO, 1948). The nobility of the Indians stands in the sharpest contrast to the behavior of Ford's protagonist.

Quincannon. Such comic questioning, which is repeated when Quincannon asks Dr. Wilkins (Chill Wills) what an arsonist is, cleverly establishes the growing rapport between the recruits and their new environment.

These comic scenes are counterpointed with serious intentions, for when the roll call culminates with Jeff Yorke's (Claude Jarman, Jr.) response, his father rises at the sound of that voice to appear and address the new troops. While the colonel's speech stresses the harshness of what the recruits are likely to face, his position in relation to Jeff, visually composed as though they were the only ones present, foreshadows the following scene in the commander's tent when Kirby further emphasizes to his son what the military life is and what it is not — a serious passage that, in contrast, ends on a comic note. After they have felt each other out, and after Jeff has stated that he would change nothing between them on a professional level, the tension is relieved. Jeff then insists on having his salute returned properly, and Quincannon guffaws, so that the strain is transformed into comedy, an alteration that is reemphasized when, after Jeff leaves, Kirby marks his son's height on the tent flap and then compares his own with it by assuming a most awkward position.

Rio Grande has fixed comic figures in the deputy marshal (Grant Withers) who suffers from corns and the stuttering bugler (Shug Fisher). While such types seem rudimentary, the film is redeemed by the comic byplay between Quincannon and many other characters. The fight between Jeff and Heinze, a sequence that culminates when the adversaries reconcile because each has refused to speak before the colonel, places Quincannon in just such a position. After he and Heinze spar verbally over the latter's insults, it is only natural that the sergeant will batter the smaller man whenever an opportunity presents itself during the subsequent fisticuffs behind the picket line. Dr. Wilkins also serves as a comic foil for Quincannon by literally acting on the sergeant's request to hit the "hand that did the bloody deed" (i.e., that burned Kathleen's beloved Bridesdale plantation fifteen years before the opening of *Rio Grande*). After he states that sending Trooper Tyree (Ben Johnson) back for trial in Dallas would not be something he would like to see happen, Wilkins allows Quincannon to mull over this advice. By then telling Tyree what to do in an oblique manner, the top sergeant stays within bounds, a process that is comically reinforced by his asking who is there when the trooper bounds out the door.

With Kathleen, Quincannon experiences a moment of comic triumph when he offers to carry her across a bridge to Jeff as the Apache prisoners caterwaul below. Quincannon's softheartedness clearly shows here, since he is the one Kathleen chooses to take her to her son. Their love-hate relationship is largely dominated by her in subsequent scenes. Whether she is calling him an arsonist (and then refining that epithet to "reluctant" arsonist), making small of his battered drawers at the wash site, or branding him as the embodiment of "Yankee" justice, Kathleen's wit is always ahead of Quincannon's.

Homes are symbolic in both films; however, in keeping with its more epic scope and scale, *Fort Apache*'s domiciles are more clearly distinguished by the objects they contain. Meacham's slovenly den exhibits a weight scale that, when Thursday tests it, proves to be rigged. The casks of whiskey (which enable the four sergeants to indulge their appetites) and rifles further define the sutler. Later, when York offers Beaufort, just returned to duty, one last drink and then throws the bottle away, Ford's symbolic intention seems fairly patent.

As a more humane officer than Thursday, York maintains better relations with the enlisted men; however, when serious duty beckons, such frivolities as alcohol must be put aside. Another symbol that is tied to a specific home in *Fort Apache* is the Bible that Sergeant O'Rourke is reading when Mickey first knocks on the door. Appropriately enough, the elder O'Rourke concludes his reading before rising to greet his son.

Within the home that Philadelphia creates for her father at such short notice, numerous objects are displayed and commented on; however, the chair that she has brought serves as the most meaningful symbol within that setting. Ford consistently uses chairs to establish dexterity and moral stature for the characters who occupy them. In *Rio Grande* General Sheridan (J. Carroll Naish) will tip back in a chair for a moment and so ally himself iconographically with such earlier Ford protagonists as Lincoln in *Young Mr. Lincoln* (1939) and Wyatt Earp in *My Darling Clementine* (1946). Given such associations, it is surely appropriate that Colonel Thursday collapses into a broken chair and is then (seemingly) unable to lift himself out of it. While Philadelphia laughingly apologizes for not having warned her father that the chair was "rump sprung," and while Thursday conspicuously does not join in her laughter, Ford's use of Fonda in such a way gains considerable resonance when we remember that the same actor played the dexterous Lincoln and Earp in the earlier films.

Throughout *Fort Apache*, Colonel Thursday is frequently seen smoking or lighting cigars, a trait he shares with many other Ford characters. While cigars traditionally symbolize the world of men and adventure (even within this film, Emily Collingwood [Anna Lee] tells Philadelphia that they should withdraw so that the men can enjoy an after-dinner smoke), lighting them becomes an act to further delineate character. In the scene with the broken chair, Fonda precedes his descent by lighting a cigar and nervously contemplating Mickey's calling card (now found on a tray). Later, Thursday needs to relight his cigar after he has been extricated from the chair.

The calling card, which has distressed Thursday and which served as the immediate cause of the earlier comic argument between Philadelphia and Mickey, operates as a symbolic talisman. This object of identity (one's name within the etiquette of the officer class) links the young lovers, for Philadelphia's desire to possess it suggests her unspoken feelings. When she must seek an excuse to confront Mickey, she uses his calling card as an entry to his home by insisting, as she takes it out of her handbag, that it represents a commitment on the young man's part. She has not been informed that her father has forbidden Mickey to see her; and this scene, with Thursday's entry into the O'Rourke household and his subsequent confrontation with the lieutenant and the sergeant major, makes her father's command overt to her as well.

Costumes and clothing also serve as symbolic extensions of personality in *Fort Apache*. On numerous occasions Thursday wears gloves, which always seem designed (and worn) to prevent him from dirtying his hands through unnecessary contact with others. The colonel's gloves are conspicuously white and figure prominently during the enlisted men's dance when he is photographed, to suggest his distaste for this obligatory situation. When trying to correct Thursday's naiveté about the military prowess of the Apaches, Captain York nervously twists his gloves as a sign of irritation. Later, when enraged by Meacham, York uses his gauntlets to strike the sutler; and at the climactic moment before the battle, when Thursday has called him a coward, York throws down his gloves in the traditional gesture for a duel. While Thursday's refusal to fight seems motivated by snobbery and shortsightedness, the impetuosity of his subordinate strikes at good military order. In a very real sense York is wrong to make the challenge, since, by acting on it, both men would place the group in even greater jeopardy.

The uniform that Thursday wears also sets him apart from the more casually dressed soldiers of his command. Though he complains about "exposed galluses," Thursday's failure to adopt regional dress once more measures the man against the background into which he has moved. Thursday never considers that the uniforms his troopers wear are practical: to him, the men are merely improperly dressed. Thursday's uniform, including his kepi, harkens back to the Civil War, while his command, in their broadbrimmed hats and neckerchiefs, personify the West in which they live and act. When he enters Fort Apache, Thursday wears a cape that, in effect, further serves to protect him from the dirt of that world.

The colonel's death is clearly foreshadowed as he loses the signs of his office — the sabre and cap both having disappeared when he emerges after being shot out of the saddle. The most striking use of Thursday's costume is, of course, in its adoption by Captain York at the film's end. Since York has become the regimental commander (as Thursday said he would during their final meeting), he now dresses in a style that embodies that of his predecessor. By wearing a kepi as he leads the troops out on a winter campaign, York shows the extent to which he has assimilated Thursday's style. York has not totally "become" Thursday, for his uniform still contains vestiges of his own past, with only the cap serving as a visual link. Within the more restricted world of *Rio Grande*, Colonel Yorke moves about in various headgear. He not

Trooper Tyree (Ben Johnson) about to kill the Indians pursuing Jeff Yorke in *Rio Grande* (Argosy-Republic, 1950). The ablest soldier makes a better man of the younger Yorke through example.

only wears the traditional cowboy hat when involved in fighting but also is seen in a Union cap and a kepi similar to Thursday's.

In *Fort Apache*, two other objects serve as prominent symbols to further delineate Thursday. The first is the watch he fingers so anxiously during the enlisted men's ball. In drawing our attention to it, Ford emphasizes the continuously preoccupied temper of his protagonist. Thursday can think only about York's return from Cochise and the possible chance for military glory and restoration of rank; thus he impatiently eyes the watch at various times during the dance. This concern about time also suggests how miserable he is in his present circumstances, merely passing time, as it were, until he can get back to a real life in the East. Given this attitude, Thursday stands in direct contrast to the rest of the cast, who, like Sergeant O'Rourke with Philadelphia, find joy in the present.

Thursday's concern with historical glory is aptly rewarded by the framed portrait of him that decorates York's wall in the film's final sequence. Thursday has become more impressive in the painting than he ever was in life; and when York corroborates the eager reporter's description of the painting of the colonel's charge in Washington as "correct in every detail," we know that society demands protective lies. York cannot dispel the newsmen's enthusiasm because the national community needs such legends to function: Thursday (Custer) must be defended and the horrors of war downplayed so that the larger group (and hopefully the greater good) can be served.

Ford's daring here is that he has showed us Thursday's real "charge" and how patently wrongheaded it was, yet he leaves us with his paradoxical concluding message. For the world at large, understanding can only be in melodramatic dimensions — heroes must be larger than life and military deeds must be glorious. For the truly initiated, the professional soldiers at Fort Apache and their like, the perpetuation of such myths is an essential part of their duty. In beginning this final sequence by pulling back from Thursday's portrait to the standing York, Ford clearly underscores the thematic direction in which his film has moved. The elaboration of the entire sequence, replete with the ghostly images of past riders in the windowpane and York's subsequent movement through his new command (including Mickey, Philadelphia, and their son), implies that the community has assimilated the values of Thursday without losing sight of its own nature and direction.

Rio Grande offers fewer symbols than *Fort Apache*, but those it uses are more obviously and forcefully employed. The coffee that General Sheridan and Colonel Yorke share represents a means for them to comment on the developing situation with the Apaches. At their initial meeting, Sheridan remarks that he has not shared a cup of coffee with Yorke since they rode through the Shenandoah fifteen years earlier. While this remark establishes the plot background concerning Kathleen's devastated home, the larger point lies in Yorke's reply that the coffee, though desirable, is too weak. Sheridan, in foreshadowing the order he will issue in their next meeting, suggests that Yorke should complain more (presumably to their superiors) and thus help make the coffee stronger. These characters are, of course, speaking about their frustrations over the government's policy of not violating the Mexican border; and Yorke even talks about his men's anguish when, after a running fight, they were forced to stop at the Rio Grande and watch the Apaches escape.

Sheridan's second meeting with Kirby, in which he countermands the orders about violating the boundary, is also accompanied by coffee drinking, so that his remark about a possible court-martial is augmented by this symbol. The Shenandoah strain is again picked up when Sheridan insists that he will handpick Yorke's court-martial panel and will be certain that it contains men who rode with them then. Coffee drinking is also featured briefly in the dinner scene between Kirby and Kathleen when she daintily puts down a cup, and he, cigar in hand, seductively eyes her. The cup that is fingered as though it would break seemingly stands for Kathleen, who, despite her repressed feelings for Kirby, cannot bring herself to openly declare her love. This symbolic mixture is quickly cast aside, however, when the regimental singers arrive and relieve the would-be lovers.

A more extended symbolic intention surrounds money in *Rio Grande*. Kathleen has secured one hundred "Yankee" dollars, with which she intends to purchase Jeff's freedom from the service. However, after being informed by Kirby that he, as his son's commanding officer, must sign any release papers and that he will not do so (and then by Jeff that he will not sign a release either), Kathleen adopts a waiting position. We see her performing domestic chores for money and charging Kirby and Quincannon for washing and ironing. Against such a background, Kirby comes courting with flowers, which, after he has dismissed his junior officers and gotten Kathleen to himself, he presents to her. She, in turn, brings out his laundered and mended coat and playfully asks for payment for services rendered. Kirby reaches into his vest pocket and offers Kathleen ten dollars, which amazes her; however, when she turns the bill over, we see that it is Confederate script. After Yorke says he has been saving the bill for just the right moment, Kathleen rushes into her tent and returns with a bag of gold coins, which she throws down as "change" for their transaction. In this exchange of currencies, with each offering the other's coin, as it were, Ford pictorializes the burgeoning love and reconciliation of his principals. That the scene subsequently moves to their open avowal of feelings is hardly surprising, given its symbolic overlay.

Ford's credit sequences in these two films offer yet another means to connect them. In both cases we see titles imposed over scenes ostensibly taken from the ensuing narratives as if these stories had already begun. Each sequence also features a mounted bugler on the crest of a hill; however, this arrangement, reminiscent of so many magnificent Fordian vistas of mounted riders along a ridge line, begins *Fort Apache*'s credit sequence and completes *Rio Grande*'s. By this difference, Ford is seemingly signing these works in an oblique way; one completes the other, as symbolized by the same figure in the credit sequences and by his position at their respective beginning and end.

The credit sequence for *Fort Apache* is also built on oppositions as scenes of mounted cavalry and Indians are cross-cut to fortify our sense of the basic generic conflict to come. Another visual clue within this sequence is the individualized figure of Captain York, so that his role as the hero-conciliator, or the man in the middle (between Thursday and Cochise, between the commandant and the lovers), is emphasized. The shots in this credit sequence are never exactly replicated in the film that follows, and the final scene is utilized as a cut to the narrative itself. This last sequence majestically opens the film by showing the stagecoach bringing Thursday to his new command against the grandeur of Monument Valley and Richard Hageman's music.

Rio Grande offers a more modest credit sequence, albeit one that again serves as an overture for what is to follow. The river itself is most prominent here, with shots of mounted troops riding to its edge as well as intercut scenes of Yorke's meeting with the Mexican officers on the sandbar. The notion of crossing seems uppermost, and this emphasis alerts us to later developments.

Just as Kirby must cross the river to rid his fortress community of its enemies, so must he cross a symbolic division within himself and go to Kathleen to achieve needed emotional, familial, and professional harmonies. When we notice that Kathleen is prominently associated with water on two occasions (when she crosses a creek to see Jeff for the first time and when she appears at the riverside doing wash) and that Kirby is most romantically miserable by a riverside (a scene that occurs after Kathleen has told Jeff that his father is a very lonely man), this pattern stands out even more as a symbolic motif.

Although Ford is not noted for camera pyrotechnics, there are moments in these films when cinematography looms large. One favorite recurrent shot uses reflections so that in *Fort Apache*, York is seen in a windowpane while speaking about the ongoing, mystical life of the regiment. This sequence ultimately finds both York's face and the mystically recalled cavalrymen in the glass surface. Philadelphia's arranging of her hatbox mirror to be able to watch Mickey on the ride to Fort Apache utilizes the same device, again to establish character relationships. Photographing the girl from below on a staircase also establishes such meaning. On the morning after her arrival, Thursday's daughter is awakened by numerous activities; when Mickey O'Rourke shows up with his calling card, she descends a flight of stairs, conspicuously framed as a passageway. In effect, Philadelphia is already more at one with her surroundings, since she can come down the stairs to Mickey. The use of a passageway, particularly as a device to join or separate lovers, occurs throughout Ford's westerns.

Such romantic associations are also apparent in *Rio Grande* when the Yorkes, at their initial meal, are photographed as "one" while listening to the serenade. The camera setups of this scene, with its contradictory, polite, and self-effacing dialogue, belay what the characters are saying. While listening to "Kathleen," Mrs. Yorke moves so as to all but put her head on Kirby's shoulder; indeed, given the camera angle, it would appear that she is resting there — an association that is reaffirmed when, as they become more aware of their surroundings (after being lost in a seeming revelry), the two principals move apart to reestablish decorum.

Dust is used throughout *Fort Apache* to veil action. The climactic massacre, containing stunt falls and stoic Indian faces raining down death, is frequently photographed in long shots. Thus, the besieged cavalry — drawn up in what can be seen as painterly or cinematic (if one recalls earlier Hollywood treatments of Custer's Last Stand such as *The Plainsman* [1936] and *They Died with Their Boots On* [1942]) style — and the charging Indians dominate the screen. There are no close-up death agonies, for the massed Apaches simply roll over Thursday's command like a tidal wave. Such visual discretion begins the process by which the massacre is transformed into a legend to support the larger needs of the nation. The same shrouding effect occurs earlier when the cavalry column arrives to rescue Mickey and the four sergeants from the pursuing Indians. This lengthy chase sequence culminates with the appearance of the fort troop, which Mickey and the others rush past. As their little group comes to a halt and turns in the foreground, the cavalry column rushes into the distant whirl of dust to rout the Apache pursuers.

Dust also figures prominently in the later massacre sequence when, as a signal to his warriors, Cochise (Miguel Inclan) releases a handful of earth to signify his displeasure and his authority. After Thursday's death, Cochise and York confront each other within still another swirl of dust. The unarmed cavalry officer goes to receive the guidon of his dead commander as a thundering horde of Apache riders circle warily in the distance. Within the swirling cloud raised by their ponies, Cochise delivers the standard, thrown at York's feet, and rides back to his people as the dust gradually rises to reveal the captain at attention.

Such calculated atmospheric manipulation occurs prominently only once in *Rio Grande*. Before Kathleen has dinner with Kirby on her first night at Fort Stark, she rummages through a chest looking for silverware and dishes. In this process, which is shot through a gauze filter to suggest that the character is reaching back into her past, Kathleen finds numerous mementos. However, as she tenderly handles a music box (which plays "Kathleen" and thus sets up various associations to the love she has always felt for Kirby), the camera focus shifts so that her face becomes a blur and the box is the only prominent object. Such technique foreshadows both the subsequent use of the song and the renewed love between Kathleen and Kirby.

Richard Hageman's musical score for *Fort Apache* offers many inspired passages that underline plot actions, particularly the accompaniment to the opening scene in Monument Valley. Such standard cues as those during the rescue of Mickey and the sergeants are, ultimately, less interesting than the traditional songs that are incorporated into the film's musical accompaniment. The dance sequences in *Fort Apache* occur to the strains of "Beautiful Dreamer," "Golden Slippers," and "Goodnight, Ladies," tunes that not only fit the time but also offer plot reinforcement. These songs emphasize the romantic tenor of events (i.e., the love between Mickey and Philadelphia) or summarize what has happened (i.e., Thursday's hasty breakup of the enlisted men's ball).

A more subtle musical comment is made through "The Girl I Left Behind Me," which is heard when Thursday leads the troops out on his final mission. This tune calls attention to another dimension of Ford's protagonist in *Fort Apache*. Unlike most of the others, Thursday has no one waiting for him, except his by-now estranged daughter, so that the music takes on a bitter and ironic overtone. The repetition of this song in *Rio Grande* occurs as an accompaniment to the scene in which Kathleen and the other women are sent away for their safety. This tune is heard as their train leaves and as Kirby, significantly, walks by the side of his wife's wagon. By declaring his love for Kathleen and acting on his feelings, Yorke contradicts the sterile leave-taking of

Thursday in the earlier film — a process of reversal that the music clearly underlines.

"Dixie" serves as another means by which the Yorkes' reconciliation is celebrated. As this tune strikes up and Kirby gets over his initial chagrin at hearing it, after Sheridan tells him that he has chosen such music, Kathleen begins to twirl her parasol and flirtatiously eye her husband. Her intention is clear, if understated; Kathleen is obviously implying that there is more to life than military parades. Her coy appearance, particularly when juxtaposed with the austere, on-duty Sheridan and Kirby standing at attention, beautifully combines the romantic and thematic resolutions of the film. Kathleen has recognized the validity of her only rival (the cavalry) in the lives of both her husband and her son, yet she is also aware that a private life is essential and, thus, has rebuilt her life with Kirby, just as she earlier rebuilt Bridesdale. Whereas the intentions of the serenading in *Rio Grande* seem fairly obvious, since "Kathleen"—with its lyrics about going back to one's original home—serves as a gloss on the Yorkes' "remarriage," a similarly arranged solo in *Fort Apache* ("Geniveve") adds little except a general ambiance of warm feeling. Of far more importance is the traditional "There's No Place Like Home," which underscores the emotional bravura of Mickey's return to his parents. This tune also counterpoints the theme of finding a home, a task at which Philadelphia succeeds and her father fails.

Naturally, Ford's handling of the action sequences creates much of their immediate appeal. The director's emphasis features movement and camera tracking. Given the epic scope and subject matter of *Fort Apache*, its principal action sequences — Mickey and Philadelphia's discovery of the massacred soldiers at the telegraph pole, Mickey's return to that scene and the subsequent pursuit by the Apaches, Thursday's futile charge and his death at the hands of Cochise — all emphasize camera tracking. Ford aims to place his characters against backgrounds, whether natural or institutional, that dwarf them so that their positions within an ordered world become more obvious. Each man's duty is not merely to himself but to the larger entities of the army and society. *Rio Grande* is colored by the same ambition, albeit there are many more close-ups and fewer expansive long shots within its action sequences. In keeping with its more overtly familial emphases, the later film individualizes death and conflict within more circumscribed areas: fighting becomes an occasion for personal communication and comic commentary rather than a time for epic gestures and results.

The two films offer similar scenes of Indian atrocities. In both cases, renegades have not only murdered but also assaulted the bodies of their victims. Unlike the noble Cochise, who seeks only redress for ill treatment at the hands of Meacham and Thursday, the renegade band that kills the soldiers sent to repair the telegraph line indulges in unnecessary sadism. Cochise is satisfied with having destroyed his immediate enemies and does not seek glory against those who have not offended him (York). Nor does the Apache leader indulge in mutilation, since he is content with returning the guidon to the remnant of Thursday's command. The renegades, however, kill and burn their victims; Mickey and Philadelphia find the soldiers' corpses tied to wagon wheels amid smoke. A considerable part of Thursday's subsequent ire with Lieutenant O'Rourke arises because his daughter has seen what has happened to these troopers. The same kind of mutilation occurs in *Rio Grande*; however, because the victim, Mrs. Bell, has obviously been raped, this sequence occurs at night and is lit so that we only gain impressions and never clearly see what later causes Captain St. Jacques (Peter Ortiz) so much distress. The silhouette of the mangled corpse, again tied to a wagon wheel, quickly gives way to a close-up of St. Jacques, whose comments are in French so as to create even more psychic distance between the victim and the audience.

Fort Apache's most extended tracking sequence involves Mickey O'Rourke and the four veteran sergeants going to bring back their comrades' mutilated corpses and to fix the telegraph. The visible struggle of the relief wagon to get to its destination is augmented by the extended chase sequence that follows. The troopers succeed in getting away, only to have the hillsides erupt with additional pursuers. This impressive sequence — in which the wagon and Mickey on horseback are chased by an initial band of "hostiles," only to have the camera track up a hill to reveal many more Apaches poised and ready — highlights the film. The momentary shot of Apache warriors set against the crest of the ridge and the scene of their rapid descent further increase the already hectic pace. Within the editing we would expect (from pursuer to pursued, with shots held for notable stunt falls), Ford gives Mickey O'Rourke some significant actions. The young man cuts loose a dangling canopy so that the sergeants can fire more effectively at their pursuers. At the same time, Ford cuts to the charging rescue party under Captain York, who, at Thursday's orders, has followed to engage in just such an action.

The major Indian raid on Fort Stark in *Rio Grande* is a rescue mission to free the renegade war chief Natchez from the army stockade. There is considerably less tracking here, for the cavalry are on the defensive, and Ford resorts to the kind of fixed positioning that one sees briefly during the massacre sequence in *Fort Apache*. Jeff, Travis, and Sandy kneel and fire as the Apache riders tear past; Sergeant Quincannon hugs the terrified Margaret Mary (Karolyn Grimes); and a comic bugler fumbles with various orders. The only mobile individual within the scene is Colonel Yorke, who, once mounted, takes total charge by issuing orders and then seeing what has happened to Kathleen. His sense of priorities is clearly illustrated in this sequence, and his order to Jeff to escort Kathleen back to her quarters further underlines the emotions Kirby feels. Ford conveys the chaos in the camp through some impressive shots of horses screaming because of fire, but the whole sequence is less technically impressive than anything in *Fort Apache*.

The same qualitative difference can be seen in the final battle sequences in both films. That of *Fort Apache* begins at the crack of dawn and pits the charging cavalry against the hidden Indian sharpshooters. After much graphic stunt work and the scene in which the colonel is unhorsed and then rescued by York, the mood changes as the charging Apaches overcome the small, valiant band. Much of this sequence is done in long shot so that the mythical nature of the events is not disturbed; indeed, the final actions of Cochise serve as a fitting end to this whole section. The staging here includes York's retreat to a nearby hillside with the supply wagons and the waiting that he and the others must endure after Mickey has been sent for help.

In *Rio Grande* when the ambushed train, except for one wagon, flees to a hillside to stand off Natchez's mounted warriors, personal relations are emphasized through much more tightly framed shots. The presence of Jeff and Sandy among the troopers being besieged and the continuous emphasis on Kathleen make this scene more personal and less epic. Mrs. Yorke is shown helping turn over a wagon, an action that underlines her increasing commitment to her husband's way of life. Although the wagons are briefly under attack here, Ford's camera remains fixed. The action sequences in *Rio Grande*, which Ford admitted were more hurried than he wanted because of producer pressures, are significantly more spotty than those in *Fort Apache*. During the pursuit of Natchez's band, for example, close-ups abound; at one point, a dead trooper's body unfortunately resembles a sack when it hits the ground. Ford also intercuts individualized actions — such as Trooper Heinze's death from a lance in the chest and Tyree's solo rescue of Jeff by shooting three pursuing Apaches from behind his own lowered horse — to cover what seems to be a shortage of means.

The same economy attaches to the final battle sequence, in which Colonel Yorke's column charges into the Apache camp at the sound of church bells, which Tyree has rung. While the three young troopers stand off the drunken assault of the Apaches against the mission doorway, Kirby and his force charge into the town from a single angle as they move away from the camera. The battle sequence is marked by the charging and recharging of Yorke's troops, with notable moments being given over to regroupings by the commander. The rescue of the children from the embattled mission church is done, in part, through one of Ford's favorite shots — of feet, in this case running down stairs. However, the enclosure of the village street circumscribes much of the action, so that we again detect economies; such shortcuts are especially noticeable when Colonel Yorke is wounded by an obviously intercut Indian with a bow. Such studio-location mixing jars by its very obviousness and, though not fatal, is disconcerting because it happens so rarely elsewhere in Ford's westerns. The constrained nature of *Rio Grande* is, perhaps, best demonstrated in the final section of its last battle sequence, when Yorke's troopers form a living enclosure around him and Jeff, by means of their horses. Within this arena, the son treats his father's wound and so restores the colonel to his horse and his command. Such action is, of course, appropriate within the plot and thematic interests of the film; however, the sweep of *Fort Apache* is most notably missed at such times.

One other type of action sequence is also important in these films. The various patrols that Kirby leads in *Rio Grande* conspicuously place him at the forefront of what are often tiresome rather than glorious activities. In this way Colonel Yorke is thrown into the sharpest possible contrast to Colonel Thursday. That Yorke is dismounted when leading the column even suggests the more noble Captain Brittles (John Wayne) of *She Wore a Yellow Ribbon*. That idyllic film is further echoed when, in *Fort Apache*, Captain York and Sergeant Beaufort go to Cochise's camp, even though their ride into enemy country is significantly longer and far more impressive visually than that of Tyree (Ben Johnson) and the protagonist in the later work. There is no such officer-enlistee mission in *Rio Grande* because there is no crisis or ultimate defeat against which the solidarity of ranks needs to be demonstrated. Such a primarily male activity would, if anything, detract from the climax of a film that strives so hard to incorporate the familial and professional obligations that were at odds in *Fort Apache*.

The Indians in these two films are noticeably dissimilar. Cochise in *Fort Apache* appears distant and dignified in trying to save his people from the machinations of crooked white officials. Like the soldiers of *Fort Apache*, he is trapped by the decisions of others who are not sufficiently aware of what is going on. Indeed, the film takes pains to establish a rational basis for the Apache leader's actions; the Indian Ring, embodied by Meacham, is formally blamed at one point by Captain York. In the meetings with York and, later, Thursday, Cochise never speaks English; thus there is no dialogue that will make him sound like a Hollywood Indian. Cochise's actions during the massacre — when he initiates the assault by symbolically casting down a handful of earth and then leads his pony soldiers on their final charge against the beleaguered cavalrymen — establish him as a leader. His sense of honor is further defined when Cochise refuses to massacre York's few troops on the ridge, for the Apache chief obviously realizes that these men have been led into this trap by a madman. His dignity will not allow him to take undue advantage of the situation, since, by destroying the arrogant Thursday, he has righted the insult to his own and his people's honor.

Though it has often been alleged (even by Ford himself) that the director's films were demeaning to Indians, such a charge is difficult to sustain when one considers the portrait of Cochise in *Fort Apache* and those of such later figures as Scar (Henry Brandon) in *The Searchers* and the tribal leaders (Victor Jory, Ricardo Montalban, Gilbert Roland) in *Cheyenne Autumn*.[1] If anything, Ford is scrupulously fair to the Indians and their motives. Certainly his films show a greater respect for these figures than do such fare as *Buffalo Bill*

(1944), *Arrowhead* (1952), or the revisionist *Soldier Blue* (1970). Of course, Natchez, the renegade Apache leader in *Rio Grande*, hardly compares to Cochise, particularly since he is using the treaty between the United States and Mexico to raid across the border. Natchez's character is further delineated when his braves steal the children and then, when next seen, indulge in a drunken dance. Natchez's lack of stature again suggests the lesser thematic ambitions of *Rio Grande*. Indeed, the plot ambiguities of *Fort Apache* have been stripped away so that a single problem — the romantic reconciliation of the Yorkes — can become central.

The enlisted men of *Fort Apache* embody the North-South division that marks so many of Ford's western characters. Sergeant Beaufort, a former Confederate officer, loudly greets a fellow ex-Rebel (Hank Worden) among the recruits; and though not developed to the same extent, Beaufort is given many of the same actions as Sergeant Tyree in *She Wore a Yellow Ribbon*. It is Beaufort who accompanies Captain York on his mission to Cochise's lair, and the enlisted man serves as a translator for both York and Thursday in their meetings with the Indian leader. The other sergeants — Mulcahy, Shattuck, and Quincannon — function primarily as comic foils, whether they are training new recruits, preparing for a dance, or serving time in the guardhouse. The lower ranks in *Fort Apache* are also used for comic knockabout and assert their presence only at the film's conclusion when two of their previously undifferentiated members emerge as parts of the new working order of command.

Rio Grande offers a more delineated group of enlisted men, partly because of the necessity for Jeff Yorke to experience assimilation and partly because of the lack of a highly developed set of antagonisms among its officers. *Rio Grande* offers no extenuating circumstances or villains to account for the Indians' behavior (unlike both *Fort Apache* and *She Wore a Yellow Ribbon*, with their evil sutlers). Tyree, Sandy, and Jeff form a unit long before their final foray into the Apache camp. At the initial horse-riding scene, when Quincannon asks who would like to try and ride in the "manner of the ancient Romans" and Tyree and Sandy take up and surpass the challenge, the rapport between these characters becomes obvious. Jeff Yorke's unsuccessful attempt to duplicate their horsemanship identifies him as their willing, if not yet efficient, compatriot. The subsequent fight scene, which individualizes Trooper Heinze, only furthers the bonds between these young soldiers and foreshadows their heroism against the Apaches. In addition, *Rio Grande* puts a large (and at times cloying) emphasis on another group of enlisted men, the regimental singers, one of whom (Ken Curtis) becomes fairly prominent in the plot.

Sergeant Quincannon — who is constantly about to be "broken," according to other soldiers at Fort Stark — performs a number of functions in *Rio Grande*. As a comic foil, he echoes the same character (also played by Victor McLaglen) in *She Wore a Yellow Ribbon*, while embodying many of the characteristics found in the four sergeants in *Fort Apache*. Not only is Quincannon fond of drink, but he is also a sentimentalist about children. When explaining the burning of Bridesdale to Dr. Wilkins, Quincannon sniffles over the memory of little Jeff, and his treatment of Margaret Mary points up his allegiance to the future even more strikingly. Whether he is protecting her from the noise of the Indian raid, setting her on a wagon to leave the post, or finally, rescuing her from the beleaguered mission church, Quincannon serves as a more overt father to the girl than her real parent (Trooper Bell). While their relationship is compromised by, perhaps, too uncaring an attitude on the girl's part (the loss of her mother seems not to phase her at all) and too much comic relief — especially when, at the height of the battle, Quincannon and Margaret Mary remember to kneel in the church aisle — the thematic point of "Uncle Timmy" as godfather and surrogate parent echoes Mulcahy's aborted speech about having that relationship to Mickey O'Rourke in *Fort Apache*.

Quincannon also functions as the trainer of the new recruits, a process that leaves him with egg on his face either when they prove to be better riders than he had figured or when they get injured (as when he urges Jeff to try the "Roman style" bareback riding). Quincannon appears shortsighted when Travis and Sandy have to tell him that a coyote's howl is actually that of an Indian and a forewarning of the raid that frees Natchez. Although Kathleen verbally berates him from the time she first appears at Fort Stark, she turns to Quincannon when she wants to see Jeff, so that their continuous comic byplay, whether when they cross a bridge or when she takes the sergeant's dirty laundry, never has a hard edge.

It is also significant that when Kathleen first appears, Quincannon, after crossing himself, says "Welcome home, darling" by a way of a greeting. Once again, a comic line resonates at a deeper thematic level, for Quincannon's remark foreshadows the principal plot development of *Rio Grande*. Later, the sergeant intercedes for Tyree after hearing the latter's account of what caused a warrant to be issued for him and, especially, after being pressured by Kathleen on the soldier's behalf. By suggesting a plan of escape to Tyree (stealing Colonel Yorke's horse), Quincannon serves the higher interests of the cavalry, which needs the young man's presence more than does a court in Dallas.

Both films feature doctors who are largely comic figures. The older physician in *Fort Apache* (Guy Kibbee) and the doctor in *Rio Grande* both further dramatic relationships within these films. Their similarity is underscored, of course, by their names — Wilkens and Wilkins. In the earlier film, the elderly physician shows up to flirt verbally with Emily Collingwood and to drink her husband's wine. His character is further enhanced at the enlisted men's dance when, assuming the role of a master of ceremonies, Wilkens sets up the grand march and the subsequent pairings of Thursday with Mrs. O'Rourke and the sergeant major with Philadelphia. Wilkens's use of this tradition is augmented by his open tipsiness and his comic business with the orchestra leader. The Wilkins of *Rio Grande* offers a comic sparring partner for Quincannon and takes delight in embarrassing the sergeant. In his major scene, Wilkins explains what an arsonist is to the befuddled Quincannon, then stops whittling long enough to crack the latter's exposed hand, before prompting the sergeant to let Tyree escape. While medical men are significant elsewhere in Ford's westerns, these two physicians clearly reemphasize why *Fort Apache* and *Rio Grande* are companion pieces.

The supporting casts in these films also exhibit some discrepancies from Ford's other works. *Fort Apache's* Meacham is one of the more delineated villains in Ford's canon; we are given an extended scene between him and Thursday, and he is present during the crucial negotiation between the colonel and Cochise. While he mouths religiously toned hypocrisies and pretends to be a patriot, Meacham's surroundings — the evil smell of his storehouse and the American flag at half-staff— establish his dubious loyalties. Since he obviously trades in whiskey and guns, with the stigma that he may have armed the renegade braves who massacred the relief party at the telegraph wire, Meacham's evil is manifest. Finally, as is so often the case in Ford's films, this villain is simply too wicked to believe; his malevolence stems from an absence of good rather than from any rationally constructed set of motives around which a recognizable human might center his life.

Although despised by both the soldiers and the Apaches, Meacham manages to stay alive in a wilderness by being a thorough hypocrite. His character is briefly redeemed by his initial reaction to Thursday ("Another exile in our wilderness"), which cleverly counterpoints the film's major plot emphasis. However, at the meeting with Cochise, who threatens and defiles the sutler, Meacham is photographed from a low angle to once more suggest his dastardly character. During this sequence, Grant Withers physically re-creates the same dumb, brooding, and dangerous character (Ike Clanton) that he portrays in *My Darling Clementine*. Given the epic proportions of *Fort Apache*, it is only fitting that Meacham be given the extended emphasis that he gets, whereas a similarly placed villainous sutler (Karl Rynders [Harry Woods]) in *She Wore a Yellow Ribbon* exists merely as a snarling character who dies because of his own greed and bravado.

Fort Apache also brings in newspaper reporters, and these easterners, whose conspicuously western dress marks them as "tourists" and neophytes, help to create the larger irony at the film's conclusion. As they extol the heroism of Thursday's final charge, by describing the painting that now hangs in Washington, one enthusiast (Frank Ferguson) illustrates how real life is transformed into officially sanctioned history. This final scene in *Fort Apache* offers a devastating commentary on the process by which the nation's media transform defeat into victory, incompetence into efficiency, and ambition into celebrity. Kirby York's patient correction of the mispronunciation of Collingwood's name and his embellishments of what the newsmen are saying ("No man died more gallantly") are but preludes to his quasi-mystical speech about how the regiment is a source of ongoing life for all its members, dead or alive. The great strength of this sequence is not that it offers a position but rather that it suggests so many possibilities. In effect, Ford's art does not demand that we take a stand for or against what he shows us here; it is enough that we appreciate the complexity of human motives that this sequence puts before us. In a genre so often dismissed as simply devoted to ritualistic action and melodramatic certainties, it is striking that such thoughtful material is even broached.

Rio Grande does not offer such rich thematic ambiguities through its distinctive lesser characters. The strongest of these figures is General Sheridan, who comes and goes between Fort Stark and some other headquarters. Sheridan indulges in personal conversation with Kirby Yorke, but his sentimental nature surfaces only in the film's final scene. Although they earlier lament that orders prevent them from destroying Natchez's base of operation, these two career soldiers largely reaffirm the professional devotion that marks Ford's genuine military men. Sheridan first tells Yorke about Jeff's failure at West Point (news that the father had not heard) and implies that he understands what has happened between Kirby and Kathleen. When the general finally orders Yorke to proceed against the Apache stronghold south of the border, he muses on their time together in the Shenandoah Valley and wonders what history will say of that event; Kirby responds that Kathleen has already said and done a great deal because of that campaign. At the dinner party in Colonel Yorke's tent, when Kathleen bids the two men an early goodnight, Sheridan is stunned — a reaction that occurs (presumably) because the general believes that the Yorkes have reconciled. His function as a conscious matchmaker finally surfaces during the concluding parade when, after the troops have been decorated and Tyree has once more escaped on a stolen horse (this time Sheridan's), the general notifies the Yorkes that he has asked the band to play "Dixie." While their rekindled love is apparent throughout this sequence, Sheridan's choice of such an obvious tune reinforces his role as romantic fairy-godfather similar to Captain York in *Fort Apache*.

Rio Grande also has a beleaguered marshal, some Mexican cavalry, and a large group of children within its supporting cast. In keeping with the smaller thematic focus and production values of the film, these characters are given primarily one-note functions. The lawman, who notes that the name "Daniel Boone" has a familiar ring to it and then proceeds to look through a set of wanted posters for a felon with that name, is a comic butt doomed to be forever too late to catch the athletic Tyree. When Tyree escapes on his commander's horse, Colonel Yorke stops the marshal from firing (ostensibly to protect the animal). However, a moment before, Kirby had been informed that Kathleen had become interested in Tyree's case; thus his gesture can also be seen as motivated by love. A brief interlude at the border river finds a Mexican officer and his patrol conferring with Yorke on a sandbar. The wounded

Mexican lieutenant, who suffers because he, like his American counterpart, is under restraining orders, engages in some friendly badinage with Ford's protagonist, only to reestablish the defining condition of the sanctity of their respective borders. *Rio Grande*'s children lend a strong sense of future, a traditional emphasis that accords with the more overtly familial plot concerns of the movie.

Ford's lesser characters in *Fort Apache* once again carry more thematic weight. The stage driver in the opening sequence (Cliff Clark) serves to throw Thursday's pique and egocentrism into sharp relief. The fidgety, precise style of the colonel has been exacerbated by his leisurely western journey, and the native driver, with his emphasis on "soldier boy," bounces local wit and psychology off Thursday. Such irreverence is echoed by the shotgun rider (Francis Ford), whose tobacco spittings reverberate in a spittoon, much to Thursday's chagrin, once the party has moved into the waystation. This latter gesture figures elsewhere in Ford's films as a device by which pomposity is deflated; the prominence of the same actor performing the same business in *Young Mr. Lincoln* again underlines how the director subtly introduces a major theme through comedy that is appropriate at both realistic and symbolic levels. The figure of Guadalupe (Movita Castenada) also highlights an aspect of the colonel's character. The servant girl displays her concern for Philadelphia when she goes to the O'Rourke home to warn her mistress of Thursday's imminent arrival; this act places Guadalupe within the moral scheme of the film by offering one more pointed commentary on Thursday's own lack of feeling for his own daughter.

Captain York has the strongest supporting role in *Fort Apache*, being not only Thursday's successor but also a source of amelioration and diplomacy throughout. York brings the young lovers together during the early-morning interview between Mickey and Philadelphia on her back porch. While the young people have managed to get themselves caught up in proprieties and pride, York rides in casually and puts everyone at ease. His own posture here, leaning against a door jamb, offers York as an obvious visual contrast to his commander, a relation that is also stressed by the captain's costuming and his gesture with gloves. York's dedication to the future is conspicuously displayed during the massacre sequence, when he not only takes Mickey out of the column to the ridge but also sends Lieutenant O'Rourke for aid and shouts after the fleeing rider that the lieutenant should "marry that girl." While the scene on the ridge is reprised in *Rio Grande*, with Jeff being sent back to bring Kirby and the others, the family emphases in both sequences are patent. York, by allowing the lovers to become a family, ensures the future that the closing scenes of *Fort Apache* celebrate; as a further symbolic touch, the child of Mickey and Philadelphia carries York's name, along with those of the O'Rourkes and the Thursdays.

Many commentators err in seeing York as the protagonist of *Fort Apache*, for this character is moved more by the conflicts around him than he is himself a prime mover; indeed, the captain is the hero of Ford's film because of his capacity for action, while Thursday remains the cause of everything that York and the others experience. In effect, *Fort Apache* postulates that the ideal soldier will combine such disparate traits as the compassion of Sergeant Major O'Rourke and the tactical abilities of Owen Thursday; Captain York, despite wearing Thursday's type of hat when leading the troops at the film's conclusion, does not completely attain this stature. It remains, in effect, for Colonel Yorke of *Rio Grande* to combine the personal and the professional sides of army life into a satisfactory whole. Thus, despite his importance in the immediate conflicts of *Fort Apache*, Captain York is not the film's principal thematic interest, a perception that will be difficult for many current viewers because John Wayne plays the role.

In *Rio Grande* the supporting officers, Prescott (Steve Pendelton) and St. Jacques (Peter Ortiz), remain ceremonial and largely undelineated types. While the former sends Jeff back to the Fort to get help for the besieged wagon train, this reprise clearly emphasizes the new role that Kathleen is assuming. She watches her son go, with the unspoken comment about bringing back help in the form of Kirby. Certainly Jeff Yorke is not being sent away to "marry that girl" (a refrain that is utilized again in *She Wore a Yellow Ribbon* when Captain Brittles plays matchmaker for Olivia [Joanne Dru] and Flint [John Agar] before sending the latter back across the river). St. Jacques and some of the other officers serve as foils between Kathleen and Kirby at dinner parties and at her tent; however, none of them are sufficiently individualized to represent any sort of serious romantic threat or even counterweight to their commanding officer.

The role of ameliorator-hero in *Rio Grande* is played by Tyree, whose prowess with horses is ultimately matched by his insights into men. Tyree, who goes on the run because of a warrant for the crime of defending his sister's honor, helps Jeff get away from three pursuing Apaches so that he can reach his father; Tyree then returns to the main body in time to save the situation. The deserter Tyree comes back by crossing a river (as the protagonist does later in *Sergeant Rutledge*), and when brought before Colonel Yorke, the young trooper suggests a strategy by which the children can be saved. York agrees and orders Tyree to pick the men who will accompany him to the Indian camp. The colonel is momentarily taken aback when Tyree selects Jeff, but in good military fashion he goes along, even uttering the phrase "Get it done" and adding that Tyree take his horse (the one the trooper had stolen earlier). The unison in which Jeff and Sandy appear when they are named by Tyree also underscores the son's burgeoning capacity as a soldier. In the earlier roll call scene, Jeff had conspicuously set himself apart from his comrades as well as alerted Kirby that his son was, indeed, at Fort Stark. By speaking together and using "Yo!," the two young soldiers demonstrate the kind of unity needed within the entire outfit.

The older O'Rourkes enact the life of duty and acceptance that constitutes the ideal military existence in *Fort Apache.* The sergeant major is the ideal
soldier and, thus, the ideal man. His courage is attested by his Medal of Honor,
while his necessary reticence comes across in his understated way of introducing that fact. As the film is at pains to demonstrate visually, Sergeant
O'Rourke stands in the strongest contrast to Colonel Thursday; their Civil
War pasts, though similar, lead to quite different reactions. Whereas the commanding officer resents his demotion, the noncom has easily accepted his own
decline in status. Thus, the ideal soldier does not complain about the ways in
which he is treated by the army or the nation because his devotion to duty,
his real love, precludes any such feelings.

The sergeant major is also clearly more of a human being than Thursday,
as seen at the enlisted men's ball. O'Rourke, ostensibly in charge and initially
beset with acting polite to superiors and demanding to subordinates, encounters the same difficulty that his commanding officer does. Since it is a tradition at this dance that the highest-ranking officer lead out the lady of the
highest noncommissioned officer (and vice versa), Dr. Wilkens's announcement of the arrival of that moment causes both men to react characteristically. Colonel Thursday, who has just upbraided Mickey and Philadelphia for
their romantic impetuosity, must now observe the amenities with the father
and the mother of the man he has dressed down. While Thursday is coldly
proper throughout, the very rigidity of his posture and his inability to ever
truly enjoy what he is doing contrasts sharply with the conduct of Sergeant
O'Rourke. He too is initially dismayed by the arrangement, albeit not as
greatly as his commander; however, when the sergeant and Philadelphia begin
to dance, a natural enjoyment bubbles to the surface. The same human warmth
appears when the elder O'Rourke regretfully apologizes for the abrupt termi-
nation of the dance. It is surely appropriate that his character brings affairs to
an end with a pointed speech about his regrets.

Sergeant O'Rourke's contrast with Colonel Thursday also extends into
oblique verbal and direct visual expressions. He remains too good a soldier to
openly quarrel with his superior (a trait conspicuously not shared by Captain
York) or to ever complain about his personal misfortunes (a trait that marks
Captain Collingwood). Sergeant O'Rourke is the kind of faithful soldier and
committed family man whom the protagonist of *Rio Grande* must ultimately
learn to imitate. The final contrasts between the sergeant major and Thursday are established in the film's last battle scenes, when O'Rourke typically
thanks Captain York for misinterpreting the colonel's order about which
O'Rourke to take back to the supply train. Although his bearing is properly
military and he comments that Thursday is mad, Sergeant O'Rourke is moved
as a father. Like a good soldier, he will follow orders even if they mean his
death; like a good father, he is delighted that his offspring will be spared; and,
finally, like a good member of the human race, he is content to realize that

his son and Philadelphia represent a future worth fighting to ensure. The sergeant major's death, like that of the entire trapped unit, is discreetly masked by the dust; but his smiling optimism about the future when Thursday returns to the doomed group ("Save your apologies for our grandchildren") underlines his role as a model within Ford's western films.

Mrs. O'Rourke illustrates most of the traits of the ideal cavalry wife. She cries when her son returns home, and she gushes excitedly when speaking about him later. She is, indeed, the "woman of the house"; after Philadelphia bursts in, she puts her foot down about who can and will stay under her roof. Mrs. O'Rourke also functions as a communal linchpin when she helps Philadelphia set up housekeeping. While she is accorded status as a homemaker within the film, her sentimentality trips her up just slightly. In a short scene with her husband, she pressures him silently about the danger into which Mickey is riding when going back to the burned telegraph wires. Although the colonel has seemingly ordered the young man to bring back the dead soldiers as a punishment for exposing Philadelphia to such a sight, and although the sergeant major has been rebuffed when volunteering to accompany his son, the real workings of the fort are not totally thwarted. Sergeant O'Rourke manages to get the four other sergeants to "volunteer" for this perilous mission, even though concern is etched on his brow as he watches Mickey and the others depart. Mrs. O'Rourke's emergence at his side and the fear in her face suggest that she is about to crack under the strain; however, the sergeant major brings her back to her duty by urging that she "go about your business." Even though such a comment undoubtedly sounds chauvinistic to some contemporary ears, Ford clearly intends that Mrs. O'Rourke must defer her feelings to the greater good of the group, in this case the cavalry and its demands.

Emily Collingwood is always the ideal cavalry wife because she never gives in to the kind of emotions that flicker in Mrs. O'Rourke. She is also used to highlight Thursday; at his initial appearance at Fort Apache, she calls him by his first name (a practice only she and her husband ever indulge in during the film), only to be coldly rebuffed. She then gravitates to Philadelphia, and we learn that Mrs. Collingwood was the "dearest friend" of the girl's deceased mother. Later, Emily Collingwood appears as the ideal hostess, balancing the mild and comic flirtations of others with her deep love for her husband. In recounting, for the beleaguered Philadelphia, how she obtained some candlesticks, Emily shows how the proper army wife adapts to changing circumstances. Her only moments of distress occur when she foresees the burgeoning love between Mickey and Philadelphia and realizes that they will need "all the help they can get," given the austere Thursday, and when she sees her own husband doubting that his appointment to West Point will ever come through. These two crises occur at the same dinner party, so that Mrs. Collingwood's role as the ideal woman can be emphasized.

She cements her status as a role model during the departure of the troops for the final battle with Cochise. Standing among the assembled wives and sweethearts on the fort's parapet, Emily is informed that her husband's appointment to the military academy has just arrived, and she is urged by Mrs. O'Rourke to get Sam to return. However, like the good soldier's wife she is, Mrs. Collingwood refuses to do so. Sam's duty lies with his regiment, and his future orders must be put aside until that obligation is met, even if (as it does here) it should mean death. To the extent that she learns to embody the virtues of Mrs. O'Rourke and Mrs. Collingwood, Philadelphia becomes a "proper soldier's wife." Once again, Ford's film takes on a heavy irony, since this expression, which Thursday urged as an ideal goal for his daughter, befits only those characters whom the colonel basically ignores.

Captain Collingwood, like Mrs. O'Rourke, approximates the cavalry ideal, for he has character traits that compromise him. The captain makes the best of his demotion from adjutant to company commander (in contrast to Thursday's dismay at being assigned to frontier duty) and then tries to warn the colonel that his new post is not a place in which to seek glory. In a bit of unresolved plotting, Thursday and Collingwood share a Civil War background in which one of them (the colonel) was a success while the other (the captain) was a failure. As Sam puts it: "You rode to glory while I came to Fort Apache." This remark dramatizes the idle kind of glory that Thursday is seeking and the real glory that Collingwood, as a faithful member of the regiment, attains by a devotion to unglamorous duty. The relationship between Collingwood and Thursday is further underscored when the colonel offers Sam a drink and the latter rejects it by saying that it's a little too early in the day "even for" him. While there are tantalizing hints about what happened between the two men (a missed assignment due to alcoholism?) during the war, in the film's present their relationship illuminates that between Thursday and Captain York.

Collingwood fails to the extent that he is alternately anxious and cynical about getting out of Fort Apache, as seen when, after leaving Thursday and the proffered whiskey, he presses Sergeant O'Rourke about whether there has been any news about his transfer. Later, at the dinner party, after Emily informs Philadelphia that they may soon be leaving, Sam initially feigns ignorance and then goes into a short and bitter tirade about his long-expected appointment. Kirby York, ever the ameliorator, suggests that the army often moves in slow and mysterious ways and, besides, Sam can take heart from the affection that everyone at Fort Apache feels for him. Mickey picks up on this note to urge that "the men" love and respect Captain Collingwood. Bucked up, Collingwood then offers a toast, and a convivial ease is reestablished. Throughout the rest of the film, Sam Collingwood functions as a good soldier, bravely following his commander to death and, by refusing to question orders, showing that Ford feels duty precedes dissension ("death before dishonor"). The final tribute to Collingwood occurs when York talks to the visiting newspapermen. One of them, in raising the issue of how Thursday is remembered while those who died with him are forgotten, ironically mispronounces Sam's name. This error is corrected by York, who then launches into his speech about the mystical life that attaches to every member of the cavalry; in effect, Collingwood has not died, because the regiment still lives.

Rio Grande offers a more truncated and impersonal view of the domestic side of military life than does *Fort Apache*. There are no delineated families here except for the Bells, who are used briefly to arouse sympathy. The female community is, instead, often shot from angles that emphasize the patient waiting and silent suffering that these women must endure. At the film's conclusion this kind of setup is dominated by Kathleen, who waits for the return of Jeff and the wounded Kirby. Earlier, she performs domestic chores — whether setting up a dinner in Kirby's tent, washing clothes so that comic byplay with Quincannon can be enacted, or ironing so that her repressed love for her husband can be expressed. Fort Stark, by its very nature, precludes extended domestic amenities because it consists of tents and settlers' wagons; indeed, the only formal arrangements remotely comparable to what we see in *Fort Apache* appear when Yorke has a formal dinner for Sheridan, and the regimental singers are heard.

By stripping down his setting, Ford suggests the more primary and unilinear design of the entire film. The loving Bells, who are shown together only once, offer the only mirror image of what Kirby and Kathleen need to become domestically. When Mrs. Bell's body is discovered raped and mutilated on the trail, Colonel Yorke operates as a "friend" to the bereaved husband, who earlier had been at such pains to say good-bye and to reassure his wife that he would diligently send money so that their family, though separated, would continue to function. Interestingly, Margaret Mary, the Bells' daughter, appears more as a child of Sergeant Quincannon, particularly when running to him for comfort during the initial Apache raid against Fort Stark. In a small way Margaret Mary dramatizes *Rio Grande*'s central thematic concerns, for her conduct reminds us that Jeff and Kathleen must both become active parts of Kirby's cavalry world. By going to "Uncle Timmy," the girl symbolizes a proper feeling toward the institution.

In *Fort Apache*, Owen Thursday lacks a comparable respect, for he is initially convinced that he has been sent to the southwestern outpost by an ungrateful war department and nation. He cannot accept the loss of his Civil War status (he was a general) or what he considers a demotion after a tour of duty in Europe; indeed, for Thursday, commanding Fort Apache is only a means to regain wartime rank and status. As a man on the make, the colonel exhibits a consistent preoccupation with his own aims and an indifference to those of anyone else. Thursday is epitomized by the number of interruptions he creates during the film. In the opening scenes, as Mickey O'Rourke and the Thursdays meet at the waystation, Ford clearly juxtaposes two styles of life. The horseplay that marks the four sergeants' greetings to Mickey quickly comes to an end when Thursday appears. Thus, the warm, nurturing character of the cavalry, its most appropriate function, is thwarted by the icy commanding officer. While Philadelphia laughs at such antics as Mickey's being spanked, her father only complains that the meeting party has not been sent for him.

This vain aspect of Colonel Thursday is further exposed when, after his arrival at the fort, the new commander walks into a dance. After the music comes to a halt, Thursday proceeds stiffly into the scene and refuses to shake hands with Captain Collingwood. After some preliminary remarks with Captain York, Thursday caustically says that the dance is obviously not in his honor, only to have York inform him that the occasion is George Washington's birthday. As Thursday stands silent, York rescues the situation by asking Philadelphia to dance. Later, Thursday terminates the enlisted men's ball by ordering the regiment to march at dawn. While this order breaks York's word to Cochise, Thursday's command also cuts gratuitously across social lines by offering insult to all who have attended. The colonel is so concerned with his own quest that he cannot observe even the most obvious amenities. This headlong chase after glory is again uppermost when Thursday undermines the meeting with Cochise not only by urging that the participants "get on with it" but also by taking offense at the Apache leader's words and so precipitating the massacre by interrupting once again. Clearly, such headstrong behavior must be eschewed by the ideal commander, for leadership must have a human as well as a professional side.

Colonel Thursday consistently demeans those who oppose him. An initial staff meeting finds him belittling the "gnat stings" of the Apaches, to the amazement and displeasure of Captain York, who tries to correct such misapprehensions. The colonel also treats Guadalupe, the Mexican servant his daughter has managed to acquire, as though she were illiterate. Despite the fact that the girl greets him in English, Thursday resorts to sign language at the end of their single scene together. In addition, despite being introduced to the servant just a few moments previously, Thursday cannot remember her name when asking for his hat and gloves. This combination of preoccupation and ethnic snobbery is underscored at the beginning of the film when the colonel mispronounces the name of the waystation and continues through his mistaken substitutions for the name O'Rourke with young Mickey. Yet such absentmindedness is contrived, since Thursday can tactlessly complain to Sergeant Major O'Rourke that there are too many men of that name at Fort Apache ("The place seems full of O'Rourkes!").

A subsequent discussion between the colonel and his top noncom again finds Thursday blundering. After learning that his aide is Lieutenant O'Rourke's father, Thursday is openly puzzled about how the young man went to West Point. The colonel states that only sons of Medal of Honor winners can get appointed to the military academy, and the sergeant major, in a typical bit of understatement, says that this is his understanding too. Thus, the colonel is once more brought up short; moreover, in this case, his correction comes from a man who has also been subjected to a loss of rank (Sergeant O'Rourke mentions having been a major in the Civil War). Thursday's demeaning of others reaches its height, appropriately, at the battle scene when he dismisses York. After calling York a coward and refusing to acknowledge his challenge to a duel, Thursday humiliates the captain further by sending him back with the supply wagons. However, York salvages the situation by saluting his troops and being cheered by them as he leaves with Mickey. Unable to extend respect to others, especially his opponents, Thursday reveals yet another of the negative traits that undermine command. Only such an egotistical character would refer to Robert E. Lee as "Captain Lee" and J.E.B. Stuart as "Cadet Stuart."

Ford's protagonist also errs drastically along other professional lines. Assuming command, Thursday demotes Collingwood from the position of adjutant. The embarrassment caused here, since the change takes place at a full staff meeting, hardly seems to be noticed by the commanding officer. Uniforms, however, are constantly on Thursday's mind; he chides his staff for appearing out of uniform at this same meeting and compliments Lieutenant O'Rourke (whom he again misnames) for being the only correctly attired soldier present. Thursday insists that he is not a martinet, yet before York sets out to relieve Mickey, Thursday upbraids the captain for the appearance of the troops and enumerates some of the particular features of their uniforms he finds displeasing.

Ford then cleverly juxtaposes Mickey O'Rourke's inept handling of the recruit drill with the manner in which the veteran sergeants instill discipline into these men. While there is a great deal of (tedious) comic knockabout in this sequence, and Lieutenant O'Rourke is distracted when his father provides him with a new horse, the larger point appears only when the recruits march past Thursday and York, and the new commander comments favorably on Lieutenant O'Rourke's future as an officer. Thursday not only is unaware of the manipulating that has been done but also is attracted to Mickey primarily because the latter is (still) the only properly attired officer on the post.

It is as a tactician that Thursday begins to redeem himself (and so move beyond being a caricature), particularly in the eyes of Captain York. After Lieutenant O'Rourke has brought back Philadelphia and the news of the repair crew's deaths and has been sent back with a burial party, Thursday issues an additional order that convinces York that his commander knows what he is doing. This plan, in which a larger force will follow the smaller detail at a safe distance in order to trap the Apache renegades, explains what had seemed like mere personal pique to Captain York and Sergeant O'Rourke. Thursday has not sent out the young lieutenant merely to revenge a personal insult but to entrap an enemy. York stands smiling as Thursday, in characteristic fashion, talks to Collingwood about his West Point past and the tactics of Genghis Khan (as reported by "Captain Lee").

After the subsequent rebuff of the Apaches, Thursday visits Meacham's store and listens to the hypocritical complaints of the villainous sutler. While York openly argues with Meacham and even ends up slapping him, Thursday maintains a formal courtesy and upbraids his subordinate's rashness. However, when Meacham makes a demand on the colonel, Thursday turns on him quickly. In a scene that foreshadows the fatal meeting with Cochise, Thursday reads out Meacham on the basis of a single word. At the same time, the colonel orders, to the delight of York and the others, that numerous contraband goods (rifles, whiskey) be destroyed.

Colonel Thursday demonstrates his best personal traits during the massacre. Although his orders are foolhardy and represent his ultimate failure to reconcile with or understand the society into which he has come, his personal conduct is above reproach. Thursday leads the ill-fated charge (a position he did not occupy during the rescue of the repair crew, although he had been conspicuously at the head of the troops when leaving the fort). After being wounded and unhorsed, Thursday's determination to return to his doomed command provides a nobility to his death. Having committed himself to a course of action, he pursues it faithfully to the end; thus, in true heroic style, the character lives up to his word. By taking York's horse and sabre and by ignoring his subordinate's realistic appraisal of the situation, Thursday performs the kind of self-sacrifice expected of the good commander (and the good soldier). When he rejoins his troops, Thursday apologizes to both Collingwood (who downplays the remark by noting that Thursday has "been late" for once) and Sergeant O'Rourke before the final onslaught. Their reactions place Thursday within the extended family of the cavalry, for these men readily forgive and forget at a time when recriminations might seem to be in order. The approval of Collingwood and the sergeant major at this point sanctifies Thursday because these men are obvious models of military behavior; in this way, the colonel earns some of the posthumous glory that comes to him in *Fort Apache*'s final sequence.

Thursday is also sharply contrasted by his daughter, who, from her opening remarks, establishes herself as a warm character trying to seek out and adopt the ways of the community in which she has arrived. Unlike her father, Philadelphia tries to build bridges to others and does not see Fort Apache as the end of the line or a place from which to escape. In the film's opening scene, Philadelphia defines her character by laughing at the stage driver's curt remarks to the angry colonel. As Thursday fumes over being late, and the stage hands humorously wonder if they have perhaps missed their destination, the girl reacts by repeating the driver's remark, using the phrase "soldier boy" to address the colonel. While appropriate when coming from a driver, the term diminishes Thursday's sense of his own self-importance, and Philadelphia's teasing repetition of the phrase further suggests that she wishes her father were less arrogant. Indeed, her repetition of this remark leads to a conversation in which the distraught Thursday bemoans his fate at being sent to Fort Apache, while his daughter insists that, since she will be with him, perhaps life there won't be all bad.

On her arrival at the waystation, Philadelphia again shows her capacity for adjustment. She eagerly allows the woman at the station (inevitably called "Ma" and played by Mary Gordon) to try on her hat, and she adjusts it to the latter's head; in this way Philadelphia wins the other woman over and shows she can operate within her new environment. The girl's capacity for adjustment is also underscored when, in another comic bit, she walks into a washroom and confronts the bare-chested Mickey O'Rourke. That Philadelphia is not shocked by such a scene (indeed, it is the young man who is embarrassed) and simply hands over a towel sets her apart from her father. Her laughter at the manhandling of Lieutenant O'Rourke by the four sergeants and her warmth when Mulcahy begins to tell her of his past with Mickey only emphasize the growing love that the girl is experiencing and, again, place her within the human family of the film. That such feelings are cut short by the entrance of Colonel Thursday is inevitable.

At Fort Apache itself Philadelphia's domestic urges — her desire to build a home for herself and her father and her growing feelings to create a similar arrangement with Mickey — are thrown into relief. On her first full day at the post, Philadelphia manages, through the intercession of Mrs. O'Rourke and Mrs. Collingwood, to put together the semblance of a home for the colonel. While such activity is conspicuously established as a woman's role (through Emily Collingwood's remark about Owen Thursday's lack of concern), it is the openness of Philadelphia's quest that makes a larger thematic point. The young girl's innocence is reinforced by her trek from her own barren and disordered quarters (the coat rack that falls) to those of the Collingwoods and O'Rourkes. As she proceeds along a lengthy porch, the colonel's "lady" greets everyone she meets without any thought as to their ranks. Once having informed "Aunt Emily" of her dilemma and been told that such matters are the special province of Mrs. O'Rourke, Philadelphia has become part of Fort Apache's military family. The onlookers now shout in sequence for Mrs. O'Rourke and thus reaffirm the easy life-style of these indigenous characters. Such behavior would be unthinkable in front of the austere commander, a point Ford emphasizes by immediately cutting to Thursday walking along another porch and silently entering his headquarters.

As a lover, Philadelphia becomes even more of a thematic icon within the film. She appears struck by Mickey O'Rourke from the moment she meets him and reveals her feelings again and again. In the scene with Mrs. Collingwood and Mrs. O'Rourke, for example, she eagerly intrudes on their conversation about Mickey's homecoming to say how "wonderful" the young man looks in his new uniform and then decorously retreats to add that she thinks he will make a fine officer. Philadelphia's feelings are clearly understood by the older women, both of whom intercede for her at dinner scenes later; indeed, as is often the case in Ford's films, the young lovers are seemingly the last ones to realize their feelings and to act on them. Ford's young couples express their love slowly, for they are bound to family, ego, honor, or peers; for most of them, romance is publicly embarrassing.

Ford dramatizes the love between Philadelphia and Mickey in familiar ways. The girl's feelings, which are more overt than the young man's, initially surface on the ride to Fort Apache when she arranges a hatbox mirror so that she can watch the young lieutenant on horseback. During her appearance at the Collingwoods' dinner, Philadelphia stays outside with Mickey after the serenade so that he can ask her to go riding with him (a suggestion that has been nurtured by Captain York earlier in the same sequence). As Emily Collingwood suggests that these young lovers will need all the help they can get because of Thursday, and the gentlemen drink to the young people's health, Philadelphia and Mickey walk along the porch and the scene fades. The same device is utilized at the end of the enlisted men's dance. Here the lovers briefly waltz and then embrace in the moonlight on another porch, a sequence that comments on their burgeoning feelings as a thematic development. The young lieutenant has been conspicuously missing from the lengthy dance sequence, presumably because Thursday has forbidden him to see his daughter; but he appears to bring this sequence to a close and so to symbolically assert the natural right of the future against the past.

Philadelphia's emergence as a full-fledged member of Fort Apache is completed at the O'Rourkes' home when she bursts in to speak to Mickey. While the sergeant major is initially reluctant to allow her to remain, Mrs. O'Rourke asserts herself and enables Philadelphia to stay despite the colonel's orders. Throughout this sequence, the difference between professional and personal obligations is stressed, for though they owe a military loyalty to their commander, the O'Rourke men must observe the prerogatives of the wife and mother inside their home. When Colonel Thursday enters to bring Philadelphia "home," that verbal irony combines with the personal defiance of Sergeant O'Rourke. The other father now upbraids his commanding officer for failing to observe that a man's home is sacrosanct and that something more serious than decorum has been breached by Thursday's headlong entrance. As the dramatic pawn in this situation, Philadelphia can only respond to the marriage proposal of Mickey and the self-righteous anger of her father. While she clings to her beloved, the older men confront the crucial issues of social status and career roles, with the sergeant major realizing that a barrier clearly exists between his class (and that of his son) and the girl's. In this prevailing scheme of values, duty and career must supersede love; indeed, proper (married) love exists as an adjunct to these higher callings, and romantic impetuosity must never be allowed to deflect the call of duty.

Philadelphia is most strongly iconographic in the film's balcony scenes when she joins the fort's other women to say good-bye to their men. The girl has become one of the women of the post, and her shawl reflects that assimilation. *Fort Apache*'s final sequence finds Philadelphia and the widowed Mrs. O'Rourke watching the troops leave under the command of Captain York. This recurrent visual motif, while underscoring the continuity of military life, also enables Ford to reemphasize the need for individual sacrifice within the human community. Mrs. O'Rourke continues as part of her society even though her husband has been killed. The younger Philadelphia, as the mother of a child who combines the Thursday and the O'Rourke families and thus embodies the social assimilation that the older fathers felt was impossible, has now become the center of the composition.

Through such a visual arrangement, and through the emergence of various characters to higher positions (Mickey is now the adjutant, and one of the recruits has become a sergeant), Ford reinforces York's comments to the newspapermen about the regiment's ongoing life. This semimystical speech, which asserts that the members of the group never really die as long as the organization continues, renders more poignant the juxtaposed final appearance of Colonel Thursday and his daughter within the film. While Philadelphia has become a wife, mother, and member of the community of Fort Apache, her father is last seen as a revered portrait that serves as the basis for a hyperbolic legend. One member of the Thursday family has become a monument, whereas the other has become a human being.

As Fort Stark's commander, Colonel Yorke in *Rio Grande* not only enjoys the same rank as Thursday but also exhibits the same devotion to duty and the regiment. However, Yorke clearly realizes that the military life is not a road to glory but one in which devotion to duty is often the sole comfort. Moreover, Yorke, who feels himself bound to obey orders even when they conflict with his own sense of propriety, exhibits another trait that the Fort Apache leader lacked. As the film establishes in its opening scene, Yorke is very much at ease with his troops; as the tired column comes into the frontier outpost, its commander not only issues orders directly but also compliments the soldiers and recognizes their need for some relaxation after what has obviously been a distressing mission. While Yorke can delegate orders to subordinates, his presence within the informal encampment and his ability to allow the soldiers to settle their own affairs, as well as his capacity to see merit in their suggestions, stamp him as a far different leader than Thursday.

In his initial conference with General Sheridan, Colonel Yorke exhibits self-sacrifice; he is required to bow to the necessity to not pursue the Apaches across the Rio Grande. Although such restraints will be lifted before the end of *Rio Grande*, this initial meeting emphasizes doing one's duty even, and especially, when it means not questioning one's superiors. Colonel Yorke is also different in that he has a commanding officer to whom he must answer; Thursday, on the other hand, has no one directly over him in *Fort Apache*.

While Kirby Yorke embodies the military and personal skills of the soldier, he lacks the kinds of love — familial and romantic — that sustain Sergeant O'Rourke. *Rio Grande* illustrates how these deficiencies are filled in for the colonel. His harsh speech to his estranged son about the rigors and requirements of the military life is juxtaposed by Yorke's presence of mind throughout as a commander. When an Apache raid frees Natchez, the colonel appears on horseback and gives orders to his subordinates. Again, when the Apaches must be trailed to their stronghold, we see Yorke as part of the regiment; indeed, he is noticeably on foot (unlike Thursday, who appears unhorsed only during the massacre) and trudges along with his unit. The colonel's position at the front of his column is further augmented by his calling for songs to help the men in their dry and dusty work. When Jeff appears at Fort Stark, we become more aware of what is missing in the protagonist's life. His austere verbal treatment of the boy is offset by his marking and comparing of their heights on his tent flap, a gesture that recalls how, on Mickey O'Rourke's initial appearance at home in *Fort Apache*, he and his father were ordered to stand back-to-back by the delighted Mrs. O'Rourke. In *Rio Grande* such measuring takes place without the obvious presence of an ameliorating woman.

The appearance of Kathleen Yorke brings the domestic shortcomings of the colonel's life even more strikingly into focus. In a bit of convoluted plotting, she has allowed Jeff to go to West Point, but now that he has flunked out and enlisted, she wants to get him away from the army life she claims to hate. When she enters Fort Stark, she is visibly shaken by the appearance of her estranged husband. The Yorkes have parted because of a quarrel over what is owed to duty and to home. Kirby burned Bridesdale, her family's plantation, during the raid through the Shenandoah Valley in 1864, causing Kathleen and her husband to separate. She has rebuilt her old home and now she rebuilds her marriage. Under orders from General Sheridan, Kirby had burned Bridesdale as an act of war against a rebellious Confederacy; now, in denying Kathleen's request to buy Jeff out of his military obligation, Ford's protagonist continues to insist on the primacy of duty and honor above sentiment. Kathleen's unspoken love is seen as she chokes when first speaking to Kirby. Later, in the colonel's tent, after he asks her to dine with him, she seems enraptured with handling the china and memorabilia in his trunk. This entire scene becomes even more suggestive when Kathleen finds an old music box and listens to it play "I'll Take You Home Again, Kathleen." In a subsequent gesture that foreshadows the more subtle romantic byplay in *The Searchers*, Kathleen affectionately handles Kirby's coat and remarks on how she would like to get her hands on another white jacket he is wearing (ostensibly, to launder it).

Kathleen's flaw is her initial resistance to the military life. This quality is systematically softened during her participation in two dinner parties, which become comparable to the dances in *Fort Apache*. When Kathleen and Kirby dine alone, their romantic uneasiness is underscored. The arrival of the regimental singers, with their rendition of "Kathleen," dramatizes the conflict between the Yorkes. Kirby says that the tune was not his choice, and Kathleen, lamenting that it was not, assumes a visual position in which she appears to be leaning on his shoulder. Shortly after, Kathleen witnesses the Indian raid and Natchez's escape. Although surrounded by Jeff and his friends, the heroine faints when the action gets close; as Kirby later tells her, such conduct is hardly decorous in a commander's wife. Kathleen's acceptance of the necessity for such courage begins at the second dinner party, for General Sheridan. On this occasion, when she is a single female surrounded by numerous officers in formal circumstances, Kathleen offers a toast to her "only rival," the "United States Cavalry." As she watches, Kirby drains his glass and turns it upside down on the table, a gesture obviously derived from their earlier life together, and she, in similar fashion, reaffirms her love for him by repeating this gesture.

Kathleen becomes even more of a soldier's wife on the trail. After the Indian ambush and the subsequent arrival of her husband and his troopers, she importunes Kirby to rescue the children who have been abducted. In pleading for the assembled mothers (who are photographed on a hill as an expectant and all but religiously iconographic group), Kathleen identifies with the military community. By going to Kirby, she has realized the necessity for violence in a good cause; it then comes as no surprise to find her eagerly awaiting his return from this mission. Thus, Kathleen and Kirby, in their literal involvements with rescuing children, simply reecho their roles in relation to each other and Jeff.

In restoring the children and so reintegrating Fort Stark as a community, Kirby and Jeff also become truly father and son. This transformation, which is abetted by Tyree, reaches its climax when Jeff pulls an arrow from his father's shoulder. Colonel Yorke, like Colonel Thursday, has been wounded and unhorsed; however, the wound is similar but dissimilar — with an arrow in the opposite shoulder. Whereas Thursday was given another man's horse to ride headlong back into a massacre, Colonel Yorke's treatment represents the symbolic reknitting of his family. Jeff, surrounded by his father's command, pulls out the arrow in an act that expresses his manhood and, at the same time, brings the two men together emotionally. *Rio Grande*'s verbal signature, the phrase "Get it done," is utilized here when Tyree urges Jeff to do so and adds the title "Reb" to his encouragement. By so labeling Jeff, and repeating a phrase that has been used in the horse training and fight scenes, Ford's film verbalizes its primary thematic evolution, in which the "Rebel" Jeff must extricate the arrow from his "Yankee" father so that the Yorke family can be reunited.

Putting the colonel back on his horse not only restores order visually but also establishes the reunification of the Yorkes and, by implication, the nation itself. The film's final scenes, in which decorations are passed out for bravery and the troops pass in review, find Kirby and Kathleen listening to "Dixie." As Jeff receives his decorations, their hands unite, and the larger historical vision of a nation optimistically reuniting (however questionable on realistic grounds) is achieved in this blend of visual and musical elements. Moreover, Kirby then intercedes so that Tyree, one of those being honored, can go on immediate "leave" and once more avoid the warrant being served on him by the beleaguered marshal. That Tyree comically steals General Sheridan's mount (he has earlier taken Yorke's horse) simply reemphasizes the personal and social unities that have been achieved.

Fort Apache is the closest that Ford ever came to making a genuine western epic. Although *Cheyenne Autumn* has all the visual and production traits of the conventional Hollywood "blockbuster," *Fort Apache* more consistently operates within the generic modes of epic filmmaking. There are individual characters with idiosyncratic problems and personalities within its narrative world, but the resolutions of these difficulties lie within the broader spectrum of society: one's communal and historical roles count for more than one's personal feelings or happiness. Thursday's death, despite its sordid immediate causes, comes to be successfully invoked within a larger social framework, so that he emerges, through his colleagues' sense of propriety, as a legendary figure.

Rio Grande exhibits no such epic designs. Its plot centers on solving its characters' more immediate personal problems. The rebirth of the Yorke family within the institutional framework of the cavalry does, of course, point up one of the implicit themes of *Fort Apache*. However, its more restricted focus, in narrative as well as production values, makes *Rio Grande* a much easier film to appreciate. It lacks the suggestive (if often ambiguous) characters and situations of the earlier film, even though its central performances, particularly that of Maureen O'Hara, are occasionally more polished than what we see in *Fort Apache*.

If *Fort Apache* is thematically unsettling and *Rio Grande* offers a more conventional melodramatic happy ending, Ford's two films are nevertheless clearly linked because of their high degree of artistic integration. Ford brings a greater degree of intellectual sophistication to what is, alas, often seen as a juvenile film genre; thus, *Fort Apache* and *Rio Grande* offer contrasted characters and situations that dialectically reinforce each other. At the same time, we see more complex Indians (especially Cochise in the earlier film) and more significantly important women than what we normally encounter in western films. Within the highly stratified world of Ford's cavalry, older characters are expected not only to train younger ones to be useful members of the community but also to lay down their lives to ensure the ongoing existence of the institutional family. The more pressing thematic issue in *Fort Apache* and *Rio Grande*, and the one that Ford answers in juxtaposing the two films, centers on the ideal qualities that a commanding officer must possess. We see these traits in opposition in *Fort Apache*, as Thursday refuses to take on the professional or personal qualities of those around him. In *Rio Grande*, Kirby Yorke is finally able to amalgamate military expertise with familial and romantic love to become the ideal commander. In addition, both films are immensely entertaining on several levels; and since they can be appreciated either for their entertainment value or for their thematic and artistic subtleties, they clearly underline Ford's stature as a filmmaker.

Chapter 7

She Wore a Yellow Ribbon and *Sergeant Rutledge*

She Wore a Yellow Ribbon (1949) and *Sergeant Rutledge* (1960) are obviously linked in terms of photographic and compositional style. Both films are in color (a process that Ford felt enhanced less thematically serious works), and their pictorialism makes them appear more "artistic" than the director's other cavalry films.[1] The images so often associated with Ford — mounted cavalry columns moving through the distinct terrain of Monument Valley — abound in these films. Indeed, although he used such visual arrangements elsewhere as well (most notably in *The Searchers, The Horse Soldiers*, and *Cheyenne Autumn*), Ford relies on his "iconographic" compositions of cavalry and Indians within these films.

Captain Nathan Brittles's (John Wayne) last mission in *She Wore a Yellow Ribbon* offers the most extended riding sequences in a Ford western; thus it is perhaps only natural that the film revels in the visuals that support these situations. We see Brittles's column riding in close shots, going over prairie or rolling terrain in more medium shots that emphasize group cohesion and relationships, or moving against the dwarfing landscape of Monument Valley in long shots. We also see tracking shots that reveal, among the rocks, Indians who seem to be at one with the terrain as they watch their cavalry enemies; and we see shots of braves riding single file in full regalia as they mass and unite against their white enemies.

Lieutenant Cantrell's (Jeffrey Hunter) mission in *Sergeant Rutledge* offers many of the same compositional opportunities; however, the later film's more elaborate narrative structure diminishes such pictorial flourishes. We again see a mounted column moving by twos across Monument Valley; in one instance, when Cantrell's force encounters the Apaches, loses Corporal Moffitt, and sees Rutledge (Woody Strode) desert, we experience a visual reprise of *She Wore a Yellow Ribbon*. Significantly, in the earlier film, Brittles manages to rescue a returning patrol at that juncture and, ultimately, to save the life of Trooper Quayne (Tom Tyler); in *Sergeant Rutledge*, a similarly designed battle leads to the death of a prominent soldier and the flight of the protagonist from his duty.

118

It is also noticeable that Cantrell, despite his youth, emerges as a far less active military leader in the field than the older Brittles. Whereas the earlier film shows its aging captain personally leading detachments (to rescue Quayne and to relieve the Sudro's Wells waystation), such moments of personal command are notably missing from *Sergeant Rutledge*. As a field commander, Cantrell contents himself with establishing skirmish lines rather than with leading charges. *Sergeant Rutledge's* most consciously photographic imagery occurs during a scene in camp when the black soldiers sing to bolster the protagonist-hero, who assumes an iconographic pose of attentive valor in the evening mist.

Ford's thematic concerns are contrasted by the different tones of these films; the idyllic surroundings and society of *She Wore a Yellow Ribbon* give way to the more compromised and tragic possibilities of *Sergeant Rutledge*. Night scenes in the earlier film are nearly always tinged with a sweet melancholy or nostalgia in which the protagonist asserts either his personality or his expertise. Night scenes in the later film generally carry a more sinister overtone, as if to suggest the racial paranoia that grips so many of its characters. While *She Wore a Yellow Ribbon* is, perhaps, Ford's closest approach to romance (in that his characters remain fixed in their natures within a plot that ends happily for nearly everyone), *Sergeant Rutledge* embodies more contemporary social problems and looks forward to the deeper pessimism of Ford's final three westerns.

It is significant, however, that Ford never allows the paradoxical unease of his 1960s westerns to totally undermine his idealism in portraying the military family of the cavalry. Individual troopers may suffer injustice (as Rutledge does) or individual commanders may be inadequate (as is Captain Wessels [Karl Malden] in *Cheyenne Autumn*), but the institution ultimately vindicates itself over time. There is, finally, no communal or social wrong (no "system" or "establishment") that individual men of goodwill cannot challenge and correct; thus, within the world of Ford's cavalry, oversights and wrongs can be rectified, so that Nathan Brittles can gain his proper place (as chief of scouts and as a colonel) and Braxton Rutledge can be reinstated in his deserved rank (as the proverbial "top soldier").

The military communities in both films are epitomized by numerous contrasted figures. The Allshards (George O'Brien and Mildred Natwick) represent the ideal military couple in *She Wore a Yellow Ribbon*. Abbey Allshard's acceptance of army life is probably never better dramatized than when she wishes Nathan Brittles a fond farewell with the comment, "Here's to our next post." While her remark foreshadows the protagonist's return as chief of scouts, Abbey's outlook derives from her acquiescence to the way things must be — she is the spiritual sister of the many good and patient wives in *Fort Apache* and *Rio Grande*.

The capacities of Major Allshard are demonstrated with Brittles, whether

the major is meeting the protagonist's objections about taking the women to Sudro's Wells or is reasonably disarming the captain's desire to go back and rescue his subordinates now that he is officially "retired." Mack Allshard speaks for the institution when, in this latter instance, he urges that Cohill (John Agar) and Pennell (Harry Carey, Jr.) must learn to operate as soldiers (i.e., under stress) without Brittles. The thematic importance of the Allshards as a couple in the cavalry community is finally symbolized by their dancing while Brittles goes out to "report" in the graveyard at the film's conclusion.

The Fosgates (Willis Bouchey and Billie Burke) are a more disturbing older couple, in keeping with the more sober tenor of *Sergeant Rutledge*. Cordelia Fosgate exhibits a decided imperviousness to military etiquette during her befuddled session on the witness stand; she questions why she has to swear on a Bible, and she remains permanently confused about the prosecutor's (Carleton Young) name, in a manner reminiscent of Colonel Thursday in *Fort Apache*. While Ford ostensibly uses Cordelia and the actress who plays her, Billy Burke, for comic relief, such shenanigans finally backfire within the more serious framework of the film, and she emerges as a symbol of society's hypocrisy. Her remark made after the sutler (Fred Libby) has confessed to the rape and murder of Lucy Dabney (Toby Richards)—"Why, Mister Hubble!"—seems innocent and comic enough until we recall Mrs. Fosgate's earlier suggestion about seeing the white girl with the black protagonist at the sutler's store. These attitudes are caught when she has trouble even saying Rutledge's name on the witness stand and when, in flashback, we see her questioning Lucy about the propriety of the girl's being friendly in public with the black sergeant. In effect, Cordelia Fosgate's last line reinforces her latent racism, for she still cannot accept that the white sutler has been responsible for what seems to be so obviously a black man's kind of crime.

Her husband, Otis, has only come to be in command at Fort Linton because of the murder of Major Dabney (Cantrell alludes to going to see the colonel at a surveying site after he had discovered his commander's corpse). At the trial's beginning, Fosgate seems unaware that Cantrell has arrived, which apparently indicates how slightly these characters know each other. Although the colonel is adamant about seeing justice done in his court through prescribed procedures, he is clearly convinced of Rutledge's guilt. He is nonplused over the defendant's not-guilty plea, and later, easily discounts the possibility of Rutledge's potential innocence with the other trial-board members during a recess. Fosgate's shortsightedness is, of course, signaled by Ford's choice of Willis Bouchey to play the part. Like Cordelia, Otis is a comic figure, with his constant cries for "water" (i.e., concealed whiskey) and his

Opposite: Captain Brittles (John Wayne), Lt. Pennell (Harry Carey, Jr.), and Sergeant Tyree (Ben Johnson) watch the death of the crooked sutler at Red Shirt's hands in *She Wore a Yellow Ribboon* (Argosy-RKO, 1949). Pennell's acceptance of the military life is symbolized by the business between him and Brittles at this juncture.

arguments with his wife over her prerogatives and testimony. Indeed, his sole military capability seems to consist in evicting Cordelia and her friends when he orders the initially hostile crowd outside; however, when the prosecutor Shattuck calls Mrs. Fosgate as a witness, even this temporary martial-marital victory is undermined. The colonel is further illuminated by his wife's reference to the chiming clock she heard when she saw Rutledge stumbling out of Major Dabney's quarters. Ford also signals Otis Fosgate's character by having the actor continuously wear a white coat so as to visually separate him from the real officers with whom he is dealing.

The same contrasts are seen within the enlisted ranks in both films. In each, an enlisted man dies as a result of a fight with Indians; however, the last moments and burials of Trooper Smith (Rudy Bowman) and Corporal Moffitt are quite different. Smith's death offers an occasion to extol the cavalry as an institution capable of taking in such beaten men as Smith and Sergeant Tyree (Ben Johnson) and providing them with useful lives. Brittles feels compelled to be generous to a defeated but gallant foe, so he allows Tyree to address the dying "General" and then offers the latter an eloquent testimonial in a full military funeral. The theme of reconciliation between the regions of the United States after the Civil War is again prominent in *She Wore a Yellow Ribbon* (as it is in *The Horse Soldiers* and elsewhere in Ford's films), and the importance of death as a communal-social fact and ritual is seen in the many burial scenes of these westerns (*My Darling Clementine, Three Godfathers, The Searchers*). Indeed, unlike so many other film genre (crime, horror) directors and unlike so many other western directors, Ford imbues personal losses with a philosophical dimension.

Trooper Moffitt's death in *Sergeant Rutledge*, the result of an Apache lance, receives an extended treatment as Moffitt dies in the arms of the central character. Moffitt's angry dismissal of Rutledge's optimism about the future (his sarcastic remarks about the sergeant's "someday") offers a striking contrast to the death of Trooper Smith in *She Wore a Yellow Ribbon*. While the earlier death brought the cavalry community together, Moffitt's end produces Rutledge's flight and an unseen burial in the sun-drenched Arizona desert. The abrupt ending of the conversation between Rutledge and Moffitt reprises the death of Smith, who could not hear Tyree's final "Sir!" Despite the visual similarity, with both bodies being laid gently on the earth, the tone in *Sergeant Rutledge* is strikingly different. Moffitt's doubts about black men ever being accepted as equals spur Rutledge to flee from the column and seek his "freedom" elsewhere; Smith's last words lead Tyree and the other former Confederates to prevail on Mrs. Allshard and Captain Brittles for a symbolic means (the Rebel flag) to commemorate their loss. Thus, one death deepens divisions within the cavalry community, and the other leads to acts of renewal within it.

Both *She Wore a Yellow Ribbon* and *Sergeant Rutledge* feature other enlisted men. Sergeant Quincannon (Victor McLaglen), by virtue of his physique and age, sets off the abilities of Tyree, whereas Sergeant Skidmore (Juano Hernandez) mediates between Rutledge and the official (i.e., white) community of Fort Linton. Both older noncoms are also used for comedy, with Quincannon exhibiting both the verbal and the physical humor associated with McLaglen's characters in *Fort Apache* and *Rio Grande*. The Irish sergeant, with his penchant for whiskey, shares a trait with many other figures in Ford's films, a connection made even more obvious by the casting of McLaglen as Quincannon. The retiring "top soldier," whose career echoes that of Brittles in its fortuitous timing, engages in some overdone comic knockout when he goes to get a suit of clothes in (appropriately enough) a bar run by another Ford icon — Francis Ford, as an obliging fellow Irishman and drinking companion. While such broad comedy, on the morning of the captain's retirement and after the relief column has been sent out under Pennell's command, serves as emotional relief in *She Wore a Yellow Ribbon*, Quincannon emerges as decidedly funnier when given comic dialogue. After Brittles shows that he has always known where a whiskey bottle has been hidden in his quarters, the sergeant's retort ("And you've been deceiving me all these years!") nicely reverses their positions while keeping Quincannon thoroughly in character. Quincannon's concern for children (as seen in his caring for the orphaned Sudro boy) and with young lovers (his intercessions on the march when Olivia is insulted by Flint) establish his acumen within the cavalry family.

Skidmore, on the other hand, does not fit as well into the larger military community of *Sergeant Rutledge*, for despite his many years of service, he bears the ineradicable taint of being black. On the witness stand Skidmore is assailed by Shattuck, who questions the sergeant's age and reliability as an observer. Here, ironically, the trial board (led by Otis Fosgate) rises to Skidmore's defense by insisting that he has always been a good soldier. On the trail of the Apaches, Skidmore emerges as a more military figure than Quincannon, for he notes the sloppiness of the enemy's retreat; and he warns Rutledge that Cantrell will never set him free because the lieutenant is a "strict man for duty." Skidmore is also used to defuse the tension surrounding the discovery of the bodies of Major Dabney and the raped Lucy. In announcing to Cantrell that Rutledge is not on the post and was last seen riding to Major Dabney's quarters because of the Indian threat, Skidmore ends with the remark that the "trouble come double." Unfortunately, this line makes the otherwise dignified sergeant momentarily sound like the comically befuddled Cordelia Fosgate and ultimately jars against the serious thematic context of *Sergeant Rutledge*.

She Wore a Yellow Ribbon offers a military community with a wide variety of supporting characters. Cohill and Pennell carry significant thematic weight, for they establish the beneficent nature of cavalry life and, more particularly, the wisdom of Captain Brittles as their surrogate father within the community.

Cohill is the more thoroughly committed to the military life, if only because of his nine years on active duty; in essence, the lieutenant represents the army tradition that Brittles solemnizes in his many references to the number of years in grade that an individual must endure before receiving a promotion. Pennell initially bridles at military discipline because he feels it stands in the way of his succeeding romantically with Olivia. When he attempts to go out with her in a buggy and is rebuffed by Cohill and the orders of the day, Pennell angrily insists he will take the girl to Delmonico's when he is free of his military obligation. In the field Pennell emerges as less competent than Cohill, especially when he questions why Brittles does not engage the Indian column, seemingly forgetting the presence of the women in their party. Cohill's jockeying of Pennell culminates when he insists that he will personally tear up any request from the latter for getting out of active duty. Thus, although the young officers are romantic rivals, Cohill feels an obligation to save Pennell from his shortsighted personal desires by keeping him in the army, where he will, finally, emerge as a better man than at Delmonico's.

Their subsequent attempt at fisticuffs shows a lack in both Cohill and Pennell, and only the film's climax demonstrates that they have grown up enough to assume command. Cohill rises to this status when he returns to hold off the Indian advance for a "long" day. His assumption of command is signaled when Brittles finally calls him "Flint" (along with the equally symbolic "son") and Olivia openly declares her love for him. Cohill's stature is thus established because his stake in the cavalry life has expanded to include the prospect of a future as a commander and a husband-father. Pennell's rise in status occurs when he takes out the troops who ride to Cohill's relief on the next morning. The formal passing of command from Brittles to Pennell is dramatized in a magnificent sequence in which they exchange salutes — the young man on horseback looking wonderfully self-assured and the older man sniffling but retaining his dignity at a hitching post. Ford also sets his two young subordinate officers apart by having them wear different hats. On the trail Cohill is seen in a traditional cowboy hat, whereas Pennell wears a kepi similar to Colonel Thursday's. This accent on costuming further reflects Pennell's apprentice role within the society of the film; indeed, the hat symbolizes both his "eastern" longings and (by association with *Fort Apache*'s protagonist) his being a stranger in the western world in which he finds himself. His final gaze at Brittles, as the dance sequence counterpoints the captain's walk to the graveyard, suggests that Pennell will model himself on the aged protagonist.

The enlisted men of *She Wore a Yellow Ribbon* are more varied than those in *Sergeant Rutledge*. Distinct types emerge in Corporal Quayne (Tom Tyler), who, though wounded, insists on finishing his patrol's report; Hockbauer (Michael Dugan), Major Allshard's adjutant and the unwilling leader of the party that sets out to arrest Quincannon; and the blacksmith Wagner (Mickey Simpson), with the notably German accent. These figures achieve their greatest importance when Brittles's company bids him farewell. Their gift of an engraved silver watch, which was brought "all the way" from Kansas City and for which they have all chipped in, moves their erstwhile commander to tears. Such generosity and spirit is obviously celebrated at the film's fadeout when these same anonymous men are praised by the narrator as the very essence of the American spirit.

There is no extended presentation of the subordinate personnel inside Fort Linton — except for minor court functionaries (like the redoubtable Jack Pennick as a bailiff) — for obviously no deeper cavalry community is present in *Sergeant Rutledge*. It is significant that the professional camaraderie we see in *She Wore a Yellow Ribbon* is still at work among the black cavalrymen, who constantly keep chiding their younger members as "rookies." This hazing becomes praise and encouragement when one of the new recruits gets wounded and is attended by Mary Beecher (Constance Towers), Rutledge, and Cantrell. In a subsequent scene, Skidmore reaffirms the bravery of the wounded youngster, and Cantrell (in a verbal bow to Brittles) sagely notes that such conduct will result in a promotion in "four or five years."

Sergeant Rutledge offers other, more sinister military types and groups. In Captain Shattuck, the legal technician, we see an officer who is neither incompetent nor shortsighted but rather bent on success at the cost of higher obligations to truth and justice. Shattuck's manipulation of testimony accords with the often symbolic nature of the court proceedings; indeed, to dismiss his character as simply a bad or dated perception is to miss the point. Ford's use of this particular actor, Carleton Young, for such a role is in keeping with what we have seen elsewhere, especially in *The Horse Soldiers*, where the actor's character (Confederate Major Johnny Miles) also embodies an outmoded historical force. The prosecutor's rhetorical flourishes during his summation, when he histrionically reminds the court of the color of Rutledge's skin (through his emphasis on the words "this man"), reveal Shattuck's racist side. In believing in Rutledge's innate guilt, Shattuck is at one with the courtroom crowd, which consists of fluttery women and a potential lynch mob. With Shattuck, we have come a great distance from the world of *Young Mr. Lincoln*, in which the protagonist defused such sentiments.

The courtroom crowd in *Sergeant Rutledge* makes threatening gestures toward the protagonist and offers the prospect of mob violence that Ford dramatizes so vividly elsewhere. Cordelia Fosgate and her friends supply a veneer of respectability for such potential criminality. *Sergeant Rutledge* never confronts these social ambiguities, for the conclusion of the trial is subsumed by Cordelia's inane remark about the murderer, while the protagonist is never shown being reintegrated into the larger (white) community of Fort Linton. Essentially, those who have admired and trusted him all along, his fellow black soldiers, Cantrell, and Mary, join in Rutledge's triumph as the various elements of the community disappear (presumably to reappear at the next trial of a black man, with all their prejudices intact). There is no open repentance or remorse within the military or civilian communities of the fort, so that we come away with no sense of a moral lesson having been internalized. Rutledge must be accepted as a brave soldier and an innocent man, but no great gain in collective humility leads to wisdom and change as a result of all that has happened.

The Indians in *Sergeant Rutledge* seem both ethereal and dangerous, if only because they emerge facelessly out of the night at Spindle Station and strike from ambush at the river. There is no figure among them who assumes the dignity of the aged Pony-That-Walks (Chief Big Tree) in *She Wore a Yellow Ribbon*; indeed, none of them ever speak nor are even as individually prominent as the rebellious Red Shirt (Noble Johnson) in the earlier film. Through Rutledge's binoculars, we see them tormenting and killing Sam Beecher and, again, leaving the indistinguishable body of Chris Hubble (Jan Styne) among some smoldering rocks. None of them openly challenge a cavalryman to man-to-man combat, as Red Shirt does when he fires an arrow at Brittles's feet. Instead, their favorite battle tactics consist of ambushes and killing from behind (the lancing of Corporal Moffitt). Their dead bodies finally prove significant when Cantrell finds Lucy's locket around the neck of a slain chief at the riverside.

Pony-That-Walks, on the other hand, is the only individual besides Brittles who understands what war means in *She Wore a Yellow Ribbon*; however, the aged chief, who has been shouted down at the council fires, has decided that there is nothing he can do. He urges his old friend Nathan to join him in hunting buffalo and getting drunk, which represents the difference between the two characters. Red Shirt is centered in a more melodramatic tradition. When Quayne's patrol is rescued, only Red Shirt rides defiantly within rifle range of Brittles's troopers, who have been instructed to fire over his head. When Mr. Rynders (Harry Woods) tries to renegotiate a higher price for his contraband rifles, Red Shirt strikes him down and precipitates the slaughter of the sutler's cohorts. His conduct when Brittles enters the Indian camp puts Red Shirt momentarily on a par with the protagonist. However, when Brittles breaks Red Shirt's arrow of defiance, spits on it, and hurls the fragments at the mounted warrior, the dramatic balance has again been tipped in favor of Ford's protagonist. The final stampede and defeat of the Indians, as a result of which they must walk and so lose face, seems a particularly appropriate fate for Red Shirt, who has been seen exclusively on horseback until this final sequence.

Because Ford rarely delineated a convincing villain, Mr. Rynders in *She Wore a Yellow Ribbon* is rarely on screen and is played by such an obvious B-movie heavy that he becomes a thematic cipher. Rynders and his associates (among whom we see veteran character actor Paul Fix) die deservedly in the fires of Red Shirt's camp. Chandler Hubble comes across as yet another histrionic villain in

Sergeant Rutledge (Woody Strode) takes the witness stand as the prosecutor (Carleton Young) accuses him in *Sergeant Rutledge* (Warner Bros., 1960). Note the contrast of Shattuck's white glove and Rutledge's face.

Sergeant Rutledge, one whose evil is more verbal than actual. Mr. Hubble's loss of his son Chris seems more than enough punishment for his character, so that his murder and rape of Lucy comes across as a deus ex machina kind of narrative convenience tacked on to bring the plot to its conclusion. His courtroom confession, made only after Cantrell physically assaults him, is accompanied by violent gestures as if to suggest that this character, who has been largely immobile until this point, has finally erupted because of repressed guilt. Chandler Hubble strikes at the psychological and sexual identity of every white man present in that he has seemingly committed what they believe is a black man's crime. A deeper irony is that his crime has led to the deaths of Lucy and Chris and scarred the future generation of Fort Linton.

Such conduct is the subject taken up most notably by the post physician, Dr. Eckner (Charles Seel), who, in attributing it to Rutledge, labels it as "degenerate." This physician, whose testimony is the shortest in *Sergeant Rutledge*, also sermonizes about the cross that Lucy wore. When Cantrell identifies the mark on the dead girl's neck by referring to a picture of her that shows the cross, Eckner states his belief that the killer had to take this symbol of the virtue that he had destroyed. In his self-righteousness, Eckner stands in contrast to the more compassionate Dr. O'Laughlin (Arthur Shields) of *She Wore a Yellow Ribbon*. That figure, who fights to save Quayne's life and then offers a fond Irish farewell to Brittles ("May the road be kind to you"), is cut from the same dramatic cloth as the physicians in *Fort Apache* and *Rio Grande*. His very Irishness separates him from the more outspoken and more Germanic-sounding Eckner.

The difference in tone between these two films is also dramatized by the position occupied by children. The orphaned girl and boy at Sudro's Wells accompany Brittles's column on its return to Fort Stark, and the adult characters (Mrs. Allshard and Quincannon) devote themselves to their future well-being, whether through talking about jam preserves or (supposed) prowess in swimming. Brittles functions as a second father to his young lieutenants, a connection he makes overt when he speaks of tanning Cohill's "hide" after Flint has insulted Olivia on the march. The romantic subplot of *She Wore a Yellow Ribbon* also implies a future with children, as symbolized by the union of Flint and Olivia; that the society's older members have seen this arrangement as natural is thoroughly in keeping with the hierarchical cavalry world that Ford is celebrating. The dead members of the younger generation in *Sergeant Rutledge* are only partly offset by the final union of Mary and Cantrell, because these lovers are emotionally distant from the larger cavalry community of the Fosgates and the courtroom mob. In *Sergeant Rutledge*, no one seems willing to wait for or to encourage love or lovers. The impatient Laredo (Hank Worden) forces the train to leave Spindle Station before the stationmaster has even been located, and such haste stands in sharp contrast to Brittles's allowing Flint and Olivia a last embrace despite military pressures on the other side of the river. Society has become more self-centered and less compassionate in the later film, traits that thoroughly accord with the mixed victory that the protagonist wins in court.

Costuming underlines thematic points and dramatic sequences to reaffirm our sense of the coherence in these Ford films. The central character of *She Wore a Yellow Ribbon* is seen in three distinct costumes, which constitute one of the more apparent symbolic devices in the film. We first find Brittles readying himself for morning inspection and listening to Quincannon's recital of the previous night's events. In his red-flannel undershirt, Brittles shows that no man is a hero to his valet; indeed, since we first see him in such unheroic attire, he can only gradually emerge as a hero through his quest for peace. If this first costume suggests the ease with which Brittles moves among all the ranks at Fort Stark, its comicality also compromises the character's capacity for athletically violent action. Brittles's morning calisthenics demarcate his age nicely, while his attention to details of dress and appearance once he is in uniform accords well with the emphases placed on costumes within the military community. When Brittles rises for his last inspection, after sleeping, symbolically, in his red undershirt and next to the pictures of his dead wife and daughters, he is persuaded by Quincannon to don his most impressive dress uniform. It is in this regalia that the protagonist receives the watch from his faithful troops; and, as if to indicate his changed role as a soon-to-be "retiree," Brittles wears a Union cap to receive their final salutation.

When leaving Fort Stark, Brittles emerges in a buckskin jacket and military trousers. It is in this costume, which combines the pioneer and the army worlds of the film, that Brittles rejoins his command and stampedes the Indian pony herd. When he is retrieved from his symbolic journey into the dying sunset of the West by Tyree, Brittles still wears this outfit; we see him only briefly in a regular uniform, leading the last column that closes the film. Brittles's various costumes underline his central role in *She Wore a Yellow Ribbon*, for their diversity emphasizes his character's capacity to adapt to circumstances and to make them work for him.

Other characters, most notably Mrs. Allshard and Olivia, also change their costumes to dramatize roles they learn to play. Thus, the women's assumption of military garb, though perfectly sensible for the trail, allows us to see that Olivia must gain character while the elder Abbey already has it. However, in both cases, these perceptions result only because of Brittles's actions with the women. Thus, his initial dismay at Mrs. Allshard's outfit (which she has borrowed from Quincannon) is offset by his pronouncing her to be a "soldier" after Quayne's operation; Olivia becomes "army" at the river, when Brittles insists she stop watching Flint's recrossing and she obeys. The most obvious costuming symbol in the film is, of course, the yellow ribbon that Olivia wears in her hair as the column leaves on the protagonist's supposed last mission. While many of the other characters assume that this token represents her love for Pennell (an idea that the young man also shares), Olivia's ribbon places her into larger contexts with Cohill and Brittles. To the former, she teasingly suggests that she may be wearing it for him, while she also makes a similar, if more comic, insistence to the elderly commander. Only the fortuitous entry of Mrs. Allshard prevents Flint and Olivia from embracing at one point, so that Abbey's comment that the yellow ribbon is for Pennell sounds even more ironic.

On the trail in *Sergeant Rutledge*, Mary Beecher wears a red blouse, riding breeches, and the appropriate western hat, while in court she appears in stiff, formal dresses of a military blue. If she is more vulnerable to her feelings on the trail, both with Cantrell and with Rutledge, her reserve in the courtroom is symbolized by her austere clothing. On the train ride into Spindle Station, during which she and Cantrell embrace, she is attired in pink; thus she encounters both love and the land's hostility (in the form of the murdered stationmaster) in "innocent" garb. Her reservations about Arizona and Cantrell are augmented by the problems she encounters on the mission vis-à-vis the central character. During these flashbacks Mary is dressed to include variations of pink (her red blouse) and blue (her riding breeches). Cantrell's defense of Rutledge finds Mary in her bluest clothing, as though she had become a part of the larger, cavalry world around her. It is appropriate that Cantrell wins her over when she is so dressed, and it is a lovely touch that, when she asks him to scold her after the trial for her wrongheadedness about him and Arizona, he repeats a line from their opening train ride ("You're still the prettiest girl I've ever seen").

This reconciliation scene between the lovers in *Sergeant Rutledge* also repeats a pattern that Ford uses in similar circumstances in *She Wore a Yellow Ribbon*. In both films the young officers feel a necessity to divest themselves of some of the trappings of their profession before approaching the women they love. The animosity between Cohill and Olivia finds the lieutenant clearly overstepping himself. He brings Olivia to tears — an action that stands in distinct contrast to the way in which women are to be treated and an arrangement that Brittles and, to a lesser extent, Quincannon observe and try to rectify discreetly or directly. When Flint and Olivia finally meet at the picket line, Cohill is properly contrite and moves to declare his romantic feelings for the girl. Before doing so, however, he sets aside his hat and gloves and throws back his cape to look less military. This symbolic casting off, which seemingly renders Cohill more open to the emotional side of life, epitomizes the extent to which romance is allowed to intrude upon the world of Ford's cavalry: the lovers can express their feelings, but only within the confines of proper military costume. Olivia is also in uniform, which further suggests that she must become part of this military world in order to be worthy of Cohill's attentions. When she and Cohill embrace at the riverside, they are still in these costumes; only during the dance scene do we see the girl in a dress and with her lover.

On the porch at Fort Linton, Cantrell more dramatically makes some of the same movements when he goes to Mary after the trial. In this case, before he approaches the woman, the lieutenant casts off various articles (briefcase, sword, gloves) that have been required for the courtroom. Once again, Ford's intention is to dramatize the subordinate role that romantic love must play within this institutionalized world. Cohill and Cantrell approach their beloveds only after they have taken care of military obligations, for they adhere to a clear hierarchy of responsibility above emotions. They have earned the right to love by having demonstrated the proper sense of values: Cohill by pressing Pennell to stay in the service; and Cantrell, on the trail, by refusing to be persuaded (by Mary and the others) to let Rutledge go. These young officers' greater allegiances to the groups they serve demonstrate their capacities for romantically happy marriages (i.e., ones like that of the elder O'Rourkes in *Fort Apache*). The correctness of Cantrell's romantic choice is, again, reaffirmed by the military-colored dress Mary wears when she "apologizes" and embraces him on the porch.

The gloves that various officers wear in *Sergeant Rutledge* emphasize the formality that attaches to the film's court proceedings. The white handwear, given added visual emphasis on the accusing hands of Shattuck, sets up a sharp color contrast. When the prosecutor assails Rutledge, generally all we see of Shattuck are his white gloves and their prominently pointing fingers. Since his charges are partially derived from an innate antipathy toward the protagonist's skin color, Shattuck's gloves suggest the repulsion his character feels toward the sergeant's very flesh. Cantrell, of course, wears the same color gloves, but since we have seen him repeatedly in close physical proximity to Rutledge (wrestling with him at Spindle Station, putting handcuffs on and taking them off during the mission), the same association does not attach to his character. Moreover, Cantrell puts these court gloves away when he returns to the larger world and woos Mary. Significantly, we never see Shattuck cast these tools of his trade aside; like the larger community within Fort Linton, the prosecutor is never shown to be repentant or to offer any sort of apology to the protagonist for what has happened.

Lost hats serve in both films as a means of identification or insight. When Tyree, after being ordered to ride alone to Sudro's Wells, finds a cavalry cap with an Indian feather in it, he sagely notes that this article has come from a brave who was present at Custer's defeat. The hero's insistence on this point reaffirms the extent of the Indian threat that Fort Stark is facing, a process that is underlined when an arrow whizzes by Tyree moments after he has found the soldier's cap, setting in motion a lengthy chase sequence in which the sergeant escapes only through superior horsemanship. Cantrell's discovery of Mary Beecher's hat outside Spindle Station, after he and the column have arrived, takes on great weight within the immediate dramatic circumstances. Since he has just ridden away from the scene of Major Dabney's death, the lieutenant now fears that the worst may have happened to Mary. The complexity here is that since the audience already knows that the girl is with Rutledge, Cantrell's fears may attach to the Indians or to the sergeant, as proverbial figures of psychological nightmare. Ford diffuses any possible racism in Cantrell in the scenes that immediately follow, for we see that the lieutenant regards Rutledge not merely as a fine soldier but also as an ideal man.

Numerous objects serve to unite *She Wore a Yellow Ribbon* and *Sergeant Rutledge*. Major Allshard's pipe compares nicely with the one scene in which Rutledge also appears with a pipe. The wisdom and goodness of the commander of Fort Stark can be epitomized in the pipe he smokes; by implication, the pipe that Braxton carries when he enters the sutler's store and when he is with Lucy encapsulates his goodness too. Indeed, Rutledge's pipe is clearly juxtaposed to the circumstances in which he is seen with it. The pipe acts as a counterweight to Chandler Hubble and the gossipy women who condemn Lucy's friendship with the sergeant. If Allshard was an ideal commander, then Cantrell's association of the protagonist in *Sergeant Rutledge* with the ideal man gains even greater resonance through the director's use of the pipe as a supporting symbol.

The central character in *Sergeant Rutledge* is also symbolically associated with other positive figures in *She Wore a Yellow Ribbon* through his use of binoculars. Just as Brittles spied the mobile Arapahoes through field glasses, so does Rutledge see the death of Sam Beecher in an extended sequence that places the Indian enemy at a discreet distance. In both instances, what is seen through the binoculars separates the heroines from situations they have associated with the idea of home. When Brittles spies the Indian column, he moves around them and thus loses the stage that would have taken Olivia back to her home in the East. Rutledge, in describing what he saw to the court, urges that Mary would not be able to go home again because of her father's death — a condition that is clearly true on an emotional level and that becomes more ironic as we realize that Rutledge has lost his "home" because of the very situation in which he speaks this line. A further irony is that, in seemingly losing their physical homes, both heroines are forced to recognize their genuine emotional homes, in the form of lovers with whom they can become useful members of the larger military community.

Captain Brittles is surrounded with symbolic objects in *She Wore a Yellow Ribbon*. The tobacco that he chews, and that he dismisses as a bad habit, becomes a means to dramatize that Pennell will stay in the service. The lieutenant remains bent on leaving the army until Brittles has him accompany the party that oversees the trading parley between Rynders and Red Shirt. Brittles, Tyree, and Pennell crouch behind a log and, in the course of seeing the deaths of the sutler and his cohorts, the captain offers a chew to the sergeant, who refuses. At this point, Pennell insists that he would like a "chaw" and bites off a piece to suggest that he has accepted his position within the unit. Brittles's subsequent remarks merely cement the connection that has already been made visually and dramatically, so that we again see how Ford subordinates dialogue to more photographic and mimetic elements. The change in Pennell is further underlined when he volunteers to remain behind with the rear guard and when Brittles, after refusing the request, notes that this offer will show on the young man's record, if he still "wishes to make one." The latter remark cleverly restores Brittles to his public role as Pennell's commander, while the young lieutenant's avidity allies him with such real soldiers as Quayne, who also volunteers to remain behind and is turned down, much less ceremoniously, by the protagonist.

The watch that Brittles receives at his retirement operates symbolically in several ways. Its inscription, "Lest we forget," brings the protagonist to tears and underlines the nostalgic feelings of those who have most clearly assimilated the values of cavalry life. Despite their often official and bureaucratized relations, the men and women of Ford's army retain a sense of group solidarity, in past and present, that is epitomized by Abbey Allshard's optimistic farewell to Brittles when the latter seemingly leaves Fort Stark for good. When Brittles consults his gold watch during the time he is "unofficially" with his erstwhile unit, it is appropriate that the essentially timeless communal life that he has led up until now should be set off by the timepiece. During his farewell to Cohill and Pennell after the Indian threat has been checked, Brittles again consults his watch to note that he has been off duty for two minutes. His restoration into the cavalry community later naturally places the captain once more in other time modes — the mythic, as seen in the horizon on which he and Tyree confer, and the historical, as caught in the list of public figures who have been endorsed his request to be head of army scouts.

Brittles's taking out his glasses to read the watch's inscription, a concession to his age, is echoed by Skidmore's appearance in court wearing spectacles. While the black sergeant's glasses counterpoint his age and Shattuck's innuendoes about it, Skidmore sees Mr. Hubble through these very glasses as the trial works toward its conclusion; thus, his spectacles symbolize the aged black soldier's earned status in the ideal military-social community that exists within the larger society of *Sergeant Rutledge*. Brittles's choked reading of the watch inscription through his glasses underlines his basic humanity: he has earned the proper tribute from the proper men and, in doing so, stands as yet another counterweight to the private goals that drove Owen Thursday in *Fort Apache*.

Lucy Dabney's cross and Chandler Hubble's coat, the connected linchpins that prove Rutledge's legal innocence, are obvious talismans whose meanings are thoroughly explored in *Sergeant Rutledge*. If the girl's cross represents her virginity, and its discovery inside the pocket of the sutler's jacket demonstrates the accuracy of Dr. Eckner's diagnosis about the villain carrying away a trophy of his perverted triumph, Chris Hubble's death while wearing the coat only further reinforces Ford's symbolic intentions. At this level, Chris dies to atone for his father's crime, especially since the younger man was riding into danger to warn a girl he presumably loved in a "decent" way.

The handcuffs that Cantrell carries also operate as obvious symbols. They are placed on Rutledge's wrists, an act that is thoroughly consistent with the plot but that serves as a reminder of the slavery from which Rutledge escaped as a youth. That the white Cantrell puts these handcuffs on the black sergeant symbolizes the prejudice that will shackle Rutledge throughout. Cantrell's own sense of duty, without which he becomes less than himself, makes him put the handcuffs back on the sergeant after the conclusion of the battle with the Indians; indeed, Cantrell's identity is tied up with reimposing these very bonds on Rutledge. Without his commitment to duty and his faith in the ultimate beneficence of army justice, Cantrell would be as lost as Rutledge proclaims himself to be when he confronts Shattuck's accusations about his conduct at Crazy Woman River. Rutledge has learned that he cannot be a "swamp-runnin' nigger," and although Cantrell's tests have not been as apparent, he has realized the same thing about himself. Neither man has a serious identity outside the army, so that they are bound in more subtle ways than through the handcuffs that link them physically.

Cordelia Fosgate's chiming clock reprises one of Ford's larger concerns about the amalgamation of North and South within American society after the Civil War. If Tyree and Rutledge positively dramatize this reunion in different ways, Cordelia and Otis Fosgate represent the downside of the process. For them, the war has provided no great trial or suffering to breed wisdom (as with the Yorkes in *Rio Grande*) but has been only an occasion to gain property that could be conveniently stolen from the vanquished. Otis Fosgate's role in the burning of Atlanta has provided knickknacks for his home; and it is surely appropriate that the colonel's other connection with the Civil War, the Confederate court-martial manual from which Mulqueen (Judson Pratt) reads, remains all but incomprehensible to him.

Ford's photographic effects in both films distinguish them within his western canon. The unreal, reddish sky that serves as a backdrop in *She Wore a Yellow Ribbon* is intended to convey a mythical framework in which memory dominates. Thus, we see it through the window of Major Allshard's headquarters as Brittles reads the casualty list from the Little Big Horn. To the refrain of a very slowly played rendition of "The Girl I Left Behind Me," the protagonist reads the names of the slain and pauses significantly at that of Miles Kehoe. At this point Ford cuts to the graveyard and Brittles's first visit there, a scene that is also bathed in the same reddish mystical light. In his recitation to his wife, Brittles notes the Custer massacre and then mentions Kehoe, someone with whom she used to dance. Appropriately, Brittles finishes his recitation by mentioning his last patrol and what he might do when he officially retires. Thus, it is no surprise when Brittles later rides off into the same-colored horizon that marks these earlier scenes; indeed, he and Tyree confer on a hillside that is swathed in the same ethereal light that has supported the graveyard sequence. In *She Wore a Yellow Ribbon* this light pattern reinforces Ford's theme: the wisdom of the old is essential to the survival of the young in an always-dangerous present.

The same light pattern is more unsettling in *Sergeant Rutledge*, for now Ford uses this tinted sky to underline a scene of great danger. The confrontations at Spindle Station, between Mary and the dead stationmaster, between the girl and Rutledge, and finally with the Apache braves, all occur against a red sky that reminds us of the setting during the massacre of the Edwards' family in *The Searchers*. Ford's manipulation of light is also noticeable in the many dissolves from present to past in *Sergeant Rutledge*; however, most of these movements away from the courtroom take us into harshly bright, natural surroundings. The sequence at Spindle Station, which is broken up because it is recounted by various witnesses, abounds in stagey lighting. The sequence in the train bringing Mary and Cantrell to the station serves as a prologue to the fevered events that later occur there; the train moves at night, a time that Ford frequently uses for important moments of confrontation. In *Sergeant Rutledge*, the night setting underlines the thematic and character conflicts that Mary and Cantrell embody.

Olivia Dandridge's initial appearance in *She Wore a Yellow Ribbon* is visually akin to that of Philadelphia Thursday's first morning at the post in *Fort Apache*; Olivia is also seen from below, poised on a balcony overlooking the events taking place on the parade ground. Significantly, however, Olivia is quickly whisked away by Mrs. Allshard, indicating that she is not yet a real part of the cavalry community. After her comic encounter with Cohill and Brittles at the gate, Olivia next appears in the graveyard bearing flowers for the captain's family plot. This scene foreshadows that Olivia will eventually become part of the ideal society represented by the protagonist and Fort Stark. Ford signals her future both verbally and visually; however, Captain Brittles makes the only verbal connection—("Nice girl, Mary. She reminds me of you.")—after Olivia's shadow has symbolically fallen across the headstone of his wife. Olivia clearly fits the mold, since her silhouette coincides precisely with the dimensions of a worthy predecessor; but she can measure up to such dimensions only by committing herself to Cohill and by being a proper army wife.

Mary Beecher has already fallen in love with the proper soldier (Cantrell) by the time she is left at Spindle Station; her test lies in rejecting and then reconciling herself to the role she has chosen. The train's rapid departure allows Ford to show Mary as the familiar waiting heroine, for she is photographed waving in the steam of the receding engine. This idyllic image is then quickly shattered when Rutledge's hand clasps Mary's mouth as she runs from the dead stationmaster's corpse. Thus, the conflicts within the heroine are dramatized much more effectively at the visual level than they are in her dialogue. By saving her by suppressing her natural instincts, Rutledge begins the process by which Mary becomes a genuine westerner. Mary later naively dismisses the sergeant's racial pessimism; she insists that Rutledge's fear of being found alone with a white woman is foolish because they are simply two people trying to stay alive in a wilderness. The heroine's real test lies in being thrown into the violent ethos that Rutledge recognizes and that is symbolized by the death of her father. Mary's integration with the black soldiers is photographically sealed when she nurses the wounded "rookie" from an angle that makes her appear to be nurturing him. Mary finally realizes that the demands of the institution—that Rutledge must stand trial and that Cantrell must ensure that he does—count for more than her own untrained feelings. Mary Beecher ultimately learns to trust in the collective wisdom of the institution and so becomes a spiritual sister to Olivia in *She Wore a Yellow Ribbon*.

Such intellectual and emotional reconciliation is tougher to sustain in *Sergeant Rutledge* because the community offers no redeeming rituals by which individual tensions can be eased. The society of Fort Linton as seen at the trial emerges as one composed of gossipy women and enraged idlers looking for trouble. In *Sergeant Rutledge*, moreover, there is no communal event, such as a dance, by which dislikes and social slights are exorcised and society is reunited. When the film supplies a final image of the black cavalrymen riding across Monument Valley, the absence of Cantrell from that end credit suggests that only the black enlisted men led by Rutledge are worthy of any honor. Cantrell and Mary will have to find solace not within the institution but with each other.

The end of *She Wore a Yellow Ribbon*, in keeping with its idyllic tone, reinforces more traditional and optimistic values with its dance and parade sequences. The party in Brittles's honor, with its lovely transformation of the film's title song into a stately waltz, pictorializes how all the conflicts within the plot have been resolved. The majority of those present luxuriate in being couples, symbolized by Cohill's announcement that he and Olivia will wed and Brittles's rejoinder that everyone except Pennell knew that all along; but three characters assume more symbolic roles. Tyree recedes from the party because his mission to bring Brittles back is finished and because his heart is given to duty and nostalgia rather than enjoyment in the present. Pennell auspiciously eyes Brittles as the latter goes to the gravesite to "report," and so Pennell like Olivia earlier, sets himself against a standard that he will try to measure up to. Brittles excuses himself to talk to the past, in keeping with his role as the embodiment of that time in the present.

She Wore a Yellow Ribbon is also distinguished by a greater emphasis on physical grace and action than is found in *Sergeant Rutledge*. Tyree's headlong ride culminates with his jumping over a gorge and leaving the pursuing Indians to howl at his receding visage, a scene that resembles Red Shirt's gestures of defiance when confronted by Brittles's skirmishers during the rescue of Quayne's patrol. The sheer pictorialism of Tyree's ride through the Monument Valley landscape is one of the greatest photographic beauties in all of Ford's westerns; indeed, this memorable sequence stands out in a film replete with celebrated images of Brittles's column moving against lightning and darkness. When the aged captain arrives at Sudro's Wells only to reflect that his last mission has been a failure, he symbolically enacts his frustrations. After telling Olivia that such shortcomings always rest with a commander (i.e., telling her of the army way of perceiving reality), Brittles kicks a prop out from beneath a burning wagon so that it can collapse, visualizing what has happened to his hopes at this point.

The night raid on Red Shirt's camp also abounds in striking visual details amid a wealth of physical action. The charging cavalrymen resemble cowhands with their yells that stampede the Indian pony herd. The extras and animals involved in this sequence outstrip anything we see in *Sergeant Rutledge*, and Ford's choice not to include such extensive second-unit scenes in that more thematic and ambiguous film is surely a conscious design. It is appropriate that the scale of action in which Cantrell and Rutledge find themselves is diminished, for these characters operate within the same military world in which Captain Collingwood found himself before the action begins in *Fort Apache*. Such nasty and largely anonymous activities do not lend themselves to glory, so that Cantrell and Rutledge are never put into a decisive final battle; all they can do is drive the Indians back to the reservation and keep a vigilant eye out for any later outbreaks. In a sense, their patrolling function, with its implicit notion of constant vigilance and no dramatic victories, may reflect a kind of cold war readiness as well as suggest the eternal struggle against prejudice that all these characters must wage.

Cantrell leads two actions in *Sergeant Rutledge*, and in both he assumes a much less commanding position than Brittles ever does in the earlier film. His purpose seems to be to get his troops assembled into lines of skirmishers rather than to lead them on horseback. Cantrell feels the imminence of danger and sends out Moffitt and another trooper to scout ahead; yet when the Indians strike, the lieutenant does not charge into them, as Brittles does so conspicuously in *She Wore a Yellow Ribbon*. At his best, Cantrell simply becomes another dismounted soldier, one who stands while others kneel and fire at his command (under the immediate direction of Rutledge). In contrast, Brittles appears gloriously on horseback, directing Quayne's patrol into safety and ignoring the rifle fire of the Indians. Later, Brittles personally leads a charge into Sudro's Wells, and the retreat to the river finds him directly supervising all the significant actions. Thus, the commander remains behind as long as he can with the rearguard, promises them he will personally relieve them, and crosses the river only at the last moment to send Cohill back to that defensive position. Ford's protagonist commands the final daring charge into the Indian camp, an action he supervises by assembling the troops and insisting on their maintaining discipline in ranks ("Bugler! Do you want to go back to horseshoeing?") until the assault can begin.

Nature is portrayed more realistically in *She Wore a Yellow Ribbon*; natural conditions shape the film's obviously "weathered" scenes. The noted sequence in which the cavalry column moves slowly across Monument Valley at night so that Dr. O'Laughlin can operate on Quayne is filled with striking shots of lightning. Ford may, indeed, have simply made the best of circumstances in this case by shooting despite the weather; however, what may seem improvisational is thoroughly in keeping with the director's artistic personality and methods of working.[2] Certainly the lightning in *She Wore a Yellow Ribbon* accords with the dramatic moment in which Brittles's column is under maximum duress within the larger background, a time when the entire frontier could turn into a war zone and set civilization back a century, as the opening narration intones. The howling wind in *Sergeant Rutledge* during the night at Spindle Station is also symbolic, but the very staging here, with its cramped interiors and avoidance of long shots, makes such a natural element seem more contrived.

Rivers are also featured to emphasize the relative scales of action within the two films. Brittles's entire command crosses a river in *She Wore a Yellow Ribbon* and is shot so as to emphasize its mobility and the majesty of such an action (as further emphasized by the musical score at this point). Moreover, once across, the group witnesses significant romantic developments between Olivia and Flint. *Sergeant Rutledge* uses a river setting to test its protagonist, whose earlier escape from Cantrell's column has been motivated by a belief that he will attain "freedom" only by getting across Crazy Woman River. Rutledge's crossing of that body of water, after witnessing the death of Sam Beecher through his binoculars, takes on significant weight when his conscience forces him to come back and warn Cantrell and the others of the Apaches lying in ambush. Thus, at the river, Rutledge does attain his "freedom" by choosing to remain what he has always been — a good soldier. His impassioned outburst under Shattuck's goading in the courtroom — with its references to "escape," "freedom," and "return" — makes Ford's visual-mimetic pattern even more apparent.

Chris Hubble dies on the trail because he has gone to warn a girl named Jorgenson, a surname that figures prominently in *The Searchers*; thus, just as Brad Jorgenson (Harry Carey, Jr.) chose to die because of his discovery that Lucy Edwards (Pippa Scott) had been raped and killed, so Chris also dies trying to save the woman he apparently loves. An even more noticeable verbal passage occurs during the opening sequence of *She Wore a Yellow Ribbon* when the narrator sets the scene by proclaiming how Custer's defeat could spell the end of the westward movement. While such hyperbole does not immediately jar, the narrator's reference to the pony express, which was essentially out of business by 1861, in the context of the 1876 massacre at the Little Big Horn represents another instance of Ford's free ways with historical events. It is as if the director wanted to incorporate as many strands as possible to underline the accomplishments of his aged protagonist. Brittles thus emerges as the ideal Ford soldier — the man who fights against having to fight and, in so doing, saves the entire course of American expansion.

Sergeant Quincannon's good heart is caught up in his remark that an Irish setter is a good dog, an aside he makes as an interruption to his speech about the men observing proper etiquette in front of Abbey and Olivia ("Watch them words!") on the patrol. If the sergeant's verbal humor seems natural enough, such as when he tells the little Sudro boy that his whiskey is really medicine (and tastes "awful"), Fosgate and his colleagues on the trial board appear in a more sinister light when they play poker and interweave small talk about Rutledge's inevitable fate with comic business about Mulqueen's bluffing. Ford's forays into verbal comedy seem more natural in *She Wore a Yellow Ribbon*; indeed, many lines in the earlier film stand in the sharpest contrast to the more obvious (and clumsy) comic antics of Cordelia and Skidmore in the later work. One such scene finds Brittles accenting every "p" while speaking to Pennell about the latter's taking Olivia on a picnic, a sequence that climaxes when numerous voices loudly urge that the young lieutenant, who is now alone and angry, be passed through the gate.

When Brittles deals with the Allshards, verbal comedy also comes to the forefront. In writing his protest about being "saddled" with Abbey and Olivia, Brittles asks how to spell "territory" and is informed by Major Allshard that the word contains two r's. The protagonist also cannot restrain himself when he sees Mrs. Allshard dressed in her soldier-style riding outfit, a regalia that Brittles finally dismisses as the "dadblastedest get-up" he has ever seen. Later, when the captain is convinced that he is going to retire, he makes plans with Quincannon for the sale of his furniture and decides that his saddle should go to Abbey Allshard. In assigning it to her, Brittles explains that this piece of equipment will be "easier on her disposition," a phrase that he delivers with significant pause between the final words to be polite.

She Wore a Yellow Ribbon also provides a notable tag line for its protagonist; indeed, Brittles's character is delineated by two phrases he repeatedly utters during the film. When the captain hears, during his first scene with Quincannon, that a Private MacKenzie has been killed on a patrol, he notes that MacKenzie might have made corporal in "five or six years" and that the private was a good man because of such a prospect. Listening to Quayne's report, Brittles encourages the wounded soldier with the advice that an additional stripe will be forthcoming in "two or three years." At the dance, after hearing that Olivia and Flint are to marry and then being told by Pennell that his day will come, Brittles does not have to add his usual comment about a number of years because the entire crowd does it for him. Brittles's other crucial phrase is his admonition to "never apologize," since such remarks bespeak weakness in a commander or a soldier. This phrase is also well-known to those around him, for Quincannon says it before Brittles can get it out on his final day at the fort. Cohill also begins his romantic speech to Olivia by repeating this phrase and then offering that he needs to apologize to her. Brittles's second tag line identifies him once more as the teacher figure among apprentices in *She Wore a Yellow Ribbon*.

The earlier film also features the kind of musical score that Ford uses in *Stagecoach* and his other cavalry films. Once again, "The Girl I Left Behind Me" is prominently placed throughout. In the opening credits it counterpoints the more expected "Yellow Ribbon," and it later suggests, especially when it is played as Brittles reads the Custer casualty list and then goes to the graveyard, the wife that the protagonist has lost earlier. When Pennell's rescue mission departs from Fort Stark, traditional shots of moving columns are again underscored by this song, now rendered in a full-blown orchestral version. Composer Richard Hageman also skillfully modulates "Yellow

Ribbon" throughout, making it more noticeable as the film moves toward its conclusion. On their return from Cohill, who has been left to defend the position on the Paradise River, Brittles's troopers shuffle despondently into Fort Stark while the strains of the song play now in a slow tempo, in keeping with the general air of fatigue and failure. The same song appears in an even more muted rendition during the final raid on Red Shirt's camp, when Brittles lines up his troops for the charge and then again as he bids adieu to Cohill and Pennell to ride off into his (presumed) retirement. The transformation of this theme into a waltz when Brittles returns offers its most significant use in *She Wore a Yellow Ribbon*. The music suggests the resolution that the plot has achieved: just as the dance reintegrates the community around Brittles's success, so does the music proclaim that all the characters have found their proper niches.

Sergeant Rutledge attempts to repeat such musical virtuosity by means of its "Captain Buffalo" theme song (written by Mack David and Jerry Livingston). This lyric, which extols the virtues of the ideal black soldier (and which is explained by Cantrell to Mary over a campfire as Rutledge poses in the distance), delineates the hero and proclaims his special place among the other soldiers. As Cantrell says, the other troopers sing to make Rutledge feel better about himself; their slow rendition, thoroughly in keeping with the protagonist's difficulties, is offset by the up-tempo treatment this melody receives during the film's end credits. Unfortunately, Cantrell's explanation diminishes the song's effectiveness; it is almost as if Ford no longer trusts the audience to make musical thematic connections, and so makes such connections on the more overt, verbal level. *Sergeant Rutledge* has only this one song, and so the film stands, as do most of Ford's other later westerns, in contrast to the musically richer atmosphere of his earlier films.

Other predictable musical themes mark *She Wore a Yellow Ribbon* and provide it with a more interesting soundtrack. "Garry Owen," the theme so prominently associated with Custer, appears when Brittles's patrol first takes the field, emphasizing the rapid initial pace at which his column moves. This musical underpinning is then juxtaposed when Brittles's command is next shown slogging over the prairie on foot (in order to rest their horses) to the accompaniment of much slower, comic musical cues. During the burial of Trooper Smith, "Bury Me Not on the Lone Prairie" is followed by "Dixie." Thus, the music emphasizes the soldier's burial (which is finally saluted by "Taps") and then brings in a tune that would have been close to Trooper Smith's Confederate heart. The appearance of "Dixie" as a theme of reconciliation also reinforces the captain's chivalry in allowing a Confederate flag to be placed on Smith's coffin, as does also his speech over this fallen comrade. Brittles's own stature is musically hailed when his ride to review his troop for the last time is accompanied by "The Battle Hymn of the Republic," another frequently utilized tune in Ford's films.

The question of position or status within the cavalry community is central to both *She Wore a Yellow Ribbon* and *Sergeant Rutledge*. Captain Brittles and Sergeant Rutledge have completely identified themselves with the army, so that retirement and arrest represent assaults on their identities: to not function as a cavalryman is to have no serious being. Whereas Brittles's plight has been brought on by aging and army regulations, Rutledge suffers because of the "unnatural" power of racism. Brittles does not have to convince anyone of his ability as a soldier or a leader. Even Major Allshard, who argues against Brittles's going back to help Cohill and Pennell, sheds tears when the protagonist bids farewell to his troops. All that stands in Brittles's way are military regulations, which, by the final fadeout, prove to be humane rather than simply bureaucratic, transitory rather than determinative. Captain Brittles's permanent "home" within the cavalry is ensured when his long-awaited orders come through; significantly for both the man and the institution, Brittles, unlike the anxious Captain Collingwood (George O'Brien) of *Fort Apache*, never has to press to see that "justice" is done.

Rutledge, on the other hand, is under attack by the very institution and system to which he has pledged himself. The circumstantial evidence against him is coupled with the unspoken assumption that he must be guilty because he is black. This guilt connection is simply assumed by Colonel Fosgate and the other trial-board members during their card game, and it is overtly argued by the prosecutor, Captain Shattuck, during his summation. Thus, Rutledge not only must prove his legal innocence but also must demonstrate that he is capable of acting as a "civilized" (i.e., white) man. The title character must win his place within the military community, even though he has served it remarkably well for years. Rutledge is finally reduced to openly pleading his love for the cavalry, and only the trial's deus ex machina ending, in which the sutler Chandler Hubble breaks down, restores the sergeant to something like his former status. If anything, Sergeant Rutledge loves the cavalry more than Captain Brittles does, for he stakes not only his own present but also the future of his race on that institution.

Ford's two protagonists also illustrate the relationship between past, present, and future. Captain Brittles's visits to his wife's and children's graves clearly establish his allegiance to the past; however, he also lives actively in the present and strives to influence the future. Indeed, against a background of incipient Indian warfare brought on by Custer's defeat, only the aged captain seems to have any plans for stopping hostilities before they start. Brittles's subsequent elevation to chief of army scouts beautifully establishes how his character links the three levels of time: the glory of the present (symbolized by the ending dance sequence) combines with the protagonist's need to "report" to the past (the last graveyard visit) while a valedictory scene, in which the narrator extols the historical role of the cavalry, finds the captain conspicuously leading a column into the future.

Rutledge's world is more constricted, for the past represents humiliation and, in an ever-increasing irony, defeat for the protagonist. Rutledge, as a manumitted slave, holds no great reverence for his earlier life; in this sentiment, he is echoed by Sergeant Skidmore and many other members of the black 9th Cavalry. The protagonist's previous years of faithful service are largely overlooked by his white superiors (except for Cantrell), who approach the court-martial as an open-and-shut case of what any black man will inevitably do in certain circumstances. Thus, the court panel speaks of Rutledge as a good soldier without ever questioning what he is alleged to have done to Lucy Dabney; only Lieutenant Cantrell has made the significant connection that Rutledge's service as a good soldier means that he must also be a good man.

Through much of the film, Rutledge's concern is not with proving his own innocence but with not besmirching the reputations of the groups (military and ethnic) to which he belongs. He remains convinced that, since he is black, there is no way he can be exonerated given the "white woman" trouble in which he has become embroiled. Rutledge thus constantly talks (especially with the dying Corporal Moffitt) about the future of his race and continuously insists that his outfit make a good record within the white man's world, as symbolized by the cavalry. Whereas Ford's film regains its moral equilibrium with the confession of Chandler Hubble, the embrace of Mary Beecher and Cantrell, and the presence of Rutledge in the field leading the men to the strains of the film's main song, *Sergeant Rutledge* offers a more disjointed sense of time for its principal character. Captain Brittles manages to embody and preserve the past in the present, and so bring them into the future in *She Wore a Yellow Ribbon*; but Sergeant Rutledge finds no sanction in his past, and his present has to be seen as an ongoing test for the sake of the future.

Both films exhibit a dichotomy between their protagonists and their heroes. Captain Brittles has heroic moments, but most of the daring-do in *She Wore a Yellow Ribbon* belongs to Sergeant Tyree. This ex–Confederate officer functions as chief point rider, goes ahead alone to Sudro's Wells, and accompanies Brittles into the hostile Indian camp. Tyree also serves as an alter ego to the protagonist in their many conversations about military strategy and possible tactics. Tyree, like many others, has come west as a cavalry volunteer because his heart still belongs to the South's "Lost Cause." To link him further with Brittles, the film notes that Tyree attained the rank of captain within the Confederate cavalry, so that his military acumen stems not merely from his physical prowess but also from his experience in command. Tyree's motives remain quite apparent throughout; his own sense of loss is indicated by the death of Trooper Smith, his erstwhile Confederate commander. Like Brittles, Tyree has adjusted to a diminished emotional life in the present and contents himself with being a permanent bachelor whose bravery and expertise constitute his stock-in-trade; in essence, Tyree is Rutledge, though he is never called on to answer for what he is or what he has done. It is thoroughly appropriate that Tyree brings the news of Brittles's promotion to the latter; their dialogue in the symbolic reddish mist of evening characteristically includes the sergeant's comment that Robert E. Lee would have made another wonderful endorsement for the protagonist. In this remark Tyree comes as close as he ever does to expressing his feelings for Brittles; indeed, his comment about Lee is the highest praise that one real soldier (Tyree) can offer to another.

Brittles's response ("Wouldna' been bad!") shows his compassion for a former foe — a trait so sadly lacking in *Fort Apache*'s Owen Thursday. While the captain demonstrated such a feeling earlier, over the grave of Trooper Smith, his role as a reconciling figure within the cavalry community, in both military and romantic matters, links him to Kirby York (John Wayne) in *Fort Apache*. The partnership forged between Brittles and Tyree is symbolized by their conduct at Sudro's Wells, where they both act to relieve the Indian siege. In contrast, the young lieutenants of *She Wore a Yellow Ribbon* are clearly subordinate. They must either be told what to do when in the field (e.g., Brittles frequently reminds Cohill to take charge of the column) or be coaxed back into following the military life as a career (e.g., Pennell's initial wish to get to New York is offset by the camaraderie extended to him on Brittles's last mission).

Lieutenant Cantrell in *Sergeant Rutledge* appears initially more comparable to the subordinate officers in *She Wore a Yellow Ribbon*, albeit circumstances throw him into a command position similar to Brittles's. Just as Cohill and Pennell were enjoined by their commander to follow the Indians at the conclusion of the night raid in *She Wore a Yellow Ribbon*, so Cantrell's job consists of trailing marauding "hostiles" back to their reservation. The scale of action has also shifted dramatically in *Sergeant Rutledge*, for the Indian raiding party does not represent a full-scale frontier uprising but is merely a group out to "blood" its younger braves. As Cantrell notes on the train with Mary Beecher, there has not been any serious Indian trouble in Arizona Territory since Geronimo's capture. Cantrell's naiveté is, of course, brought out repeatedly: the Indians kill a stationmaster, a young man on the trail, and Mary's father before they are driven back to the reservation.

Unlike the more experienced protagonist and hero of *She Wore a Yellow Ribbon*, Cantrell cannot appraise the overall situation, even if he does show a sense of awareness when he muses over the unconcealed trail his Indian enemies have left. It is also obvious that Cantrell never considers that having Mary Beecher along on the patrol may serve as a deterrent to engaging the enemy. Brittles, on the other hand, who is aghast because his last mission has been hamstrung by the presence of Olivia and Abbey, always takes measures to avoid exposing these women to any direct danger. Cantrell is the apparent protagonist of *Sergeant Rutledge* because his actions connect the plot. He is the only one who finally fights for Rutledge, yet in Ford's overall scheme he pales beside the title figure both as a hero and as a leading character. In effect, Cantrell's outrage is the most noble and notable thing about him; his romantic longings for Mary Beecher ultimately reduce him to the stature of Cohill.

Rutledge's dual role within the film is muted because, however daring *Sergeant Rutledge* may have appeared to contemporary audiences, the dilemmas of its central character have been outstripped by later screen developments and social changes. If made today, *Sergeant Rutledge* would offer more extended and overt motivations for its main character; indeed, Rutledge would take up the bulk of screen time, and Cantrell would be reduced to a legal technician who saves the accused within the military's institutional framework. Rutledge's heroic status arises at the very beginning of the film when he rescues Mary from the three Mescaleros who have trailed him to the railroad station. This scene begins with Rutledge's strong, black hand across Mary's mouth, and that image lingers because Ford then cuts back to the courtroom. The sergeant's expertise as a soldier is shown when he is released from the handcuffs and takes charge of the firing skirmish line and, later, when he rides to the aid of the stricken Moffitt. Rutledge demonstrates his devotion to the cavalry life when he recrosses the river to alert Cantrell about the impending Apache ambush. The protagonist's ability to operate alone again links him to Tyree in *She Wore a Yellow Ribbon*: like the ex–Confederate, the ex-slave seems devoted to a life as a bachelor soldier, as further symbolized at Fort Linton with Lucy Dabney when Braxton appears as a kindly "uncle" figure. Indeed, Rutledge seems on the way to becoming another Quincannon, a figure who loves children and has "never done anything peaceably."

The trial clearly places the sergeant in the center of the narrative, and his impassioned climactic speech establishes him as the protagonist in the larger drama. On one level, *Sergeant Rutledge* is about uncovering the mystery of the deaths of Lucy Dabney and her father; on another, it explores the racism inherent in the society of Fort Linton. This second theme constitutes Ford's most extended criticism of the cavalry his films celebrate, for the taint of racial prejudice extends to the high command and, more ominously, to the women of the fort. The equivocality of these characters — whether it be that of Mary Beecher, whose protests about not noticing the color of Rutledge's skin are offset by her initial terror when he silences her at Spindle Station, or of Mrs. Fosgate, with her innuendoes about and raised eyebrows over the friendship between the central character and Lucy Dabney — symbolizes the depths to which such feelings permeate this military society. In such an environment, the histrionics of Captain Shattuck appropriately summarize community feeling. Given this emphasis, the central confrontation in *Sergeant Rutledge* is between the title character and the prosecutor, and the greatest dramatic moment in Ford's film occurs when the sergeant is so moved by Shattuck's charges that he declares that he has never been "a swamp-runnin' nigger!"

Rutledge's self-defense shows that he is both the hero and the thematic protagonist of the film that bears his name.

The heroines of both films also dramatize their different ambiances. Both women are novices who have either come or returned to western society only to be put off by its initially ruder ways. When Olivia Dandridge is first seen, her inexperience ("She ain't army!") offers distinct difficulties for the men in charge at Fort Stark. Her dismay when Lieutenant Cohill, under orders, refuses to let her go on a picnic with Lieutenant Pennell stands in the sharpest contrast to Philadelphia Thursday's conduct with Mickey O'Rourke at the telegraph wire in *Fort Apache*. Olivia's greatest mistake is encouraging the two young officers in their romantic pursuit of her — an attitude that, in spite of Brittles's remark that there is never anything wrong with embarrassing junior officers, strikes at the overall cohesion of the cavalry society. Olivia keeps Pennell on the hook in spite of her feelings for Cohill, also in contrast to Philadelphia and her open desire for Mickey.

Those around Olivia gradually educate her. Mrs. Allshard, who serves as the girl's chaperone during the ride to Sudro's Wells and who teaches Olivia through her talk of uprooted gardens and her unspoken devotion to her husband, is all that the ideal cavalry wife should be and is the most apparent of these influences. Abbey Allshard receives her ultimate sanction from Captain Brittles after she has assisted in the dangerous operation on Quayne. The protagonist thanks her as a "soldier," whereas he jokingly refers to Olivia as a "proper trooper" in much less serious circumstances before the patrol has begun. When Olivia makes her feelings for Cohill known, after her young rivals have almost come to blows on the night of Trooper Smith's burial, the older and wiser Brittles and Quincannon simply nod. Lieutenant Pennell, who has been coaxed back into army life by witnessing the death of the sutler Rynders, reaffirms military etiquette by being "an officer and a gentleman" and in acquiescing in the heroine's choice. Pennell's gentlemanly acceptance solidifies his position in the system, a status that is reaffirmed by his final actions and appearance at the dance-reception for the restored Brittles.

Mary Beecher's initial uncertainties about coming back to the West (after twelve years at an eastern finishing school) are deepened by what she experiences at Spindle Station and by the death of her father. While she is attracted to Cantrell during their initial train ride (enough to suggest that he will find a welcome at her father's ranch), Mary turns away from her cavalry suitor when she subsequently witnesses his treatment of Rutledge. Like Olivia, Mary is at odds with army regulations, albeit her dismay arises from humanitarian reasons rather than personal pique. If Mary initially reconciles the conflict between her sense of justice and the demands of military procedure by casting aside Cantrell's love, she sounds a more ominous note when she insists that Arizona is a worthless land and certainly a place not worth fighting or dying for.

Rutledge saves Mary from immediate physical danger, while Cantrell dispels the girl's gloom and dismay over the army and Arizona. By proving Rutledge's innocence, Cantrell shows Mary that military justice and mores are ultimately as humane as her own sympathies. Although the issue of the value of the Arizona land is never verbally resolved, the final scene between the reunited lovers clearly establishes that both of Mary's dilemmas have been eased. In overcoming her problems, Mary is never helped by Cordelia Fosgate, who offers the starkest kind of contrast to Abbey Allshard; indeed, these two characters never even speak in *Sergeant Rutledge*, let alone assume any sort of extended relationship, as their counterparts do in *She Wore a Yellow Ribbon*. In keeping with its more ambitious and ambiguous social themes, *Sergeant Rutledge* finds its heroine largely working through her own misconceptions alone, by means of what she sees and experiences. Mary, as someone who grew up in the West, presumably has less to learn than Olivia Dandridge, who, as more of an outsider, has to be shown and told what to do and how to behave.

She Wore a Yellow Ribbon and *Sergeant Rutledge* ultimately stand in sharper contrast to each other than do *Fort Apache* and *Rio Grande*. Despite their similarities in color and photographic style, as well as their similar plots, which center on missions into hostile territory rather than focusing on army post life, these two films exhibit significant structural and thematic differences. The protagonists' quests to hold on to their positions within the cavalry both end triumphantly, but the societies in which Brittles and Rutledge move are quite dissimilar. *She Wore a Yellow Ribbon* features a conventional plot moving through discernible stages. Such a linear arrangement enables Ford to mute the threat of a good man's being forced out to pasture by having Brittles spend much time as the teacher-father to so many of the other characters. The plot and Ford's thematic emphases both suggest a more idyllic worldview underlying *She Wore a Yellow Ribbon*; doing one's duty becomes a natural obligation in such a setting.

Sergeant Rutledge uses a more elaborate plot and stresses more troublesome themes, in keeping with Ford's own sense of how the contemporary world was changing. The theatrical staging of some of the film's flashbacks makes *Sergeant Rutledge* far less easy to interpret or to immediately enjoy; indeed, the plot's ambiguity is increased during the trial's summation scenes when events that have not been shown are mentioned. While familiar themes of apprenticeship and fidelity to duty are present, *Sergeant Rutledge* treats more pressing issues in its emphases on the pervasiveness of racism among seemingly good people and on how a man must struggle for freedom only to find it within himself at the end. The characters in *Sergeant Rutledge*, by giving voice to such concerns as the need to sacrifice in the present for the future, also reflect the greater unease that surrounds them. In this film we see Ford's cinematic genius working in revisionist directions that will appear even more noticeably elsewhere.

Chapter 8

My Darling Clementine and *The Man Who Shot Liberty Valance*

The surface unities of *My Darling Clementine* (1946) and *The Man Who Shot Liberty Valance* (1962) initially mask the great dissimilarities between the two films. While both present the taming of a town by ridding it of its outlaw elements through a cathartic gunfight, *The Man Who Shot Liberty Valance* critically reexamines and all but undermines many of the themes and values in *My Darling Clementine* by virtue of its more complex narrative structure. The relationship between the male leads is fragmentary on both the physical and psychological level in both films, with Ford's later film offering the more enigmatic and melancholy rendering of the "bonding" that is central as an organizing element in his other westerns. The director's increasingly darkened perception of human possibilities is presented in a significantly more stagey manner in *The Man Who Shot Liberty Valance,* so that it comes off initially as a more formal exercise than *My Darling Clementine.* The earlier film, with its linear plot, presents a more archetypal rendering of the West: it is a classic western in which the hero even leaves at the end. *The Man Who Shot Liberty Valance* uses its more convoluted plot to point up ambiguities that are easily resolved in the earlier film.

Ford deliberately calls attention to the similarities of these works in their credit sequences. Both films list their contributors on signposts; however, even the slight variations in these title designs suggest significant differences between them. *My Darling Clementine*'s credits all appear on a single post, down which the camera tracks. Such a movement reinforces the unity of the story that is to follow: from the opening of *My Darling Clementine*, all the elements are linked in a straightforward fashion. The credits for *The Man Who Shot Liberty Valance* start with the same signpost design; however, two notable variations are introduced. The individual credits are initially on separate posts, dominating the center of the screen but set apart, with no post to link them. Halfway through this sequence the credits appear against a solid

background, as if to suggest that much more troubled and insulated tone we experience at the opening of *The Searchers*. The wall design also points up the communication problems that beset so many of the characters in *The Man Who Shot Liberty Valance*; indeed, Stoddard's (James Stewart) having to reveal his past turns on the same notion, for the aged senator must expose a truth that lies behind a public facade he has maintained (for ostensibly good reasons) since his early days in Shinbone. The film's credits then revert to the signpost design, as if to imply that the world we are entering is a mixed and complicated one. At the same time, Ford's signposts foreshadow the introduction and manipulation of Stoddard's professional shingle — a symbolic object that is featured prominently throughout *The Man Who Shot Liberty Valance*.

The two films also exhibit similar musical patterns in their use of numerous traditional songs (sourced music) in place of lush or elaborate original underscoring. The songs and tunes of *My Darling Clementine* nearly always augment character relationships; however, these tunes are played so quietly in many instances that such patterns are not always readily apparent. Chihuahua's (Linda Darnell) singing of "Ten Thousand Cattle" and "The First Kiss" delineates her as the proverbial bar girl of the western film. At the same time, these songs resonate thematically, since the earlier tune is associated with the Earps on the trail, the rustling of their cattle, and the death of James (Don Garner). The second song sparks a confrontation between the singer and Doc Holliday (Victor Mature), the man she loves, when the latter urges that Chihuahua go someplace else to "squall [her] silly little songs." Later, the girl rationalizes her dalliance with Billy Clanton (John Ireland) and her acquisition of the incriminating Chingadera as the natural result of Doc's coldness.

The film's title song, most obviously used to accompany Clementine Carter (Cathy Downs), is heard earlier than her arrival. Appearing in a disjointed rendition as background to the Earps' initial entry into the wild, nighttime world of Tombstone, it suggests the order that they (and eventually the heroine) will bring about. The final idyllic and platonic meeting between Wyatt (Henry Fonda) and Clementine, now about to become the schoolmarm of the increasingly settled town, is also plaintively underscored by this tune to imply that there will be no coming back for the hero. Wyatt will be loving Clementine with regret for the rest of his life, just as the (unsung) lyrics imply. The use of "Shall We Gather at the River" during the celebrated church social-dance sequence is perhaps only to be expected, since this hymn was a favorite of Ford's and its lyrics convey the emerging group solidarity within the town and the larger community.

Opposite: Chihuahua (Linda Darnell) tries to console the estranged Doc Holliday (Victor Mature) as Mac (J. Farrell MacDonald) looks on in *My Darling Clementine* (20th Century–Fox, 1946). The gambler's indifference provokes the saloon girl into a fatal liaison.

The most important musical theme in *The Man Who Shot Liberty Valance* harshly offsets the more romantic (and borrowed) cue that is heard when feelings of love are uppermost. This somber main theme appears when Stoddard, Hallie (Vera Miles), and Link Appleyard (Andy Devine) arrive at the undertaker's to view Doniphon's (John Wayne) coffin and comfort the grieving Pompey (Woody Strode). Cyril Mockridge's harsh theme operates in conjunction with Alfred Newman's more romantic love theme to indicate changes between Stoddard, Hallie, and Doniphon. After Liberty Valance (Lee Marvin) has been killed, Hallie realizes her love for Stoddard on the literal level (to the accompaniment of Newman's music); and when Doniphon enters to see the embracing lovers and to announce that he will "be around," Mockridge's main cue forces out the softer music.

The injured Stoddard's initial entry into Shinbone in the back of a buckboard reveals the town to be a far less noisy place than Tombstone; at five in the morning we hear only one tired honky-tonk piano, whereas the noise in Wyatt's town went on all day and all night. Later in the film, the political convention in which Stoddard is nominated features a rowdy interlude in which a horse appears on the dais to the comic accompaniment of "Home on the Range." Ironically, Doniphon, who reveals the truth to Stoddard moments after this interruption, leaves the convention hall and passes a sign for Langhorn, the candidate whom Stoddard defeats. Doniphon, who had been conspicuously building a home for Hallie, has already burned part of it down so that, while he continues to live, he has lost whatever might have been his own "home on the range."

Alfred Newman's borrowed cue (taken from Ford's *Young Mr. Lincoln* [1939], where it most noticeably underscores a brief sequence between the protagonist and the doomed Ann Rutledge) works well in *The Man Who Shot Liberty Valance*, for it implies the death of a loved one and the regret that those who remain will feel. We first hear it when the aged Link takes Hallie to Doniphon's deserted ranch and she persuades him to pick a cactus rose from the garden. Hallie's feelings for Tom, as well as the nostalgia she feels for her home and her past, suggest layers of sentiment within her character; unlike most other Ford women, Hallie seems capable of having loved both men and now being aware of it. Her love for Doniphon is symbolized by the cactus rose — for her, he is the path not taken and the ultimate cost of all choices, whether communal or personal, centered on love or duty. *The Man Who Shot Liberty Valance* later uses Newman's cue to underscore Hallie's burgeoning affection for Stoddard, the man who wants gardens in place of wilderness, education in place of ignorance, and statute law in place of guns. We hear it when, after some brief and uneasy moments, Hallie persuades Ransom to teach her to read, when the girl importunes Pompey to find Doniphon so that Valance will not kill Stoddard, and when Hallie dresses Stoddard's wounds and confesses that she could not have borne his death. Such musical placements cleverly imply the complexities in Hallie's feelings toward the male leads; that such emotions are present but muted is in keeping with Ford's often subtle integration of form and theme.

Several camera angles and setups distinguish *My Darling Clementine*, which is probably the most interestingly photographed of Ford's black-and-white westerns. In accord with the tenor of the time and with the releasing studio (20th Century–Fox), *My Darling Clementine* features some of cinematographer Joseph McDonald's best work, replete with touches that lend this western an air of film noir. McDonald's expressive use of light and shadow, particularly when photographing Holliday's face, sets up later events, especially the deaths of Doc and Chihuahua. Holliday's persistent cough and symbolic handkerchief also make his demise all but inevitable; however, the numerous times in which he is photographed in darkness (as when he argues with Clementine on the saloon balcony, with the evening sun bathing her face and reflected off his, and when he tells Chihuahua how brave she has been during the operation, with his face almost completely in shadow) establish this plot development visually.

A characteristically Fordian sequence features establishing shots of the Clantons as they enter the Tombstone hotel during the rainstorm and confront Wyatt, who informs them he has lost his cattle and has become the town marshal. Each of the villains is shot in close-up or intimate two-shot, and their countenances are edited against shots of Wyatt to establish the confrontational relationship — a noticeable heightening of feeling when contrasted with the first meeting among the protagonist, Pa Clanton (Walter Brennan), and Ike (Grant Withers), when animosity ran in only one direction. *My Darling Clementine* also briefly focuses on the feet at the church social-dance, in a photographic signature that can be seen elsewhere in Ford's westerns.

While all is not technically perfect in *My Darling Clementine*, it contrasts photographically with *The Man Who Shot Liberty Valance* by constantly emphasizing the openness of Tombstone and the surrounding country, in contrast to the crowded and angular terrain and sets of Shinbone.[1] Even the climactic gunfight, which brings the Earps and the Clantons into more restricted quarters, begins with long shots that emphasize the length of Tombstone's main street. The gunfight in *The Man Who Shot Liberty Valance* takes place on a crowded, stagey set and is photographed to emphasize the angular buildings that jut into the street and the relative positions of the principals in the scene. Ford also emphasizes frontality in both films, although he is much more taken with such staging in *The Man Who Shot Liberty Valance* than in *My Darling Clementine*. This kind of composition results in a cramped or cluttered look because crowds appear to be at the very edge of the set nearest the camera. Ford's use of such frontality in *My Darling Clementine* is almost glaring; many of its interiors contain intervening objects (wooden bars and their railings or tables) that are prominently featured. When Miss Carter comes to the saloon to wait for Doc, she is seated next to the kitchen door, and in a reverse shot, we see Morgan (Ward Bond) and Virgil (Tim Holt) enter against a cluttered background at the truncated end of the bar. The same restricted pattern occurs during the town meeting to elect territorial delegates in *The Man Who Shot Liberty Valance*; in an unusual bit of staging, Stoddard runs the assembly while crowded under a stairway. At the same time, the citizenry of Shinbone seems to be crowded up to the edge of the scene; when the reverse angle is shown, with Doniphon seated prominently on the bar, these figures appear to be spilling into the audience's lap — an illusion that is reinforced by the ubiquitous pushing, shoving, and unseating that is done to this group both by Doniphon and, after his cyclonic entry, by Liberty Valance.

The later film also features crowded yet "flat" scenes during much of the territorial delegation meeting when cluttered benches and a highly prominent doorway convey the illusion that the debating conventioneers are caught in a much smaller place than they initially appear to be. The same spilling-over quality can be felt in Stoddard's classroom, where the assembled students appear huddled around the teacher's desk, and their formal recitations contrast with the appearances of the editor Peabody (Edmond O'Brien), Link, and Doniphon. Ford also photographs Doniphon in settings and lightings that make his fate all too apparent. The side door of Lars's (John Qualen) restaurant serves as one such frame as Doniphon leaves and Hallie stands silhouetted there in an early scene. Doniphon's "retreat" from the same exit after he realizes that Hallie loves Stoddard, and his lighting of a cigarette, with the attendant shadows on his face, make his demise predictable.

At the territorial convention, Doniphon appears bewhiskered and bedraggled after, ironically, having refused a nomination to it because he wanted to "get on" with his life with Hallie. He again strikes matches and, appropriately, emphatically closes the hall door so that some overly inquisitive females cannot continue to gawk at the proceedings. While Doniphon is rational enough to despise what he hears from the high-blown Starbuckle (John Carradine), he sits on a flight of stairs whose railing resembles, given his position, the bars of a jail cell. Doniphon's slouching in such a place, a posture he has never assumed before, reverses his earlier consistent appearances as an erect (and usually the tallest) figure in virtually every scene in which he is present. Indeed, one of the recurrent visual patterns that organize *The Man Who Shot Liberty Valance* thematically is physical positioning. The original men of the West, Doniphon and Valance, end up in horizontal positions, whereas the new man, Stoddard, starts in a prone position and gradually becomes vertical and dominant.

A more revealing bit of camera work occurs when Liberty and his "minions" (Lee Van Cleef, Strother Martin) enter Lars's restaurant, relieve some cowhands of their seats, and are then challenged by Doniphon over a dropped steak. On his initial entry, Valance leers suggestively at Hallie, who runs toward the reversed camera after it has tracked in on her for a close-up from another angle. Since this scene is the only time that the outlaw and the heroine are ever on screen together, such elaborate (for Ford) camera movements suggest a deeper level of meaning. The forward tracking of the camera, when combined with Valance's expression, enforces the implication of rape, as though the nefarious Liberty would not be above such behavior were he and Hallie alone. At the same time, the more overt verbal and visual linkages between Valance and Doniphon—Tom's comment that Liberty is the toughest man south of the picket wire "next to me," and Tom's drunken rage in the saloon and at his ranch after killing the outlaw—are well served by this earlier movement. In effect, Hallie subliminally sees the other side of Doniphon, the Liberty side, when Valance erupts into the restaurant on Saturday night. The outlaw's capacities for rape and murder suggest that the same qualities lie buried within Doniphon; and Hallie, by withdrawing so abruptly from Tom's mirror image at this juncture, makes her choice of Stoddard even more convincing. The character and thematic ambiguities within *The Man Who Shot Liberty Valance* are thus captured by such a noticeable camera movement.

These two films also share a common theme, but once again the classically simple plot of *My Darling Clementine* stands in contrast to the more complex and rambling narrative of *The Man Who Shot Liberty Valance*. Wyatt's celebrated speech at James's gravesite underlines the duty imposed on all the "good" people in Tombstone to create a livable civilization (i.e., a law-abiding town) out of a frontier wilderness. The means for the next generation to grow and flourish must be put into place by the sacrifices of the present generation—an activity to which Wyatt dedicates himself at his brother's headstone. Hallie and Stoddard embody the same theme in *The Man Who Shot Liberty Valance* when Tom brings a cactus rose to the girl and Ransom asks if she has ever seen a flower in a "real" garden. Later, on the train, they talk of having transformed Shinbone from a wilderness into a garden. However, this civilization theme is now extended to dramatize the losses that have accompanied its realization. Hallie has spent her life away from her roots (as has Stoddard, to a much lesser extent), while Doniphon's aborted life represents the archetypal sacrifice necessary to ensure that the advantages of civilization will be achieved. In this regard, Doniphon's unseen life after Valance's death counterpoints the line in *Stagecoach* when Doc Boone, after sending Ringo and Dallas to their idyllic home on the other side of the border, proclaims that the happy couple has been freed from civilization's "blessings." Ironically, the unshown middle years of Hallie and Ransom and their being childless further suggest that a civilized life is not without costs even for those who do not flee from it.

The Man Who Shot Liberty Valance also presents other themes more prominently and dialectically than does *My Darling Clementine*. Stoddard is the embodiment of formal, written law in the territory; on those grounds alone, he enrages Valance during the opening holdup when the frenzied outlaw insists that he will show the interloping Ransom "western law," in the form of a whip. Valance's ripping of the codebook before he beats Stoddard, and the protagonist's subsequent mending of and reading from that text over the washtub at Lars's, dramatize the obvious thematic clash between these figures. Doniphon's allegiance to the same kind of "law" as that followed by Liberty — he keeps insisting that the "pilgrim" Stoddard must master and carry a gun if he is to survive — places him within an older, violent society, one that Tom is attempting to perpetuate by building his ranch as a retreat from even the primitive civilization of Shinbone.

Doniphon's ranch raises the theme of finding a home, for the major characters clearly do not achieve the residential permanence traditionally thought to embody happiness. If Valance can insist, at the sign-in table before he enters the territorial delegate selection meeting in Shinbone, that his home is where his hat is, then, paradoxically, Stoddard lives the same kind of life once he has "killed" Liberty. The newspaper editor's (Carleton Young) account of Stoddard's fame as a senator and an ambassador points up the transient, political existence that Ransom and Hallie have lived; her wish to return to Shinbone exposes the emotional and physical fatigue she has experienced in leading that peripatetic life. Naturally, Doniphon is the character most acutely deprived of any home; for despite his remaining in one place, when he burns the addition to his ranch he destroys the only meaningful home he could ever have.

A third overt theme in *The Man Who Shot Liberty Valance* concerns apprenticeship and is at the basis of the relationship between Stoddard and Doniphon. The rancher constantly extols armed force as the only means by which problems can be settled in the territory; thus he undertakes, at Hallie's behest, to teach Stoddard to use a gun. However, this training sequence finally reveals the independence and jealousy of the two male principals, since Doniphon concentrates on embarrassing rather than instructing the lawyer and gets knocked down for his trouble. Doniphon abuses Stoddard by shooting paint cans so that they splatter over the attorney, as if to suggest that the only chance Stoddard has against Valance would be through trickery or flight. The connection between Doniphon and Liberty is also brought out during this scene, for in the street later, Valance shoots a water jug whose contents spill on Stoddard. The larger thematic and plot movements of *The Man Who Shot Liberty Valance* are, however, brought out more clearly by the lawyer's punch; indeed, Stoddard's eventual superiority is visually established as Doniphon falls into the dirt, for the first time, when Stoddard strikes him. After Valance's formal challenge to Stoddard, all Doniphon can suggest is that the lawyer flee, in keeping with his own jealousy over the impression that Stoddard has made on Hallie.

A much more ambitious theme within *The Man Who Shot Liberty Valance* centers on reading and the world of print. This emphasis is implied by

Valance's assault on the lawbook, but it comes even more to the fore when Hallie reveals that she cannot read and Stoddard, taken aback, offers to teach her. The subsequent emergence of Ransom's school divides the characters into print, antiprint, and aspirant-print people. Prominent among the first group are Stoddard and Peabody, who get elected to the territorial convention precisely because of their literacy. Hallie, Nora (Jeanette Nolan), and Pompey compose the last group; they want to acquire the rudiments of education, but they are thwarted by Valance and Doniphon. The outlaw and the rancher can both read, as seen when Valance sputters over newspaper headlines and when Doniphon takes note of what Stoddard has painted on his shingle. Doniphon assaults the world of print, and of education and civilization, when he storms into the schoolroom and orders Pompey to leave. Valance's most extended attack on the world of print takes place when he and his gang destroy the newspaper office. Liberty symbolically forces Peabody to "eat his words" by stuffing a newspaper down the editor's throat, representing the most overt visualization of this conflict. Surprisingly, Valance appears to be aware of the forces that will eventually destroy the kind of life in which he and Doniphon shine, more aware than is the rancher, whose animosity is always softened by his love for Hallie.

The gaseous orator Starbuckle, who opens his speech denouncing Stoddard and praising the cattlemen's sycophantic candidate, Langhorne, by throwing away an ostensibly prepared text (which is actually a blank scrap of paper), reveals the degeneracy that even print and education can assume when used for the wrong reasons. In this broadly drawn figure, and throughout the entire histrionic convention sequence, Ford shows the loss of nobility that accompanies the physical death of Liberty and the emotional demise of Tom. In the new society, individual character must take a backseat to machine politics. An even more unsettling note is sounded when Scott, the modern-day editor of the *Shinbone Star*, after insisting that he be given the "truth" about Stoddard's return to the town, casts the "facts" into a stove and declares that in the West, one prints the "legend" when popular images and the truth clash. As in *Fort Apache*, Ford once more has presented a richly paradoxical situation in which we are made aware of the ambiguities of the "written record" rather than just being given the "myth" (as so many standard westerns do). Such obvious dramatic irony supplies *The Man Who Shot Liberty Valance* with a thematic depth that casual observers all too often deny to westerns.

My Darling Clementine, by virtue of its linear plot, in which there are no digressions in time, does not place its characters in such equivocal positions. Wyatt's frequent remarks about the kind of town that Tombstone is (or should be) alert us to the formal movements by which he undertakes to make it civilized. If he does not succeed in ridding the town of "all evil" (a suggestion Holliday tauntingly advances during their first meeting), Earp does manage to liberate Tombstone from the Clantons. He also encourages Clementine to stay and become the archetypal symbol of eastern civilization on the western frontier — a schoolteacher — and Doc to once more practice medicine and so (hopefully) save the wounded Chihuahua. In bringing together the decent elements of the midnight world of Tombstone, in transforming these characters, Wyatt assumes the central civilizing role within the film. It is his organizational ability that leads to the night operation in which, for a time, the gaudy and raucous saloon world of *My Darling Clementine* becomes a hospital, and the brothel madam (Jane Darwell) and such figures as Mac the bartender (J. Farrell MacDonald) are changed into veritable angels of mercy. Wyatt also endorses the quest for civilization by his conduct at the church dance, when his desire to court Clementine comes into the open. In this sequence Ford visualizes the civilizing process by which a frontier man is transformed, through love, into a pillar of society. In *My Darling Clementine*, the embodiment of law and order participates in a communal dance and meal to endorse his legal (and thus civilized) values at an everyday level.

There is no such optimistic social unity in *The Man Who Shot Liberty Valance*, not only because the marshal of Shinbone is the innocuous Link but also because this film contains characters who are far too engrossed with their professional and personal roles to ever want to step into the public limelight as Earp does. Ford's enclosed and unnatural sets, as well as his systematic casting that makes the earlier Shinbone seem a hauntingly old place indeed, further undercut any unbounded celebration of the emergence of civilization on the prairie. If anything, in *The Man Who Shot Liberty Valance*, such an advance has become something that is talked about rather than acted on, except in the most incidental ways; print and statute law ultimately triumph over the other values of the past. Certainly the circular narrative, signaled by the film's opening and closing shots of a train entering and exiting in a semicircle, enriches the motive and character ambiguities that Ford wants to suggest. When Stoddard is pressured into telling why he has come to Doniphon's funeral, his narration begins with his walking off the screen to stage left, while the return of the story to the present finds him ensconced in a tilted chair that reminds us of Wyatt Earp on the hotel porch. Photographic dissolves assist both of these moments, as does a similar technique when Doniphon tells Stoddard what really happened on the night Liberty Valance was killed.

Doniphon's narrative-within-a-narrative characteristically begins with Tom blowing smoke, to effect the dissolve using a prop (a cigarette) with which he has been associated throughout the film. At the same time, Doniphon's flashback is essentially wordless, since he adds nothing, except one or two whispered instructions to Pompey, to what we have already heard. Thus, Doniphon's allegiance to a world of action is reaffirmed not merely by what he does in the flashback but also, and perhaps even more tellingly, by the way he presents his "version" of that past. While Doniphon feels guilty because he betrayed the western custom of man-to-man confrontation, he appeals to love

Ransom Stoddard (James Stewart) teaches civics and reading in *The Man Who Shot Liberty Valance* (PARAMOUNT, 1962). The inscription on the board ("Education is the basis of law and order") quickly becomes obsolete when the outlaws return to Shinbone.

(as the embodiment of civilization) to excuse such conduct. If he is a murderer, and if he can live with this because his feelings go deeper than any allegiance to an institution (such as Stoddard's to the law), he has done so because Hallie's well-being guided him. The relatively sparse embellishment that Doniphon's flashback does provide stands in sharp contrast to Stoddard's narrative, which opens with Ransom babbling on about why he originally came out west as a young man — just before his flood of words is halted by Liberty and the other robbers. As a kind of clue to Ford's intention to link these films, we hear Doniphon mention the deaths of "Old Man Holliday and his son" during the schoolroom scene in which he details the return of Liberty and his gang to the territory. This kind of verbal echo can also be found in the earlier film when Wyatt speculates, with the enraged and everdrunken Holliday, about all the men who would like to make their reputations by becoming the "man that shot Doc Holliday." Still another echo in *The Man Who Shot Liberty Valance* occurs when Peabody mentions that Stoddard is the first lawyer "west of the Rosie Buttes," in a line that resembles Doc's comment to Wyatt that Tombstone has the largest graveyard "west of the Rockies."

The topography or symbolic geography of the towns in *My Darling*

Clementine and *The Man Who Shot Liberty Valance* reveals the same contrasts that have been made thematically, photographically, and histrionically. The arrangement of Tombstone is not only more open but also more coherent; structures or locations are explored and utilized in a linear fashion, so that the narrative literally ends at the limits of the town in order to send Wyatt back into the wilderness from which he emerged at the beginning. If there is an obvious beginning and ending to *My Darling Clementine*, we never sense the kind of enclosed circularity that we find in *The Man Who Shot Liberty Valance*. Wyatt's initial appearance and his exit occur within and against much more linear patterns, especially the winding trail to the horizon down which he follows Morgan as Clementine watches at the film's end. In between these extreme points, the plot moves us into increasingly more intimate quarters (as if to suggest the greater rapprochement Earp achieves with his surroundings) and symbolic locales to dramatize the increasing conflicts between its characters.

The outskirts of Tombstone not only bring the Earps into conflict with the Clantons at the film's opening, but they also contain James's gravesite, the waystation at which Wyatt stops in his pursuit of Holliday, and the Clanton ranch, where Billy is laid out and Virgil is gunned down. Their brother's grave serves as an appropriate family icon for the Earps; Wyatt's speech at that site gives James's death the same aura that attaches to Trooper Smith's burial in *She Wore a Yellow Ribbon* and to the interment of the mother in *Three Godfathers*. During his pursuit of the bullion stage, Wyatt stops at the waystation to get fresh mounts, and after inquiring if Doc has just been there, he characteristically goes to a washbasin to neaten himself for the rest of his ride. The Clanton ranch, which is reduced to tight quarters in shots that emphasize a porch, a narrow dining room, and a bedroom, visually reinforces the coiled menace of Pa Clanton, who shoots Virgil in a doorframe as the latter unsuspectingly retires. The brief scene of the Clantons at dinner emphasizes the animal-like nature of the family members, who appear huddled over their plates in a suspicious manner, in contrast to the Earps, who dine often and in relaxed circumstances.

Scenes in Tombstone's main street subtly imply the control that Wyatt exerts over his environment; indeed, a daylight calm dominates once the protagonist and his brothers begin policing the place. This process is underscored when the hero instructs an arriving gambler to get some breakfast and take the next stage out. While Doc drives out a tinhorn cardsharp and is reprimanded for overstepping himself by Wyatt, Ford's protagonist discretely arranges that no such types will stay in Tombstone. Even at night, the town streets yield to silence, as seen when the Clantons invade that calm with Virgil's dead body and their challenge to Wyatt and Morgan. Noises can, of course, still be heard within the saloons of Tombstone, but even there Wyatt's influence is powerful, especially when he arranges for Chihuahua's operation.

The relative calm of the town is also stressed in two long shots. The first finds the actor Thorndyke's (Alan Mowbray) stage leaving to the accompaniment of muted saloon music, and the second features the long walk to the O.K. Corral by Wyatt and his cohorts on the brilliant morning of the gunfight.

Individual buildings within Tombstone are also used for larger dramatic purposes. The barber Mr. Bon Ton's (Ben Hall) shop serves to bring Wyatt and his brothers pell-mell against the rowdy night world of the town in the form of Indian Charlie (Charlie Stevens), who is shooting up a brothel across the street. While this sequence begins with some joking dialogue about what the Earps want and who they are, the barbershop takes on an added significance after Wyatt subdues the Indian and still insists on having a shave. At the protagonist's next visit to Mr. Bon Ton's, the proprietor remarks that he has another new chair coming in from the East (after he nearly injured Wyatt through his clumsy handling of a chair in their first meeting); this scene finds the marshal primping in accord with his new status and (subconsciously) in an attempt to impress Clementine.

The saloon-brothel in which Wyatt confronts Indian Charlie is featured throughout *My Darling Clementine*; indeed, we hear noises coming from it during the operation on Chihuahua, as though that part of the town's life could not be curtailed at any time. It is in this setting, with its largely Mexican audience, that the Clantons torment Thorndyke into a recital of the "To Be or Not to Be" soliloquy from *Hamlet*. After Wyatt knocks out Ike and brings the other Clanton boys under control, Pa Clanton emerges from a back room; he later whips his sons for their failure to kill Earp ("When you draw on a man, kill him!"). Although the prostitution angle is not pushed, the appearance of a raucous group of whores at the aborted theatrical performance counterpoints a later moment when the youthful hotel manager (Arthur Walsh) tells his chambermaids to be back in time for lunch. The presence of the madam and her employees at the theater, and their lusty cheering when they are referred to as "ladies," accords with the general informal tenor of that setting. Even in this theater, Wyatt emerges as the agent of civilization when he rescues the bedraggled impressario (Don Barclay) from being carried around town on a rail.

Doc Holliday's saloon is a much more important setting, for it brings the principals together, establishing and then reinforcing their feelings about each other. At the first meeting of Wyatt and Doc, the latter challenges the new marshal's purposes in Tombstone and then draws on the protagonist. Wyatt, when directly challenged to go for his gun by Holliday, pulls back his vest to reveal that he has no weapon ("Can't"); when Doc says that he can rectify that situation, he finds himself caught between the Earp brothers. Wyatt has Morgan's pistol in his hand before Doc can react and then slides the weapon back to its source, again before Holliday can react. Appreciating his precarious situation and realizing he has been outthought, Doc backs off, the first sign of his growing respect for Wyatt.

Later, this saloon serves as the background for the meeting between Doc and Clementine, for Holliday's dismissal of Chihuahua, and for the operation on the mortally wounded girl. Holliday's saloon is also featured when Wyatt, after discovering the Chingadera around Chihuahua's neck, comes looking for Doc and learns that the latter has ridden out on the stage. At this juncture, the Clantons emerge en masse from stage right, and for a moment, it appears that there will be gunplay between them and the lawman; however, Pa Clanton, thoroughly in character, contents himself with watching Earp leave and then demands a drink by thumping his quirt on the bar and ordering Mac about. After the operation, Wyatt and Mac salute Holliday with a symbolically shared drink; when the rejuvenated Doc leaves, Wyatt asks the aged bartender about love — in what has to be one of the drollest moments in any Ford western. Mac's matter-of-fact denial of any knowledge on that subject, though not spoken humorously ("No, I been a bartender all my life"), strikes a thoroughly deflating note to the love-lorn Wyatt's entreaty for generalized advice ("Were you ever in love?"). The verbal wit, relatively rare in Ford, is quickly dispelled when bullets ricochet off the saloon door as Wyatt steps out into the street.

Other significant settings in *My Darling Clementine* are the jail and the church, which are linked by John Simpson (Russell Simpson), who excuses the Earps' refusal of his invitation to the church dance by noting that serving the law is as important as serving God. Simpson's later willingness to fight beside Wyatt and Morgan reinforces this association of church and law that is bringing civilization to Tombstone. The unfinished church, with its fluttering American flag, remains Ford's outstanding symbol of the new, civilized life that Tombstone will enjoy after the climactic gunfight; it is appropriate that Clementine prompts Wyatt into taking her there. In this famous dance sequence, much attention is focused on the anonymous couples and groups to suggest that these larger social forces will eventually supersede the principal characters on this historical stage. The members of the band who play at this dance — John Simpson, the hotel attendant Dad (Francis Ford), and Mac — also suggest how the town's various social strata can come together and act as a unit.

The gradual enlarging of the crowd of dancers culminates when Wyatt finally builds up enough courage to ask Clementine to dance, after she has not too subtly cued him by clapping her gloved hands to the music. Once more, Ford's protagonist is relatively taciturn ("Oblige me, ma'am"), in keeping with his role as a man of action. The celebrated dance between Wyatt and Clementine, certainly the high point of their romance, is masterfully presented to suggest Wyatt's potential for life within the kind of settled community that the churchgoers want to supply for the town. Doc's dismay, signaled in the very next scene when he intrudes on Wyatt's meal with Clementine and the Simpsons, shows Holliday to be like Liberty Valance in that he recognizes the potential end of his way of life in the atmosphere bred by society.

Doc's and Clementine's rooms, which are across the hall in the hotel, are used at various points in their stormy relationship. When Miss Carter first comes to this floor, attended by Wyatt, she opens Holliday's door and wanders in briefly, noting various items. Wyatt appropriately stays just outside (in the door frame) and only comments that Doc's picture of Clementine is pretty. Doc's rejection of the eastern girl is later symbolized when Chihuahua opens Clementine's door to be certain that Miss Carter is packing; the saloon girl then goes to Holliday, who, in a drunken depression, suggests that they marry, much to the singer's delight. When this plan fades with Holliday's precipitate exit on the bullion stage, Chihuahua again confronts Clementine in the latter's room. After throwing Clementine's clothes on a bed, Chihuahua is cut short by Wyatt, who once more treats the saloon girl as though she were an undesirable element within the town. Wyatt confuses Chihuahua with an Indian both now and earlier, when he dunks her in a horse trough, a confusion that could point to a streak of racism within the marshal; but such a revisionist reading hardly seems worthwhile when we consider Ford's relatively enlightened views on such matters. Doc's room is also the setting when Holliday reveals his self-loathing by destroying (or at least shattering) his image in the mirrorlike framed diploma facing him. Doc has told Clementine that one of them must leave, and now, after getting away by himself, he begins to mock his past as a physician. Glancing at his face in the reflection, he hurls a glass at the diploma to shatter it and the disheartening spectacle of what he has become.

The saloon kitchen is where Doc and Clementine are together for the first time in the film. As she enters this cramped setting, Holliday and Wyatt are eating; after the marshal excuses himself, the girl and Doc discuss her decision to come to Tombstone. That Wyatt is next seen eating with his brothers simply reiterates the protagonist's sociability; unlike Doc, who rarely eats but always drinks, Ford's hero savors life with others. In the kitchen, Doc and Clementine engage in talk that includes his dismissal of her coming ("It was ill advised"), as well as her comment that trailing him from "cow camp to cow camp" has not been easy. Clementine's remark about Doc's past trail echoes Wyatt's earlier line that Holliday's path is one marked by gravestones from town to town.

Two other settings at the hotel also deserve attention. In the parlor, Clementine prepares to wait for the Sunday stage and is encountered by Wyatt, who enters whistling her tune. His statement that he thinks she is being hasty in leaving, and her retort that he does not understand a woman's pride, supply a fitting prelude to their going to church. This process is considerably abetted by the appearance of other characters, the chambermaids and the mayor, who pass through the same setting. The second hotel setting is the porch outside, which offers possibly the best stage for Ford's acute talent for creating "business." Here we see Wyatt exercising in his chair and surveying the town. Such a setup keeps the hero properly occupied, for his physical dexterity subconsciously asserts his larger mastery: if he can avoid falling from a chair despite his many gyrations, there can be no doubt that Wyatt will be able to handle the Clantons. Earp's mastery is further extended by his relative indifference to others while he sits in this chair: he dismisses the incoming gambler and pretends not to listen when Chihuahua threatens him with Doc's wrath. This latter scene further enhances the hero's prowess when Chihuahua throws milk over Morgan, an act that shows that her fear of Wyatt does not extend to his less-threatening brother. Wyatt's infatuation for Clementine begins when he rises from his comfortable chair at the first sight of her alighting from the stagecoach. This transformation from mastery to awkwardness is embodied magnificently by Fonda, who continues to appear awestruck throughout his many moments with Clementine.

Shinbone in *The Man Who Shot Liberty Valance* also has dramatically significant settings. Even an opening location like the telegraph office, with its telephone on which the neophyte reporter calls his editor, establishes the degree to which modern civilization has come to the town. The outskirts of Shinbone are immediately brought into play as Hallie and Link ride to Doniphon's ranch; their journey is contrasted by Stoddard's presence in the newspaper office, whose large picture windows set up a safe "distance" between his listeners and the wilderness/garden outside. "Out desert way" lies Doniphon's symbolically charred house, and the film ventures into this natural setting on only two other occasions. It is as though Ford, one of the most location-conscious of directors, suddenly decided that such visual opulence was detrimental to his later version of the West. Although some commentators insist that the director was simply running out of energy and so felt more comfortable manipulating stagey interiors and exteriors in *The Man Who Shot Liberty Valance*, Ford's ability to create memorable location shots is later reaffirmed in *Cheyenne Autumn*, which contains some of the most resplendent outdoor shots in all of his westerns.

In the earlier outdoor moment in *The Man Who Shot Liberty Valance*, Stoddard and Doniphon engage in the shooting lesson at the latter's ranch, a sequence that ultimately establishes how independent the lawyer can be. When we next return to Doniphon's ranch, it is after Tom has seen Hallie's love for Stoddard and has resolved to burn the addition to his house. His moments of madness are symbolized by his frenzied driving of the buckboard in a manner that echoes Holliday's fury aboard the gold stage, with his constant attempts to make the horses run faster. This association of Tom Doniphon and Doc Holliday is carried even further in the similarity of their dress: both men wear hats tied at the back of their necks when they are about to kill or be killed. Holliday is so attired when he comes to assist Wyatt against the Clantons. Doniphon appears dressed this way when he enters the territorial convention and symbolically throws away his life by explaining the truth to

Stoddard for Hallie's sake. Ford also links the two characters by showing their affinity for random violence. In many ways Doniphon acts like Valance; Doc, in his drunken rage after dismissing Clementine, shoots up his own saloon in an action similar to that of Indian Charlie in the brothel. Holliday shoots a lamp and starts a fire to suggest that he, like the drunken Indian, has an irreducible wildness that would inevitably bring him into conflict with the emerging civilization of Tombstone.

The streets of Shinbone, both before and after Valance's climactic death, appear to be crowded and twisted. The stagey central portion of the old town, with its saloons and Lars's restaurant, exhibits the same basic arrangement as does Tombstone. However, this setting is more confined in *The Man Who Shot Liberty Valance*, so that when the outlaw and his cohorts ride roughshod and shoot wildly after being faced down by Doniphon and Pompey, they appear visually trapped in a narrow street in which their horses barely fit. Once again, Ford's crowded frontal compositional style greatly contributes to this effect while his treatment of the later gunfight, especially Doniphon's account of it, continues to emphasize the enclosed atmosphere by placing Liberty within a triangle of fire in which he must die. The crowded nature of modern Shinbone is, perhaps, best caught when Hallie and Ransom proceed to the undertaker's through back alleys and narrow passages — a progress that compares strikingly with the spaciousness of Tombstone, in which Doc and Morgan appear for only a moment in a narrow alley on their way to the O.K. Corral. Stoddard's only extended moments in the town's old streets occur when he crosses over to Peabody's beaten body and then challenges Liberty; nearly all his other appearances find him in a buckboard, whether in the modern or the older town.

The railroad station provides our first view of Shinbone, in keeping with the modern character of the town. The platform, with the waiting Link and the unctuous Jason (Willis Bouchey), offers Ransom and Hallie's point of entry into their old life. As the senator will proclaim when he begins his narration to Scott and the others, the coming of the railroad has made a quantum difference between these men's lives and the lives of Stoddard and his contemporaries during the stagecoach days. At Junction City the presence of the railroad represents an additional step up for that town, a point that is stressed by the political manager (Robert F. Simon), who is eager to get Ransom nominated over Langhorn. Scott's newspaper office, into which the elderly Stoddard settles to do some political fence-mending while Hallie goes out to find the cactus rose, resembles a museum in that we see a picture of Peabody on one side of the frame as Ransom concludes his initial remarks to the editor, the mayor (Paul Birch), and the cub reporter.

When we go back into Shinbone's past, this building becomes the domain of Dutton Peabody, the man of words and eloquence. His drunken stand against Valance resembles what might have happened if, say, Doc Boone had

had to face Luke Plummer in *Stagecoach*. Peabody is an obvious later version of Boone, albeit without the latter's wisdom or compassion, since he is devoted to getting a story even at the expense of human sympathies. That Peabody lives alone, with only the drunken Doc Willoughby (Ken Murray) for occasional company, illustrates the flaw in this great wordsmith, and the two men being equally drunk once more points up the ambiguity with which Ford has structured the film. Valance's assault against Peabody stops short of actual murder, since Liberty expends most of his energies in destroying the machinery by which Peabody manufactures his words (the power of the press). While Valance's henchman believes the editor to be dead, Liberty is more concerned with destroying the physical setting than with killing Peabody. In this assault, we are reminded that the editor has allowed Stoddard to teach school and to hang his lawyer's shingle here, so that Valance is, of course, striking at Ransom and the law he represents as well.

Shinbone has two saloons. Although neither one is as prominent as those in *My Darling Clementine*, we first see the cantina into which Liberty's Mexican allies disappear, along with some convenient saloon girls, after they have returned from the robbery at which Stoddard has been left for dead. It is to this saloon that the drunken Peabody goes, with Link's aid, to get whiskey ("courage") before he is beaten senseless by Valance; and it is out of this place that festive music pours when the outlaw's corpse is removed in a buckboard after he has been pronounced dead by the hard-drinking Doc Willoughby. This setting also brings out Peabody's verbal power, for he gains admittance there because of his (drunken) promise to make Link into a figure resembling Buffalo Bill. The other major saloon in Shinbone carries more dramatic weight, although it too never approaches the importance of Holliday's establishment in *My Darling Clementine*. This second saloon in *The Man Who Shot Liberty Valance* is a mere backdrop, a place from which noise and drunks emerge with about equal regularity. The delegate election transforms this setting by making drinking briefly off-limits, but once the selection process has been completed, the saloon returns to its primary function, much to the relief of the parched male citizenry.

Liberty Valance's death is foreshadowed by his actions in this saloon before he goes into the street to face Stoddard. Ford deliberately imbues this sequence with echoes from *Stagecoach*; like Hank Plummer, Liberty is shown playing cards and winning with the famous dead man's hand (aces and eights). Link, searching for Doc Willoughby to help the battered Peabody, notifies Liberty that Ransom is waiting outside. Willoughby taunts Valance with the prospect of the day when he will be called in to pronounce the outlaw dead, and their exchange of money harkens back to Liberty's earlier actions in Lars's restaurant. Link, surprisingly, stands up to Valance by asking the outlaw to show mercy to the inexperienced Stoddard (who, according to the portly sheriff, couldn't shoot the hat off his own head); however, Liberty quickly opines that any shootout will be a matter of self-defense. Shouting to the crowd to bear witness to this claim, Valance rises and goes to the bar, where he takes a preparatory drink. As he moves there, Liberty puts his chips into his hat, just as Wyatt did before he moved down the length of the bar to confront Doc for the first time. Valance, even more tellingly, repeats a gesture of Holliday's after he does not elicit any enthusiasm from the crowd for his "legal" explanation of what he is about to do. When one gambler fails to respond, Liberty knocks off his hat, in a reprise of the way that Doc struck the offending cardsharp in his saloon. Valance, however, knocks off the gambler's hat as a means of intimidation rather than confrontation, and significantly, he does so from behind, underlining his villainy.

When Doniphon enters this saloon, after he has murdered Liberty, the atmosphere is rife with accusations and threats as Valance's accomplices insist that Stoddard be lynched. Once again, the citizenry appears passive in the face of this verbal tirade, so that it remains for Doniphon to step in when the noise disturbs his own somber mood. He has come there ostensibly to drink himself into oblivion because of what he has just done, as well as witnessed at Lars's, but he is still not about to allow Valance's "myrmidons" to reassert their sway over the town. As a means of exorcising them and some of his own bottled feelings, he turns on Floyd (Strother Martin) and hurls him into the street, in the same way that the bartender (Jack Pennick) tossed out an unruly drunk to the delight of some mocking women earlier. Doniphon then turns to Reese (Lee Van Cleef), who represents a much more worthy adversary, if only because he has checked Valance on two occasions (and because we have already seen Doniphon kick Floyd out of the way during the earlier confrontation with Liberty). Reese attempts to draw his gun, but before he can unholster the weapon, Doniphon has coldcocked him with his own pistol; this confrontation literally repeats scenes in *My Darling Clementine* when Wyatt, in rescuing Thorndyke, lays out the cretinous Ike and, later, saves the drunken Doc from himself.

At this juncture, however, the situation becomes more ambiguous in *The Man Who Shot Liberty Valance*. Law and order are asserted (as they were in *My Darling Clementine*) because of what has been done; however, their embodiment in the suddenly swaggering Link remains comic, especially when he is struck by a swinging saloon door. At the same time, Doniphon becomes increasingly crazed and hostile; he fights against the racism that prevents Pompey from joining him in the saloon, in a nice reversal of his earlier action when he prohibited the black from attending school. He throws a glass against an offscreen mirror, as if to shatter his own image in the same way that Doc did in his room. Then Doniphon throws money about, to pay for his drinks and to stir the house band into action, in gestures that once more recall the dead Liberty. Tom's exit is complete when he pushes Link into a door, whose glass promptly breaks.

Lars's restaurant is the most featured setting in Shinbone, for within it Stoddard is nurtured both physically and emotionally. His couch in one corner takes on greater symbolic importance as the film proceeds, while the actual kitchen, with its washtub and skillets, serves as a veritable atrium for much of the action. Ford's ensemble style works to good advantage in these scenes, particularly after the confrontation between Valance and Doniphon during which Stoddard has been tripped up. The enraged Ransom goes to his couch while the other characters attempt to comfort him in various ways: Hallie through compassion; Doniphon through reassurance; and Peabody through an impulsive challenge. Stoddard's response is, of course, to accept the editor's offer to hang his shingle in public view, a choice that he insists he will not have to back up with a gun. The kitchen setting achieves further significance because Tom and Hallie meet only within its cluttered quarters, as if to show that their "love" has never gotten to any more serious or intimate stage.

Peter's kitchen is also where Link, the public embodiment of law and order in Shinbone, most often cowers from Liberty and lives "on the cuff" as comic relief. Stoddard's position in Shinbone is further symbolized by his doing dishes for the Ericsons as a matter of honor, a sense of debt, and a feeling of gratitude that he apparently does not feel toward Doniphon, the man who initially supplies him with credit. Stoddard continues to work as a dishwasher after he hangs out his legal shingle and is elected a territorial delegate; indeed, his dalliance over a washtub constitutes the immediate reason he does not leave Shinbone on the night he is to face Valance. Stoddard subconsciously cannot leave Hallie because staying contradicts the wishes of Lars and Nora, who urge him to go.

The dining room provides the backdrop for the central confrontation between Valance and the emerging civilization of Shinbone, as defended by Doniphon. The outlaw's rambunctious entry is followed by Stoddard's emergence carrying Doniphon's steak. A close-up of Liberty's whip from Ransom's angle of vision symbolizes both men's feelings; the camera tracks away from that object in Valance's hand and thus nicely balances, by reversing, Liberty's earlier movement toward Hallie. As Stoddard tries to brazen his way past the mocking Valance and is sent sprawling, Doniphon moves into the frame with the remark that his steak is the one that has just hit the floor. The rancher and Valance then spar over who should pick up the dirty meat, a verbal confrontation that barely disguises their allegiance to guns as the basis of law. When Valance insists that Doniphon is outnumbered, Tom calls the outlaw's attention to Pompey in the kitchen doorway with his cocked rifle. Tom has managed to get Liberty into the same situation that Wyatt maneuvered Doc into during their first meeting in *My Darling Clementine*; however, unlike the principals in the earlier film, Doniphon and Valance never have a traditional, western face-off. Whereas Wyatt confronted Doc, proved to be the better man, and gained Holliday's allegiance, there is no such classical or therapeutic fight in *The Man Who Shot Liberty Valance*. Stoddard rises between the quarreling westerners, holding the steak and asking a terrible question ("Is everybody kill crazy?"), which only temporarily checks the symbolic antagonism of two men caught by the emerging civilization around them.

Given its more traditional plot, *My Darling Clementine* makes more obvious use of symbolic objects to advance its narrative. James's Chingadera (bought for his fiancée in California) serves as a veritable "MacGuffin" to establish who has committed his murder and how Wyatt solves that crime. Ford characteristically avoids an overt presentation of James's death, for it is the remaining brothers' reactions that are most important. By placing the Chingadera on Chihuahua's neck so that Wyatt can find it there, Ford creates a final bonding between the marshal and the gambler. Wyatt's subsequent pursuit of Doc derives from allegiances to law and family, and their sudden gunfight on the trail serves to unite them. Indeed, if Doc feels he no longer has any real physician's skill after the death of Chihuahua, he refuses to abandon his other identity as a fighting man and friend to Wyatt.

Doorways also carry symbolic weight, as seen when Wyatt enters the mayor's room to claim the vacant marshal's job and then emphatically slams the door after he has accepted the position. Ford's intention here seems patent enough — the slammed door marks a stage in the hero's life, an irrevocable commitment. Holliday bursts through the doors in his saloon on his initial appearance (and his confrontation with the tinhorn gambler) and later when he wants to challenge someone because of his disgust at the course his life has taken. The doors in the hotel rooms are also manipulated to suggest Holliday's ultimate inability to fit into society; significantly, Doc never enters Clementine's room, but she is seen in his. The swinging doors of Doc's saloon are also featured when Wyatt goes through them in a euphoric mood only to be shot at and have Virgil's body thrown at his feet.

The central characters in *My Darling Clementine* are surrounded by objects that become symbolic identifications. Pa Clanton's whip is seen when he first appears and when he uses it to intimidate his sons and Mac. We also see the old man slouched in chairs, both on his ranch and at the corral, as if to distinguish him from the hero. Wyatt's chair and the ease with which he manipulates it place him in another category, as does the graceful slouch he assumes when playing poker in the saloon before Holliday's entry. The hero is also characterized by his hat, which he places on his head carefully after his Sunday-morning session with Mr. Bon Ton. At the theater Wyatt has to dodge a hat thrown by an irate spectator; he gracefully catches and returns it as he struggles with the impresario and listens to Dad's message about the beleaguered Thorndyke. That thespian begins his recital from *Hamlet* only after he has thrown off his hat melodramatically, and this same casting off of one's hat before action recurs when Wyatt casts aside his hat and asks Clementine to dance.

The hero is also associated with the badge that he accepts when he takes over as "Mr. Law and Order." This symbol is temporarily worn in his belt during the gunfight, which both Wyatt and Morgan define as a matter of family honor; at the same time, Earp carries warrants for the Clantons, so that his feud is sanctified by the larger institutions of law and society. Holliday is symbolized by the mirror (in the form of a framed diploma) that he breaks when full of self-loathing, by the ubiquitous handkerchief that lends him a certain dainty as well as dying air, and by the sack of coins that he hurls at Chihuahua as he rushes out of town. Throwing money and appearing with his hat tied back on his neck links Holliday to Doniphon and Valance in *The Man Who Shot Liberty Valance*, thus establishing that each of these characters has become anachronistic in the new emerging West.

Symbols underscore the coming of civilization to Tombstone. The frequent long shots of pioneer wagons establish the melting-pot nature of the town. Whether in Thorndyke's exit or Clementine's entry, stagecoaches represent a lifeline between Tombstone and the outside world. The juxtaposition of the appearance of the heroine, the ringing of a dinner bell, and Wyatt's dismissal of the incoming gambler symbolically tie the stagecoach to the advancement of civilization, femininity, and law and order. Doc's furious ride out of Tombstone — motivated by disgust with himself, Clementine's appearance, and Wyatt's reaction to the eastern girl — uses a stagecoach to dramatize the character's rage, as Holliday cannot get the horses to run fast enough.

The headlong course of this stagecoach, with its dusty wheels surging through the desert, masks the world for Doc and stands in the sharpest visual contrast to the images of Wyatt in pursuit through Monument Valley. The fortuitous appearance of a later incoming stagecoach at the O.K. Corral offers yet another visually masked sequence as Ike challenges Wyatt and then dies when the marshal fires from out of the dust that has been raised. The larger historical confrontation between the settlers and the wilderness is caught in the scenes of wagons moving past the outskirts of Tombstone, presumably bound to new lands and the promise of independence. Buckboards represent the civilized people of the town, for in such vehicles we meet John Simpson and we see the Earps riding out to visit James's grave. The initial appearance of Pa Clanton and Ike in a buckboard is the only time they are seen in such a vehicle, so that its later association with civilized characters underlines the emergence of Wyatt as a force in the town.

The Man Who Shot Liberty Valance does not rely on objects to carry its immediate plot in the same overt ways. Within this film, Liberty's whip represents his authority and his inability to act in a civilized fashion in the midst of an emerging society. Valance uses this object to beat Stoddard senseless, and it is only Reese's wrestling Liberty away from the prone protagonist that prevents murder at their first meeting. The relationship between Valance and

Stoddard is next dramatized by the close-up of the whip on the restaurant table immediately before Ransom is tripped by the outlaw. Liberty also uses his whip during the choosing of delegates when, after nominating himself, he waves it at the assembled "sodbusters" to remind them that they will not be as brave when they have separated and gone home. Here the villain's whip is juxtaposed to the makeshift gavel that has passed from Doniphon to Stoddard during the meeting. Thus, the gavel, an obvious symbol for law and order, wins out over Valance as the townspeople elect the attorney. In the saloon, after Liberty's death, Floyd swings a rope as he urges that Stoddard be hanged, and his striking of a table with the lasso symbolizes his attempt to stand in for Valance. The crazed outlaw's assumed status is, however, quickly cut out from under him when Tom throws Floyd into the street.

Doniphon is symbolized by the many cigarettes he lights and the matches he strikes; although such business seems standard, Ford clearly manipulates these objects and actions to foreshadow how the westerner will destroy his ranch and any hope for a future with a "home" in it. Doorways are also prominently associated with the character at those times he leaves Hallie and, especially, at the territorial convention. There, Doniphon jerks the door closed on some gawking women similar to the ones seen earlier laughing at a drunk in Shinbone. Thus, Doniphon imposes decorum on the political proceedings, which, until his arrival, have been supplying delight to these busybodies. The rancher also reasserts a traditional male prerogative by showing that politics is serious (i.e., manly) business; indeed, even the henpecked Colonel Fosgate of *Sergeant Rutledge* could temporarily clear the courtroom when female noise became too much for him to stand.

Entering the convention hall, Doniphon strikes a match on the door he has just closed and lights a cigarette, actions that visually reprise his last leave-taking of Hallie and that look forward to his narrative that enlightens Stoddard. In essence, the match and the cigarette symbolize that Doniphon becomes extinct in Hallie's world. Tom, by virtue of ridding Shinbone of Liberty, has made himself superfluous: his only talent (gunfighting) has become anachronistic in the world that Stoddard and the new, politicized citizenry are building. When Doniphon follows Ransom, after the latter has bolted out of the hall, he again closes a door with decided emphasis to separate himself and the lawyer for their final confrontation. The ensuing discussion, which leads to the flashback within the flashback, reveals how Stoddard loathes basing his career on his (alleged) killing of Valance; interestingly enough, Ransom charges back into the convention, and so assumes the same double life that Doniphon has taken on, only after he is assured that he did not kill Liberty. If Doniphon can live with being a murderer, Stoddard can live with being a hypocrite; thus, each man reconfirms his love for Hallie by surrendering some part of himself for her happiness. Stoddard's actions are, of course, sanctified by considerations of public good, whereas Doniphon's are equated with a more primitive and "noble" morality. Tom's exit from the film is also visually and symbolically rendered, for we last see Doniphon as he walks past election posters for Langhorn, suggesting that he too, like the candidate who ultimately fails, has become a thing of the past.

Stoddard is initially symbolized by the lawbook that he has brought to the territory and that Valance attempts to destroy. If Ransom is a walking personification of codified (i.e., civilized) law in a society whose major representatives are set against it, the importance of this object changes after the film's opening scenes. All that Stoddard ever seemingly gains from subsequent readings of his mended lawbook is the knowledge that Hallie cannot read or write; indeed, his discovery of statutes that will allow Link to arrest Liberty consistently runs afoul of the de facto powers in Shinbone. Thus, although the lawbook epitomizes the de jure allegiances and procedures that accompany civilization and social compromise, Ransom must put it aside to confront Valance in a more meaningful western way. The same process is reemphasized by the shingle that Stoddard paints shortly after he has recovered from his beating by Liberty. Hanging this shingle outside Peabody's office coincides with Stoddard's returning with the names of new voters and teaching a class in civics. After the dismantling of the newspaper office, Ransom finds his shingle hanging precariously, as Valance left it. In his rage at what has happened to Peabody, and as a sign that he will finally fight Valance with the means (the gun) that men of the West understand, Stoddard tears down his shingle as he announces to Link that he will be waiting for the outlaw. Thus, Stoddard has become a man of the West after holding out against the warnings of Doniphon and the tauntings of Valance; to create the kind of civilization he wants, Ransom must use the very means that he sees as antithetical to that civilization. Naturally, this larger irony is compounded because Stoddard must base his new civilization not on his own actions but on those of Doniphon, who violates his own older code by bushwhacking the outlaw.

As we have seen, Stoddard is also prominently associated with the couch in Lars and Nora's kitchen; this serves as his first resting place after being brought in from the trail. His delirious efforts to get up from the couch, motivated by his obsession to get even with Valance through legal channels, lead to Nora and Hallie's initial ministrations. At the same time, Ransom's real awakening is symbolized by his reaction to Doniphon, who, appropriately enough, towers over him in the same way that Valance did earlier. For a moment Stoddard is startled, as though he has mistaken one man for the other; this hesitation brilliantly suggests Ford's linking of Doniphon and Valance. Indeed, it is only natural that the neophyte Stoddard would confuse such men, who live by the gun in a world where personal prowess represents the only workable kind of "law." The love between Hallie and Ransom also develops around this couch. Stoddard retires there after his angry confrontation with Valance and Tom over the spoiled steak, and Hallie goes to him.

Later, after Valance has been killed, Stoddard again rests on the coach to have his wounded forearm bandaged by the tearful Hallie, who now confesses her love. This scene climaxes when Doniphon enters, sees the affection between them, and beats a hasty and bitter retreat.

In yet another symbolic gesture, Ford summarizes the major plot movement in *The Man Who Shot Liberty Valance* by having Stoddard erase the school blackboard, which contains a statement on the connection between education and civilization. In essence, once serious physical danger threatens, the tools of civilization — education and the written law — are helpless and must be forgotten. In Stoddard's abandonment of the legal way and his assumption of the personal, western way to stop Valance, this erasure marks a distinct step. At the same time, Stoddard's action upsets Hallie, who has made a choice between the lawyer and the rancher. Her dismay at the collapse of the school and at Stoddard's resort to arms reinforces her role as the feminine embodiment of civilization à la Clementine Carter. Indeed, the erstwhile waitress blossoms within the schoolroom, and in the tender care she exercises while picking up after the abrupt class dismissal we see the same understated visual love that occurs when Martha Edwards caresses Ethan's coat in *The Searchers*. Earlier, Hallie rings the school bell in Stoddard's ear, dramatizing both the girl's dismay at his tardiness and her own sense of organization.

Hallie is anything but a helpless female; indeed, she is in total command, whether cutting through Peabody's persiflage on where the cutlery should be placed or taking the order of the stuttering Kaintuck (Shug Fisher), whom she humors. We see this same practicality when Hallie learns that Stoddard is training for a potential showdown with Liberty. Hardly has she become aware of this development from Peabody than she appears on a porch shouting for Doniphon; against this setting, Hallie recalls the abiding wives and lovers of *Fort Apache*, *She Wore a Yellow Ribbon*, and *Rio Grande*. Liberty's death is also brought on by Hallie's intervention: when Ransom goes into the street, she urges Pompey to run and get Tom. In an interesting verbal aside, Pompey informs Hallie that Doniphon is down the street playing cards — an activity that again links Tom with Liberty. While we never see Doniphon playing cards (and we wonder where he could be playing, since Valance is in one saloon and the other is full of Mexicans), it is surely appropriate that the rancher, who is about to exorcise the outlaw by the latter's means, should be so engaged.

Ford also imbues the emerging civilization of Shinbone with numerous symbols that relate to travel. The train, of course, puts us immediately into a later historical time than that of either *My Darling Clementine* or of the internal narrative of *The Man Who Shot Liberty Valance*. The railroad, which Stoddard insists has changed so much, makes Shinbone similar to the more politicized Junction City that we see at the territorial convention. The presence of a telephone in the railroad station office further underlines the passing of the frontier. By virtue of their circular entrance and exit, the film's opening and concluding scenes remind us that the railroad has made possible the public life of Ransom and Hallie, the life that took them away from Shinbone and their "roots" in order to bring a garden out of a wilderness.

Within Stoddard's flashback, stagecoaches and buckboards take over, as seen when Ransom dusts off an old coach before he relapses into recollecting. Ford then uses this vehicle to effect the transition to the past in which Liberty and his band stop the stage. The artificiality of this night setting further underlines the symbolic and figurative nature of what Stoddard relates; indeed, Valance's archaic diction ("Stand and deliver!") and Doniphon's costume hearken back to historical and cinematic pasts. The outlaw speaks like an eighteenth-century highwayman, whereas the rancher looks like a movie hero of the 1920s, a veritable reincarnation of the character Harry Carey played so many times for Ford. Buckboards also reinforce the circular patterns of the plot, for one brings the bedraggled Stoddard into Shinbone and another removes Valance's corpse along the same street, albeit out of the opposite side of the frame and the town. Buckboards are also featured when Stoddard returns from his political and business canvass and when he rides out to practice with a gun, as well as when Doniphon returns to burn down the "future" at his ranch.

Still other objects that symbolize civilization include the pin that the frightened passenger (Anna Lee) gives up during the stagecoach robbery; it is Valance's insistence on the surrender of this souvenir of the woman's dead husband that moves Stoddard to challenge the outlaw. A picture of Dutton Peabody is conspicuously featured in the office of the *Shinbone Star* as a token of respect for the past; oddly enough, the town remembers the man who recorded its past news while it seemingly has forgotten Doniphon, the man who ultimately made it possible for the town to exist at all. In this ironic juxtaposition, which is signaled when the new editor, Scott, cannot place Doniphon, Ford once more comments on the nature of recorded history. Thus, *The Man Who Shot Liberty Valance* suggests that written history often ignores, or never even recognizes, the true agents of social change.

Numerous other symbols delineate relationships between the principal male characters in *The Man Who Shot Liberty Valance*. Tom Doniphon's coffin, a stark and cheap pine box supplied by the county (and out of which the undertaker will make no money, as he reminds Stoddard), symbolizes the relationship of the male leads. The survivor Stoddard ironically tries to reimpose the past by insisting that Doniphon's boots and gunbelt be restored. When Link notes that Tom hadn't carried a gun for years, we not only are reminded of the inroads of civilization in Shinbone but also are prepared for the eclipse of Doniphon's heroic way of life in Stoddard's recollected flashback. The last shot of Tom's coffin, with Hallie's cactus rose adorning its lid, illustrates the emotional ambiguities felt by the major characters in *The Man Who Shot Liberty Valance*. The past may die physically, but it remains alive emotionally to guide the feelings of those who survive.

Within the lawyer's story, Ford deftly juxtaposes the use of lamps by Stoddard and Doniphon to suggest their paths diverge. Ransom carries a lamp into Peabody's office after the editor has been beaten, and the light seems to spur him to face Valance. Stoddard has been an intellectual light to the people of Shinbone, both as a teacher and as a politician, but he now decides to abandon his civilized ways in favor of gun law. Doniphon uses a kerosene lamp to burn the addition he has built for Hallie, so that the light becomes a symbol of destruction for him. Having both characters use such objects at critical moments suggests that civilization, in the form of Stoddard, has swept Doniphon under and destroyed the rancher's future. The relationship between Valance and Stoddard is caught up by the lawbook that the outlaw mutilates and that Ransom later patches up. This juxtaposition is also reinforced by Valance's assault on Peabody, yet another representative of the print culture that Liberty despises. Although the outlaw can read, he does not want a world in which that skill ultimately governs, in the form of codified statute law.

Liberty and Doniphon are further tied together by the hats they wear at haphazard angles to reflect their feelings. The outlaw's hat is often pushed up on his forehead, as though Valance were challenging social decorum by his very dress. The importance of hats is further implied in an early scene when the obsequious and cowardly Link, who has managed to avoid any direct confrontation with Valance over the holdup and then has received yet another meal "on the cuff," gets his hat knocked off by Doniphon and then kicked by Hallie. Whereas the girl's action arises from frustration with the sheriff's lack of concern for law and order, Doniphon's movement foreshadows the moment when Liberty knocks off the gambler's hat in the saloon in order to reassert his dominance. Once again, Ford cleverly and subtly links Doniphon and Valance by suggesting the latter's traits in the former. When Doniphon realizes that Hallie is no longer his girl, he appears hatless (during the burning at his ranch) and then dressed in a manner that resembles both Liberty and the distraught Holliday of *My Darling Clementine*. Thus, Tom's headwear delineates his mental state, for he has been conspicuously neat until this point. That he has changed to a black hat after wearing a white one may also be suggestive, if not overly conventional. In Valance's final appearance, as a corpse being hauled out of town, his hat is thrown contemptuously after his body by one of the crowd.

Doniphon and Liberty are also united by their disdain for money; indeed, both men are shown dropping or throwing money in public. Valance taunts Doniphon by urging the latter to have a steak on him at the same time that he drops coins on the floor of Lars's restaurant. Valance's initial insistence that Ransom pick up the spilled dinner is checked by Doniphon's insistence that the outlaw pick it up ("I said you, Liberty. ... You pick it up"). When Ransom throws the steak back on the plate after rising from the floor, he diffuses the immediate cause of the quarrel without cutting the tension between the two antagonistic westerners. Valance then sprinkles coins on the floor to challenge Tom to pick up the money and, thus, to do physically what Tom has just insisted Liberty must do. The outlaw later trades insults with Doc Willoughby in the saloon by means of money. When the outraged physician proclaims that he awaits the day when he will be called to tend Valance, Liberty contemptuously throws him a coin and chortles about paying for such service in advance. Significantly, Willoughby throws the coin back at Valance; although the outlaw laughs, their exchange prepares us for the postmortem scene in which the doctor will announce the villain's death. Doniphon's final appearance in the same saloon after he has gunned down Valance finds him hurling money at the band and urging them to play as he lunges drunkenly out the door.

Ford further links these two westerners by the "gunfights" they have with Stoddard. The confrontation between the lawyer and Tom takes place at Hallie's behest and suggests the deeply ambiguous feelings that Doniphon has toward his romantic rival. Tom tricks Ransom, an action similar to what Valance does later in the street, but the larger point here is that Doniphon's initial instruction in firing a weapon quickly turns into an occasion to embarrass Stoddard. Doniphon turns to the paint cans as a means of showing Ransom exactly how devilish Liberty can be; however, another motive derives from the rancher's earlier conduct at the delegate election. Tom's refusal of a nomination and, his subsequent nomination of Ransom, reasonable enough on the surface, seem designed to destroy or displace the man who has emerged as Hallie's favorite. Doniphon clearly knows how Valance will receive anyone else's nomination; indeed, if Tom had the best interests of Shinbone at heart, he would not have declined the nomination because, by his own admission, he is the only man who can stand up to Valance. Instead, Doniphon places Stoddard in extreme peril and then urges him to think seriously about leaving town. Ironically, Doniphon becomes the embodiment of Liberty's wishes, for getting Stoddard away from Shinbone will effect what the outlaw wants. The visual similarity between Doniphon's splattering the whitewash on Stoddard and Valance's spilling the water over him simply makes this connection more apparent. Doniphon finally murders Valance because he cannot stand to see Hallie hurt; thus, he possesses a residue of civilized feeling that is completely lacking in the outlaw. The same limit is suggested when Liberty wounds Ransom and makes him grovel for his weapon; Tom is content with merely illustrating what will happen, and he takes a punch from Stoddard without retaliating.

The community is much more unified in *My Darling Clementine* than in *The Man Who Shot Liberty Valance*; indeed, in the later film, politics and fear prevent people from coming together in any unaffected way. The homey atmosphere of the Earps' evening meal on the trail, with the brothers alternately kidding and praising James, establishes the kind of feeling that should exist between people. The later meals of the Earps continue to emphasize their rapport, with Morgan's appetite being comically echoed by Link in *The Man Who Shot Liberty Valance*, and the Clanton meals stand in marked contrast to the Earps'. Most tellingly, the confrontation between Doc and Clementine after the church dance occurs over a meal, to make the point that Holliday has transgressed the bounds of good society. Wyatt tries to get Doc to join the celebration, but the gambler refuses to be placated and even informs the marshal that they will now have to communicate with guns. In *The Man Who Shot Liberty Valance*, Link's comic intrusions into the Ericsons' kitchen ultimately demonstrate how weak the law is in Shinbone, for Appleyard never performs any substantially heroic action within the film. His most daring moment is when he tries to persuade Liberty not to shoot Stoddard on humanitarian grounds — a process that is undercut by his later bravado in dispatching Floyd and Reese after Doniphon has knocked them out.

The same contrast can be seen in the funeral scenes in these films. The death of James brings the brothers together in a mournful solemnity in the rain, a scene that is briefly reprised later by the almost religious framing of Wyatt and Morgan over the fallen Virgil in Tombstone. Much of the ritualistic solemnity attached to funerals elsewhere in Ford's westerns is repeated here as they cover their youngest brother in the midst of a thunderstorm. Wyatt's delivery of a major thematic message at the gravesite shortly after he has become town marshal reprises another situation we see in other Ford films. A different feeling emerges at Doniphon's funeral, which consists essentially of a wake to which each of the mourners brings a different and thoroughly personal set of values. If these aged survivors are grieving over their own vanished youth, their different reactions signify the disparities between them; indeed, they have become the atomized individuals that a higher civilization seemingly demands. The rule of law may ultimately be more rational than that of the gun, but in the attainment of that civilization, many of the personal relations that went with the earlier, wilder society have vanished. In place of the garrulous Peabody we now have the super-inquisitive Scott; meanwhile Clute (Joseph Hoover), the undertaker who whines about not making any profit and who tries to steal Doniphon's boots, has become the representative tradesman who has replaced the humane and warm Lars and Nora.

Stoddard's angry and mercenary reactions to Clute clearly establish that the senator is at home in the newer world. Ransom cannot feel as the others do because his heart has never been attracted to the individualistic world of Doniphon. He could never understand its violence, but he also could never understand its beauty — a process that is signaled by his reaction to Tom's gift of the cactus rose to Hallie. Feelings of nostalgia and melancholy are, of course, expressed by Hallie, who can dwell on the past enough to realize that part of her has always loved Doniphon and the world he symbolizes. There is, finally, no group activity in *The Man Who Shot Liberty Valance* to match the church dance in *My Darling Clementine*. When Shinbone comes together, it does so in an all-male meeting about territoriality versus statehood without any softening (civilizing) females being present. The absence of an extended feminine community in Shinbone is striking. Only Hallie and Nora resemble the nurturing women of Ford's earlier works, and in this oblique way the director once more suggests the costs of creating the civilization that Stoddard embodies.

The citizens of Tombstone exhibit the solidarity and interaction of a united community almost from the first moment we enter the town. If they are initially frightened by Indian Charlie, Tombstone's citizens ultimately work to remove this scourge from their midst. In contrast, the citizenry in *The Man Who Shot Liberty Valance* can only cower in the face of Valance and his men. Shinbone has no one comparable to the mayor in *My Darling Clementine*, who recognizes Wyatt's talent and tries to persuade him to be marshal after the sequence with the drunken Indian. Jess, the mayor, also marvels at the sound of church bells in Tombstone, further indicating his desire for more civilization in his frontier town. His later presence as the Earps await their rendezvous with the Clantons also attests to his civic-mindedness, as does the presence of the church elder Simpson. Unlike the timid denizens of Shinbone, who appear only after serious fighting has been done, Jess and Simpson initially accompany Wyatt in a show of support against the Clantons.

Thorndyke also represents the civilization that is impinging on the frontier in *My Darling Clementine*, for he brings Shakespeare to Tombstone. As one of a gallery of amiable drunks in Ford films, Thorndyke illustrates verbal daring in telling off the Clantons after Earp has delivered him from their clutches. ("Shakespeare was not meant for taverns. Or for tavern louts!") The actor's relationship with Dad establishes his essential goodness, and he is an obvious symbol of new ways in the town. This last fact is noted by Holliday, who marvels at the coming of dramatics to Tombstone. Thorndyke will be followed in short order by Clementine, who brings another, more permanent kind of civilization, as well as by John Simpson and his church. All these manifestations of growing order within Tombstone ultimately rest on Wyatt and his brothers, who are providing the safety necessary for such advances.

The Clantons are associated with animals. Pa Clanton, after passing the time of day with Wyatt and having his offers for the hero's cattle refused, moves his upper lip like a dog to express his instinctive enmity. His oldest son, Ike, lumbers like a bear when he challenges Earp at the dust-strewn corral. The other Clantons gravitate around the father; unkempt, they stand in sharp contrast to the Earps. Though the Earps are also unshaven initially, their appearances become gracious and civilized once they settle in town. In contrast, the Clantons remain bearded despite living where a barber is available.

Thus, the Earps' opening goal of going to town to get shaved represents an allegiance to higher values; the juxtaposition of their activities in Tombstone on that night with those of the offscreen Clantons establishes good against evil. The murder of James, certainly one of the most visually accented minor characters in all of Ford's films, further bespeaks the barbaric nature of the outlaw family.

Ford deliberately adds to the villainy of the Clantons by consistently photographing them in darkness. They are almost literally creatures of the night, so much so that Pa Clanton and Ike appear somewhat out of place when they first meet Wyatt in the light of day. This thematic pattern is reinforced by the setting of the climactic gunfight at dawn. The deaths of the Clantons in the redemptive morning light signal how civilization, in the form of the Earps, ultimately triumphs over barbarism, in the form of these night creatures. The end of the gunfight finds Pa Clanton calling on his dead sons (even Billy, who died the night before) in a pattern that is repeated by Uncle Shiloh in *Wagonmaster*. At this point Wyatt thinks about his own father, who has lost two sons. During his soliloquy at the gravesite, Wyatt claims that the bereaved Earp patriarch will never get over James's death. Thus, to even the score, Wyatt sends the elder Clanton off to suffer from the pangs of memory. But Pa Clanton prefers to go down fighting, in keeping with his thorough hatred and "honest" villainy, and Morgan must kill the unrepentant father.

Chihuahua links the Clanton-Earp conflict to Holliday by flirting with Billy Clanton. Before that time, the saloon girl has doted on Doc, even though she assists the tinhorn gambler whom Holliday orders out of town. Chihuahua also reacts to Earp's refusal to flirt with her by being forever insulting to the marshal. The girl's capacity for violence is symbolized by the glass she hurls at Doc and the milk she pours over Morgan. Chihuahua's impulsiveness is accompanied by her clumsiness, whether emptying the remnants of a pitcher in a hotel hallway or knocking things over as she enters Doc's room, further indicating her lack of civilization. The girl's passions and spontaneity are thrown into the most obvious contrast by Clementine, who stands for more decorous values and conduct. Rushing to Clementine's room after she has seen Doc leave on the stage, Chihuahua is all fuss and fury—qualities that are graphically established by her headlong run through the town and the agitated musical cues that accompany her movements. The singer's rush to pack Clementine's bags, as if by exorcising Clementine's presence Chihuahua could restore the idyllic daydream between herself and Doc, is sharply juxtaposed to the serenity of the eastern nurse. When Wyatt breaks up this confrontation by manhandling the saloon girl, Clementine calmly insists, in her nicest clinical voice, that hysteria is all that is wrong. Chihuahua's death, which precipitates the final crisis in Holliday, again underlines the duplicity in her character, for she has obviously given her favors to the youngest Clanton by the time Wyatt and Doc return to town to establish where Chihuahua got the incriminating Chingadera.

Clementine Carter offers a more idyllic vision of feminine civilizing traits than we ever see in *The Man Who Shot Liberty Valance* because she is more literate and self-assured than Hallie. Her dress shows her as an obvious (if not clichéd) contrast to Chihuahua; indeed, Clementine's civilized feelings prevent her from ever throwing herself at Doc, as the singer does. In essence, Clementine foreshadows Stoddard, the individual whose emotions remain checked by social decorum, whereas Chihuahua presages Doniphon and the more elemental feelings that control his character. Clementine ultimately decides with her heart rather than her head, for she comes to love the town, as she announces on the morning of the church dance. Her stately procession on Wyatt's arm again contrasts her to Chihuahua. As a lady, Clementine allows Wyatt to court her; the more hot-blooded Chihuahua cannot prevent herself from openly showing her passion for Doc. In both *My Darling Clementine* and *The Man Who Shot Liberty Valance*, those spontaneous forces that live by guns and the indulgence of personal feelings — the Clantons, Valance, Doc Holliday, Doniphon, and Chihuahua — must all be killed or displaced so that civilized communities can be established. Holliday's death at the O.K. Corral is thus the necessary prelude for Clementine to become the town's schoolmarm; and this progress is dramatized verbally and literally by the antagonism between them.

Doc Holliday oscillates between the violence and spontaneity of Chihuahua and the more civilized values of Wyatt and Clementine. Doc can and does communicate through physical actions. At his initial entry he touches the joyful Mac's arm as a signal of mutual affection and then knocks the hat off a gambler's head. The same resort to action occurs during the headlong stagecoach ride in which Holliday seems bent on escaping from all that has happened in his life by going from town to town, starting with Boston, where he left Clementine. The same rage continues as Doc nearly kicks in Chihuahua's door when he returns with Earp and the Chingadera.

Holliday's more pensive moments emphasize his death, such as when we see him in the Mexican saloon-brothel checking the Clantons so that Thorndyke can finish Hamlet's soliloquy. In discussing Earp's newfound status with the marshal, Doc challenges Wyatt on several levels: initially, by insisting that the lawman drink champagne, which the hero obviously dislikes; then, by suggesting that Earp has a holier-than-thou attitude; and finally, by daring the man across from him to draw a gun, which Wyatt does not carry. In this memorable first meeting Doc moves from conversation into action — a process that is rather consistently reversed by Wyatt, who goes into action only to preserve or restore a rational equilibrium. Holliday's attempt to complete Thorndyke's speech clearly focuses on death, especially since Doc begins choking and stops just after he has reached the point where Hamlet speculates on the afterlife and the conscience that makes "cowards of us all." Holliday's being marked for death is Ford's way of underlining the precarious position that such a figure occupies on his historical-mythical stage. Doc, like Doniphon, is marked for extinction because more civilized and modern men like Wyatt and Stoddard have arrived to take control. Whereas Holiday still wants to die in an ostensibly good cause, Liberty Valance knows who and what he must oppose. Doc and Wyatt, after their initial meeting, often appear in the same clothing, to suggest visually what is happening between them. We see them so attired at the theater, and when Doc's initial rage over Clementine erupts and he tries to drink himself into forgetfulness, he bursts into the saloon still attired to match the protagonist. Later, Holliday's all-black outfit matches Earp's as they fight each other and the Clantons.

Wyatt's delineation is more verbal than physical. His opening comment to Pa Clanton about how "rough looking" the country is sets up his reaction after entering Tombstone and being shot at while in the barber's chair ("What kind of town is this, anyway?"). If Earp subsequently refines this latter perception to note that Tombstone is a "hard town" in which to enjoy a poker game, his initially perplexed question is clearly echoed by Stoddard's first reaction to Shinbone ("What kind of place have I come to?"). Wyatt's taking command of his environment derives from this question, for he proceeds against Indian Charlie only after the town marshal (Harry Woods) quits. He symbolically becomes the manifestation of law and order, dramatized by his putting his foot literally to the Indian and, later, figuratively to the incoming gambler. Wyatt also reveals his identity by the ways in which he gives his name; indeed, until asked by the mayor to stay on as marshal, Ford's protagonist has not told anyone who he is. The mayor is awestruck by the hero's name, and the soundtrack underlines the moment with the sound of thunder, which links this scene to the offstage murder of James. The protagonist later elicits fear from the Clantons when he tells them who he is after he has taken over as town marshal. Such portentous announcements of his name bespeak the mythical nature of the character that Ford is delineating. Everyone, it seems, has heard of Earp by reputation; whether Pa Clanton or Doc Holliday, they react noticeably. Indeed, Doc and Wyatt are quickly placed on a comparable level because of their foreknowledge of each others' names and pasts.

Wyatt is also allowed some verbal humor in *My Darling Clementine*. He is initially nonplussed when the barber keeps asking him why he has come into his shop. To the bearded and bedraggled Wyatt, it seems obvious that he needs a shave; however, within a Tombstone that includes the Clantons, such behavior is not always expected. The sparsity of Wyatt's dialogue with Clementine and the appropriately tongue-tied ways in which Fonda acts correspond with Earp's gentlemanly reticence. It is apt that Wyatt must leave Clementine, for the "legend" is clearly being celebrated in *My Darling Clementine*. The film's visual and auditory elements (especially the placements of its music) make clear that this final meeting will be the last one between these surviving characters.

The world of *The Man Who Shot Liberty Valance* offers no such clear-cut choices for its principals. Not only are its inhabitants elderly, but the freedom represented by the frontier has also passed on. In the opening of the film we encounter Jason, the obsequious railroad conductor, whose role reemphasizes the circularity of the entire plot. Just as the train will enter and exit to suggest this pattern visually, Jason's final remark ("Nothing's too good for the man who shot Liberty Valance!") closes the film on an appropriately ironic note. Society, it seems, is more than happy to propitiate the legend that has surrounded and abetted Stoddard for years. This lesson is, of course, made even more apparent when Scott, the newspaper editor who presses Ransom for the real story, decides that myth and legend are better copy than the truth. Although Scott seems pushy and ill-informed (why doesn't he know about Doniphon's death?), his instincts are consistent with a society that needs to believe in Stoddard (and not Doniphon) as its savior.

Link Appleyard's very name shows his function, for he brings together the past and present of *The Man Who Shot Liberty Valance*. That things have changed in Shinbone is made obvious by his comments that he is no longer sheriff ("Folks haven't elected me in a dog's age") and by his pointing out that Doniphon had long since quit carrying a gun. If his first name marks his plot function, his surname emphasizes how Shinbone has evolved from a wilderness into a garden. Ironically, this evolution has deprived Link of his role even though he has managed to survive; indeed, he resembles what we imagine Doniphon must have become — a harmless, wistful, old man living out his time. Link provides comic relief, a trait that he shares with the stuttering Kaintuck and that supplies his character with some additional dramatic weight. The cowardly sheriff represents another anachronism that Shinbone must remove if it is ever to achieve the degree of civilization that Stoddard wants for it.

Pompey, fiercely loyal to Tom, basically operates through action, even though he would like to become part of the refined verbal culture that Stoddard embodies. His fumbled recitation of the opening of the Bill of Rights offers Ransom a chance to reiterate antiracist sentiments in keeping with the tone of *Sergeant Rutledge*. It is while planting the cactus rose and aiming a rifle at Valance that Pompey serves most notably. In Doniphon's narrative, the black man appears as the only other person who knows the truth; his subsequent silence thus reaffirms his deep commitment to Doniphon, as does his rescue of the frightened horses at the ranch when Tom sets the fire.

Pompey's silence stands in sharp contrast to the histrionics of Dutton Peabody. As the purveyor of words, the editor engages in constant barrages on the possibility of Doniphon and Hallie getting married or on the injustice of his own election as a territorial delegate. Peabody resembles Thorndyke in reciting long Shakespearean and other purple passages when drunk. Peabody's association with words continues: inebriated, he missets the newspaper headline; he verbally describes Valance and his men; and he emphasizes the word "liberty" when he briefly awakens to tell Ransom what has happened on the night of his beating. At the territorial convention, Ford's editor serves as a verbal counterweight to the oratorical Starbuckle, and their debate demonstrates how the world of the West has become the world of the East, with speech replacing action. Peabody, in recounting the evolution of the West, clearly belongs to the newer, sophisticated, and decorous world of Stoddard.

Liberty Valance breeds silence around him, and his physicality is established by his first attack on Stoddard. The outlaw's masculinity is further emphasized by the ways he pushes into meetings. At Lars's restaurant, Valance unseats Kaintuck because he is too impatient to wait for anyone to leave. He displays the same precipitate quality in the saloon when he knocks off the gambler's hat because the latter does not agree with him quickly enough. Liberty's aggressiveness is further dramatized when he enters the delegate-selection assembly and surges through the crowd as though he were a tidal wave. His excess is also seen in his beating of Peabody and in his glee at winning the final poker hand (with the symbolic dead man's hand). His subsequent gunfight with Stoddard emphasizes Valance's overconfidence. His slouched posture and the ease with which he torments the overmatched easterner show that Liberty is sure that he is operating within "western law." He never expects that Doniphon, or anyone else for that matter, will step outside the bounds of that code to strike him down.

Hallie offers the greatest acting challenge in *The Man Who Shot Liberty Valance*, for her character must not only age but also embody the ambiguities of a woman who loves two men across a lengthy span of time. While her love for Stoddard emerges almost in spite of herself, Hallie's feelings for Doniphon are clearly more central to the themes of the film. Her rejection of Tom's suit, in spite of the urgings of her parents and the town's assumption that the two are all but betrothed (a view perhaps most strongly articulated by Stoddard), dramatizes the notion that the requirements of civilization must loom larger within the individual's consciousness than the claims of personal happiness. Hallie must do the work of civilization; however, she can realize, in retrospect, that choosing against Doniphon was not an altogether unmixed bounty. Ironically, since she and the senator have no children, there has never been any symbolic flowering in her marriage to Stoddard. Hallie's stature as an embodiment of the future and the natural promoter of settlement puts her in the center of the conflicts that mark *The Man Who Shot Liberty Valance*. Her desire for change can be seen when she asks Ransom to teach her to read and when she wistfully thinks about the water that will someday make the desert bloom. That Hallie's desires for the future come to center on Stoddard can also be seen in her rage and disappointment when the school closes because of Valance's renewed threat. When she sees Ransom once more in an apron, she can only surmise that reading and writing have done nothing for him; and this practical view is later echoed by Doniphon's insistence that Stoddard go back into the convention and give Hallie something worth "reading and writing about."

Hallie chides Ransom about his manners with women by insisting that he does not need to rise every time she brings his supper; her comments serve as a prelude to asking if his offer to teach her was serious. Her brusque manner also appears, significantly, in the ways she treats Doniphon. When Tom brings her a cactus rose and even gets dressed up for Saturday night to win her, Hallie receives his overtures in an offhand way. Although grateful for his attentions and compliments, she never acts in any ecstatic manner; indeed, in their first scene together, Hallie complains because Tom has wakened her at five in the morning to look after the injured Stoddard. More significant, we never see Hallie and Doniphon, at this time or any other, in anything resembling a romantic embrace. Tom can compliment her by noting how a color makes her pretty, and even by saying that she is prettier when mad, but when he attempts to manage her life she rebels. When the school closes because of Tom's news about Valance, Hallie angrily dismisses her would-be lover by stating that what she does is "none of your business!" Her defiance, indicative of her growing feelings for Ransom, is quickly compromised when she asks for Doniphon's aid after learning that Stoddard is practicing to meet Valance. The very understated nature of their scenes together ultimately implies the depth of feeling that Doniphon has for Hallie; her often unthinking treatment of her suitor is hardly commensurate with what he does for her. Only in modern Shinbone does Hallie show her awareness that she has lost as well as gained both romantically and personally by choosing Stoddard.

Tom Doniphon's potential dismissal by Hallie is foreshadowed very early when he attempts to join Stoddard in drinking some brandy. While Nora has provided this stimulant as a medicine for Ransom, Tom takes up the bottle and states that drinking alone isn't sociable in the West. In this sentiment, Doniphon once again resembles Valance, for he is teaching Stoddard about how the West should work. Hallie prevents Tom from drinking, providing an obvious comic touch but also making the point that the woman must control the man within civilization. Stoddard's greater capacity to adjust to the newer, feminized society is asserted ironically by Doniphon, who jokingly notes that the newcomer is a "ladies' man" because he has gotten beaten for trying to protect a woman. His calling Stoddard "pilgrim" also delineates Ransom, who has come west as a naive and innocent figure who must learn the ropes to seek his fortune.

Doniphon's later entries into the Ericsons' kitchen all call attention to Stoddard's emergence as Hallie's beloved. When Doniphon sees them standing together, just after Hallie has decided to learn to read, he notes that Stoddard is "still protectin'" the ladies. After Valance's death, Tom enters to overhear Hallie's tearful declaration of love to Ransom, the ultimate defeat of Doniphon's own romantic dream, and exits with the bitter phrase, "I'll be around." Doniphon is trapped by a single, all-consuming passion; indeed, he resembles such earlier Ford protagonists as Captain Yorke in *Rio Grande*, whose love for Kathleen was just barely subsumed by his duties, and Ethan Edwards in *The Searchers*, whose passion for his sister-in-law spurs him to seek a revenge to which he must devote years. Ford's cinematic artistry comes to the fore once again in his delineation of Doniphon, a character not only played by the same actor who had those earlier roles but also limited to his articulations by both temper and locale.

The more verbal Stoddard insists that all his obligations must be paid, and he works for Nora and Lars to "square" his account even up to the time when Valance comes gunning for him. He also needs to act within the framework of the law; thus he becomes most animated and daring during the delegate election. Not only does Ransom provide and enforce the formal rules by which the town meeting is conducted, but he also nominates Doniphon, and then, after Valance has intruded, he ensures the election of Peabody and himself. Stoddard is at his most self-assured in the schoolroom and when he peruses Peabody's political editorial; these scenes clearly anticipate the loquacious older politician that Ransom appears to be in modern Shinbone. Indeed, Senator Stoddard has become adept at talking to reporters and spinning out "copy" that they can use — a process he signals by telling Hallie that he will have to mend some fences while she and Link ride out to Doniphon's ranch. Stoddard's earlier desire to put Liberty in jail naturally runs contrary to western ways, for the eastern newcomer wants to make a prisoner of a man who defines himself by his ability to move. Such a legal trap, though an understandable expression of Stoddard's character, represents a way of dealing with outlaws that is anathema to Doniphon, the traditional westerner.

The evolution of the society of the West is underscored by Stoddard's success after the death of Valance. Because he appears to have played the hero's role, he is accepted as a hero (and duly rewarded) by the citizens of the territory — a process to which he accedes readily enough after Doniphon has informed him of the "truth." Stoddard can salve his conscience at this point because he possesses a larger social vision than does Doniphon. Ransom can excuse his duplicity on the grounds that such behavior will ultimately make the territory a better place for people to live (the sort of environment in which James Earp could have had a chance to grow up), whereas Tom's betrayal of his western conscience has been motivated by more tangible and personal values. Stoddard might well have sustained a life without Hallie, but for Doniphon, losing her spelled the end of his real existence. Thus, Stoddard's emergence as the kind of leader needed by a newer society counterpoints the eclipse of Doniphon, the hero without whose sacrifice the new order could never have emerged at all. Underneath Ford's historical-thematic lessons in *The Man Who Shot Liberty Valance* we see the director's revision of his earlier portrait of the ideal western hero in *My Darling Clementine*: Wyatt Earp does not die, he simply becomes an embarrassment.

Chapter 9

Wagonmaster and
Two Rode Together

At first glance, *Wagonmaster* (1950) and *Two Rode Together* (1961) seem the least likely pair of Ford's westerns. The first, long a favorite among the director's aficionados, represents one of Ford's most personal efforts; the latter, which has not received equal accolades from either fans or critics, is often dismissed as merely a studio assignment.[1] *Wagonmaster* resembles the more classical and optimistic tones of *My Darling Clementine* and *Three Godfathers*, whereas *Two Rode Together* seemingly reworks ground already covered in *The Searchers*. Although such thematic and tonal disparities loom as reasons for not coupling them, both films tie the fate of a wagon train to the actions of paired heroes. From this angle, and in light of their elaborate emphases on courtship, *Wagonmaster* and *Two Rode Together* emerge as similar, even though the easy optimism of the earlier film, in which clearly apparent enemies and obstacles are overcome by heroic and collective action, all but disappears in the more resistant and unrepentant world of the later work.

Two Rode Together represents Ford's distillation of a more unsettling vision of the West, for his heroes are weaker and more psychologically scarred than heretofore. At the same time, Ford accentuates the ambiguous and hypocritical sides of evil through casting that occasionally runs contrary to what he has done elsewhere. Thus, the dark side of human nature assumes a more permanent and domesticated character in contrast to the melodramatic and, finally, more stable world of *Wagonmaster*. Whereas each different social or religious group in the earlier film has its own distinct territory or values, all layers in society blend in *Two Rode Together* to create a more sophisticated and depressing aura.

The credits in these films immediately announce their differences. In *Wagonmaster* we see the movements of opposing forces toward an inevitable meeting — a process that is augmented notably by the prologue in which Uncle Shiloh (Charles Kemper) and his "boys" (Floyd [James Arness], Reese [Fred Libby], Luke [Hank Worden], and Jesse [Mickey Simpson]) rob a bank and kill a teller. The outlaws' subsequent riding in single file through various mountain passages is then juxtaposed to the Mormon wagon train moving across rivers and plains to the accompaniment of a song by Stan Jones. If such lyrics serve to create a historical distancing by virtue of their emphasis on "1849," the Mormons' unremitting quest for a "promised land" is also accentuated by these opening credits. *Two Rode Together* uses a neutral background for its opening credits — a design that is even less suggestive than that found in *The Searchers* but one that makes the same point by emphasizing the static quality of what we are about to experience. Ford's more sober views about the effects of heroic action on society are caught by this design; of his final five westerns, only *Sergeant Rutledge* uses the "shot over" credits that had been so prominent in his westerns (with the exception of *My Darling Clementine*) through *Rio Grande*.

The same dichotomy arises in the musical scores that accompany these films. *Wagonmaster* consistently features tunes that comment on the action through their lyrics, so that the entire film begins to take on the air of a ballad. In its most musically poignant and important moment, Travis Blue (Ben Johnson) and Sandy Owens (Harry Carey, Jr.) decide to join the Mormon train after watching the immigrants' wagons go by. They do not verbalize their decision but, rather, reach it by singing a song about joining a wagon train — in what has to be the closest that Ford ever came to opera. The religious tenor of the Mormon expedition into the wilderness is underscored by various hymns, including the obligatory "Shall We Gather at the River." When the promised valley is reached at last, the grateful travelers celebrate their good fortune by singing a hymn, which quickly segues into the final scenes, in which the principals pass by in a kind of curtain call similar to the end of *The Quiet Man*. Whistling is also prominently featured, and music is part of the workaday world of Denver (Joanne Dru) and the other members of Doctor Hall's (Alan Mowbray) theatrical medicine show company. A square dance enables the Mormons to relax after a hard day on the trail; when their festivities are interrupted by the outlaws' entrance, the music appropriately stops.

The same kind of musical manipulation can be found in *Two Rode Together*, although there is little joyfulness in the score that accompanies Guthrie McCabe (James Stewart) and Lieutenant Jim Gary (Richard Widmark) as they go into Indian country. At the post dance, source music (waltzes by Johann Strauss, Jr.) is noticeably interrupted by the confrontation between Elena (Linda Cristal) and the society of the fort, whose feminine contingent includes, in a startling bit of revisionist casting, Anna Lee as an unspeaking but suspicious-eyed member. The rest of George Duning's original music for *Two Rode Together* functions unobtrusively to suggest various character feelings and dramatic situations. In keeping with Ford's more sober views, there are no songs or even instances when such materials could be brought into play — a departure that separates this film from *The Searchers* and *Sergeant Rutledge* (with their ballads) and links it to the darker visions of human possibilities we encounter in *The Man Who Shot Liberty Valance* and *Cheyenne Autumn*. Ford's visual imagination works more conspicuously in *Wagonmaster* perhaps because it is an Argosy-RKO picture and perhaps because its plot needed considerable fleshing out in light of its often Spartan production values. Certain shots are repeated, most notably the river crossing sequences that bring *Wagonmaster* to its close, to suggest that the mystical wagon train is still driving on somewhere. The shots of struggling drivers and pioneers battling up ever-steeper inclines, whether at a stream bank or during the final mountain crossing, make the landscape more of an immediate presence in *Wagonmaster* than in virtually any other Ford western. The relationship here between the ongoing wagon train and the terrain it must cover suggests that the environment is a hurdle that can be overcome only by group expertise, willingness, and sacrifice: the good Mormons can traverse a difficult terrain when the need arises because of their social spirit. At the same time, the confrontations between horses and villains never occur in rugged terrain but rather on flat ground (in *Wagonmaster*) or in obviously stagey settings (in *Two Rode Together*). The familiar long-distance grandeur of Monument Valley often dwarfs the characters in *Wagonmaster*, as it often does in other Ford westerns. In *Two Rode Together*, while much occurs on flat ground, Ford ventures into a new terrain, one whose woods and fallen trees resemble the westerns of Anthony Mann in which James Stewart is always psychologically flawed.

Ford embellishes *Wagonmaster* with obvious visual devices that become veritable stylistic signatures. The combination of slower music with passing wagons augments the fatigue of the trail, a motif that is further amplified by the recurrent shots of feet trudging through dust. Even Dr. Hall is shown instinctively beating time during the Mormon hoedown, while the sheer drudgery of the journey is repeatedly emphasized by views of the pioneers' feet. This motif extends to Denver when Travis offers her a pair of Miss Prudence's (Kathleen O'Malley) shoes in a scene that initiates their love affair. Such conscious visual effects are much less apparent in *Two Rode Together*, where style plays a secondary role to the tale. It is only during the death of Stone Calf (Woody Strode) that the struggle between white and red cultures is made strikingly manifest. Ford's final shot of McCabe holding Elena in the mystically lit atmosphere, after he has stopped her from praying over her dead warrior husband like a Commanche, is the most memorable composition in *Two Rode Together*. This fadeout symbolizes the central thematic conflict by showing McCabe rescuing Elena at the cost of wrenching her free from the Indian culture embodied by Stone Calf.

In both films, dances are prominently featured as occasions that reveal conflicts. The dances in *Wagonmaster* are ultimately more hopeful and, once the outlaws have been destroyed, truly more festive than those in *Two Rode Together*. The "Chuckawalla Swing" allows the show folks and the Mormons

to play together. Elder Wiggs (Ward Bond) instigates this dance by which the two groups come together because of his innate compassion and humanity. Asking Miss Fleuretty (Ruth Clifford) to be his partner reprises Wiggs's earlier intercession for the show people when they were discovered drunk and dying and were assailed by the prim and priggish Elder Perkins (Russell Simpson). This notion that human compassion must override doctrinal purity is reemphasized in the dance at the Indian camp, when Perkins is discomfited and Sister Ledyard (Jane Darwell) thoroughly enjoys the embrace of her partner. Both of these dances are, however, brought to a stop by the outlaw "family." The Cleggs' initial entry into the Mormon camp, with Uncle Shiloh's lame story about being shot while out hunting and his hypocritical allusion to "good Christian folk," ends the first dance; Reese's assault on an Indian woman leads to Wiggs and Shiloh's confrontation, which motivates the rest of the film. That the Cleggs do not fit into the civilized world that Ford celebrates in these dance sequences comes as no surprise. A quick reprise of a shot from the first dance as part of the epilogue of *Wagonmaster* suggests that the Mormons' world has been reintegrated after the killing of the outlaws: the unnatural force has been exorcised, and normal life can now resume because of the heroics of Travis and Sandy.

Dances provide less optimistic tones to *Two Rode Together*, for if one of the characters is symbolically reintegrated by going to a party, another figure's suffering and the larger racial issues of the story are made manifest on the same occasion. Marty Purcell (Shirley Jones) does not attend a wagon-train dance, despite being pressed to do so by her father (Paul Birch), who fears that she is not behaving as a young person should. At the same time, in refusing the invitation of the nefarious Clegg brothers (Ken Curtis and Harry Carey, Jr., in other examples of role-reversal casting), Marty shows her good taste and gets embroiled with both these villains and Lieutenant Gary. By the time of the second dance at the fort, Marty has emerged from her shell, gotten engaged to Gary, and become an eager participant in the fun. However, her feelings quickly become secondary because of the treatment accorded Elena by the ladies and officers at this dance. Marty can only leave when Gary does. Thus, the final dance in a Ford western becomes a means to show the internal divisions within a society rather than an occasion when a community's sense of itself can be celebrated (as in *My Darling Clementine*) or when various social ranks can intermingle (as in *She Wore a Yellow Ribbon*).

In *Wagonmaster*, the heroes' profession, horse-trading, allows them to sell to the sheriff (Cliff Lyons) a bucking horse whose gyrations they can control — a process triggered by their whistling to the animal when the beleaguered lawman tries to ride it. This comic device becomes an important plot element on

Opposite: The wagon train in *Wagonmaster* (Argosy-RKO, 1950). This group activity is a major character in the film.

the prairie when Travis and Sandy short-circuit the sheriff's suspicions about whether the outlaws are with the wagon train. Travis's own mastery with horses is shown on various occasions, most especially when he rides to escape from his Navajo pursuers, in a reprise of the sequence in which Sergeant Tyree fled in *She Wore a Yellow Ribbon*. Ford later uses Travis's horsemanship to bring the lovers together: when Denver inadvertently splashes the wagonmaster's mount, the protagonist is thrown. Of course, Travis's fall represents a visual equivalent of the way that he "falls" romantically for Denver. Their subsequent dispute about taking a bath, while containing some innocuous double entendres, brings this association to an appropriate end when Travis says he will "join" the retiring Denver and does so by letting his horse wallow in the nearby stream.

Of even greater significance is whittling, which links Travis and Wiggs at their first meeting. While such business keeps both men in character, their shared habit foreshadows Wiggs's subsequent expertise in card playing (hardly a Mormon concern, as the ubiquitous Perkins reminds him), as well as Travis and Sandy's joining the train. Ford uses whittling to underline the horse-trading between Wiggs and Travis. The elder's temper is nicely symbolized by his vicious actions with the wood on which he carves, whereas Travis's shrewder business sense is emphasized by the control that he exerts on his piece of wood. This sequence suggests that these characters will not merely coexist with but prosper because of each other. It is one of those numerous instances when Ford's proclivity for merely showing existence rather than adhering too strictly to plot and dialogue is beautifully realized.

Objects and gestures are more tied to such narrative considerations in *Two Rode Together*, for even a bed frame similar to the one that Dr. Hall had in *Wagonmaster* takes on a special sense because of the quest on which the pioneers-seekers are bent. The metal frame in front of the Purcells' wagon represents the past that has driven them into seeking their long-lost son and brother; indeed, it stands in sharp contrast to the wilderness, and the savagery within it, later found on the trail in the camp of Quana Parker (Henry Brandon) and within McCabe himself. The music box, with its Boccherini minuet, crystallizes Marty's guilt over not being taken prisoner along with her brother and, later, identifies Running Wolf (David Kent) as, indeed, the lost Purcell child. If the contest between civilization and savagery is implicitly symbolized by such an object, Marty's destruction of the music box after realizing that her brother has been lynched by the irate mob frees her from her past.

The girl's progress has been abetted by Jim Gary's patient insistence that she is not responsible for what happened when she was a child and by her own revulsion when Running Wolf is brought in for "reassignment" because of McCabe and the lieutenant's trek into the wilderness. Marty realizes the futility of trying to reassemble the past, and her brother's actions as a prisoner in a white man's world only underline this theme. When the captured boy spits at the adult pioneers who gawk at him and when he empties a slop bucket over Henry Wringle (Willis Bouchey at his most obnoxious), he enacts a poetic justice. However, the ambiguous nature of Ford's film (and by implication of life itself) is caught when Running Wolf kills the demented Mrs. McCandless (Jeanette Nolan) so that he can never return "home."

Elena's inability to find a home in Fort Grant's white society is symbolized not only by the cost of her rescue (the death of Stone Calf) but also by her vicious treatment at the hands of the ladies and the gentlemen of the post. Her flight from that society ironically brings her into Tascosa and the ministrations of Belle Aragon (Annelle Hayes), who plans to make a whorish novelty of her. When Elena decides that she must seek a new life elsewhere and is joined by McCabe, who now wants her rather than Belle or the town, Ford reprises two symbolic objects to present the relationship. The lovers escape like Dallas and Ringo in *Stagecoach*, albeit not in a buckboard. In addition, Elena watches McCabe by using a mirror, in a way that repeats Philadelphia Thursday's maneuvering of a similar device to see Mickey O'Rourke during their initial ride into *Fort Apache*. In both instances, the mirror symbolizes the love of the characters; the difference, of course, is that because the romantic pair in *Two Rode Together* have been exposed to the world and its bullying ways, their love will be worked out offstage, instead of being a major portion of the ensuing narrative.

Wagonmaster presents camping for the night as a means by which its weary travelers find space and time to rest as a necessary end to long days. Encampments in the more sober *Two Rode Together* serve as backdrops to further action and conflict, whether it be Marty's dismissal of the first dance or the insults that are swapped between McCabe and Gary. The delusions of the parental seekers — both those of the hapless Mr. Knudson (John Qualen), who only wants his daughter back, and those of the berserk Mrs. McCandless, who wants her infant returned — surface within these encampments. McCabe's initial entry into their midst and the later scene when the addled Mrs. McCandless rushes into a river while the sanctimonious Mr. Clegg (Ford Rainey) fires at some nearby Indians also occur within the nightmare world of such camps. The stops that McCabe and Gary make on the trail to and from Quana's village reveal the disparity between them. Their somewhat comic relationship, as delineated on the way to Fort Grant, becomes considerably harsher when they meet in the early morning, after Gary has "deserted," and they discuss who will give orders to whom. On the way back, McCabe's establishment of a camp to ambush Stone Calf provokes a savage confrontation between them. McCabe, after drawing on the lieutenant without any advance warning, insists that he will shoot Gary if need be. This streak of mad violence in the lawman stands in contrast to the coldly calculating way in which Ethan Edwards engineers the same kind of ambush in *The Searchers*. McCabe's underlying fury emphasizes the tough-minded world of *Two Rode Together*.

The plots of *Wagonmaster* and *Two Rode Together*—a linear journey in the earlier film and a circular trip in the latter work—stand in contrast. The meeting between the outlaws and the Mormons in *Wagonmaster* and the final struggle between them are characteristically short and sharp. Indeed, the plot serves to exemplify the ideal lives of the Mormons and to demonstrate why the characters most influenced by them (Travis, Sandy, and Denver) choose to become part of their society. *Wagonmaster* contains characters who can decisively affect one another and who change because of the course of events.

Two Rode Together, on the other hand, is circular and repetitious in both characters and plotting. The comic buffoon Ward (Chet Douglas), who replaces McCabe both as town sheriff and as Belle's kept man, appears to be a veritable double for the protagonist when McCabe and Gary return to Tascosa after the post dance and the insults to Elena. Ford's circular plot then finds McCabe riding out with Elena in a scene that finishes the circuit of the stagecoach that entered during the film's opening scene. Such visual circularity foreshadows *The Man Who Shot Liberty Valance* and, though perhaps not as overtly thematic, establishes that McCabe and Elena can find salvation and happiness only through escaping from Fort Grant and Tascosa. That McCabe's journey should also start and end in Belle Aragon's saloon is, again, thoroughly in keeping with the film's thematic emphases. The madam's offer to put Elena to work as a kind of Indian-specialty whore crudely repeats the treatment that Miss Madriaga has experienced at Fort Grant. Thus, Elena and McCabe's exodus represents the only answer — escape — to the permanent social evils with which they are confronted. The settled community from which Dallas and Ringo had to flee, for legal reasons, in *Stagecoach* has become considerably more powerful and less hospitable in *Two Rode Together*.

The more classic nature of *Wagonmaster* can also be seen in its main theme, which might be reduced to the familiar bromide about good inevitably triumphing over evil, albeit with a considerable emphasis placed on man's sheer ability to transcend the physical circumstances that beset him. The destruction of the outlaw clan by the essentially peace-loving Travis ensures the first proposition, while the overcoming of the various rivers and mountains by the wagon train represents the film's second pressing thematic interest. We see a looseness of plotting in *Wagonmaster* because the mere existence of the characters ultimately represents more to Ford than any machinations they undergo. *Two Rode Together*, on the other hand, opens with a joke about the "widow Gomez," who has delivered a child despite the fact that her husband died a year ago. Such an exchange implies the more relaxed ethical sense of McCabe and the town. We cannot imagine Captain Brittles or Wyatt Earp greeting such news with the protagonist's ironic retort ("You just can't trust some men

(On the top: Stewart with a pistol; on the bottom: Stewart with a rifle.) The evolution of Guthrie McCabe (James Stewart) in *Two Rode Together* (COLUMBIA, 1961): on the top, he threatens to kill Jim Gary; on the bottom, he lets Elena know that he is going with her in the film's finale.

to stay put"); and so, McCabe's "heroic" dismissal of the newly arrived gamblers, in a sequence that reprises *My Darling Clementine*, is already compromised. An even larger irony surrounds the notion of "home" in *Two Rode Together*, for the pioneers have come, ostensibly, to restore their loved ones, but their efforts simply rebound on their heads. There is, finally, no home to which Running Wolf or Elena can go within the confines of civilized society. McCabe and Gary are also men who have no real homes but who find such places because of their journey into the wilderness; their prospective domestic arrangements suggest that love represents the only genuine refuge any character ever gains in Ford's westerns.

A more subtle theme arises from McCabe's role as a restorer of the past, as one who has been called on to right the wrongs of bygone days. The sheriff's candor in urging the pioneers not to seek their long-lost relations is chastised as cruelty by Gary; however, when Running Wolf is returned to "civilization," McCabe's words seem wise. Major Frazier's (John McIntire) reaction to the savage boy stresses a "cruel lie to the living"; in essence, Fort Grant's commander speaks for nearly all the pioneers who are appalled by what they have tried to do. Their attempt to restore the past has finally made them aware of the seemingly inevitable clash of cultures. What has been seen initially as a problem is now shown to be a tragic condition, and the death of Mrs. McCandless at the hands of Running Wolf only makes the point more dramatically.

Mr. McCandless's acceptance of Running Wolf, before the murder, raises the issue of past reality versus present necessity. The distraught husband does not believe that Running Wolf is his son, but he takes the young Indian because he feels there will be a "comfort in the lie" for his demented wife in pretending that "Toby" has been restored to them. The murder of Mrs. McCandless, who is killed in the very act of freeing her supposed child from bondage, leads to the lynching of Running Wolf by the pioneers, led by the "Bible thumper" Clegg and his two mad sons. Their action is symbolically preceded by the defeats of the legalistic, elder Purcell and of Gary, who is unable to halt the mob through physical intervention. Thus, a comforting lie leads to a catastrophe and suggests, once more, the altogether darker nature of *Two Rode Together*. Lies do not always work; heroes and societies have severe limitations — so severe, in fact, that outcasts can no longer be easily reintegrated into society as Debbie Edwards was in *The Searchers*.

Social groups define individuals more rigorously in *Wagonmaster* and *Two Rode Together* than in Ford's other westerns. The earlier film, in particular, emphasizes the dichotomy of social allegiances by setting up five distinct groups: the Mormons, the outlaws, and the theatrical troupe members are all on the run from society, which constitutes the fourth entity, while the Navajos represent a final group that has learned to deal with different white men in appropriate ways. The Indians recognize Travis and force him to pretend to be a Mormon, in a bit of obvious foreshadowing; their invitation to a tribal dance precipitates a crisis by showing Reese and the other outlaws for what they are. Throughout *Wagonmaster*, Ford stresses the assimilation of other groups by the Mormons, so that the actors become part of their ongoing trek as do Travis and Sandy. The killing of Uncle Shiloh and his "boys" is followed by Travis's casting his gun into the desert to symbolize his choice of the pacifist Mormon way. He and, to a lesser extent, Sandy have turned their backs on the life of the town, and their conversion dramatizes the spiritual strength of Elder Wiggs. If Sandy chooses to stay with the Mormons because of his infatuation with Prudence, Travis brings Denver into their fold along with himself. His choice ultimately represents a more adult commitment that includes his sense of being part of a larger social order, as opposed to his younger companion's more romantic decision.

Crystal City is epitomized by its sheriff, who initially suspects that Travis and Sandy may be part of the Clegg family. The lawman's role as a moral guardian also includes his insistence that the wagon train leave town by nightfall, an order he backs up with a group of armed riders who enter the Mormon camp to "remind" Wiggs that he must lead his people out or suffer the consequences. When the sheriff plays cards with Travis, he remains suspicious and antagonistic as he conspicuously checks a winning hand and questions the protagonist about his cards. The shortsightedness of the sheriff (and of the town itself) is further symbolized by the bucking horse that the gullible lawman not only buys but also suffers from whenever Sandy whistles to excite the animal. The society of Crystal City may be prejudiced against Mormons and actors (as well as outlaws and Indians), but ultimately it is too preoccupied to impose its viciousness in any extended way. Unlike Tonto in *Stagecoach*, Crystal City has no group that openly demonstrates to get undesirables out of town, even though such people are forced out. *Wagonmaster* implies that one can and should escape from this town and its prejudices in order to build a better life.

The possibilities for such escape are considerably lessened in *Two Rode Together*, where the sleepy village of Tascosa is quickly transformed into the cynical materialism of Madam Aragon's saloon. McCabe has assumed a comfortable life as a sheriff-grafter who enforces the rules from a chair with a glass of beer in hand. His experiences on the trail and within Fort Grant finally convince him that his town life should be abandoned. Belle's saloon represents no home for him; Ford uses her establishment to delineate those who are worthwhile and those who are not. The final scene there only deepens Madam Aragon's casual amorality, which was so noticeable at Gary's initial entrance. That earlier scene finds Belle speculating, in supposedly comic fashion, about the predictabilities of men and the poverty of army life. Such easy cynicism keeps Madam Aragon from ever gaining any sympathy because it shows that she cannot see her own viciousness. Belle's offer to make Elena a showpiece in her brothel ("Mrs. Stone Calf!") forces McCabe to realize that a modicum of idealism is essential, even for an ostensible realist and materialist like himself. Madam Aragon represents a more blatant expression of the civilized cruelty that Elena experiences at Fort Grant and among the pioneers; the key symbol of the saloon owner's character, the stiletto she carries in her garter, wonderfully epitomizes her mercenary nature. If Belle combines an easy sexuality with her own profitable business, her strictly mercenary personality is caught up by this weapon and its proximity to her sexuality. Ultimately, she is like the town itself, for she is quite different under the surface.

The same facility for role-playing exists among the theatrical troupe in *Wagonmaster*; however, they gradually emerge as better than what they initially appear to be. While Denver becomes not only Travis's fiancée but also, as seen in her change in clothing, a member of the Mormon community, Dr. Hall is not too far behind during the final, climactic crossing of the last pass. If Miss Fleuretty accuses "Gus" of simply showing off, her decision to go along confirms that their essential goodness has come out because of their contact with the Mormons. Dr. Hall has gradually taken charge of his life and now confronts the outlaws as much as he dares. The medicine-show doctor, like Thorndyke in *My Darling Clementine*, is given to wordiness, especially when he says good-bye to Wiggs at the California cutoff; but this trait is ameliorated when he offers to drive the second wagon through the trench that has been dug. Hall is not given any moment of verbal victory over those who torment him (as the actor was given in Tombstone); instead, he triumphs more convincingly by transforming himself so as to be able to act openly against them. Miss Fleuretty adjusts to her surroundings much more quickly and easily when she accepts Wiggs's invitation to join the dance and, thus, bridges the gulf between the theatrical troupe and their reluctant Mormon hosts. Her essentially normal outlook appears later when she teases Denver about Travis, whereas her desire for monogamy explains her long-standing adherence to Hall.

The Navajos in *Wagonmaster* offer a test to the wagon train; the Cleggs, who initially have to be restrained from shooting it out when Reese violates the Indian woman, conspicuously fail this test. Their mindlessness is underscored by Luke's remark, made when they initially confront the Navajos on the trail, that he has never killed an Indian (the same line that the equally cretinous Joe speaks in *Cheyenne Autumn* before shooting down and scalping a hungry brave). The social solidarity of the Indians is seen in their dance, which integrates both groups and even includes the austere Elder Perkins. However, this spirit of accommodation is threatened by Reese's attack on the Indian woman, who symbolizes her outrage by casting dirt on herself in a gesture similar to what Elena does when she cries over the fallen body of Stone Calf. Wiggs's handling of this crisis, along with Travis's warning to Uncle

Shiloh that they are outgunned, demonstrates how the group must assume control over its individual members to ensure justice and life itself. Reese's whipping, which so nettles Shiloh and the other outlaws, is the only way a massacre can be avoided; in keeping with their stupidity, only the villains fail to grasp this elementary point.

Division abounds in the Indian society of *Two Rode Together*, with its conflicting leaders, Stone Calf and Quana Parker. The latter is cut from the same calculating cloth as Major Frazier, a connection that is reaffirmed when Gary's commanding officer is delighted to hear of Stone Calf's death. At the same time, Quana is linked visually to the rabid Elder Cleggs through his attraction to the rifle that McCabe wants to trade. Quana, being a realist, sees Stone Calf as a mad anachronism, a warrior who literally believes that shields can turn aside bullets. That McCabe kills this war chief accords with his increasing importance in Elena's life; indeed, Stone Calf's foolhardy charge into the light of the campfire dramatizes the change in Elena's life and allegiance in a sequence whose visual symbolism outweighs its verbal consistencies. Like the anachronistic Confederates who die so foolishly at Newton Station because of Yankee ingenuity in *The Horse Soldiers*, Stone Calf succumbs to McCabe's more realistic perceptions so that the struggle between the ambush-setting sheriff and the brave if precipitate Indian is brutally short. The death of Stone Calf forces McCabe to tear Elena away from her Indian allegiances in an act that belies the sheriff's cynical views about reintegrating a "captive" into civilized life. McCabe's insistence that Elena stop acting like a squaw represents his initial commitment to her and is their first step in escaping from the society of Fort Grant and Tascosa.

In *Two Rode Together* Major Frazier colors all activities associated with the cavalry, and his duplicity prepares us for Captain Wessels of *Cheyenne Autumn*. Frazier's avowed aim is to use McCabe to get the army out of a public relations bind. He sends Gary along as a "deserter" to keep rein on McCabe, but this decision stands in direct contrast to a similar maneuver in *Rio Grande*. Sheridan sent Yorke into Mexico without official orders, and the general was willing to share the blame if anything went wrong. Frazier exhibits no such willingness, for he tells Gary that any consequences will fall strictly on his subordinate's head, a prospect that is softened only by the lieutenant's remark that death will mark his failure more permanently.

Frazier's treatment of McCabe is even less defensible, for he sees the sheriff merely as an instrument to use and cast aside at the army's whim. The major believes there is "no reason to honor" any promise made to McCabe; however, such moral superiority diminishes quickly when he auctions off Running Wolf. Unlike even Wringle, Frazier does not see that sending the boy back to the Commanches would be more humane. As the presiding officer at the dance, the major enjoys the status of Thursday in *Fort Apache*; when the affair turns into a confrontation between Elena, McCabe, and the citizens,

Frazier becomes clearly identified with the society's persecutory forces. That nothing serious ever happens to Frazier is simply another indication of Ford's increasingly cynical vision; in essence, his favorite institution is now controlled by an opportunistic cynic. If Guthrie McCabe's dour views enable him to protect people from their own worst desires, Frazier's outlook simply perpetuates those wishes. McCabe has honor and feelings; the major has neither.

In *Wagonmaster* the Mormons are seeking a new land in which they can build a life apart from the society that persecutes them. The seekers-pioneers of *Two Rode Together* are trying to restore parts of their communal lives. Given such aims, it is only natural that the religious community exhibits more unity than the more temporary group. The Mormons are bound by their faith and by the perils they encounter, whereas the seekers in *Two Rode Together* have only their individual reasons for restoring the past. The latter group exhibits such strikingly varied types as Wringle and Knudson. The businesslike cynicism of the former stands in sharp contrast to the forlorn but dogged hopes of the latter. The pioneers in *Two Rode Together* never face the same degree of hardship that the Mormons do because they are protected by the army and are quickly escorted back to Fort Grant after McCabe and Gary have departed for Indian country; thus they are never bound together by any serious common peril. It is only in the lynching of Running Wolf that they ever act as a unit — and then under the sway of the Cleggs. At the end of *Wagonmaster*, the Mormon community has found a home in which it can prosper; *Two Rode Together* offers only the relief that its wagon-train society has disbanded and gone home.

The Mormons' initial appearance within Crystal City immediately sets them apart. Their costumes and their solidarity, as caught in the grouping of Wiggs, Perkins, and Prudence, clash with the less-restrained western garb and manners of the townspeople. Wiggs's conversation with Travis, who gradually realizes these people are Mormons, gently mocks the popular superstitions about this faith. The elder's capacity to make fun of himself establishes him as the true spiritual leader of the group, the man who can and does rise to the challenge of getting to the promised land. Once again, we see a character in Ford whose concern for the group overrides his concerns about his own personal well-being. Travis's later argument with Sandy about how precipitate gunplay leaves the wagon train to the mercy of the elements marks him as another such figure.

The Mormons' hope for the future is, of course, symbolized by their grain wagon, which, as Wiggs says, is worth more than gold because it contains seeds that will support those who will join them in the spring. Since getting this cargo over the mountains to the fertile valley of the San Juan is the major goal of the Mormons, the outlaws' jeopardizing of the grain wagon epitomizes their barbarism. The triumph of the Mormons over their human and natural adversaries is celebrated when they arrive at the river country and assemble to the accompaniment of a hymn. That their exploit is set within such an overtly religious context raises it to mythical heights, while Ford's reprised shots of the journey emphasize the Mormons' persistent strength. *Wagonmaster* celebrates the power of a community within both a geographical and a historical context: the Mormons literally become parts of the mythical past that Ford creates so magnificently here and elsewhere. The wagon train in *Two Rode Together*, which perhaps better illustrates reality in being closer to the way things actually might have been on the frontier, represents the darker side of Ford's social vision.

The priggish Elder Perkins and the earthly Sister Ledyard also illustrate the tolerance of Wiggs. Perkins, who constantly upbraids Wiggs's near lapses into profanity, is judgmental rather than compassionate, as seen by his insistence that the show folks be left to the desert elements rather than brought along. When Travis opposes that suggestion by insisting that he will also have to remain behind, Wiggs cleverly overrides Perkins by taking the elder aside and arguing that the appearance of the theatrical troupe is part of God's larger design and that anyone who opposes such a scheme is obviously misinformed. Perkins's subsequent discomfort at the Navajo camp nicely sets off Sister Ledyard's joyful acceptance of the same affair. Her caterwauling on a horn each morning underlines the unity of the Mormons just as buglers do in the cavalry films. Sister Ledyard's raised eyebrows when Wiggs describes the medicine show's "hoochy-koochy" act emphasizes her earthiness. However, her basically innocent heart is symbolized when she cooks for Uncle Shiloh when he arrives in camp. The outlaw insists on having hot pepper with his eggs, irritating Sister Ledyard, who is later amused when Travis says that he has used his gun only on snakes (a line that is repeated when the outlaws are dead and Wiggs asks about the young man's prowess with a weapon). Sister Ledyard's intuitive dislike of the Cleggs indicates that she is a woman of the world, one who must wrestle with the faith that demands that she care even for such obvious "trash" as the outlaw band.

Wiggs dominates through his good sense, which causes him to appeal to others on practical grounds. Thus, he initially approaches Travis and Sandy as a businessman prepared to buy their stock and throw in something extra if they will consent to guide the train. Wiggs hopes that the young men will go along, but he never begs for their aid. The appearance of the posse that insists the Mormons be out of town by nightfall only causes Wiggs to give his people a short sermon about what they are going to face. While the elder is tempted to use profanity once again (and is comically checked by Perkins), he emphasizes how the Mormons have always had to be tough and how he knows that this group will rise to the challenge. Wiggs's compassion, as opposed to Perkins's pity, seemingly arises from his past. The elder's more dissolute days are briefly implied when he asks Travis what kind of card game he is going to play. By showing that he is familiar with its variations, Wiggs reveals that he must have spent some time at the gaming tables. At his best, Wiggs conveys a sense of a lived past in the present and shows that history, for good or ill, is indeniably part of the human condition. In this regard, Ford continuously emphasizes that men are shaped by the historical times through which they have lived. Wiggs's rejection of his previous life for that of the Mormons provides the model that Travis and Sandy will finally emulate.

Wiggs is in control when he breaks up the dispute with Perkins about the theatrical troupe and, later, the fight between Sandy and Sam Jenkins (Don Summers), as well as when, in the Navajo camp, the attacked woman's honor must be restored. Wiggs's compassion extends to the acting troupe because he realizes that they too have been "invited out, like we were." The scuffle between the young men, ostensibly brought on by their disagreement over Sandy's language ("Hell's not swearing, it's geography!"), shows the elder operating comically to reinforce his thematic position. His waltzing around with Sandy and Sam, and the subsequent tearing of his pants — to the delight of Sister Ledyard — shows Wiggs to be a leader whose mistakes mark him as very human. While he can accept the Indians' back-handed compliment about the Mormons (who in Navajo eyes are only little crooks, as opposed to most white men), Wiggs sets the whole tone of this meeting by insisting that the trigger-happy Cleggs put away their weapons. Within the Navajo camp later, the elder immediately takes charge when Reese oversteps himself. By ordering the latter to be tied to a wagon wheel and whipped before the entire gathering, the elder engenders Shiloh's undying hatred. The beating of Reese, who howls and struggles throughout like an animal, also foreshadows Sam Jenkins's killing by Uncle Shiloh.

The more compassionate side of Wiggs is caught in two moments with Travis and Sandy. When the three men are riding on the point, they discuss the Cleggs and the threat the outlaws pose; Wiggs asks Travis if he is frightened. The wagonmaster answers that he is, but Sandy blusters that he is not; Wiggs, after listening to the latter's defiance, wisely adds, "That makes three of us." In this remark, the Mormon elder suggests that real heroism consists in dealing with ongoing difficulties rather than in bold, short-range actions. As a scared but patient and religious man, Wiggs takes it on himself never to reveal his fears to his flock in what is yet another obvious trait of heroic leadership. Later, when the elder and Travis scout a river crossing for quicksand, Wiggs falls off his horse and nearly curses once more. This time he is stopped by Travis in what resembles a parody of Perkins's earlier admonitions. The elder's ongoing propensity for anger, which stamps him as imperfect but human, is thus used to dramatize Travis's growing affinity for the Mormon style of life.

The tensions between the seekers in *Two Rode Together* are never reconciled through leadership; indeed, these people are bound together only by a goal that, when reached, will cast them apart. The wealthy Henry J. Wringle quickly dispels his authority by cynically insisting that he will pay for any reasonable facsimile of the boy his wife has lost. Ole Knudson wants simply what he ironically thinks will be best for his lost "Frieda," and the Cleggs are merely looking for an excuse to kill Indians rather than find the wife and mother they have lost. Mr. Purcell's ineffectiveness is underlined by his failure to persuade Marty to attend the group dance and his failure to defend Running Wolf at the offscreen kangaroo court that precedes the Indian boy's lynching. Mr. Purcell represents the shortsightedness of the seekers, for he is appalled by Running Wolf's appearance and then, rather too late, wishes that he had never set out on such a quest.

In this regard Purcell symbolizes the relationship between the seekers and McCabe, the army's answer to their aims. The sheriff is initially hailed as a "blessing" and a "Moses" by them and Major Frazier. These hopes are not dispelled by McCabe's attempts to dissuade any search for long-lost relatives; it is not until he has returned with two captives that the seekers realize the sordid reality of what he said. The death of Running Wolf establishes that the Cleggs are the arbitrating power within the wagon-train community; their violence precipitates the most communal act the seekers ever undertake. The community's complicity is further underscored by the participation of Mr. Purcell and the heretofore (relatively) stable Mr. McCandless, who drives the wagon in which the young Indian is taken and lynched. That the entire group overwhelms Gary's resistance clearly separates this guilty assembly from the Mormons of *Wagonmaster*.

Three figures soften this picture somewhat, while suggesting the divergent outlooks within the wagon-train community of *Two Rode Together*. The forlorn Mr. Knudson, whose daughter turns up alive (and thoroughly acculturated as an Indian mother) in Quana's camp, represents the ideal suffering parent. McCabe gently tries to dissuade Knudson, but finally the sheriff accepts the task of finding Frieda even though the father lacks the money to pay him. McCabe is swayed when Knudson comments that it will make no difference to him if Frieda has turned into a "savage." When last seen, Knudson reinforces his unquestioning love by humbly asking if Frieda was ever seen during the protagonist's trek into Commanche territory. Ironically, the girl fled from McCabe and Gary, who allowed her to remain with the Indians out of compassion, offering another point at which Ford explores the relationship between truth and legend. In this case, McCabe's lie about never seeing Frieda suggests that the truth must often be guided by compassion in human affairs.

Mrs. McCandless has the same determination as Knudson, although her quest is the result of obvious madness. Her need to find "Toby" and so restore the past reflects the insanity of the entire undertaking and suggests how Ford's protagonists increasingly put their lives on the line for equivocal, if not worthless, goals. In *Two Rode Together*, the institutional needs of the army and the ostensibly enlightened wishes of public opinion (who can argue that a parent should not look for a lost child?) come together in Mrs. McCandless's demand for restoration. McCabe and Gary are, ultimately, sops to prevent "bad press" from coming to the larger institution: they must risk death so that Mrs. McCandless can be soothed, in what is certainly a great departure from such heroic and rational motivations as those of Ringo in *Stagecoach* and Wyatt in *My Darling Clementine*. Mrs. McCandless, in a further irony, is victimized by her own will and the ways in which others try to spare her feelings in allowing her to take Running Wolf. The cynicism of Frazier, the dismay of the other seekers, and the supposed kindness of her husband all contribute to her murder. Out of a combination of motives, some of which at least seem praiseworthy, Ford fashions an instance of tragic results emerging from good wishes.

Sergeant Posey's (Andy Devine) role as comic relief in *Two Rode Together* does not prevent his being a moral agent. The running gags about his weight and the strain it puts on his horse, jokes instigated by McCabe, fix the sergeant as the butt of the fun; however, as the guardian of the wagon train after Gary and McCabe have gone into Indian country, Posey capably guides the seekers back to Fort Grant. During the comic fight between the Clegg boys and Gary, Posey rescues his commanding officer. Knocking Ortho and Greeley into a nearby stream by means of his stomach elicits laughs from the drunken McCabe, but Posey's relative ease in handling these buffoons foreshadows Gary's later failure to stem the mob violence that kills Running Wolf. When Posey breaks up the riverside discussion between McCabe and Gary earlier, he chides the lieutenant for failing to fill his canteen, in a comic instance of extending his aid to his superior. At the post dance Posey offers silent support for the actions of the two couples. In a pantry the sergeant finishes and then tosses aside a bottle to affirm his feelings for McCabe and Elena, who have just told the assembly why she could not kill herself, and for Gary, who has challenged his fellow officers because of their treatment of Elena. Sergeant Posey stands for the ordinary run of mankind, so his expression of approval indicates how we should react to this dramatic situation.

The centripetal plot in *Wagonmaster*, which brings disparate elements together as a society, also unites the film's various women, who accept their positions within the Mormon community. There are no romantic rivalries between them, with only small amounts of jealousy being seen when some Mormon wives look askance while their "men folk" dance in the Navajo camp. The centrifugal plot of *Two Rode Together* is dramatized in its women and the choices they make for themselves and their loved ones. The only romantic rivalry, a rather muted one between Belle Aragon and Elena, is designed to open McCabe's eyes about his erstwhile partner and bedmate. In *Wagonmaster*, Sister Ledyard, Prudence, Miss Fleuretty, and Denver finally emerge as members of the same community. By contrast, any society that could include Mrs. McCandless, Marty Purcell, Belle Aragon, and Elena Madriaga, the women in *Two Rode Together*, would hardly be a community, since their aims and temperaments are so at odds. Such groupings again emphasize the central differences between these films: in *Wagonmaster*, there is the prospect of a merging of the individual and the community so that the aims of the one can be incorporated and nurtured by the purposes of the other; there is no such possibility in *Two Rode Together*, where the best that any individual can hope for is an escape from the society that surrounds Tascosa and the military base.

Denver offers the most extended female portrait in *Wagonmaster* and, as such, is provided with significant bits of business. Her initial appearance finds her holding a cigarette, which she quickly throws away; later, after she has rejected Travis's proposal, we see her smoking while staring wistfully back at the trail that has led her away from the protagonist. The lovers are also united by water, which Denver asks for when she first sees Travis; that she and the others have been drinking Dr. Hall's alcoholic "elixir" to stave off thirst is not immediately apparent. Denver's initially brazen appearance disguises her essential goodness, which emerges only as she somewhat reluctantly realizes her love for Travis. On the trail before the wagon train reaches more water, Denver resembles Hall when she wastes this precious commodity. She throws away her bathwater and causes Travis to lose control of his horse and fall, to the delight of the other pioneers. In spite of his discomfort, Travis is awed by Denver's very presence. When she asks to be helped out of the wagon, she appears to be undressed and thus causes the hero to hesitate; the girl's being clothed serves notice that she is aware of the great attraction she holds for the wagonmaster. At the river, Denver again indulges in sexual innuendo when she asks Travis if she is free to bathe now and proceeds into the hills to hide from prying eyes; the protagonist's own response is characteristically ambiguous—he says he will "join" her but does so by spurring his horse into the nearby river.

Denver consistently belittles Travis to Fleuretty, who sees the wagonmaster's interest and teases the girl about it. If Travis is "that rube," Denver's deeper feelings come out when he offers her Prudence's walking shoes; after first ascertaining that he is a bachelor, the girl borrows the footwear. Denver also rejects Travis's later proposal out of a fear that her acceptance would precipitate further trouble with the Cleggs. She is certainly a temptation to the outlaws: Reese makes an advance toward her, a move that Travis checks by insisting that a lady has a right to choose her partner in this particular dance, and at the posse's approach later, Floyd carries her kicking into the back of a wagon. In her efforts to keep Travis at bay, Denver resembles Dallas in

Stagecoach, for she cannot believe that her romantic luck has changed so suddenly and so dramatically; Travis offers Denver life on a small ranch as an inducement to marriage, just as Ringo did in the earlier film. The girl is even shown primping at a mirror before Reese and Travis argue over her, and she states that she can "take care of myself" after their tête-à-tête has broken up. Her insistence that Travis not address her as "Ma'am" will be picked up in *Two Rode Together* more vehemently when Belle Aragon chastises Lieutenant Gary for the same thing. In both cases the male responds, in accepted comic fashion, by immediately using the offending term. Denver offers this rebuke only once (and does not insist on it even then) before she accepts such formal language as part of Travis's gallantry.

Hannah Clegg (Mae Marsh), who appears briefly in Quana's camp when she comes to McCabe and Gary's tent, embodies another version of the duality that so colors *Two Rode Together*. This elderly woman fondly remembers her sons, is willing to reveal white captives for whom the main characters might trade, and yet insists she cannot return to civilization herself. Gary again indulges in the kindness of a lie by telling Hannah that her sons are "fine boys," although neither he nor McCabe says anything about her husband. At the same time, they do not protest when Hannah insists that she must stay with the Commanches because she could never be reassimilated into white society. Paradoxically, if Mrs. Clegg can insist on her own inability to go back, she exhibits no such compunction about revealing the identities of other captives. She quickly identifies Running Wolf and Frieda Knudson and then, unwittingly, adds that "Stone Calf's woman" is also white. Thus, Hannah serves as an essential plot device while at the same time illustrating, in miniature, the larger perception of human isolation at the center of Ford's vision in *Two Rode Together*. It is, of course, the integration of such a minor character into the film's thematic mainstream that marks Ford's directorial genius again and again in his westerns.

Elena de la Madriaga changes most in *Two Rode Together*. She is wrenched out of the Indian culture by McCabe, then thrown into a hostile white environment only to be whisked off again by her rescuer, who, finally, realizes how much he loves her. To enrage Stone Calf, Quana brings her to McCabe and Gary and insists that she be part of their deal. Elena, resigned to an early death through overwork in the Commanche camp, states that no man will ever want to fight over (or for) her because she has been the wife of a Comanche chief. McCabe discerns her Mexican ancestry and, in so doing, distinguishes himself from Lieutenant Gary, whom we have already seen as physically weak. Elena's retort that going or staying "does not matter" conceals her deeper feelings, in a manner similar to Denver's dismissal of Travis. By the time McCabe and Gary arrive at a campsite and argue about whether to stay there, Elena has changed enough to want to remain behind with the sheriff. This alteration is signaled by Elena's removal of her serape, which has concealed her shape and her striking red clothing. This symbolic baring of herself to McCabe dramatizes the burgeoning relationship between them.

During the night, as they wait for Stone Calf, Elena anxiously moves over to McCabe as a potential lover, while telling of her abduction by the Comanches. McCabe is, of course, only using Elena as bait and moving her into the light to further enrage (and hopefully unsettle) his Indian enemy. During Elena's recital, she crosses herself when she mentions the death of her mother — a religious act violently contrasted by her behavior over the fallen Stone Calf. Her Comanche lament over the dead chief enrages McCabe, who seemingly cannot stand such conduct from a "white" woman he is starting to love. His embrace of Elena, after she pulls away from Stone Calf's corpse and so symbolically saves herself from her Indian past, instinctively reveals the sheriff's deeper feelings through a memorable composition.

At Fort Grant, however, McCabe errs by giving Elena over to Mrs. Frazier (Olive Carey) — a choice that leads the girl to chastise him for having brought her back to civilization at all. Elena explains that the people around her have "eyes that bite" and make her feel unclean, things she never experienced with the Comanches. McCabe is distressed that Elena gives in to such pressures, so he decides they must appear at the dance; in a sequence that resembles the Pygmalion legend, he talks about redoing her hair and getting her a more civilized dress. Once again, McCabe's feelings are guided by outward considerations, but his real self emerges when he reenters to wordlessly kiss Elena. At the dance Miss Madriaga attempts to answer the pointed questions of "ladies" who wonder about whether she had any children with Stone Calf. McCabe finally answers another unspoken question when he notes that Elena could not commit suicide because of her Catholic faith; thus the sheriff shames the assembly by pointing out the moral dilemma in which Elena found herself and which they have unfeelingly overlooked.

Miss Madriaga's subsequent flight from Tascosa, precipitated in part by Belle Aragon's treatment, is the only way that she can ever find a rational, if not a happy, life. While Elena can speak to the local porter in Spanish (and thus exhibit a talent no one else in Tascosa has shown), she is repelled by the indecencies that Belle proposes. Their confrontation in the saloon again raises the film's central question of who the real barbarians are. Like many other films and novels, *Two Rode Together* suggests the possibility that civilized man contains the savage very close to the surface (as witnessed by McCage's rage on the trail with Gary), while society's supposedly refined elements often fail to rise above imposing vicious racial stereotypes.

Marty Purcell changes more slowly, within the confines of a settled society. Her gradual blossoming into Gary's intended, marked by her alteration from a horse-riding girl in a cowboy outfit to a demurely dressed lady at a ball, dramatizes the easing of her guilt over losing her younger brother to the Comanches. Marty's earliest extended appearance finds her throwing flour over the Clegg brothers in a bit of comic knockabout that illustrates her dislike of them, particularly the more surly Greeley, who regards her as "his girl." The flour-dusting scene brings Ortho and his brother into open conflict with Gary, whom they regard as a "Yankee" intruder preventing them from massacring Comanches. Their rage resembles the religiously toned zeal of their father; and their true selves emerge during the lynching of Running Wolf, when their demented grins resemble those of Uncle Shiloh's dissolute brood in *Wagonmaster*. Marty also refuses their offer to go to the dance because she has no interest in such activities; despite her father's urging, she prefers to go on "torturing" herself.

When Marty holds hands with Jim Gary by the riverside where the wagon train makes its first stop on the way to Comanche territory, earlier situations immediately come to mind. This type of setting has already been used in *Two Rode Together* in the remarkable scene between the lieutenant and McCabe during their ride to Fort Grant, and Ford has associated Denver and Travis with a similar setting. Gary's romantic notions are obvious and domestic right from the start, since he compliments Marty on her practical choice for a campsite. His relieving her of the water bucket and their spontaneous walk further underscore what is developing between them. Marty soon trusts Gary enough to show him a picture of her lost brother in the hope that it will help McCabe in the search. All these good feelings come to a halt, however, when Sheriff McCabe, now drunk because of what he has been asked to do, assails Marty with a graphic description of what her lost sibling would now be like and would do to her if given the chance. Gary's solicitude leads him to rail at McCabe while trying to comfort the distraught Marty. His embrace of the girl then precipitates the fight with the Clegg boys; the fight, though funny, establishes the physical limits of the lieutenant's heroism. Marty ends up being his nurse after the brawl, and their relationship is extended.

After Gary has returned from Quana's camp, the lovers' next meeting finds Marty asking if Jim is proposing when, amid numerous remarks about the nature of army life and his abiding loyalty to the service, he asks her to dance. Their kissing scene on a moonlit porch reprises a similar setup in *Fort Apache*; however, Gary, unlike Mickey O'Rourke, looks around to be sure no one is watching. Thus, even love has become less spontaneous in this later film. Marty's emotional growth is further symbolized by the music box that her lost brother so enjoyed. While she can listen pensively to its chiming tune, her reaction after the lynching of Running Wolf clearly shows that she has freed herself from the past. The young Indian, on his way to death, pauses briefly when he hears the music box playing and utters what sounds like "mine." If Running Wolf is, indeed, Marty's brother, his reversion to English is telling. Yet the girl shatters the music box after she has dismissed that possibility; in effect, Marty chooses not to remember such a "truth" because it would not be useful in the present or the future. Once again, a conflict arises between the truth and its usefulness in human affairs, and though Ford is keenly aware of society's need to create a usable past, he is consistent in portraying the ambiguous realities out of which such history is manufactured.

The outlaws in *Wagonmaster* are stock villains out of melodrama, for they never do anything to ameliorate (or even explain) their personalities. Uncle Shiloh mouths religion but has no real feeling for it, and his brood, with their strains of incest and madness, are close-mouthed or babbling degenerates. While the villains in *Two Rode Together* are also bent on their own ends, such figures as Major Frazier, Quana Parker, and Henry Wringle have all gained positions of respect or authority within their different communities. Thus, evil wears a more authoritarian face and even sounds reasonable in the later film. Indeed, given the characters of the story's villains, it is only fitting that the principal confrontation between McCabe and Stone Calf takes on an air of tragedy: the efficient modern man destroys an anachronistic, but physically heroic, opponent who represents an older, more chivalric ethos.

The nature of the Clegg family in *Wagonmaster* is established by the prologue when they rob a bank and then trek toward their seemingly inevitable meeting with the Mormon wagon train. Uncle Shiloh's supervision of the robbery is marked by his return to "pay back" a teller for firing at them. His whining admonition ("I wish you hadna done that, son") establishes Shiloh's hypocrisy, since it proceeds his gunning down of the offender. The outlaws' entry into the Mormon camp harkens back to *My Darling Clementine*, for they are shown in close-up as were the Clantons when they met Wyatt on the night of James's death. Ford alternates shots at the Cleggs with close-ups of Travis, Sandy, Elder Wiggs, and Sam Jenkins to establish that the entire community of the wagon train is threatened by the outlaw brood. Another close-up sequence occurs when the Mormons succeed in crossing the final mountain pass by means of the trench they dig. While Uncle Shiloh and his boys enjoy the crash of the first wagon, they gradually become gloomier as wagon after wagon succeeds in making this passage. The final gunfight between them and the film's leading characters again harkens back stylistically to *My Darling Clementine*; at its conclusion, the stricken Shiloh calls on all his dead "boys," just as Pa Clanton did, as a prelude to his own last defiant gesture before Travis kills him. The villainy of the Clegg family is further signaled by the absence of music during their appearances. When they initially ride into the Mormon camp after hearing the square-dance music, all music stops except for a short, ominous cue that underlines the outlaws' emergence. The music also stops when they appear by a riverside. The happy Mormons are whistling as they start another day, but as soon as the camera moves to the outlaws with whom Wiggs has struck a bargain concerning their remaining with the wagon train, all music ceases.

Uncle Shiloh carries a whip, which he is not adverse to using on his brood, and so he calls Pa Clanton and Liberty Valance to mind. Shiloh enjoys disarming his enemies with soft-spokenness; indeed, his method used with the bank teller, whom he approached as if he were going to use some lesser degree of retaliation, is repeated during the mountain crossing. After Shiloh has chuckled over the supposed "gold" that the Mormons feel they are transporting in the form of grain, he insists that Wiggs must drive this precious load without benefit of the trench and at full throttle. Sam Jenkins is already in the driver's seat of this wagon, and his slight hesitation, when Shiloh commands him to get down, costs him his life as the outlaw shoots him and then as Floyd pumps another bullet into his prone body. Uncle Shiloh's biblical allusions, which include a reference to the providence that marks the sparrow's fall, provide yet another hypocritical facet that masks the antisocial rage within him. His taunting of Wiggs with the phrase "the promised land" and his angry casting down of dirt to announce that hostilities have commenced are further instances of his style. When entering the Mormon camp, Shiloh proclaims that the pioneers' wholesome "mountain music" in the wilderness guided him and his boys because they knew that no Indian would make it. This dialogue echoes the reactions of Travis, Sandy, and Wiggs when they first heard sounds emanating from the actors' camp (and, again, decided that no Indian would make them). Shiloh's rotundity also provides him with a comic physical character; however, he is as great a beast and as instinctual a killer as Pa Clanton or Liberty Valance.

His sons run a gamut from total silence (Jesse) to loquacious madness (Luke), with variations of insanity marking the bearlike Floyd and the libidinous Reese. If Jesse is simply a scowling presence who dies voicelessly, Luke is the most simpleminded of the bunch, and much of what he says irritates the outlaw leader. Luke, whom Shiloh describes as somewhat "light-headed," is constantly fascinated by guns and killing, as seen in his awareness that only Travis and Sandy are armed when the Cleggs enter the camp and, later, when they take control. When the whole brood descends on Dr. Hall, believing him to be a physician, and when the con man demurs, Luke menacingly insists that he "hates liars" and feels that killing is none too good for them. Floyd, on the other hand, is a tower of strength that Shiloh uses against his enemies; speechless, like Jesse, Floyd enjoys violent physical action such as throwing away Travis's and Sandy's weapons or carrying the struggling Denver into the back of a wagon. Floyd's shooting of the fallen Sam identifies him as a true son of Shiloh.

Reese, the most active in seeking the comforts of the Mormon camp, is the most precipitate of the outlaws. His approaches to Denver suggest his potential for rape, and his nighttime encounter with Hall further reveals his essential animosity. Reese forces the medicine show impresario to read a sign to him and then insists that Hall treat Shiloh's wound. The appearance of the rest of the Clegg gang, accompanied by their leader's remark that finding a physician and a bed, as well as a bottle of good whiskey, is truly "providential," puts Hall in even further danger. After Reese's attempt to escort Denver to the Navajo camp is checkmated by Travis, Reese's libido runs amok in the camp, with predictable results. When the theatrical troupe separates from the wagon train, it is Reese who goes after them and returns with them to the main party. His grinning lechery is rarely varied; thus his death, like those of the rest of his family, goes unlamented. Travis's earlier analogy to shooting snakes is totally appropriate, since the removal of the Clegg band has as much moral significance as the killing of vipers.

The villains in *Two Rode Together* survive, for the most part, by virtue of the same character trait — hypocrisy — that marks Uncle Shiloh. Customary cinematic sources of villainy, particularly Indians such as Stone Calf and Running Wolf, emerge as embodiments of anachronistic ways of life rather than as purveyors of evil. More characteristically, Henry Wringle's hypocrisy just barely conceals his malevolence. Wringle sees his wife's pursuit of her long-lost child as a simple impediment to making money; as a result, he approaches McCabe, as "one man to another," with what he considers a sensible business proposition. The merchant's offer of one thousand dollars for "any kid" ties together many of the thematic strands in *Two Rode Together*, for his price clearly meets McCabe's earlier declaration to Major Frazier that the cost of rescuing the captives would be "whatever the market'll bear." Although the sheriff has been consistently presented as a greedy capitalist up to this point, McCabe is dismayed by Wringle's offer. In insisting that he has always made "his own luck," the merchant exposes yet another unseemly side of the pioneers' search; indeed, their group embodies all the evils of the society that Ford delineated in *Stagecoach* and that are here moving to the center of his dramatic canvas.

The ultimate victim of Wringle's offer is, of course, the unfortunate Running Wolf, who seemingly fits on neither side; Quana Parker is willing to sell him to the whites, who, when confronted with his savagery, want no part of him either. The howling Indian boy framed against the bars of his cell clearly symbolizes such dehumanization, and the bucket of water he throws in Wringle's face offers an appropriate verdict on the older man's actions. Wringle naturally refuses to accept Running Wolf as the "kid" who would satisfy his wife and, at the same time, declares that the entire expedition has been a "fool's errand." Like Major Frazier, who also feels no obligation to McCabe, Wringle steadfastly refuses to pay the sheriff for the captured boy, thus signifying that there is indeed no honor among thieves.

The more openly vicious style of civilized villainy in *Two Rode Together* is embodied by another Clegg family, this one with a fire-and-brimstone father and two slightly simpleminded sons. Their identification with the South, as witnessed when Greeley chides Gary as a "Yankee" in a "soldier suit," puts them on the same moral level as the deserters whom Marlowe interrogates and then returns to Confederate justice in *The Horse Soldiers*. Ortho's and Greeley's capacity for violence initially seems limited to rocking Marty's wagon and to engaging in a comic bout with Gary and Posey, instances in which they are easily bested by the girl and by the rotund sergeant. During the lynching of Running Wolf, the Clegg boys appear in the forefront of the mob, and their gestures serve as a kind of mad commentary on all that happens. These brothers embody the same demented violence as seen in the Cleggs of *Wagonmaster* and among the trail hands in *Cheyenne Autumn*. It is significant that these characters suffer no indignity greater than some comic discomforts; apparently, there are no longer any means to exterminate idle maliciousness from the world.

Their father, Henry, appears like an avenging angel whose only mission seems to be the extermination of Indians. He is a variation of Ethan Edwards in that the loss of a family member has caused him to go to war against an entire race. We first see him, with his trusted rifle in hand, bragging that he is certain he has killed, or at least wounded, an Indian on the other side of the river. At the same time, Mrs. McCandless is thrashing in the water, so that both extremes of the pioneers' madness are on display. When Running Wolf is about to be killed, Henry appears with his rifle and his Bible, the two sources of his inspiration, as a kind of Old Testament judge waging a holy war against the heathen. The essence of this man and his sons is best caught when Greeley grumbles because the soldiers have prevented them from going into Comanche territory and wreaking their own kind of havoc. With this second Clegg family, Ford shows how racial enmities become crippling when revenge is the primary motive; the men of this family are incapable of learning the lesson that Ethan Edwards finally grasps in *The Searchers*.

Sandy Owens represents the more impetuous half of a heroic partnership in *Wagonmaster*. His actions are nearly always direct and occasionally foolhardy, as seen in his almost immediate romantic reaction to Prudence and the comic excess of his bowing to her at nearly every opportunity. It is Sandy who initially pushes Travis into joining the wagon train because of his concern about the women and children; however, when the outlaws take control, Sandy's discretion gives way to his need to "make a play." In checking such enthusiasm Travis slowly emerges as the more rational of the two, a perception that is solidified when the Mormons finally reach the long-sought river in the desert. Sandy sights the stream, but his shouts create a stampede among the tired pioneers. The chaos that he precipitates, the action of a boy, stands in sharp contrast to the behavior of Wiggs and Travis, who stay behind to see that no serious damage is done. Travis's rescue of an unhorsed rider, from whom he receives an obligatory thank-you, serves as the counterpart to Sandy's rashness and, again, establishes Travis as the primary hero. In addition, the opening scene initially establishes Travis's primacy: the partners calculate how much their horses should bring in Crystal City, a comic interlude in which Sandy shows that he does not know elementary arithmetic.

Sandy does, however, augment his partner by preparing to fight the Cleggs and forcing Travis to act at the climax. Despite the rapport that has been established between them, and Travis's own recognition that Uncle Shiloh intends to kill Wiggs, only Sandy is ready when the moment of confrontation arises. Sandy's less exalted rank is consistently emphasized: he is goaded into a fistfight with Sam Jenkins (again in opposition to Travis, who deals with the Clegg family more diplomatically); he uses exaggerated gestures with Prudence; and he accepts and subsequently handles the hidden gun. Sandy swaggers a bit more than Travis because he seems younger; this trait is marked during the film's later stages when Sandy wants to battle the outlaws and Travis reminds him that sixty lives will be in jeopardy if such a confrontation takes place too soon.

As a horse trader, Travis Blue seems to have a past that is almost as suspect as that of Wiggs. His initial reactions in Crystal City to the sheriff's inquiries suggest that he has dealt, and not always scrupulously, there before. Their card game reveals Travis's capacity for bluffing; but once he commits himself to being the wagonmaster, he reveals his more compassionate side as the "shepherd" of all the members of the group. Travis's quiet intercession for the stranded theatrical troupe shows his nature, for he persuades the Mormons through a patient determination; indeed, his posture at this juncture reprises the watchful ease he embodied at the corral when dealing with the sheriff and Wiggs. Travis's capacity for quick thinking is abetted by his superior horsemanship; after he has evaded the Navajo riders, he easily deflects the Indian chief's remark that he resembles someone who earlier fleeced them in a trade.

If Travis quickly passes himself off as a Mormon and quiets down the entire row, his comic actions foreshadow that the young man is coming to accept the life-style of those he serves. Travis gives in to the Clegg band because he — unlike Sandy, who has to be slapped before surrendering his gun — recognizes the danger to all from the demented outlaw family. Later, however, when the opportunity presents itself, Travis retaliates. The arrival of the posse from town forces the outlaws to hide within the wagons, and to prevent a direct confrontation, Travis goes to get some bacon for the lawmen. As he exits from this wagon, Travis manages to slap Jesse in the face with his burden, thus showing that he is prepared to confront the Cleggs when necessary.

Travis's patience is coupled with his innate dislike for violence, thus giving him a greater depth than his sidekick. While Sandy courts Prudence in the most affected and obvious ways, Travis's pursuit of Denver never violates his own sense of what he is. He never pleads with her or attempts to be something he is not — a process that is underscored by his constant gentility with the girl. At the same time, Travis has grown to distrust violence as, at best, a necessary evil; thus his approach to destroying the villains is tinged with reluctance and then marked by his own rejection of the very means he has used. By throwing his gun into the wilderness after the shootout, Ford's protagonist dramatically signals his acceptance of the Mormon way of life. His last appearance behind the reins of a wagon, with Denver at his side, reveals not only that Travis has won her love but also that they have both become integral parts of the Mormon community. Travis's "retirement" from point rider to covered wagon driver couples with Denver's more sedate clothing to show the alterations that both have made.

The friendship between Travis and Sandy is more clear-cut and uncomplicated than any other between male characters in Ford's westerns. There is none of the complexity of motives that surrounds Wyatt and Doc or Doniphon and Stoddard; at the same time, the world in which they operate, unlike that of *Two Rode Together*, still allows for successful heroic action. The affinity between these young men is best caught by their decision to join the wagon train, and their ongoing humor marks their easy rapport. Travis admits to being lost on the trail at one point, but there is no panic because Sandy remembers that they have passed this way before. Sandy's prowess also comes forward with the Navajos; he speaks their language and negotiates for Travis and Wiggs. The moment of greatest tension between the two young leads occurs when their perceptions of Uncle Shiloh force them to acknowledge that Wiggs will die unless something is done. Their campfire discussion, which reinforces their earlier immediate recognition of the outlaws at the band's arrival, again reveals Sandy's precipitate character and Travis's greater patience. The wagonmaster does not quite know what to do, but he is certain that his partner's rashness will only lead to more trouble. The teacher-apprentice relationship between them is reaffirmed when Sandy brandishes the pistol that Prudence has clandestinely placed in his hands. When Travis snidely remarks that Sandy had better be careful not "to blow your brains out," Owens is at that very moment putting the gun into his pants with its barrel pointed at his buttocks. Even if such wit is lost on its object (in keeping with Owens's unsophisticated nature), the relative innocence and idealism of Sandy and Travis mark them as proper heroes for a story in which good and evil exist in absolute terms.

No such easy rapport marks the relationship between Gary and McCabe in *Two Rode Together*. Although they are old friends, their trek into the wilderness reveals the differences between them in order to create a more stable friendship. Initially, the sheriff and the lieutenant are drinking acquaintances whose joy at seeing each other is, probably, in direct proportion to the amount of time that has lapsed between meetings. This somewhat idyllic mood lasts until McCabe learns why he has been brought to the army post, and then the two men become virtual sparring partners until they return from the Comanche camp. Their disagreement about tactics almost boils over into violence when they argue about how to confront Stone Calf. At this juncture their verbal sparring takes on a savage cast when McCabe's pistol and psychotic leer cause Gary to back down. The more unsettling tone of *Two Rode Together* is perhaps best caught in this emotional standoff; here McCabe in threatening to murder his partner if he is contradicted, descends to the level of the outlaw family in *Wagonmaster*. There is not even any pretense of a duel or a gunfight, since the sheriff simply draws his weapon and states that he uses it only when he means to kill and never to bluff. Although McCabe softens his position somewhat after Gary has backed down, there is still no question that their relationship is more conditional than any we have heretofore seen between male leads in a Ford western.

Jim Gary remains a career soldier throughout, for even if he disagrees with particular policies, he never revolts against military decorum. At the dance, as he prepares to leave with Marty as a result of all that has happened to Elena, he still goes through the motions of military etiquette. Gary never challenges Frazier but accepts his orders as part of the routine to which he has given his life. His proposal to Marty stresses the patience and suffering that inevitably attend military existence while also emphasizing that she will have to agree to those conditions if they are to marry. The lieutenant initially manipulates McCabe, for much of what they discuss (e.g., Belle's amorous advances and her reduction of the protagonist's name to "Guth") is used by Gary against his erstwhile friend once the sheriff becomes angered by what he is being asked to do. While Major Frazier neither understands nor approves of the private needling between these characters, he goes along because Gary's provocations sway McCabe into doing the army's business. The lieutenant's military ethics are also shown when he is challenged by the flour-besmirched Greeley: duty might forbid an officer from brawling, but there is always tomorrow, when he will be free and "glad" to oblige the cretinous Clegg. Gary finally emerges as prophetic when he opines that McCabe has found something he wants "more than ten percent of" in Elena. If the older lawman succeeds in fleeing from the comforts of civilization, Gary can only establish a future with Marty in which he will continue to be Major Frazier's errand boy.

Guthrie McCabe is capable of significant moral growth and finally acts decisively on what he has learned. Though cut from the mold of Wyatt Earp, as seen by his dismissal of the arriving gamblers, McCabe is much less of an idealist than is the savior of Tombstone. Indeed, McCabe, in seeking the comforts of office, presages Link Appleyard. For McCabe, all human relationships seemingly turn on money, and in the beginning of the film that subject is his favorite topic of conversation. Gary is a failure in McCabe's eyes because of his relative poverty, and only the prospect of "getting what the traffic will bear" out of the "sodbusters" seems to motivate the sheriff's decision to go to Quana's camp. However, such cynicism is belied by McCabe's dismay at encountering Henry J. Wringle and by his compassionate advice to Mr. Knudson. He is, finally, so disgusted at the prospect of what he is about to do that he gets drunk and speaks a "sober man's mind" to Marty when she asks about the prospect of recovering her brother ("Sister, he'd rape you!"). Before he goes off with Wringle's jug of liquor, McCabe argues with Gary in the latter's tent and, mocking military ritual, rises to salute the lieutenant in a manner that parodies the first meeting between Kirby Yorke and Jeff Yorke in *Rio Grande*. Once again, a tent proves too low when McCabe's head touches the fabric.

The sheriff's calculating nature is most obviously dramatized in the ambush he sets for Stone Calf. While others want the Indian leader dead, it remains for McCabe to use the tactics of the modern world against the anachronistic warrior. It is during this sequence, however, that McCabe's moral and racial senses emerge, when he makes Elena cease mourning over Stone Calf. In adopting such a role, McCabe assumes an abiding responsibility for the "senorita" and sets up expectations that will prompt them to escape from the morally chaotic world of Fort Grant and Tascosa. If McCabe becomes a veritable Pygmalion to Elena, he is also now reviled by the disappointed pioneers, who want nothing to do with Running Wolf. The same degree of antagonism greets Elena: the army women prefer to whisper about her depraved life with Stone Calf rather than offer the compassion that would mark a more humane society. McCabe rises to this occasion by calling out Major Frazier and pointing out that the latter has never actually dealt with the Comanches. McCabe's final fury is directed at Belle, who belittles Elena yet again; however, he realizes that beating the "hell" out of his former mistress would serve no lasting purpose, so he bids her good-bye (by symbolically throwing coins on the bar) and says farewell to Gary instead. As the shotgun rider on the outbound stage, McCabe makes his own and Elena's lives complete in a typically backhanded fashion.

It is this very understated quality that distinguishes the relationship between the two male leads in *Two Rode Together*. In one of the most celebrated scenes Ford ever filmed, McCabe and Gary converse at a river crossing quite early, in a sequence remarkable for its sustained acting and its unusual camera position. Ford places his camera within the river, and the sparse dialogue between the principals represents the trimmed-down quality that marks the director at his best. Their conversation about Belle's aggressiveness explains McCabe's desire to "get away for a while," and the rapport between them is further established when McCabe states that Madam Aragon carries a stiletto in her garter. Gary's less-than-startled reaction causes McCabe to do a double take, and the lieutenant's subsequent insistence that he "knew" this fact only because he just heard it hardly refutes that he may have slept with Belle.

The final return to Tascosa, and McCabe's discovery that his position as sheriff has been filled by the slow-witted Ward, show that the two leads have grown even more in tune with each other. Gary appreciates his friend's plight, but he heartily wishes the ex-sheriff well and then calmly proceeds to inform Belle about what has happened to her former lover. McCabe, like Travis Blue, has found a new way of life — in this case, one based on something other than cash relations. The receding stagecoach, which leaves Tascosa in the opposite direction from which it originally entered, further symbolizes McCabe's escape from the predatory worlds through which he has traveled in *Two Rode Together.*

Chapter 10

Three Godfathers and
The Searchers

Three Godfathers (1948) and *The Searchers* (1956) center on journeys into a wilderness, with the rescue of a child as the ostensible aim in both films. They are among the most sharply contrasted of Ford's westerns. Although two of the three main characters in the earlier film die, it is far more comic and optimistic; the later effort embodies the first expression of the director's darker vision of the West. *Three Godfathers* contains little violence, whereas *The Searchers* abounds with physical and psychological hostilities. Sentimentality is hedged by humor in the earlier work, but human feeling emerges only after a tremendous emotional struggle in the second. The plot of the earlier work, adapted from a Peter B. Kyne novel, is dated, sentimentalized, and predictable. The narrative of *The Searchers*, based on an Alan LeMay novel, is circuitous and self-conscious, in keeping with its darker and all but obsessive thematic interests and characters. Whereas the earlier film appears relaxed, Ford never eases up in the later effort; we tend to feel mildly consoled by *Three Godfathers* but exhausted by *The Searchers*. The first work seems designed to reinforce relationships that are already patently clear. Monument Valley and Ford's propensity for visual images have never been better presented than in the later film. Ultimately, *Three Godfathers* is controlled by a tone of melodrama, and *The Searchers* moves into the more difficult emotional terrain of tragedy.

The linear and progressive nature of the plot in *Three Godfathers* is caught by the trains that appear in its opening and closing scenes; they ultimately come to represent the amalgamation of Bob Hightower (John Wayne) into the society of the town of Welcome. That town has achieved a serious level of civilization, as shown by the train in the credit sequence, and Sheriff Buck Sweet's (Ward Bond) chase after the outlaws by rail only further underscores how the West is being tamed by eastern technology. When Hightower goes to Yuma prison on the outbound train, nearly all the townspeople gather to bid him farewell. The opening arrival of the three outlaws at a waterhole just outside Welcome establishes the importance of water very early in the film,

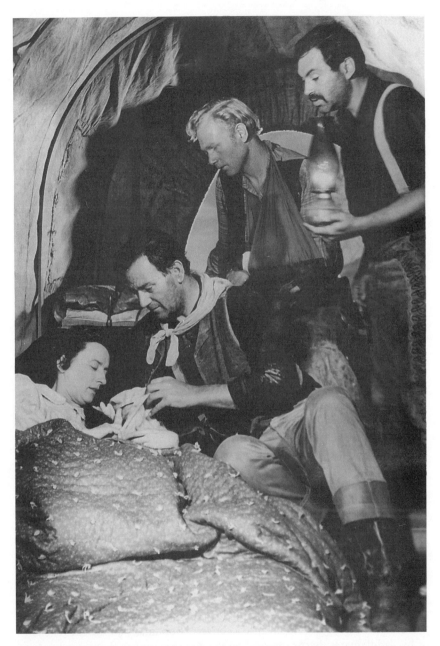

The three outlaws imitate the Magi in *Three Godfathers* (Argosy-MGM, 1948). Bob Hightower (John Wayne), the Abilene Kid (Harry Carey, Jr.), and Pedro (Pedro Armendariz) agree to be godfathers for the child of the dying woman (Mildred Natwick). Ford's inclusion of the wagon canvas supplies a Renaissance style to this scene.

and nothing ever diminishes this crucial need in the desert country through which they trek. Hightower's remark to the Abilene Kid (Harry Carey, Jr.) that they must be certain to fill their water bag sets up the significance of Buck's well-placed shot that destroys the bag.

At Mojave Tanks, the arrival of the train with the sheriff and his posse prevents the outlaws from getting water and further underscores their great need. Their subsequent flight to Tarapin Tanks and the discovery of how "the tenderfoot" has destroyed that well lead the outlaws to seek water from cactus, both for themselves and for the newly born infant. The struggle for water is best dramatized in those scenes of gathering it, scenes in which Bob and the Abilene Kid work to the accompaniment of clearly supportive musical cues. A larger symbolic pattern centers on the physical losses the three godfathers experience as they travel through the desert. Their disposal of saddles, bedrolls, and other gear, as well as the catastrophic loss of their horses, dramatizes how they must lose their lives in crime to attain better lives on earth or (presumably) in heaven. The three bad men's selfless conduct with the infant places them clearly on the side of the angels, so that Ford can, once again, treat villany in a melodramatic way. Pedro (Pedro Armendariz) and the Abilene Kid die to ensure that the future may live—a seemingly natural human arrangement to which even these lawbreakers acquiesce; however, their sacrifices also bring Bob to an appreciation of biblical faith.

Throughout the course of *Three Godfathers*, religious symbols and motifs abound, with the discovery of the woman (Mildred Natwick) about to give birth on Christmas Eve being the most obvious and important. The relation of the three bad men to the three Magi is patent, as is the association of the deserted wagon with the manger. The gifts that are brought to this special child are more secular than in scripture because the heroes sacrifice their own lives and freedom to ensure the infant's earthly existence. Bob's dismissal of the Bible as a source of truth gradually weakens as he follows the lead of the Kid, who has mystically found passages describing where they must go. Hightower feels all religion is useless and, at one point, ironically declares that their chances of finding water are about as good as his chances of becoming a believer. Later, he rails against the "punk" child who has been thrust into his care just after he has denounced the Bible as foolish. Nevertheless, the Kid's trust in the "good book" and Pedro's deep religiosity eventually turn Bob around: when he consults the Bible at what he thinks are the final moments of his life, he learns that he will be rescued by a donkey. The appearance of that animal, at the end of a long, nightmarish tunnel through which Hightower travels, turns the outlaw into a convert. Bob finally appreciates the faith of his saddlemates, best expressed by the Kid's insistence that what has happened has all been part of a design set forth in scripture. *Three Godfathers* demonstrates that the conversion of an erring man will lead to his acceptance by society at large.

The *Searchers* begins with a note stating that we are in Texas in 1868. Subsequent references to the passage of time establish the length of the quest that Ethan Edwards (John Wayne) and Martin Pauley (Jeffrey Hunter) undertake, while past events are narrated from different present perspectives to keep the audience distanced from what takes place. The massacre of the Edwards family and the kidnapping of the girls comes about because of a trick by which Scar (Henry Brandon) gets the Rangers and Ethan out on a wild-goose chase, and this pattern of pursuit without result foreshadows much of what follows. After finding the dead Lucy (Pippa Scott), as well as losing Brad Jorgenson (Harry Carey, Jr.), Ethan and Martin return to the Jorgenson ranch after approximately two years. On that evening Ethan tells Lars (John Qualen) where they have been, providing continuity to the plot. Later, when Laurie Jorgenson (Vera Miles) receives Martin's letter, another lengthy stretch of plot is told in a retrospective way; the events that are covered represent after-the-fact details about which the listeners can do nothing.

At the same time, a new note is struck in Ford's portrayal of the cavalry, which is shown bustling through a wintry landscape (to the symbolic music of "Garry Owen"); their principal accomplishments are the recovery of mad, white captives from Indians whom they have slaughtered. Their winter quarters resemble what the Cheyennes will encounter at Fort Robinson in *Cheyenne Autumn*, while their treatment of the restored captives suggests the thematic ambiguities that abound in *Two Rode Together*. The destruction of the Indian village in which Martin discovers Look's (Beulah Archuletta) body epitomizes this new cavalry, one that, like Ethan, seems bent on waging an all-out race war. The other side of the cavalry is represented by Lieutenant Greenhill (Patrick Wayne), whose naive exuberance almost disguises the fact that his military father (Cliff Lyons) arrives only after the serious fighting at Scar's camp has ended in a battle during which the Rangers drive off the Comanches' horses (as is done at the end of *She Wore a Yellow Ribbon*).

Ethan's earlier dismissal of such a tactic suggests the racial hatred that boils within him: in wanting to confront the Comanches in direct combat, he emerges as the least civilized character in the film. It is his anger (a trait often attributed to John Wayne's screen persona) that drives *The Searchers*. Although he softens enough (through a process never made very overt) to bring Debbie (Natalie Wood as an adult, Lana Wood as a child) back to the white community, Ethan's evolution never leads to his being fully accepted by the settled civilization. The famous closing door that ends *The Searchers* clearly shows that the protagonist, like the dead Indian whose eyes he shot out to ensure that the corpse would wander "between the winds" for eternity, must himself forever search for a permanent home. The central characters' journey through time and terrain ends with Ethan remaining as much of an intruder within society as he was when he first arrived at his brother's ranch.

Ethan drives Brad and Martin across desert terrain that resembles the land-scape in *Three Godfathers*; when Brad returns with his fatally ironic news about having seen Lucy, their physical positions resemble those of the three outlaws before Mojave Tanks; and Martin collects dripping water after Ethan has been wounded during the battle with Scar's force at the cave, just as Hightower did after the baby's birth.

Three Godfathers abounds in familiar Ford camerawork. The opening credits feature dramatic shots over which are superimposed the film's indi-vidual contributors. While a train briefly appears, this sequence emphasizes the desert and its rocky terrain, as well as the opposing groups of outlaws and lawmen who will dominate the ensuing action. A tracking shot of the initial pursuit sequence is also employed, in which the camera cuts from pur-suers to pursued in accepted classical fashion and in which a central devel-opment (Buck's destruction of the outlaws' water supply) is shown. Feet are also featured in shots that resemble moments in *Rio Grande* and *Wagonmas-ter*; we see the horses' hooves, the outlaws' feet stumbling over ridges in the salt lake, and finally, Bob alone collapsing during the last stretch of his trip. On the desert a notable panning sequence finds each of the bad men, now on foot, trudging past the camera; as each man goes by, the camera returns to its original position to show the next man. Through such obvious visual repetition, Ford dramatizes the sheer drudgery faced by these characters as they trek to New Jerusalem with their precious cargo.

At Tarapin Tanks, after the dying mother has been discovered and Pedro has been sent to her aid, the framing of the outlaw in the back canvas flap of the wagon resembles Renaissance-style painting in its circular outline. Given the religious emphasis of *Three Godfathers*, such style is in keeping with the film's overall thematic intention, as is the prominence of this same frame in the following scenes between the outlaws and the dying woman. The hud-dled group, in which Bob holds the infant while Pedro maneuvers the can-dle and the Kid listens attentively, clearly resembles a nativity scene. When Buck discovers the wagon and ascertains that his niece has been aboard, he is also framed by the back canvas to imply his essential goodness, even though he is enraged at this point. Since he immediately offers an additional reward for the three outlaws, whom he earlier refused to kill during the chase out of Welcome (despite his obvious proficiency with a rifle), the sheriff is clearly blinded by a need for vengeance. However, by framing Buck within this sym-bolic background, Ford suggests that the lawman's anger will be only tem-porary. The many shots of the Abilene Kid with his eyes raised heavenward and with "angelic" lighting on his face underline the young man's goodness. He is photographed with these effects at the funeral for the dead mother when his song serves as the only accompaniment to her interment; later, in the wagon when he urges that he and his comrades have been chosen to fulfill predestined roles, the light seeks him out as he again looks up to heaven.

The burial of the mother, presented in long shot at night, finds the godfathers posed as mourners around a cross, which they place over her grave.

On the trail a repeated gesture also attains symbolic weight. The Abilene Kid shields "little Robert" from the sun by holding up his hat, and during the youngest outlaw's own death, when he reverts psychologically to being a child (by reciting "Now I Lay Me Down to Sleep") Hightower holds his hat in the same position to keep the sun off. Through these repetitions of a simple but realistic gesture, Ford implies that, in the face of life and death, we are all like little children. Pedro's death is also treated reverentially and discreetly, for while his prayers resemble those of the Kid, his suicide is registered only through Bob's reaction. Though both men know why Pedro wants Hightower's pistol, the actual gunshot causes Bob to stop for a moment, as if to register the weight of this loss visually on his already burdened frame. Miss Ruby Latham's (Dorothy Ford) affection for the reformed outlaw Bob, feelings suggested by her comic gift of a cake with a file inside, leads to their saying good-bye on the train platform and to a scene that resembles so many other leave-takings in Ford. Miss Ruby, waving good-bye to Bob, is photographically linked to Clementine Carter in *My Darling Clementine*, Lana Martin in *Drums Along the Mohawk*, and a host of the director's other heroines.

The Searchers opens less dramatically on a brick wall against which its credits are listed. Such a design suggests not only the emotional prison in which Ethan lives but also the adobe house in which his beloved Martha (Dorothy Jordan) lives and dies. The most obvious visual pattern in *The Searchers* arises from the many passageways and entrances through which scenes are shot. The opening and the closing of doors begin and end the narrative: Martha opens the Edwards' door to a new day and to Ethan's arrival in the distance; and the wind fortuitously blows shut the Jorgensons' door after the protagonist has wandered away from the reunited inhabitants inside. Martin first appears jumping off a horse and skittering into dinner within the framework of a door at the Edwards' ranch, and his return from the initial phase of the search with Ethan begins with another shot through the front door at the Jorgenson ranch. After Debbie has revealed herself to Ethan and Martin and begged them to leave her with "her people" in the Comanche camp, Scar's force chases the white men into a cave from whose mouth they fight off the Indians and bring the chief down from his horse. Such imagery also rises when Ethan chases Debbie into another cave after the final, successful raid on Scar's village. The protagonist's earlier desire to kill his niece again seems dominant, for Ethan has insisted once more that a direct raid into the Comanches is advisable even though such a tactic may get Debbie killed, and he then scalped his dead Indian antagonist. That Ford now uses a setting that has been earlier associated with defeating the Indians as the background in which Ethan reclaims Debbie (and to some degree his own humanity) nicely suggests that, if only for a brief moment, any man can change. Ethan's ultimate inability to settle into society because of what he feels he has lost is, of course, symbolized by the door-framing pattern in the film.

The nightmarish destruction of the Edwards' ranch by Scar depends heavily on lighting and color schemes. The reddish dusk that envelopes the family as Aaron (Walter Coy) and Martha wordlessly realize that they are surrounded emphasizes a color that is often associated with savagery in Ford's westerns. Such impulsive Indians as Red Shirt in *She Wore a Yellow Ribbon* and Running Wolf in *Two Rode Together* wear this color, and Ethan wears a red shirt when he searches for Jorgenson's cattle and when he shoots out the corpse's eyes, clearly strengthening this association. The camera track toward the young Lucy foreshadows her offscreen physical violation; given the censorship standards of 1956, it makes this point briefly and subtly. Other noticeable close-ups focus on Ethan to emphasize that his unspoken feelings are uppermost in a scene. Given Ford's propensity for relatively simple camera placements and movements, these trackings noticeably restrict his customary field of vision to a single character and, by their very rarity, call attention to themselves. Such tense moments occur when Ethan wipes down his horse after the headstrong Martin has left to go back to the ranch; the older man realizes the tragic possibilities but also recognizes the need to rest his mount — a wisdom that is underscored later when the horseless Martin is passed by Ethan and the garrulous Mose Harper (Hank Worden) on the way to the ruined ranch.

At the fort where the captives have been assembled to be shown to prospective relatives, Ford again tracks to a close-up of Ethan after the protagonist has stated that these people are "no longer white." The hatred and the disgust he feels are plain, for he would obviously like to treat these returned captives as he did the dead Comanche in the rock grave, the wounded Indians at the river battle, or the buffalo he slaughtered to keep Comanches from having food during the winter. Ethan's resolve to destroy Debbie because she has "been living with a buck" is also reaffirmed by his psychological handling of the pistol after Mose has revealed the whereabouts of Scar's camp. Ford's visual emphasis on mounted columns is featured when Scar's braves surround and chase the Rangers over the river and, again, when the Mexican trader, Emilio Figueroa (Antonio Moreno), takes Ethan and Martin to the Comanche camp. Ethan's rage at Martha's death is also translated into striking visual terms. His angry stomping through the center of her funeral establishes the protagonist's savagery, especially since such rites have been accorded so much respect in *Three Godfathers* and elsewhere. The ensuing scene shows him darting past the camera at extremely close range, so that his image literally cuts through the domestic scene of Martin with Laurie and the pensive Jorgensons behind him. Such a noticeable photographic style makes the rage in Ford's central character quite apparent.

Ethan Edwards (John Wayne) has finished writing his will which disowns his niece Debbie in *The Searchers* (Warner Bros., 1956).

The Seachers is replete with compositions that call up earlier Ford westerns. The scene in which Ethan prevents Martin from following Brad into the Comanche camp and certain death resembles the scene in *Stagecoach* in which Ringo halts before the distant sign of Indian smoke and Curly and Dallas join him to form a tableau at the side of a cactus. Ethan's restraint is guided by pragmatism, for he realizes that there is no sense in following the suicidal Brad. This same practicality arises later when the protagonist and Martin realize in winter that they must go "home" to refit, and Ethan delivers a speech about the inevitability of their quest for Debbie. The final charge of the Rangers into Scar's camp also features tracking shots that resemble similar sequences in *She Wore a Yellow Ribbon* and *Rio Grande*. Indeed, the atmosphere of both of these films emerges: the emphasis on movement by which Brittles defeated Red Shirt by driving off the Indians' pony herd now combines with the more bloody emphasis that attached to Yorke's being wounded and then treated by son Jeff. This last charge in *The Searchers* also features comic relief in Clayton's warnings to the young Lieutenant Greenhill and the subsequent treatment of the Reverend/Captain (Ward Bond) for an accidental wound from the lieutenant's sabre. However, these sequences are clearly subordinate to more sobering moments, such as when Ethan scalps the dead Scar and throws Martin to the ground in his pursuit of Debbie.

Ford's placement of the family around the dinner table on Ethan's first night home also resembles a similar occasion at Apache Wells in *Stagecoach*. Ethan's position on one side of Martha provides him with a romantic link, while his conversation with Martin establishes his hatred of all Indians. We learn that Martin was rescued by Ethan after an Indian raid, in a situation that ironically foreshadows what is about to happen to Debbie, and that he was brought to Martha to raise. While the latter pattern will be repeated when the Jorgensons take in Debbie at the end of the film, Ethan's dismissal of what he did and his present emphasis on Martin's mixed ancestry signal more ominous possibilities in his character. Ethan's reserve and hatred set him apart from Aaron, who symbolically is seated next to Martin, as well as from Martha. The editing of this sequence also emphasizes the division in feeling between the characters, for though Ethan and Martin are on the same side of the table, they are rarely shown together.

Ford's penchant for shots of waiting women is also featured in *The Searchers*: Ethan rides off with Clayton and the other Rangers, and Martha stands and watches him go. Since these characters have just engaged in their most overt display of feelings when Martha fondles the "Johnny Reb" coat of her brother-in-law and Ethan kisses her forehead, this lingeringly photographed parting makes the protagonist's subsequent loss only more poignant. When Pauley and Ethan arrive at the burned-out Indian camp, Martin kicks down the remains of a tent, recalling the moment when Captain Brittles kicks over the charred remains of a wagon in *She Wore a Yellow Ribbon* to symbolize his own displaced anger. If Martin's gesture contrasts with that earlier moment because the destruction has been brought about by opposing forces (Indians in *She Wore a Yellow Ribbon*, cavalry in *The Searchers*), a similar sense of failure attaches, since he and Ethan have again been too late to find Debbie. Ford's use of such an obvious photographic parallel also underscores the more cynical perceptions that mark his westerns. In the cantina, where Ethan and Martin meet up with Mose and the Mexican trader, Ford repeats another moment from *Stagecoach* when the protagonist interrupts Pauley's meal with the news that Scar ("Cicatrice") has been seen and that they must go at once. After refusing to allow Martin to drink at the bar, Ethan picks up the younger man's glass of tequila and throws its contents into a fire. This gesture vividly recalls the moment when Doc Boone threw away a drink because he could not bring himself to imbibe with Gatewood. The two scenes are staged from opposite angles, but their visual similarity is striking: Ethan's disposal of the drink is, of course, in keeping with his hellbent quest for revenge.

Music is much more prevalent and noticeable in *Three Godfathers* than in *The Searchers*; however, both films use traditional tunes to make additional or ironic comments on major plot developments. During the credit sequence for the earlier film, "Goodbye Old Paint," a lament about parting, is heard when the dedication to Harry Carey is shown. Given the Christmas setting of *Three Godfathers*, it is hardly unusual that "Silent Night" and "O Come All Ye Faithful" are heard when Bob arrives in New Jerusalem. His sighting of the donkey is underscored by the latter hymn, whereas the patrons of the saloon into which he stumbles are engaged in a caroling session that features the former tune. "Bringing in the Sheeves" is performed by a large female chorus on the morning that Hightower is taken away to jail, as a sign of the outlaw's reacceptance by civil society. The tune obviously underscores Bob's conversion into both a god-fearing and a future member of the town. Richard Hageman also provides situational cues to augment idyllic and "heavenly" moments on the desert when the three outlaws act for the mother and the child. Bob and the Abilene Kid's task of getting water out of cacti is supported by musical effects to suggest dripping, and the appearance of the train at Mojave Tanks with Buck and his deputies aboard is accompanied by sound effects that "Mickey Mouse" is coming into view. Other aural distortions are designed to emphasize the conflicts of the main characters. Thus, the sounds of their feet on the salt lake are exaggerated to suggest their physical struggle, just as an earlier step-up in sound accompanied their movement away from the oasis where they weathered the sandstorm but lost their horses. In this second instance, an auditory emphasis on their feet reinforces their being reduced to walking, a condition that has almost caused Bob and Pedro to come to blows and that has been diffused only by the wounded Kid's comment that they had better get started.

"Shall We Gather at the River," the most repeated tune in Ford's films, is heard when the outlaws bury the mother; the Abilene Kid sings as much of it as he can remember. After Bob has been placed on the train to prison (and assured Buck that he will not let the latter's deputy, Curly [Hank Worden], get lost in delivering him to Yuma), his sendoff, in which even the sheriff is shown with his tearful wife and the symbolic infant, also features this tune. *Three Godfathers* ends similarly to *Wagonmaster* in that the assembled community celebrates its renewed good fortune by engaging in song. The tune that receives the most extended treatment in the film, however, is "The Streets of Laredo" which is both sung and played. The Abilene Kid initially sings this tune as a lullaby to the infant; its lyrics, with their emphases on a dying young cowhand who has "gone wrong," nicely foreshadow the Kid's own end. As the outlaws leave the mother's gravesite with their new burden, the same air is reprised as a solemn march to celebrate their acquiescence in the dead woman's wishes. When Bob collapses in the tunnel, he is egged on by the spirits of Pedro and the Kid, and the latter sings this melody, which Hightower then takes up. By means of this tune and the super-imposed shots of the other (now dead) outlaws, Ford hammers home the point of mystical unity between these men, a condition that has been strength-ened (if not ensured) by their assumption of responsibility for their godchild. Bob's singing at this point and his subsequent use of Spanish symbolize the notion that the infant is, indeed, the child of all three godfathers.

The Searchers features harsher musical cues, especially those designed to suggest the Indian world dominated by Scar and invaded by Ethan as a sort of spiritual twin of the Comanche chief. Max Steiner's most dissonant pas-sages are heard when the credits are shown, when the Edwards' ranch is in flames, and when Ethan takes his final revenge on Scar's corpse. In addition, there is a theme song (by Stan Jones) whose lyrics emphasize the eternal wan-dering of Ethan, in contrast to the more sociable behavior of the other char-acters. The lyrics and orchestral variations of this tune are invoked to suggest the passage of time. During the initial pursuit of the Jorgensons' cattle, the subsequent quest for the girls, and the final prelude to the battle between the Rangers and Scar's tribe, Steiner provides this melody with sharp accents and headlong tempi to suggest the striving men and unrestrained action. A slower rendition accompanies Ethan and Martin's first return to the Jorgen-sons' ranch after two years of looking for Debbie, and the association of this music with that place (so important at the end of the film) is clearly estab-lished. The final rendition of this melody — when its lyrics support the return of Debbie, the reuniting of Martin and Laurie, and the shot of Mose in a rocking chair on the Jorgensons porch — adds to the overall poignancy of Ford's resolution. While the other characters can put aside the ills that have beset them and begin more normal lives, Ethan can only stand aside and dis-appear — or literally "ride away," as the Jones lyrics proclaim.

"Shall We Gather at the River" accompanies Martha's funeral and the aborted wedding of Charlie McCorry (Ken Curtis) and Laurie; at both occa-sions, its associations with community seem appropriate. Nevertheless, in keeping with the gloomier tone of The Searchers, this melody also augments sequences in which its lyrical expectations are defeated or altered. Ethan's interruption of Clayton's eulogy while this tune sounds in the background foreshadows its underlying irony in the wedding sequence. Ethan violates civ-ilized decorum in the earlier scene, and his appearance with Martin destroys the marriage that has been planned by the Jorgensons. Whereas Ford's favorite tune may replace more traditional wedding music (Mendelssohn, Wagner) because of Reverend Clayton's presence, this melody also foreshadows Lau-rie's choice of Martin over her guitar-playing suitor.

At the beginning of this sequence, "The Yellow Rose of Texas" allows those assembled to engage in an old-fashioned hoedown, in keeping with their frontier milieu. Ford emphasizes the dancers' feet, as he does in *My Darling Clementine*, *Fort Apache*, and *She Wore a Yellow Ribbon*; however, the sprightliness of this dance, with its intercut shots of Lars and Mrs. Jorgenson (Olive Carey) as nervous hosts at the front of the visual plane, and the arrival of Clayton and Charlie create a more uneasy atmosphere than those of the earlier dances. Ethan's first appearance at his brother's ranch features "The Bonnie Blue Flag" to suggest his Confederate sympathies and, perhaps, to imply why he has not come home before now—points that are addressed later in dialogue. "Skip to My Loo" juxtaposes Martin and Charlie. We hear Martin singing it while taking a bath at the Jorgensons, with an emphasis on "Got me a gal prettier 'n you" just before Laurie appears and chides him about being embarrassed. After Laurie reads Martin's letter, with its tale about Look, her dismay is augmented by McCorry's singing the same song with an emphasis on "Gone again."

Steiner's manipulation of Jones's main theme provides the musical support necessary for the end of *The Searchers*, since its sentimental tone stands in contrast to the more traditional and original melodies heard elsewhere. Its first striking appearance accompanies Ethan's contemplation of the possible death of Martha as he remains reasonable long enough to take care of his horse before riding to try to rescue her. Much later, after Debbie appears as one of Scar's wives and shows off the scalps he has taken, this theme reappears at the camp that Ethan and Martin have set up outside the Comanche village. The girl's appearance on a distant rise and her progress down that incline are augmented by this theme, with its associations to Ethan's longing for the love he has never had. Martin initially senses Debbie's approach and runs to protect her from Ethan. Their would-be duel is, of course, fortuitously stopped by an Indian arrow; and it is not until the final moments of the film that this main theme is heard again. When Ethan says, "Let's go home, Debbie," after lifting the distraught girl above his head, this music underlines the protagonist's newfound love and forgiveness.

Numerous objects are given symbolic weight in *Three Godfathers*. Buck Sweet's shingle on the fence outside his house causes Bob to laugh and brings the sheriff into view from behind a rosebush. Buck's willingness to acknowledge that people call him "Pearly" only adds to Hightower's merriment while showing just how socially "sweet" the lawman is. Buck's sign does not include his profession—an omission that is rectified when he puts on his vest with its prominent tin star to the accompaniment of an ominous musical cue and the sudden suspension of conversation among the three outlaws. Trains, stagecoaches, and buckboards also fill the landscape in *Three Godfathers*, with their symbolic connections to civilization being suggested by the characters who occupy them—Hightower, Miss Ruby, and Buck. The deserted wagon at Tarapin Tanks in which the infant is born becomes a Christmas manger because of the ministrations of his three godfathers. The mother's death within this symbolic setting is augmented when a candle placed at the rear of the wagon is extinguished, marking the actual moment of her passing.

Additional shots of the wagon on the following morning, when the godfathers search for food and clothing, and at their departure only further emphasize its symbolic importance.

The initial meeting between Buck and the outlaws is marked by what they wear. Mrs. Sweet (Mae Marsh) recognizes the Texas backgrounds of the godfathers by their hats, a recognition that prompts Buck to ask if they have come by the Mormon Trail and New Jerusalem. Since he does not totally believe that they could have come that way and missed his niece and her dissolute husband, who are on the same route, Buck resumes his official position as sheriff, as signaled when he puts on his vest. The costumes of the main figures, though not elaborate, allow certain obvious facts to emerge, such as Pedro's Mexican ancestry (seen in his hat) and Bob's losses (seen in his casting away of canteen and gun). The sling that the Abilene Kid wears after being shot in Welcome and his boots, whose heels he knocks off to walk more comfortably over the salt lake despite realizing he will be unable to move in the rocky terrain that lies beyond this flat stretch, symbolize his self-sacrifice.

Clothing and costuming loom even larger in *The Searchers*. Ethan's Confederate coat epitomizes his thwarted romantic feelings for Martha, as well as hers for him. Her reactions to this garment, whether in taking it from Ethan or in lovingly bringing it out to him before the original search party rides out, show Martha's repressed feelings for the protagonist. She loves both brothers but realizes that staying with Aaron and her children to create some kind of civilization out of a wilderness is her higher calling. Handing the coat to Ethan, while the Reverend/Captain Clayton discreetly looks elsewhere because he is embarrassed by the open feelings between them, is as close as Martha ever comes to expressing her romantic sentiments. Ethan's later use of the coat to bury Lucy completes his descent into an emotional hell, for he loses the item most associated with his beloved Martha. Lucy's blue dress, which is never seen, causes Brad to believe he has identified his fiancée in the Comanche camp and precipitates his death when Ethan explains the "truth" of what young Jorgenson has seen. Debbie's plaid dress, part of which falls into the mercenary hands of Jerem Futterman (Peter Mamokos), serves to identify the girl, since Mrs. Jorgenson recognizes it and so sends Ethan and Martin into the second, more protracted phase of their search.

Among the Indians, Scar's ceremonial headdress, which he dons when he enters the river battle and again when Ethan and Martin are chased into the cave, marks him as the Comanche leader (and gives the protagonist something to shoot at). When the principals start trading among the Indians, the most popular items seem to be hats, two of which create the "marriage" tie between Look and the unwitting Pauley. The Reverend/Captain Clayton's hat serves as a means by which he exercises his temper, for we see him throwing it at Ethan after the latter has tossed him a pistol (with the sarcastic advice that it is loaded) during the river battle. At the end of that confrontation, when Ethan refuses to stop killing wounded Indians, Clayton again casts off his hat, but this time he does so to express a genuine rage at the inhumanity he is witnessing. His appearance at the wedding is replete with his assumption of a clerical collar: once again, identity and costume are linked. Laurie Jorgenson's costuming includes both dresses and jeans, with an apron being featured as her most prominently manipulated piece of clothing. She casts aside her apron on both occasions when Martin returns, as if to symbolize the drudgery she has endured for the sake of her love. We see her in a dress on the night she interrupts Martin's bath and kisses him in front of Ethan; at her "wedding," her elaborate bridal gown nicely calls attention to her delight in Martin's return, to her rapture when Pauley and Charlie fight over her, and to her zeal in urging that Debbie should be killed after having lived so long among the Comanches.

Ethan's outfits are manipulated in terms of where he is. His brutal nature is symbolized by the red shirt he wears when he initially searches for the cattle, when he shoots out the Indian's eyes, and when he wreaks havoc on the Comanches during the river battle. When he slaughters the buffalo herd, he is in a winter jacket, and he is so attired when he examines the deranged and dead victims of the Indians at the cavalry outpost. When he finally meets Scar face to face, Ethan wears a plaid shirt and galluses he wears during the final sections of the film. Objects primarily associated with the protagonist are the gold locket he has given Lucy, which turns up on the trail, and the medal he gives Debbie, which appears around Scar's neck during the trade conference in his tent. Ethan is also associated with money when he offers to pay Aaron "freshly minted Yankee dollars." The mystery of the protagonist's immediate past arises when he denies going to California, as his brother assumed he had, and when he chides Clayton for having been at the surrender of the Confederate cause they both served. The possibility of Ethan's having been a thief is surely suggested, while his dislike of northerners reappears when he teases young Greenhill about the yellow stripe down his back. Paradoxically, Ethan defends his oath to the defeated Confederacy on the grounds that a man can have only one master at a time, yet he founders on the oath that exists between Aaron and Martha.

The geography in *Three Godfathers* is fairly elaborate; paths of flight are discussed in detail by both the outlaws and their pursuers. While the action begins in Welcome, which according to Pedro has changed its name from Tarantula, it moves to Mojave Tanks, Apache Wells, and Tarapin Tanks, all points where water is supposedly to be found. New Jerusalem, the town into which Hightower comes with the baby, symbolically lies to the east and is found by following a star and the words of the Bible. The Old Mormon Trail connects that town with Welcome by means of Tarapin Tanks, while the railroad links up the other watering spots as it heads north. Mexico lies only sixty miles to the south, and Bob urges the Abilene Kid to go there before the bank robbery. Hightower and Sweet emerge as well-matched rivals by virtue of the maps they draw to counterpoint the tactics they adopt with regard to each other. After being thwarted at Mojave Tanks, Bob and his cohorts move unpredictably to Tarapin Tanks rather than to Apache Wells as expected. Arriving at the latter point, Buck soon realizes that he has been outsmarted. Hightower introduces this change of direction to Pedro by drawing a map in the sand, while the lawman uses a railroad chalkboard to illustrate how his adversaries have "doubled back."

These specific geographical locations are less significant than the terrain in which such actions take place. The rising ground over which the outlaws pass during the initial phases of their escape soon gives way to the more rolling country of the desert, with its sandstorms, and to the dried salt lake, whose cracked underfooting causes them to stumble because of their new burdens (the baby) and losses (their mounts). Hightower must finally carry the infant up another incline in blistering heat, and his moments of supreme trial and despair occur in the echoing rocks and tunnel immediately before his discovery of the means by which he will get to New Jerusalem. Dust is especially prominent anytime the outlaws move on horseback on the outskirts of civilized (town) life; at the waterhole just outside Welcome, they are all-but-enshrouded in it. On the desert they are beset by wind-stirred sands. While blowing sand denotes the passage of time, its most striking use occurs when the outlaws must battle a storm that nearly swallows them up in what has to be the most visually striking sequence in the entire film.

Welcome emerges as a highly civilized place; by contrast the more stagey-looking New Jerusalem, which is approached by night, resembles the older, less settled towns seen in *Stagecoach* and *My Darling Clementine*. We are made to wonder if Tarantula wasn't a more open, brawling kind of place, especially given Pedro's description of the cantina and the girl he knew there. By the time the bank robbers arrive, Welcome has developed most of the trappings of a settled western town — a stage line, a bank, and a railroad station. On the street where Buck Sweet lives, large trees and wide avenues indicate the "respectable" character of the neighborhood. When the sheriff looks at wanted posters because of his suspicions about the three visitors, he examines them in a parlor rather than in the jail in which Hightower is finally incarcerated.

The central street in Welcome is considerably wider than that in front of Buck's home, for it serves as the major traffic artery, as can be seen when Miss Ruby arrives by stage only moments before the outlaws rob her father's bank. The public life of the town occurs in this street: the returning daughter is greeted by her father (Charles Halton) and two would-be suitors whose formal clothing again emphasizes the extent to which eastern civilization has taken over in Welcome. The local saloon is seen only when Hightower comes up for sentencing before the kindly judge (Guy Kibbee), who is moved by the outlaw's parental feelings. The transformational power of Welcome is subtly caught when Miss Florie (Jane Darwell), the boisterous and ribald operator of Apache Wells, arrives there costumed in an appropriately demure dress. On the desert, seemingly in her own element, Florie is costumed in western garb and is full of suggestive remarks; in Welcome, she appears indistinguishable from the other good, God-fearing ladies who serenade Hightower as he departs.

The geography of *The Searchers* is in keeping with the frontier society that is being depicted. There are no large towns, only cantinas and trading posts set within the terrain between large, scattered ranches and transient Indian encampments. The one fort that the searchers go into proves only that the soldiers' lack of compassion on the prairies is matched by their treatment of the mad captives whom they have ostensibly "rescued." Jerem Futterman's trading post, like the man himself, appears dark and cramped, with its bar front serving as the place from which the proprietor sells what he knows for whatever price the market will bear. The exchange of coins between Futterman and Ethan, an exchange that is completed only when the protagonist takes back his money from the corpse of the trader, symbolizes their relationship. The stagey-looking campsite that Ethan sets up to beguile Futterman and his allies stands in sharp contrast to the natural terrain we see nearly everywhere else in *The Searchers*. Futterman's death in such a setting underscores his villainy; unlike Scar, who represents a worthy antagonist to Ethan, the trader and his bushwhacking friends are simply "scum" to be destroyed. By having them die as and where they do, Ford again reveals the often melodramatic way in which he regards and presents evil.

The artificial light that surrounds the sequence in the marsh, when Ethan and the Rangers come upon what they believe to be Scar's camp only to discover that the Comanches have already left and so reversed the roles of pursuers and pursued, repeats the symbolic atmosphere that colors the massacre at the Edwards' ranch. Ethan's rage at Clayton's culpability foreshadows their later argument after the battle and their subsequent parting. Thus, the river where the pitched fight between the Rangers and the Comanches takes place serves as the symbolic point at which Ethan parts from Clayton, since the Reverend/Captain interferes with his shooting of the wounded Indians. Their separation is verbally prompted by Clayton's urging that they are both "too many and too few" for what needs to be done, but the deeper division is emphasized by the long shot in which the reverend/captain's party rides off while Ethan, Brad, and Martin recross the river and return to their quest.

The ravine in which Ethan finds Lucy's mutilated body represents another symbolic division: passing through it hastens Brad Jorgenson's death and reduces the searchers' quest to simply finding Debbie. The various camps that Ethan and Martin set up include the trap for Futterman, the more natural setting in which they settle down with Look, and the riverside camp to which Debbie comes and in which Ethan attempts to kill the girl. Look's adherence to the land is symbolized by the stone arrow she leaves as a marker after she flees when Martin and Ethan ask her about Scar. Martin's doubt about whether Look was simply running to the Comanches or trying to help him is dramatically undercut when she is found dead in a burning Indian camp that has just been visited by the 7th Cavalry.

In the Comanche village, on the night before the Rangers' attack, Scar reacts to noises that Martin makes, but only after the Indian leader has been shown hurling a stone at a whimpering dog. The tent in which Martin finds the sleeping Debbie and then turns to kill Scar resonates with meaning because earlier Martin and Ethan appeared there as supposed traders. On that occasion Scar's demonstration of his scalp pole put the white men on notice, as the Mexican trader saw clearly; on this later night, Ethan tries to dissuade Martin from attempting to save Debbie by appealing to the younger man's past. Ethan insists that one of the scalps they viewed belonged to Martin's mother, thus suggesting that all Comanches are subhuman and that Debbie must be treated as one of them. Martin's freedom from the past, in contrast to the protagonist's fixation on it, is then shown as the younger man dismisses this appeal and demands that Clayton allow him to go into the Indian camp. By shooting Scar inside the tent, Martin rescues his half-sister and exorcises the demons that Ethan sought to invoke.

In *Three Godfathers*, the discovery of the books among the effects the mother left in the wagon at Tarapin Tanks provides the means by which the words of the Bible loom ever larger in Hightower's consciousness. Initially, the outlaws are pleased to discover a book about infant care to guide them with their young charge. When it comes to coating him with grease, Bob is admonished to "follow the book"—a notion that is extended to scripture. The Abilene Kid's embarrassment over the word "toilette," a term he does not want to utter in front of his godchild, quickly restores a comic atmosphere and prepares us for Kearney's being the source for subsequent biblical allusions. Hightower's final reading from the Bible, in which he encounters a passage about being taken into New Jerusalem by a donkey, shows the most cynical of the badmen accepting its guidance; despite his immediate doubt and despair about finding or even stealing a mule in such country, he soon sees the wandering animal that will take him and the infant to safety. Hightower's attempt to get rid of the Bible when he collapses during the final stage of his journey is belied when he crawls back to look at it after Pedro's ghostly advice to "follow the book."

In *The Searchers*, letters represent the only permanent kind of communication possible between the disparate characters. Futterman's letter to Ethan, which Lars keeps for nearly a year, starts the second stage of the search by offering proof that Debbie is alive and with the Comanches. On the ensuing morning, when Martin kisses Laurie, their short idyll comes to an abrupt halt when Martin learns that Ethan has already left to pursue this new lead. Laurie has stolen Futterman's letter so that Martin will know what has happened, and the first instance of his quasi-literacy leads her to become further exasperated and to read it aloud. Ford thus foreshadows the later sequences in which Laurie will read Martin's letter and Martin will read Ethan's will before railing against its terms. The first of these reading sequences is augmented when Laurie pushes Martin over a bench in the same way that Charlie knocks him over the same piece of furniture later, at the "wedding." Her frustration over Martin's desire to follow Ethan is completed by the angry way in which Laurie gives him her own horse and then, most significantly for a Ford heroine, refuses to watch as he rides off in pursuit of the protagonist. Laurie's petulant rage as she clings to a hitching rail is in keeping with her immaturity, a trait brought out well when she gloats about the fistfight over her and then advises Martin to let Debbie die at Ethan's hands.

The letter that Martin sends to Laurie, by way of Charlie McCorry, offers one of the most complex narrative sequences in all of Ford's films. The resultant flashback conveys information that occurs before it is actually encountered in the girl's reading. While Laurie initially reacts as though she has received a private love letter, she agrees to the demands of her parents and reads Martin's missive aloud. The letter recounts how Martin and Ethan became traders to cover their continuing search and how the older man stumbled into something at one of the Indian camps. Martin's own naiveté results in his buying Look as a wife, a decision that is read by Laurie only after this process has been completed by Ethan's insisting that the trailing Indian maiden join "our merry band." Such news prompts Laurie to throw the letter into the fireplace, causes Lars to insist that any young man should be married, and finds Charlie chortling over the "squaw" that Martin has acquired.

Martin's letter then tells of how Look ran away after being asked about Scar, the horrors of the massacred Indian camp, and the presence of the restored captives at the army post. Martin also presents Ethan's fury with the buffalo as "Something I ain't quite got straight yet"; indeed, the young man's shortsightedness is offset only by his decision to rescue Debbie at the end of the film and by an earlier awareness that prompted him to continue riding with the inhospitable Ethan. At the conclusion of this lengthy narrative device, Martin announces that he and Ethan are on their way to New Mexico (where they meet Scar), and Lars sagely, but ironically, adds that they will never find Debbie.

When Ethan is wounded and must be nursed back to health, he prepares a will leaving all his property to Martin, who manages to spell out this testament but, instead of being pleased, becomes enraged at the protagonist's insistence that he has no living "blood kin." Martin objects that Debbie is still alive, and when Ethan insists that her life with the Comanches has made her dead for all practical purposes, he hurls the notebook that contains the will at the older, wounded man. Martin's impotent rage is symbolized by his inability to kill Ethan at this juncture, for all he can do is declare through angry tears that he hopes the protagonist will die soon. Ethan's inevitable "That'll be the day" once again demonstrates the coldness of his character; like the natural forces he alluded to when they gave up the search in winter, he is seemingly above feelings and inevitably able to function.

The solemnity that surrounds death — as seen in the gentility of Hatfield when he covers up the dead woman's body at Lee's Ferry in *Stagecoach*, in the speech that Wyatt offers at his dead brother's grave in *My Darling Clementine*, and in the ceremony that surrounds the interment of Trooper Smith in *She Wore a Yellow Ribbon* — is certainly caught by the ceremony for the dead mother in *Three Godfathers*. Even these three outlaws, who have lost their horses and for whom time is of the essence, stop to formally bury the deceased and offer words over her grave. The Abilene Kid's singing provides a ritual austerity, and Hightower's studied "Amen" only underlines how deeply moved he has been by the whole experience. Bob's earlier soliloquy, when he insisted that he wasn't tough enough to deal with the birth of the baby, and his courtly treatment of the dying mother have already revealed his humanity. The solemn framing of the three godfathers on the burial hill at night under the stars associates them with the Gospel story they partially reenact, while the entire tone of this sequence, replete with its symbolic candle and consciously framed wagon setting, further emphasizes religiosity.

The burial of Martha in *The Searchers* reverses these emphases by providing Ethan an occasion to show how antisocial he can be. The protagonist's actions are so contrary to what happens both before and after in Ford's westerns (e.g., Rutledge's tender care of the dying Moffitt in *Sergeant Rutledge*, and the elaborate solemnity with which the survivors treat Doniphon's death in *The Man Who Shot Liberty Valance*) that this sequence all but jumps off the screen. Clayton's sermon is heard indistinctly until Ethan urges that the reverend/captain put "An amen to it!" When the religious leader counters that he still has more to say, Ethan simply shouts "Amen!" and brings the service to a close by stomping through the mourners to get on 'the trail for revenge. By storming out of the tableau that Ford has established on the hillside, Ethan cuts through the social bonds by which communities come into being and survive. Although he may eventually appear compassionate when he brings Debbie "home," Ethan will never fit into society because of his rash disdain of such a rite. He will appear more lonely at the end of the film, but Ethan is nowhere more alienated than when he flaunts his rage at Martha's funeral. His headlong act is quickly augmented by the anger and ~ivility he shows when moving through the very next scene as he leaves with Brad and Martin. The protagonist's indifference to Mrs. Jorgenson, who wants to urge moderation ("Don't let the boys waste their lives in vengeance") in Martha's name, only reinforces the visual points made by his exit at the funeral and his pellmell entry into this setting. Ethan's tunnel vision is shown further by the way in which he listens to Mrs. Jorgenson: his eyes remain fixed on Brad and Martin, who are not getting mounted quickly enough to suit him.

Hightower's acceptance of religion causes his personality to change, and the script must make such a transition plausible. The naming of the infant introduces the first thematic-verbal device to effect this development, for the dying mother insists on using all three outlaws' names for the child, with the proviso that his surname be Hightower because Bob was the one who found her. As Robert William Pedro Hightower, the child is variously hailed by his three godparents, who alternately omit each of the other names but not their own in moments of comic anger. Pedro argues that Bob must be the one to "grease up" the infant because he is the "head wrangler" by virtue of being the first one mentioned in the baby's name; in other moments, the Mexican outlaws insists that "Pedro" be added to the child's names. Bob's demand that Pedro not speak Spanish around the child, a point he makes on three occasions, sets up the poignant moment when Hightower says good-bye to the godchild with a Spanish phrase as a recognition of the infant's shared legacy. Thus, Bob brings the past and present together in a meaningful way so that he can live at peace with himself and his dead comrades. Hightower's allegiance to the Abilene Kid and Pedro forces him to reject Buck's offer to set him free in exchange for totally giving up the child.

The crucially repeated line in *The Searchers* is Ethan's phrase "That'll be the day," a prescription he uses to vent his rage and frustrations with those around him. While this verbal signature underlines the central character's enduring power, its exact repetition also demonstrates Ethan's failure to become part of the community with which he is ostensibly concerned. When Ethan and Clayton quarrel over what strategy to use in pursuit of the Comanche raiding party, they quickly reach a point where Ethan agrees to take orders but only for a brief time. Their debate over stampeding the pony herd or raiding directly into Scar's encampment and causing the likely deaths of both the girls brings on this crisis. When they subsequently discover that the Comanches have given them the slip, Ethan sarcastically asks if there are any other "orders" that the reverend/captain would like to issue now that they are about to be killed. The protagonist closes off this angry dialogue with his first "That'll be the day" to suggest that he is now forever removed from Clayton's authority. Their later argument after the river battle makes this breach more apparent, since Ethan now insists that the head of the Rangers' interference "tears it" as far as any relationship between them goes.

On the trail with Brad and Martin, the protagonist enrages the young

Jorgenson by too often mentioning the possibility that Lucy may be dead. After Brad insists that he will fight Ethan if he hears that phrase once more, the older man dismisses this threat with another "That'll be the day." Ethan's phrase suggests the distance between himself and the younger men because it so clearly implies that there will never be a day when he will recognize them as equals or even as men worth listening to. This attitude does not change throughout the search; he never consults with anyone before making a decision, so that even his final sparing of Debbie comes as a shock. An even more symbolic use of Ethan's key phrase follows Martin's angry wish that the protagonist would die soon, a remark made after he has read the will and heard the denial of any blood ties to Debbie. At this point, the wounded Ethan's phrase raises his character to all but mystical heights: it is as if nothing on earth, or at least no one in the narrative, will ever be able to exercise any significant power over him. The last appearance of the phrase occurs when the protagonist and Martin return to undo Laurie's "wedding"; again, it denotes Ethan's seemingly invincible determination. He will stop only when Scar has been killed, Martha revenged, and Debbie (presumably) destroyed because of her "defilement"; thus, Ethan's tag line emphasizes everything that the character wants to do.

Mrs. Sweet, Ruby Latham, Miss Florie, and the mother all exhibit various degrees of responsibility in *Three Godfathers*. Buck's wife is the embodiment of settled domesticity, willing to entertain on a moment's notice because of her good-heartedness. She is in her element when she gives coffee to the three outlaws who have stopped at her front gate and when she makes small talk with the Abilene Kid, who says she resembles his own mother. Mrs. Sweet's maternal instincts are also seen when she mutely nods as the judge insists that the baby's education and future needs must be taken care of. Her concern over Hightower's welfare is amusingly caught when she gives him more breakfast than she supplies Buck, who complains about the disparity. At the outlaw's sendoff, she promises to take care of the infant until Bob can return, and then she sings and cries as the train pulls away.

Ruby Latham is much more boisterous, as seen when she speaks to Bob and his compatriots in the street after her arrival in the town. Her high spirits are caught when she insists how much she enjoys seeing real western men after being away at an "eastern" finishing school in Denver. Despite his crime against her father's bank, Ruby appears melancholy, pensive, and doting at Hightower's trial. At the train station Ruby becomes another Ford woman waving good-bye to her beloved. Thus, Miss Latham actively courts the man of her choice as seen in their comic repartee about the file in the cake she sent to Bob in jail and in Hightower's agreeing to write to her from prison.

Florie's greeting to Buck's posse on her doorstep in Apache Wells reveals her far less inhibited view of life. The older woman continuously jokes about getting remarried and sees the group that has arrived as a "Christmas present" of "a whole passel of men" from whom she can select or trap a husband. When Buck decides to seek the outlaws at Tarapin Tanks, he leaves some men at Apache Wells, and Florie insists that she may well have a new mate before the New Year, when she will be coming to town to see "Cousin Carrie Lou." Buck's earliest exchange with Florie includes the observation that her cat, which died, must have been a "tomcat"; the older woman does nothing to dispel this notion when she insists, "If I'd seen anything with pants on around here, they wouldn't have to beg for anything." Such verbal ribaldry is considerably softened by Florie's final appearance in Welcome; indeed, her lustiness proves to be more verbal braggadocio than anything else, for her relationship with Mrs. Sweet clearly establishes her goodness within the moral hierarchy of Welcome.

The dying mother embodies Ford's most idealized portrait of womanhood within his westerns. This veritable Madonna thinks only of her child's fate; in a particularly syrupy speech about no one being there to kiss his little bruises, etc., she prepares for her death by getting the outlaws to pledge their aid. Her role is symbolically reiterated when she dies after kissing the infant for the last time; her angelic concern with her child, to the extent that she disregards her own fate and that of her derelict husband, marks her as one of the most melodramatic and idealized figures to be found anywhere in the director's work. In essence, the mother derives from the same uncomplicated vision that colors the drawing of such simplistic outlaws as the Clantons and Uncle Shiloh's brood.

Curly, Buck's deputy who is bald, constantly has trouble handling horses, which he is always being asked to load on and off train cars. He struggles in Welcome as the posse sets out for Mojave Tanks, and at Apache Wells he can barely get the animals off the train. Naturally, when Buck asks Hightower to look out for Curly, who has never been far away from home before, the deputy stumbles when he takes the outlaw up an incline to the waiting train. Luke (Jack Pennick), the conductor, constantly tries to hurry Buck and his posse on and off the train, which is chronically late. At Welcome, when Luke asks whether the engineer can "drag her," the train is eight hours behind schedule; at Apache Wells, when he repeats the same request to the sheriff, it is sixteen hours late.

The judge, who operates out of a saloon, emerges as a kind of fairy godfather solely concerned with Hightower's welfare and that of the infant. When Bob opines that he would rather serve a maximum sentence than be permanently separated from his godson and get a lesser sentence, the kindly magistrate is delighted by the outlaw's familial feelings and rewards Hightower with a minimum penalty so that he can return quickly to the child and Welcome. The judge's wisdom, coupled with his fondness for alcohol, as signaled by his urging that the bar reopen the moment after he has finished with Bob, marks him as a variation of Don Boone in *Stagecoach*.

Buck's posse also functions as a character, for their reactions counterpoint those of their leader. When the banker, Latham, insists that there are not enough men in this group, Buck thanks him for adding a one-hundred-dollar reward for each of the outlaws, and so do the men who head for the train. At Mojave Tanks, the three men the sheriff leaves are armed with Winchesters and cannot be rushed by the watching outlaws; at the same time, their basic cupidity, caught earlier when they argued about how much pay they were to get, arises once more when Buck asks for the cards they have hidden because he doesn't want them merely idling away their time on the taxpayers' money. While the foursome that chases Hightower into New Jerusalem is shown trekking on horseback and on foot through the rugged desert terrain, their actions at Tarapin Tanks underscore Buck's own anger there. The discovery that the mother has been there occurs when Curly describes a wedding dress to Buck, who then adds fifty dollars to the reward money and says he would prefer to pay for dead men. The dynamited tanks, which have been destroyed by the tenderfoot husband, whom Buck earlier described as so shiftless that he had tried working at everything except being a preacher, are attributed to the outlaws by the deputies. In New Jerusalem these men support Buck after he has challenged the exhausted Hightower to a shoot-out, and in Welcome they function as a kind of chorus. Curly, who clearly has it right when he notes that Mrs. Sweet is "the boss" of her household, joins the other deputies to say good-bye to Bob in the final scene.

The lesser characters in *The Searchers* all suggest thematic or plot ambiguities that mark them as more than mere comic diversions. The shavetail Lieutenant Greenhill may epitomize naiveté, but at the same time he is part of the very cavalry that destroyed the Indian village and the mild Look. Greenhill's father, who arrives too late to help against Scar, myopically congratulates his son, whose only accomplishment has been wounding Reverend/Captain Clayton in the derriere. Look, who agrees to answer to that name after Martin has inadvertently purchased her, suffers the brunt of comic antics that, by current standards, appear racist and cruel. The very idea of an interracial marriage is mocked by Ethan, and the physical proportions of the actress playing the role make such a coupling even more mismatched.

The protagonist's enjoyment of Martin's discomfort hardly disguises the older man's hatred of Indians; indeed, he can enjoy Martin's distress because the younger man is also an Indian in Ethan's eyes, as is made plain during their conversation at Martha's dinner table. Look's desire to please leads to her getting kicked down an incline by Martin when she beds down next to him — a bit of "fun" certain to upset anyone sensitive to feminist and racist slurs and stereotypes in older movies. Her fear after hearing Scar mentioned prefigures her death, an event Martin more compassionately underlines by wondering (in his letter to Laurie) what she had ever done to deserve such a fate.

The Mexican trader, Emilio Figueroa, initially appears to be controlled by money and not sentiment, but then he proves unwilling to compromise his conscience. Figueroa accepts a bag of coins to lead Ethan and Martin to Scar's camp, but he is wise enough to see that revenge and not trading is what is on the protagonist's mind. On the next morning, the trader pulls out because he wants no part of a blood feud. Figueroa warns Ethan that Scar knows why the white men have come and will surely attack them, then he returns the money and states that he does not trade in blood.

Charlie McCorry is comic in his slow-wittedness and his exaggerated accent, a veritable Gomer Pyle of the plains. He first appears when he delivers Martin's letter to Laurie and stays to court her. His gift of a box of sweets and the guitar he carries symbolize his intentions; when he guffaws on hearing of Martin's Indian wife, Charlie clearly suggests his hopes about Laurie. His serenade to the distraught girl, set in a window frame as she tearfully ponders the news that Martin has sent and the lack of romantic feeling with which he presented it, underlines her unhappiness. Charlie's emphasis on "Gone again" reiterates Laurie's sense of loss, for while she seemingly cast Martin aside when he rushed to join Ethan on the trek to Futterman's, her romantic feelings have not subsided. Charlie's next appearance, as a would-be bridegroom, sees him uncomfortably decked out in a suit and under the direction of Clayton. Martin's reappearance and Laurie's desperate throwing of herself into his arms precede Charlie's entrance. After hearing Martin state that Laurie couldn't seriously want to marry someone as inconsequential as himself, McCorry proceeds to knock Martin over the bench. Laurie's insistence that there be no fighting inside the house sets the stage for the comic bout that follows. Martin and Charlie engage in various exaggerated bits of etiquette — urging each other to go first through a doorway and then passing through it simultaneously, ritually spitting over a piece of firewood — to formalize their antagonism.

The brawl is designed as a commentary on the observers, for during it Laurie gleefully watches two men fighting over her. At the same time, Ethan forces Mrs. Jorgenson into the house by stating that she must remember she is a lady and should not be seen outside with the men watching this scrap. Mrs. Jorgenson quickly forces her way to the front of the window at which other "ladies" have crowded in order to enjoy the spectacle. Clayton's insistence that rules be observed, Charlie's interruption of the fight to find the owner of a fiddle, and the comic resolution in which apologies are made all divest this struggle of any serious intention. Indeed, only after it is over, and Charlie says that there will be no wedding until some things have been clarified, is a more serious note struck. The reverend/captain's insistence that

Ethan and Martin will have to answer for the death of Futterman follows Clayton's ironic comment that it was certainly a nice "wedding" considering that no one got married. When Martin offers some further resistance to the Ranger commander's orders, Charlie scuffles with him within the house, and Clayton must separate them once more.

The most interesting minor character in *The Searchers* is Mose Harper, a madman whose seeming incoherence enables him to move between Indian and white societies. Mose is first mentioned when Ethan arrives at his brother's ranch and Aaron asks him about California; Harper had earlier brought news that Ethan went there after the Civil War. Ethan states that someone should have buried Mose long ago, and thus the age of this character is emphasized before he ever appears. In his desire for a place to rest, which Mose first mentions when he thanks Martha for the "use of the rocking chair," Harper ultimately succeeds in his quest as Ethan so obviously fails in his. During the initial search for Jorgenson's cattle, Mose stays with Ethan once the Comanches' intention has been discovered. On the way back to the Edwards' ranch, he chides Martin for foolishly exhausting his horse; and after Ethan has denied the younger man any sight of the mutilated Martha, Mose keeps Pauley in tow while sitting in a chair.

Mose continues to be a mirror image of Ethan, albeit with a curious overlay of biblical rhetoric that reasserts the weakness of his mind. When the initial Comanche trick is discovered, Mose arouses Ethan's disgust by dancing about and whooping like an Indian—behavior that gets the light-headed Harper kicked squarely in the seat of his pants. Mose's essential childishness, his inability to perceive what the protagonist must be feeling at such a moment, is reechoed by his conduct during the second phase of the search under Clayton. He grinningly gestures after Ethan has shot out the eyes of the Comanche corpse; in answer to the reverend/captain's question about how far a river is, he answers that he has been "baptized," to the dismay of the man (Bill Steele) riding beside him. At the cantina, where Ethan recognizes his mule, Mose offers that he knows someone who has seen Debbie and that he will trade such knowledge "for a roof over Old Mose's head."

When next seen, Harper is brought to the Jorgenson ranch after having lived for a time among the Comanches, an ordeal he dismisses by pleading that he cleverly ate grass and acted like a madman to fool them. His entry into the ranch house finds him once more seated before being adjured by the others to tell where Scar's camp is now located. In a symbolic sequence, Mose refuses to tell Ethan (and even goes so far as to stick out his tongue at him) but does agree to inform Martin, who is able to decipher the message ("Five Fingers") which the addled old man then delivers. Mrs. Jorgenson characteristically dismisses Mose's rhetorical question about his sanity by saying that he is only "sick and tired," while Lieutenant Greenhill insists that since there is no place such as Mose has named on any of the army's maps, the cavalry has not been able to make any sense of his story. Mose last appears smiling in a rocking chair on the Jorgensons' porch, a position that he has earned by his deeds and one that offers a striking contrast to Ethan's final lonely exit after the last door swings shut. Mose claimed this status earlier when, as he was brought into the parlor, he declared that he had "come for my rockin' chair." His assimilation into the society of the film, despite his biblical mockery ("Thank you, Lord, for what we are about to receive") at being able to kill Comanches earlier, serves as a further devastating comment on the central character's permanent estrangement.

Lars Jorgenson's fears, wishes, and feelings register almost immediately, and he never ventures to present any of them extensively. His rage over the loss of his prize cattle (he fumes that he should have raised pigs instead) quickly gives way to outright fear when he realizes the Comanche raid was a diversion. When Ethan and Martin return after their initial two-year quest, Lars greets the protagonist by lamenting how harsh the country has been in costing him his only son. This pessimism is countered by his wife, who offers one of the recurrent themes in Ford's westerns as a rationale for their lives. On the porch with Lars and Ethan, Mrs. Jorgenson insists that although the country may need their sacrifice in order to become civilized, in time it will become a place in which young people can grow and prosper.

By linking Mrs. Jorgenson with Martha, for she insists to Ethan that his dead sister-in-law would have wanted him to care as much for the living boys as for the captured girls, Ford illuminates both women. Aaron Edwards compliments Martha because she made him stick it out and build their home in the wilderness, and Mrs. Jorgenson's philosophy of sacrifice extends this perception to her and Lars; once more, Ethan's alienation can be seen when, in his rage, he not only cuts short Martha's funeral but also, just as tellingly, insults Mrs. Jorgenson by barely listening to her (and thus symbolically ignoring Martha again). The older woman triumphs at the end of *The Searchers* when she takes Debbie from Ethan and guides the girl into the protective aegis of her house, which now represents the settled civilization from which the nomadic and egocentric protagonist is forever excluded.

Brad's loss of Lucy connects him to Ethan, for the younger man runs amok when confronted with the truth. Brad's youthful exuberance is caught when he shouts for the others to join him at the scene of the butchered cattle. On the trail he parodies Ethan by wanting to further destroy the Comanche corpse with a rock; since his action precedes Ethan's act of mutilation, Brad is linked even more closely to the madness at the core of the central figure. Their brief quarrel foreshadows the moment when Ethan confesses how he found Lucy and how she must have died ("What do you want me to do? Draw you a picture?"). Brad's subsequent charge into the Comanche camp represents his futile suicide, and Ethan restrains Martin because he fully understands what has driven the younger man to such desperate lengths.

Indeed, Brad's symbolic death raises the question of why Ethan doesn't also run amok because of his repressed love for Martha. It is seemingly his racist-tinged need for revenge, a trait that clearly places him at odds with any future society that might be built, that keeps Ethan pursuing a more "rational" course by which he may be able to kill Debbie.

Aaron and Martha, by simply going to bed while Ethan sits on their porch steps with a dog, dramatize the anguish within the protagonist. Their settled, married life represents all that Ethan has ever wanted and will never have. Martha's adherence to her family comes out fully during Scar's raid when her primary concern is with getting Debbie away from the house so that some kind of future may be ensured. If she harbors serious feelings for Ethan (as seen by her handling of his coat), Martha does not want to break up her home for them. Her only son, Ben, is given his uncle's sabre and asks why Ethan has not come home before now; in the massacre sequence, the boy remarks that he would feel considerably better if Ethan were there.

Lucy exhibits a similar prescience during the attack once she becomes aware of what is about to happen. Martha and Aaron, who have suspected for some time what is going on in the brush outside, quietly try to prevent panic, but Lucy does not immediately understand and keeps wanting to light candles. When Martha snuffs out the candle the girl is carrying, Lucy finally realizes their danger and suffers a brief hysterical outburst that ends when her mother slaps her. The elder daughter's fate at the hands of the Comanches is never explicitly shown, in keeping with Ford's sense of decorum, although we are supplied with a telling track-in close-up of the girl — which is similar to what happens when Liberty Valance and Hallie have their only direct confrontational moment in *The Man Who Shot Liberty Valance* and which, again, implies rape. Of course, the absence of any scenes showing Lucy being assaulted or manhandled in any way merely makes her fate seem worse; Ford knows that we can imagine greater horrors than he could ever film. Ethan's fury when he returns from burying Lucy's corpse further underscores this technique and adds to the "nightmarish" aura of *The Searchers*.

Debbie, the most important member of the family from the standpoint of plot, initially greets Ethan by pointing out that she is not her older sister as he lifts her up. When Clayton and the Rangers appear the next morning, we learn that Debbie has not been baptized — an omission that is symbolically rectified by the experiences she endures throughout the rest of the film. When Debbie is finally seen in Scar's tent, she recognizes Ethan and Martin, as they do her, so that her later appearance at their encampment comes as no surprise. With Martin she breaks down and admits that initially she wanted to be rescued from her captors; however, her nostalgia ("I remember. From always.") quickly gives way to her argument that the Comanches are now her "people." Appropriately, Debbie uses her Indian tongue to urge Ethan and Martin to leave; however, Martin's later rescue of the girl from Scar shows her willingness to abandon Indian life. In her flight from Ethan, whom she intuitively recognizes as a danger, Debbie tries to defend herself; she raises her fists just before his urging that they "go home," an action that demonstrates a return to her white childhood. In lifting her up, Ethan recognizes the child he once held and realizes that her individual life transcends anything as transient as having lived with Scar. Debbie's return to white society finds her quickly comforted by Mrs. Jorgenson; she does not go through any of the trauma that Elena experiences in *Two Rode Together*.

Buck Sweet, of *Three Godfathers*, is certainly among the gentlest of lawmen to be found in any western. The religious strain in Buck is suggested by his nickname ("Pearly") and his desire to save Hightower, in order to play chess with the outlaw once the sheriff has him securely in the Welcome jail. His deliberate breaking of the outlaws' water bag and his subsequent moves and countermoves against them underscore Buck's perception that he is not being paid to kill people. At Tarapin Tanks, when he discovers the death of his niece, Buck temporarily loses control by offering an additional reward for the "dead" outlaws. In New Jerusalem, however the sheriff comes back to himself and relents when Hightower collapses on the saloon floor. In this ability to forgive, Buck stands in the sharpest contrast to Ethan Edwards, for with similar provocation, Buck still observes the standards of decency that community life teaches. The sheriff remains firmly in control of the posse he commands, and such competence is exhibited earlier when his instincts cause him to look at wanted posters and to finger the Abilene Kid, after saying that he will be seeing the three outlaws in the future. The sheriff's association with flowers and domesticity clearly demonstrates that he is a model citizen, similar to the role Ward Bond embodies in *Fort Apache* and *Wagonmaster*. The courtroom exchange, when Buck and Bob chide each other about their full names, quickly rebounds on the lawman, who takes the crowd's laughter in good spirit. Buck's final appearance — heartily singing Bob out of the town — underlines his treatment of "that big Texan" both in and out of jail.

The Abilene Kid is characterized more by gentleness than by any proficiency with a gun, despite his early bravado when he insists that he "ain't backin' down" even though Bob urges he head for the border without participating in the robbery. His being wounded in Welcome imposes the first serious burden on the outlaws, who take him along in spite of the loss of his horse. For a time, the others treat him deferentially because of that injury; however, as their burdens increase, the Kid emerges as a moral leader. After the sandstorm and the loss of their remaining mounts, Kearney understatedly asks "What are we waiting for?" when Bob and Pedro engage in mutual recriminations. After the birth of the infant, the Kid takes delight in merely holding the child, whom he comes to see as his only legacy; his belief in scriptural wisdom enables him to impose a design on the others by insisting that they go to New Jerusalem. Kearney's special status is established when he asks his companions: "Do you think this was all chance?" and "Can't you see the star?" The Kid's willingness to sacrifice for the godchild underlies his refusal to drink more water than the others because he does not want to "steal" from the infant. On the salt lake, when Bob warns that the rocky terrain beyond will be tough, the Kid, now wearing heel-less boots, prophetically answers that he does not plan to go that far; and when he feels the final ebb of his strength, he runs to take the infant as close to safety as he can. Bob's eulogy for his fallen comrade, in which he notes, that the Kid has returned to being a child in heaven, anticipates Kearney's angelic return to guide Hightower at the end of his trek.

Pedro acts out of impulse and anger when confronted with problems. He and Bob have obviously traveled together for some time as cattle thieves, and their new excursion into bank robbery does not sit well with either man. Once the holdup is discovered and the Kid wounded, Pedro throws bullets around the town to cover their escape. In doing so, he nearly starts a riot on the streets of Welcome and foreshadows the anger with which he will react to Bob's later questions. Pedro's politeness with Mrs. Sweet and Ruby Latham foreshadows his role as the midwife at the desert nativity. His exceptional deference to the expectant woman, despite his noting that she is a "gringa," raises Pedro to the exalted status that all three godfathers come to enjoy. When Pedro is framed within the arch of the wagon flap, an obviously religious-sounding musical cue adds to this effect. He later examines the infant's clothes that have been left by the mother and comically imagines how they will be used by his godson. In so doing, the Mexican outlaw aligns himself with Martha and Mrs. Jorgenson in *The Searchers*, who see the necessity for their present generation to make sacrifices to ensure the well-being of future generations. Pedro's reverence for scripture causes Bob to react violently at one point ("Don't give me any more of that Bible stuff!"), but their argument is quickly resolved by their mutual desire to see that the child, who begins fortuitously to cry, is fed. When he collapses after accepting the burden of carrying the child after the Kid's death, Pedro knows that his broken leg has finished him, and he proceeds to recite the "Our Father" after Bob has left him with a pistol. It is surely fitting that when Hightower experiences the ghostly aid of his former saddlemates, Pedro appears as an angry figure who tries to shame Bob into going on.

Hightower, as the character who changes most during *Three Godfathers*, learns to accept a providential view of existence, in finding something to live for besides himself. His compassion can be seen in his opening remarks when he tries to persuade the Kid to go south; once Kearney has refused, Hightower reminds the younger man that he is there only to hold the others' horses. At Tarapin Tanks, the main character delivers an extended speech to establish that "this fine old state of affairs" necessitates that Pedro serve as midwife because he himself isn't smart enough or tough enough for such a chore. His position as leader of the outlaw band is again emphasized when he begins to cut cactus for water once the Mexican has assumed that task. Hightower's greasing of "little Robert" leads the threesome into convulsive laughter, and his awkwardness in diapering the infant supplies still another comic-sentimental moment.

When he collapses in the rocky tunnel, Bob gives his remaining water to the infant and then crawls to retrieve the Bible he has cast aside. His skepticism about the scriptural message that he will be saved by a donkey is followed by yet another collapse, which he takes as final ("This is the end of the trail"). At this juncture his dead comrades appear as ghostly images at his heels, and their singing and talking prod him onward until Bob looks back and breaks the illusion; however, by this time a donkey is visible at the end of the tunnel, and the "miracle" has been accomplished. Hightower's reformation has certainly been completed by the time he gets into New Jerusalem, and he wishes everyone in the saloon a merry Christmas. His regeneration is further symbolized by one of the bar's habitués (Francis Ford), who identifies Bob as the "baby's pappy" after Buck has arrived and the protagonist has fainted.

The mystical power of the three outlaws, their ability to influence each other and to function as a group, becomes more marked as their journey progresses. Their initial exuberance at Mojave Tanks is cut short by the arrival of Buck and his deputies. Bob's joy there consists of imagining how good a bath will feel, while the Kid is thankful for the prospect of some relief for his injured arm, and Pedro laments that there is only water and not whiskey to slake their thirst. When the forces of the law arrive, Pedro wants to attack, but Bob realizes they would have no chance against the other men's rifles. Hightower then immediately turns to devising a strategy that will enable them to elude their capable opponent, the sheriff of Welcome. In the sandstorm, the three outlaws get to shelter and, as their waking-up scene shows, arrange themselves with the Kid resting between the other two. Their deference to women reaches an apogee when they are summoned into the presence of the dying mother and they drop their gunbelts before entering her wagon. Their sense of decorum clearly foreshadows the consummate care they will lavish on their godson. It is, finally, this sense of the three of them working together that serves as the principal thematic emphasis in *Three Godfathers*. With Bob, Pedro, and the Abilene Kid, Ford shows how a small society goes about building the future and achieves what is implicit in Martha's life and Mrs. Jorgenson's "Texican" speech in *The Searchers*.

The major characters in the later film are more striking and problematic than the three principals in *Three Godfathers*. The most straightforward among them, the Reverend/Captain Clayton, serves as a means by which Ethan is illuminated rather than as the embodiment of any superior religious or leadership skills. Clayton is given far too many comic moments, and his tactics, which ultimately prove sound enough, are too thoroughly overridden by Ethan for him to ever achieve the stature of Buck Sweet. Clayton's noisy arrival at the Edwards' ranch, replete with his inquiries about Debbie's baptism and his fondness for the donuts that Martha and Lucy serve, foreshadows his appearance at the truncated wedding when he bursts in with Charlie and immediately sweeps up Mrs. Jorgenson in a rough-and-tumble dance. Clayton's earlier exuberance is checked when Ethan — arriving and taking Aaron's place in the posse — chides the reverend/captain about being at the Confederate surrender; and the latter greets Ethan as the "prodigal brother." Clayton's weakness in dealing with Ethan later surfaces at Martha's funeral and on the trail.

The Ranger leader is reduced even further during the final battle at Scar's camp, when he serves primarily as a comic foil for the inexperienced Greenhill. Clayton calls out the young lieutenant for failing to take off his hat in the presence of women; and later, before Scar's village when Greenhill pleads to stay, he gains comic points by urging that he, and not the Indians, is "the hard case you're up against out here." Such rhetoric is dispelled, however, by our final view of the reverend/captain: he gets his backside sutured because of an accidental wound from the lieutenant's sabre. Since he has called attention to Greenhill's flourishes with that weapon, what the reverend/captain most feared has obviously come to pass. Clayton's compassion is shown in one of the most telling and celebrated scenes in *The Searchers* when his reactions to Martha and Ethan call attention to their repressed feelings. Clayton's averted eyes reveal him to be not a judge but one who forgives when he can and overlooks when he must. In the doorway, where Martha stands gazing after the departing Ethan, the reverend/captain manages to squeeze past and, in yet another telling mimetic bit of business, tips his hat to the enraptured woman.

Martin Pauley works diligently to belong to the Edwards' family, which has taken him in as an orphan, and it is finally his loyalty to them that saves Debbie and enables Ethan to atone. Martin naively believes that finding the girls is the real purpose behind his "uncle's" pursuit, and even after he intuits that Ethan has the capacity to "go crazy," he adheres to that aim by refusing the protagonist's testamentary gift. Martin is unfortunately too emotional to kill Ethan, as we see when he is in tears during the battle with Scar's forces at the river and, again, when Ethan denies that Debbie is his kin after having lived with an Indian. Ironically, Martin manages to rescue Debbie and kill Scar precisely because he adheres to the "idealistic" notions that enable him to dismiss a painful fact — that his mother's scalp is in the Comanche chief's collection — as irrelevant to what must be done in the present.

Martin's relationship with Laurie seems consistently unfair to the girl until it becomes apparent that he embodies a compassion that she needs to learn. Her patient devotion, seen when she states that they have been "going steady since the age of three," represents the idyllic kind of domesticity that good women must possess in Ford's westerns. However, she later chides Martin for making her live in such a place for so many years, and her movement toward Charlie McCorry, though obviously half-hearted, causes her to be just a bit flawed. If Laurie's delight over Martin and Charlie fighting for her is real enough, emphasized when Ethan tells her that her protestations about stopping are phony, her later zeal with Martin about letting Ethan kill Debbie is chilling. When Martin earlier repeats his need to bring Debbie back, she challenges him by asking "Fetch what home?" Laurie even goes so far as to insist that Martha would not want her child returned now. In Laurie's mind, Debbie should be killed, as Ethan wants; by saving the girl from this fate, Martin demonstrates how his mercy and compassion must be acquired by his future wife. Their entrance into the Jorgenson home after Debbie's return cements the bonds between them and implies that theirs will be a fruitful marriage for them and society.

Ethan Edwards dominates *The Searchers* to the extent that any changes the other characters experience result from his presence. The individual closest to him emotionally is Scar, who has lost sons and seeks revenge against all white men. The Comanche chief initially appears as a shadow across the gravestones before which Debbie kneels, and this image relates him to the very forces that drive the protagonist. The similarity between Scar and Ethan is borne out further in the insults they exchange about each other's languages in the Indian camp. Thus, we see that these men are joined together by hatred of each other and by the misunderstandings between the larger societies each man personifies. At the river battle Ethan deliberately tries to kill Scar, who has donned his ceremonial chief's headdress. At the cave battle, Ford's protagonist again manages to unhorse his rival, but in the end, he can only take a sadistic revenge on Scar's corpse. In scalping his nightmare Indian, Ethan practices the same behavior he deplores when trying to persuade Martin not to go in alone because Scar had scalped the younger man's mother.

It is, of course, such contradictions within Ethan that make him an arresting figure within Ford's westerns. Other later characters, McCabe in *Two Rode Together* and Doniphon in *The Man Who Shot Liberty Valance*, carry around bitter and defeated psyches, but they do not operate as close to lawlessness as Ethan does. Although he restores Debbie to society, Ethan remains forever alien to that world, for there is surely no place in the Jorgenson home for a man who mutilates dead enemies. Ethan becomes heroic only because he abandons his race hatred long enough to allow emotion, in the form of love for a child as the embodiment of the future, to guide him, finally, with Debbie. Once back in civilization, however, he realizes that he is just as lonely and alienated as he was when he first appeared with the newly minted money at Aaron's door. Ford's heroes and villains have heretofore been melodramatically pure; with Ethan, the director creates the more ambiguous possibility of a man who is tragically torn between good and evil. Because he can scalp Scar moments before he raises Debbie up and says "Let's go home," Ethan remains the most disturbing character in all of Ford's westerns and one of the most arresting creations in all of American cinema.

Chapter 11

Stagecoach and *Cheyenne Autumn*

Stagecoach (1939) and *Cheyenne Autumn* (1964), the first and last of Ford's twelve sound westerns, represent his most and least romantic endeavors in the genre. Both films feature journeys in which characters undergo significant emotional, personal, or social changes. Although many lesser characters in these films experience significant changes, the eventual fates of their lovers most notably reflect Ford's increasingly sober outlook. The trip from Tonto to Lordsburg in *Stagecoach* climaxes with the killing of the Plummers and the escape of Ringo (John Wayne) and Dallas (Claire Trevor) from "civilization"; the trek from Indian territory to the Yellowstone country in *Cheyenne Autumn* drives a permanent wedge between the tribe's ranks when Little Wolf (Ricardo Montalban) kills Red Shirt (Sal Mineo) and then rides away into a symbolic sunset. If conventional heroics dominate and are rewarded in *Stagecoach*, those virtues prove ineffectual in *Cheyenne Autumn*. Even Ford's usually benevolent cavalry has become controlled, in the later film, by madmen and weaklings.

Such an alteration, of course, reflects the director's increasingly skeptical and pessimistic outlook on the western movie mythology that his films had endorsed and helped to create; while many explanations can be advanced for the commercial failure of *Cheyenne Autumn*, the most apparent ones are physical and economic. Ford's artistic capacity may well have been on the decline by the early 1960s, although critics heap praise on *Donovan's Reef* (1963) and *Seven Women* (1965), which were made before and after *Cheyenne Autumn*.[1] Ford's last western may also have suffered because Warner Brothers viewed it as a kind of "insurance policy" for their more elaborate production of *My Fair Lady*, which was to be the studio's leading film of 1964. However, the somber and revisionist cast of *Cheyenne Autumn*, despite all its efforts to "redeem" the Indians, whom Ford felt he had misrepresented, finally palls because it presents themes that are too negative for the box office. Ford's last western contains diminished expectations and too much overt didacticism, qualities that were not palatable for much of its audience; his most obvious western epic is

249

thus similar to Anthony Mann's *Fall of the Roman Empire* (also 1964) in emphasizing more thoughtful and less melodramatic solutions to the thematic issues it raises.

Stagecoach proceeds through distinct geographic points, in keeping with its linear plot. The preparation of the coach in Tonto as the passengers are assembled is followed by significant developments in Dry Fork, where the group decides to continue despite the absence of a military escort; in Apache Wells, where Mrs. Mallory (Louise Platt) gives birth; in Lee's Ferry, with its difficult river crossing; and in Lordsburg, in which climax and denouement occur. The compact structure of *Stagecoach*, in which virtually every scene supplies additional momentum, reflects Ford's capacity to hone a story down to its essentials so that single camera shots and gestures do the work of more elaborate sequences. In the ethically fixed world of *Stagecoach*, there is no need for excess, whether of action or of emotion. The very pace of the journey, in which the stage rarely moves at a less-than-rollicking gait, and Ringo's face-off with the Plummers with only three bullets merely epitomize the economy of the narrative.

The impending confrontation with the Apaches is underscored at each stopping point. If Billy Pickett (Francis Ford) and his wife (Marga Daighton) are preparing to run from trouble at Dry Fork, Chris (Chris Pin Martin) lives among the Indians at Apache Wells because of his trust in his (ultimately duplicitous) wife, and Ringo's escape attempt there is checked by distant smoke signals. The burned remains of Lee's Ferry, symbolized by Hatfield's (John Carradine) gentlemanly concern for the dead woman, bring the Indian danger even closer. This last step adds to the irony of Doc Boone's (Thomas Mitchell) toast to their successfully having avoided the Apaches — just before Peachcock (Donald Meek) is hit by an arrow.

In addition, the strains within the group arise at these various points, and their united resolutions represent a working out along the lines of classical democratic political assumptions. Curly (George Bancroft) polls the other passengers about going on without a military escort and thus implies many of the tactics by which political leaders work within the context of "one man, one vote." Deeper tensions and shifting emotions color the dispute at Apache Wells when Gatewood (Berton Churchill) presses to leave immediately while the others decide on a day's rest for Lucy and her baby. On the final leg of the journey the group fights for its collective life against the Apaches and runs out of ammunition just as the cavalry arrives. The nighttime and nightmarish world of Lordsburg is then invoked to underline the escape of the lovers from the "blessings" of community life; as Ringo so aptly puts it, the town is no place for a girl like Dallas.

The narrative structure of *Cheyenne Autumn* is both more formal and more elaborate; indeed, the later film is at considerable pains to distance the audience from it by means of its very telling. Ford's use of a narrator here is more extended (than, for example, the occasional voiceover comments in *She Wore a Yellow Ribbon*) and more generalized (than, for example, those sections of *The Searchers* and *The Man Who Shot Liberty Valance* that are recounted by characters who were part of the action). Archer's (Richard Widmark) narration consistently focuses on the Cheyennes and their difficulties, and the very detachment of his tone stands in sharp contrast to his frequent arguments with others within the narrative itself. The journey of the Cheyennes is, of course, undertaken to return to a better place, one associated with their collective past. If the lovers in *Stagecoach* escape from society by going across the border to Ringo's ranch, Archer and Deborah Wright (Carroll Baker) must presumably return to the point at which the Cheyennes' trek began.

The actual stopping points in *Cheyenne Autumn* feature a battle site, in the rocks; Dodge City, with its cast of cutthroats and cynics; Fort Robinson, in which half of the Indian party suffers; Victory Cave, where official Washington intervenes to prevent more bloodshed; and finally, the Cheyennes' regained homeland, where they settle the feuds that have developed over the course of their journey. Little Wolf's revenge of his honor ultimately shatters the community that has endured the trip. The much slower tempo at which the Cheyennes move simply underlines Ford's more somber outlook, and such episodes as the Dodge City interlude and the brief glimpses of newspaper reactions to the Indians' flight create ambiguities within the narrative. Archer's mentioning of the actual date on which the story starts, and his later allusions to the number of miles the Indians still have to cover, provide an internal chronology that is abetted by shots of the changing seasons. His final narration, in which he notes that the Cheyennes still have "wounds to heal" before the shootout between the two warriors, underscores the Indians' muted triumph. That Archer never rounds off the plot with a concluding comment, as the narrator does so conspicuously in the epilogue section of *She Wore a Yellow Ribbon*, only adds to the sober ending of *Cheyenne Autumn*.

Ford's filmmaking techniques can be seen from the opening of *Stagecoach* through the final moments of *Cheyenne Autumn*. Although his admonition about the need to make thematically serious works in black and white and less demanding ones in color might be applied, the larger scale of *Cheyenne Autumn* undoubtedly conditioned some of Ford's visual approach. Once more we are confronted by a signal difference in credit arrangements: *Stagecoach* uses the kind of pictorialism found in the majority of Ford's earlier westerns, whereas *Cheyenne Autumn* incorporates the kind of static design found in *The Searchers* and *Two Rode Together*. In *Stagecoach* alternating shots of the stagecoach and the cavalry column establish the same kind of expectancy as seen in the opening of *Wagonmaster*, while the accompanying music sets up an aural contrast between the forces that will clash. This type of arrangement is augmented by musical cues; and the director's penchant for violent visual juxtaposition is prominently on display when the Apache finally appear in

force. The equestrian statues that serve to backdrop the credits for *Cheyenne Autumn* stress the historical and legendary emphases that Ford's plot pushes so hard; these static figures, suggestive of Remington, and Alex North's somber music cast a pall of melancholy over the entire proceeding. Once again, a placid background implies a more controlled world, one in which the characters' efforts will be held in bounds. The credits of *Stagecoach* show us men acting, whereas those of *Cheyenne Autumn* show us men as monuments.

Many of the camera setups and shots in *Stagecoach* strike us as much fresher than those in Ford's later westerns. The visual grandeur of the Monument Valley locations in *Stagecoach* was, of course, somewhat attenuated by the time *Cheyenne Autumn* appeared. By then, two of the photographic elements being utilized — the cavalry and technicolor — had been thoroughly explored in *She Wore a Yellow Ribbon*, *The Searchers*, and *Sergeant Rutledge*; thus, though there are characteristic shots of mounted columns against the backdrop of Monument Valley, a sense of déjà vu operates in the later film. The slower pace of the moving groups in *Cheyenne Autumn* also detracts from the epic photography, for fatigue and hunger rather than exuberance mark much of the action. This photographic lushness jars with the extreme staginess of much else in *Cheyenne Autumn*; indeed, the cinematography in *Stagecoach* seems more integral and far less obvious, despite its frequently spectacular qualities.

Initially, *Stagecoach* exploits the photographic possibilities of Monument Valley as the coach and its cavalry escort travel through that terrain. Numerous high-angle shots foreshadow later developments, particularly the emergence of the Apaches on an overlooking ridge, while establishing the symbolic function of Ford's landscape. The terrain of Monument Valley often operates as a sort of commentary on the human actions in the foreground, and this tendency is clearly at work in *Stagecoach*. Shots of the coach battling to get up steep grades emphasize man's capacity to surmount difficulties. In other instances, the camera is cleverly moved. Ringo's first appearance, when he halts the coach, is emphasized as the camera tracks to a close-up. If this series of shots "made a star" out of John Wayne, it also establishes his character's importance. That Ringo's entry is photographed in distinct stages also implies that there is more to the character than a first impression is apt to yield; his emergence as a real gentleman finally belies his jailbird status. The dinnertable confrontation between the supposedly genteel (Mrs. Mallory, Gatewood, and Hatfield) and the supposedly unworthy (Dallas and Ringo) enters a different phase by means of the tracking shot that brings Lucy into the center of the frame and leads to one of her inconclusive conversations with the

Opposite: John Wayne, (but actually stuntman Yakima Canutt) jumps onto the racing team in *Stagecoach* (Walter Wanger-United Artists, 1939). This is but one of a succession of great action bits during the battle over the salt flats.

gambler about his past. A reverse process sets off the destruction at Lee's Ferry: Ford's camera pulls back from the coach, which has stopped to reveal the smoldering waystation.

Other shots clearly emphasize thematic and narrative points. Thus, in the scene showing the parting of the stage and the cavalry escort outside Dry Fork, a road branching off in two distinct directions is shot from a high angle to emphasize the separation of the groups. Another extended shot, in which the coach becomes gradually smaller, more isolated, and alone, then occurs against a magnificent sky as if to suggest that nature exhibits no necessary sympathy for the fate of the passengers. At Apache Wells a shot of a coyote is intercut with the birth of Lucy's baby to account for the nickname given to the infant. The ever-solicitous Hatfield, Ringo, and Buck (Andy Devine) constitue a kind of holy trio at the end of the hallway. When Dallas subsequently shows off the newborn, the same threesome assembles, along with Peacock and Curly, and the camera moves in closer to gradually omit Hatfield and to concentrate on the blooming love between Ringo and the girl.

Ford's comment that actors' eyes should always be watched is, perhaps, nowhere better demonstrated, for the ostensible object of discussion seems lost on Ringo and Dallas, who, as the cliché has it, only have eyes for each other. In addition, the absence of Gatewood is surely consistent with the hypocritical banker's compromised moral standing. Ringo's subsequent proposal to Dallas corresponds to what has happened, since he insists that he has been moved, in part, by the way she appeared with the Mallory baby. Hatfield's being edited out of the scene is undoubtedly another way in which his demise is foreshadowed. The prominently featured long, darkened hallway with a door at its end, through which Ringo will pass to propose to Dallas, obviously symbolizes love and the future.

The sequence of the crossing at Lee's Ferry also offers a notable example of editing and staging. The coach is photographed from angles that alternate between an intimate view from the driver's box and a long shot in which the whole vehicle is shown. The alternation of close-up, with its emphasis on physical movement and struggle, and long shot, in which the coach seems to float through the water, offers a nice contrast in rhythms of action. The same fluid quality attaches to the juxtaposed shots that mark how the Apaches are assembled en masse before their pell-mell assault on the coach. This abrupt transition, by which the ironic tranquility within the stage gives way to Geronimo's armed warriors preparing to attack, again illustrates Ford's deft sense of timing. The Indians have been signaled by smoke on distant hills and by Ringo's aborted flight from Apache Wells when he stopped in the courtyard. The shot of Ringo, Dallas, and Curly, all facing offscreen right, underlines the danger, as do the frantic getaways from there and Lee's Ferry.

When the travelers arrive in Lordsburg, darkness increasingly marks the photographic style. If this final town is similar to Tonto in that it has numerous

Spanish Woman (Dolores Del Rio) and the Quaker teacher Deborah Wright (Carroll Baker) share a pensive moment on the trail in *Cheyenne Autumn* (Warner Bros., 1964).

citizens milling about, Lordsburg is also distinguished by the raucous sounds that emanate from its saloons and brothels. A street idler quickly informs Hank Plummer (Tom Tyler) of Ringo's arrival; at the same time, he exhibits little or no interest in the other passengers. Inside the saloon where he has been gambling, shadows are manipulated so that when Hank stands up after hearing of Ringo's arrival, his face is bathed in darkness to imply his death. On the main street in Lordsburg where the actual confrontation takes place, the villains enter from the rear while the hero appears in the foreground. Ford's cutting away from the gunfight serves *Stagecoach* by bringing Hank Plummer back to his proper milieu, the saloon, to die and by emphasizing the great love of Dallas and Ringo.

Long shots of escaping Indians and pursuing cavalry retain their visual impact in *Cheyenne Autumn*, for if nothing else, Ford was one of the supreme visual artists ever to work in film. An early long shot reprises the scenes in *Wagonmaster* in which the Mormons get their wagons over the final pass; thus, the Cheyenne column is shown ascending a rise in the distance as Deborah confers in the foreground with the chiefs. Tall Tree's (Victor Jory) burial in the rocks is set off by a scene of mounted braves riding over rolling terrain in the background, in a visual arrangement seen most notably in *She Wore a Yellow*

Ribbon and *The Searchers*. The arrival of Archer's column on a plateau also resembles *She Wore a Yellow Ribbon* with its frequent evocations of mounted men riding over rolling terrain in all kinds of weather. The river crossings in *Cheyenne Autumn* harken back photographically to *Sergeant Rutledge*, when the title character foiled the Indian ambush, and to *Wagonmaster*, when the train crossed a stream and ascended the steep shore on the other side.

The arrival of Archer's command at an undermanned army post is highlighted by an entry scene reminiscent of such moments at the beginnings of *Rio Grande* and *Sergeant Rutledge*; in addition, this setup is repeated at Fort Robinson, which the cavalry column enters in the same listless fashion that Brittles's tired patrol entered Fort Stark in *She Wore a Yellow Ribbon*. The division of the Cheyennes into groups led by Dull Knife (Gilbert Roland) and Little Wolf is heralded by a ground-level shot of their parting, a shot similar to that of the cavalry and travelers in *Stagecoach*. These dividing parties trudge through forbidding snows toward the camera, accentuating their separation, a point that is further dramatized when Little Wolf's youngest wife bolts to join the headstrong Red Shirt and go to Fort Robinson.

The musical score in *Stagecoach*, composed of American folk songs arranged by various hands, neatly augments the narrative.[2] In Tonto, when Doc Boone and Dallas are driven out by the ladies of the "Law and Order League," we hear "Shall We Gather at the River." While this tune appears elsewhere to celebrate the benevolence of community (most noticeably in *My Darling Clementine* and *Wagonmaster*), in *Stagecoach* it accompanies a sequence in which the community treats individuals unjustly. Since the subsequent narrative is at pains to demonstrate the goodness of Doc and Dallas, their early treatment establishes the basis for the film's final scene; indeed, anyone would want to avoid the "blessings" of the civilization that we see on the streets of Tonto and Lordsburg. The religious hypocrisy of the "good citizens" of the first town is also abetted by this comically skewed rendition of "Shall We Gather at the River," which is deftly juxtaposed by Doc Boone's acceptance of the community's judgment and his proceeding with head held high. His remark about the trouble that awaits him and Dallas turns them into doomed nobility while it makes prosecutors of those who want them out of town.

"I Dream of Jeannie" is associated throughout with Lucy Mallory, who, as a daughter of the Old South, infatuates Hatfield because he associates her with his past. The wistful romantic sound of this Stephen Foster standard nicely emphasizes the gambler's chivalrous feeling for the army wife while, at the same time, suggesting the "Lost Cause" for which he has suffered. Hatfield has not adjusted to the defeat of his beloved Confederacy, as seen in his initial disagreement with Boone over what to call the Civil War, so that he appropriately dies protecting what he (ironically) believes is its essence in Lucy Mallory. She, on the other hand, though embodying much of the supposed delicacy of the southern belle, has married and is adamant about rejoining her husband. Lucy recognizes the filigree work on the drinking cup that Hatfield offers her in the coach, but she is finally too much a part of the present to be caught up in the nostalgia that controls the gambler.

The music in *Stagecoach* also scales appropriate heights during the storm sequence when the passengers are buffeted by snow in the higher regions into which Buck drives to avoid the Apaches. The swirling weather is augmented by similar musical effects that, in turn, nicely emphasize the central dramatic action(s) at this juncture. Just as all the characters are caught in various emotional storms — whether bred by the Apache threat, their own clandestine desires, or the emergence of new relationships — so the music emphasizes the chaos surrounding the stagecoach. The birth of "Little Coyote" is hailed by fittingly sentimental cues, while the pursuit of the Apaches across the flats is marked by a driving ostinato to mark the furious action. The interruption of such music by a distant bugle call, nicely timed to emphasize the symbolic disparity between Lucy Mallory and Hatfield by showing his death at the precise moment that she hears its sound, brings this chase sequence to its conclusion. The tawdriness of Lordsburg's night life is emphasized by the sound of a honky-tonk piano. The saloon in which Hank Plummer is seen features such music, which is, symbolically, brought to an end when news of Ringo's arrival reaches the villain.

Alex North's score for *Cheyenne Autumn* supplies an appropriate epic gloss to the film. His principal themes, by virtue of their tempi and orchestrations, emphasize the mixed results of the Indians' accomplishment. Somber and brassy, North's cues never allow us to be too hopeful about what we are watching. Although Hollywood gossip has it that Ford was not pleased with this score, the music surely does not detract from the thematic messages of *Cheyenne Autumn*. The secondary love theme exhibits the same tentative character as does North's main theme for the Cheyennes: in both cases, the composer has wisely opted for restraint to catch the antiheroic tone of the film. Within the Dodge City sequence, however, *Cheyenne Autumn* reverts musically to the format of *Stagecoach*. Traditional tunes are heard in the saloon in which Earp (James Stewart) and Holliday (Arthur Kennedy) are gambling, and these melodies are performed by an ensemble whose forced gaiety matches the artificial nature of the entire episode.

Once Earp and the others dash out of town in their drunken and bumbling pursuit of the Cheyennes, "Camptown Races" becomes a constant musical background. This jaunty tune, with its connotations of gambling and race tracks, nicely catches the sporting artificiality of the events. The sighting of a single Indian in the distance (a figure who, with one rifle shot, manages to blow up their ammunition wagon) sets off a veritable stampede among the drunken pursuers; for such frenzied comic activity, "Camptown Races" provides splendid support. The embarrassments of Guinivere Plantagenet (Elizabeth Allen), as she races skirtless across the prairie and then wrestles with her would-be rescuer, Doc Holliday, hardly calls for anything more elevated. The narrator's summary of the "battle of Dodge City" with its casualty of "one silk dress" brings this interlude to a fitting end as the music slowly dissipates and disappears.

In Washington, when Archer manages to discuss the Cheyennes' plight at Fort Robinson with Secretary Schurz (Edward G. Robinson), other derived music is featured. The older man's grappling with the problem of the Cheyennes, a situation that has been made worse by pressure from the army to remove the Indians from the control of his department and turn them over to the ministrations of "land grabbers," leads him to seek solace from the picture of his beloved friend Abraham Lincoln. As Schurz looks at the portrait of the dead leader and asks for advice, "The Battle Hymn of the Republic" rises, appropriately, as a kind of easy identification of the Civil War president.

Ford's reasons for making *Cheyenne Autumn* included a claim that he had treated Indians badly in his other westerns. For many revisionist critics, Ford's portrayals of Indians are inaccurate or racist or both; however, their treatment in *Fort Apache* and *The Searchers* hardly shows them as either simple-minded or savages. Cochise shows chivalry and nobility when he defeats Thursday but does not destroy the remainder of his command in *Fort Apache*; the burning village in which Look's corpse is discovered and the motivations behind Scar's conduct make the struggle between white men and red men thematically ambiguous in *The Searchers*. The Indians in *Stagecoach* are not highly developed; indeed they are at best a kind of elemental force that threatens to destroy the principal characters. As such, they emerge as a highly mobile cavalry lacking even the headstrong or vicious figures in *She Wore a Yellow Ribbon* or *Rio Grande*.

Chris's wife (Elvira Rios) at Apache Wells represents the most extended portrait of an Indian in *Stagecoach*, and her initial entry frightens Gatewood, who is hardly the most reliable witness of moral worth. Her duplicity, seen when she sings to disguise the vaqueros' horse thievery, places her at odds with the travelers; and her disappearance on the following morning marks her as an enemy. Some observers may object that Chris's subsequent grieving over her taking his beloved horse is sexist, since he says he will not be able to replace the horse but that getting another wife should prove easy; however, the comic status of the stationmaster belies such a reaction. Chris may indeed feel that his wife's ancestry will protect him from raiding Apaches; but, as a comic foil, his views on her stature hardly represent a serious commentary.

Cheyenne Autumn offers a more sincere portrayal of its Indian characters, if only by virtue of the extent to which they are drawn. In a kind of dialectic movement, the Cheyennes are given qualities that belonged to the cavalry in Ford's earlier films, and the question of whether such simple role reversal significantly redresses any possible stereotyping must remain moot. Their group solidarity is initially stressed when they wait for the congressional party that is supposed to inspect the miseries of the reservation. Their unity and endurance are symbolized by Tall Tree, who refuses water after he has collapsed and whose word remains law. Their subsequent decision to flee leads to a sequence in which the Indians smoothly rearm themselves and pack up their belongings; their trek to the north soon finds them crossing a river as a unit and battling successfully against the cavalry in a ravine. This later section, in which their ambush is short-circuited by the overanxious Red Shirt, shows the Cheyennes to be clearly superior to their army pursuers. The shelling of their women and children demonstrates Major Braden's (George O'Brien) inhumanity; appropriately enough, he is the only casualty in this skirmish. The Indians defeat Archer's column by stampeding the soldiers' mounts, in a manner that distinctly resembles Brittles's defeat of Red Shirt in *She Wore a Yellow Ribbon*.

When some cowhands later encounter two begging Indians, and the cretinous Joe (Ken Curtis) kills one of them, another sequence from *She Wore a Yellow Ribbon* is reprised. The other brave escapes in the same way that Sergeant Tyree evaded his Indian enemies — by jumping over a gorge and leaving his angry pursuers behind to fire futilely at his retreat. Such reversals demonstrate the status accorded to the Cheyennes in Ford's last western. After discovering that the buffalo herd has been extinguished for sport, their despair dramatizes how the Indians continue to be victimized by unthinking white men. Their sagacity appears once more when they cross under a railroad bridge at night, despite the troops who are guarding it. Although the narrator has insisted that these railroad tracks represent a veritable prison wall to the Cheyennes, the Indians easily work their way through this alleged difficulty. Later, at another river crossing, the infantrymen on duty are also unaware that the entire Cheyenne column has passed them by, for only Trooper Plumtree (Ben Johnson) notices the book that Deborah has dropped there.

The division between the Cheyennes, in which Dull Knife accedes to the claims of the hungry and leads a group into Fort Robinson, ultimately reaffirms the coherence of the tribe. When the martinet Captain Wessels (Karl Malden) places these prisoners in a warehouse without firewood in order to break their spirits and force them to go back to the reservation, the Cheyennes continue to exhibit the same group solidarity that has distinguished them earlier. Thus, within the freezing warehouse, they rearm themselves so that they can break out and fight their way once more into open country. The guilt-ridden officers at Fort Robinson appear more interested in ideologically flagellating Wessels, who is removed from command shortly before the Cheyennes escape in what seems a heavy-handed plot development. These soldiers' laments over the many casualties on both sides seemingly forstall any armed pursuit of the escaped prisoners.

The cavalry escort that accompanies the coach from Tonto to Dry Fork in *Stagecoach* is led by Lieutenant Blanchard (Tim Holt), who follows orders to the letter, even if he must endure Curly's calling him "soldier boy" and Gatewood's ignorant pomposities. The young officer is committed to duty, so much so that he silences the banker by stating that he will place the older man "under restraint" if necessary. This threat is more than sufficient to cow Gatewood, and Blanchard's ability to command a situation is confirmed. The last image of the lieutenant finds him waving and smiling to the departing stagecoach as Lucy unfurls her handkerchief in response; then, as Blanchard puts his hat back on and returns to duty, we see the doubt that marks his real evaluation of what the future may hold for the passengers.

The later cavalry force that saves the travelers emerges as a unified fighting group riding gloriously to trumpets and sweeping down on its Indian adversaries in efficient splendor. Ford presents this battle impressionistically, so that swirls of dust surround a distant encounter as the stagecoach arrives safely "behind the lines." In effect, the dust becomes a curtain behind which supposedly heroic, if violent, deeds are performed; once again, had Ford been as much of a racist as his detractors claim, his visual emphasis here would have been significantly different. Instead of any sort of cathartic bloodbath in which "savages" receive their "just" comeuppance, the director quickly transforms this battle into a triumphant march in which the victorious cavalry ride briefly four abreast to accompany the stagecoach into Lordsburg.

The cavalry of *Cheyenne Autumn* is considerably diminished. In addition to the defeats at the ravine, due to Braden's rashness, and on the trail, when the headstrong lieutenant Scott (Patrick Wayne) replays Thursday's charge in *Fort Apache*, these troopers appear disgruntled from the start. The assembling of the soldiers to await the congressional delegation is colored by the cynicism of Archer and the telegraph operator (Bing Russell), both of whom appear to be weary as well as wary of anything having to do with political higher-ups. Archer's sour reaction to the bad coffee he is served foreshadows Schurz's later dismissal of the same beverage with the admonition that conditions in the army have not improved since his own time in the service; no one in *Cheyenne Autumn* finds any of the "stronger coffee" that Sheridan and Kirby Yorke enjoy in *Rio Grande*. The only truly efficient cavalrymen are Troopers Plumtree and Smith (Harry Carey, Jr.), who are constantly sent out to scout ahead. Plumtree resembles the beloved Sergeant Tyree of *She Wore a Yellow Ribbon* in his insistence that he is "not paid for thinking" whenever he reports to Archer. At the same time, Plumtree exhibits the same perspicacity that Tyree did, for he discerns a potential ambush, finds Deborah's diary, and after some hours of waiting as an advance guard, insists that the original congressional party will not be coming.

Unfortunately, Plumtree cannot alter the weak and bad commanders under whom he must serve, and so he must simply bide his time and hope that

Lieutenant Scott does not get him, and many other good men, killed through foolish bravado. Unlike Tyree, whose background as a Confederate cavalry officer made him knowledgable about tactics, Plumtree can only serve as an advance scout. His partner, Smith, resembles Peacock in *Stagecoach* in that, like the whiskey drummer, he must keep insisting that his name is "Smith" to Captain Archer, who persists in calling him by other names. Archer's comic inability to remember Smith's name underlines the relative weakness of the captain, who is competent as a tactician but not bold enough to gain a victory. Smith's succeeding appearances are increasingly minor, but when he is draped in a blanket, as if suffering from the cold more than any other trooper, his huddled posture once again recalls Peacock when he was being cared for by the solicitous Doc Boone.

The cavalry's principal function in *Cheyenne Autumn* is, of course, to follow the Cheyennes; the troopers' inability to catch up, despite the Indians' slow pace because of the women and children, offers an oblique criticism of these heretofore always magnificent fighting men. The arrival of Archer's column at Fort Robinson stresses the hardships this group has endured through seasonal changes. His command's extended stay at the Nebraska post reveals the dismay with which the men under Archer perform their duties. While Top Sergeant Wichowsky (Mike Mazurki) has earlier spoken about not wanting to be a Cossack, that spirit has infected all the men, as seen when they eagerly support Archer's decision to go to Washington. The massacre at the fort emphasizes Wichowsky's comment that he and his comrades are not the Cossacks now. The final confrontation between the cavalry and the Cheyennes at Victory Cave offers yet another example of incompetent military command. The officious colonel, who only wants to attack the beleaguered Indians (a figure played by Willis Bouchey, who is always associated with hypocrisy or ethical blindness in Ford's later films) is clearly more like Braden than the chastened Scott; it is only the presence of the determined Secretary Schurz that prevents more bloodshed.

In *Stagecoach,* the town of Tonto features a duplicitous atmosphere in which we initially see cowboys roaming the streets in broad daylight. Its society is apparently controlled by the priggish women who chase Dallas out, a group that gathers strength from its numbers and has, as its spiritual leader, Mrs. Gatewood (Brenda Fowler), whose Valkyrie-like demeanor seemingly prompts her aged husband to abscond with the payroll. The landlady (Nora Cecil) who evicts Doc Boone becomes quickly assimilated into this female band, and the beleaguered deputy (Leroy Mason) who must escort Dallas and Doc to the coach performs his duties as society demands. Dallas's boarding of the coach, when the sight of her ankle offers a highlight to two gawkers, and Doc's comic dismissal of the women who have come to gloat over their "moral" victory, clearly establish these exiles' superiority over those who have condemned them.

Tonto also supplies a visual shorthand by which the characters are introduced. Thus, Curly is found initially as the master of the jail; Gatewood, seen inside his bank is prattling about why it would be good business for payrolls to be deposited six months in advance; and Hatfield, after noticing Lucy Mallory, is shown at a saloon window playing poker and philosophizing about an "angel" in a "jungle" before committing himself to the trip. Such visual expositions serve the streamlined plot of *Stagecoach* well, just as later arrangements serve to demarcate the characters. At Dry Fork the seating of the characters at opposite ends of the dinner table, after Hatfield has convinced Lucy that a seat by the window would be cooler, reasserts the social divisions between the supposedly refined and the lower classes, ironically reinforcing the thematic changes that will occur as a result of the journey.

Lordsburg is conspicuously a city of night, a place that has the same crowded streets as Tonto but lacks the censorial types of the latter town. Law and order are present in the sheriff, who greets Curly and then arrests Gatewood, who has (characteristically) made an ass of himself. The barroom in which Hank Plummer presides resembles similar locations in *My Darling Clementine* and *The Man Who Shot Liberty Valance*. His bravado is underscored by the deliberate way he drinks after learning that Ringo is in town; the false courage of his brothers can be seen when they fumble with drinks and then when, out in the streets, they miss shooting a cat at "four feet." Dallas's descent into Lordsburg, where she will presumably live as a prostitute, sets this town even further apart from Tonto, if only because prostitution appears openly. The response Dallas elicits from Ringo, who seemingly appreciates and yet discounts her past, elevates her to heroic status. It is love that finally proves that Doc Boone's warning ("You'll be hurt, child") is shortsighted, for the hero operates as though their future life were a given, whereas the heroine fights against this perception as being too dream-like. When Dallas descends toward the place where she will stay in Lordsburg, Ringo reassures her that his confrontation with the Plummers will work out. Moments later, after the shots have been fired, Dallas has risen back to street level to embrace the protagonist and to symbolize that he has, indeed, brought her up from a life of sin.

Ford includes a brief scene in which the local newspaper editor rushes in to inform his pressman that the front page will have to be remade. Insisting that the Ringo Kid will be shot within minutes, the top-hatted newsman represents the earliest portrayal of a recurrent theme in Ford's westerns. His penchant for "making" the news foreshadows the more extended treatment of that subject in *Fort Apache*, in the memorable interview between York and the eastern reporters; in *The Man Who Shot Liberty Valance*, which centers around the efforts of a local editor to uncover why Stoddard has come back to town; and in *Cheyenne Autumn*, when a cynical press chief (Charles Seel) supports the Indian side simply to be different. In all these figures, Ford raises the issue of the relationship between historical truth and those who report it, and he nearly always suggests that there is a great disparity between the two.

The only developed town in *Cheyenne Autumn* is, of course, Dodge City, which first emerges as a boy hawks newspapers proclaiming the imminence of the arrival of the dangerous Cheyennes. The arrival of Guinivere Plantagenet and her "girls" establishes the wide-open character of the place, and her subsequent outrage at being referred to as "madam" by Doc Holliday links the prostitute to the nefarious Belle Aragon of *Two Rode Together*. Guinivere suffers some proper comic pratfalls, just as the same actress (Elizabeth Allen) does in *Donovan's Reef*. Nevertheless, her essentially mercenary outlook emerges when she declares that she and her girls are simply following the flag as the expedition sets out after the Indians. Earp's failure to recognize Guinivere until she has lost her dress and been thrown into his buckboard with her legs resting against his chest makes the same point comically.

The lawman's overriding interest in poker (he's so expert that he knows when a deck has only fifty-one cards) dramatically reverses the portrait of the frontier legend found in *My Darling Clementine;* Doc Holliday, played by an older actor (Arthur Kennedy), here seems like a physical buffoon and is costumed like a businessman. The third card player, Major Blair (John Carradine), comes off as an older and more tired version of Hatfield because of his marked southern accent. Blair not only lacks any lady in distress whom he might offer to rescue but also shows no inclination to ever leave the gaming table. Throughout the game, Blair is constantly being looked at askance in ways that Hatfield would never have tolerated. When last seen, Blair is weighing cards to ascertain how Wyatt could have known that one was missing. The cowardly mayor of Dodge City (Judson Pratt), who is also its major saloon owner, rises naturally to the threat of the Cheyennes, for he has lived among drunken mobs all his life. This official's brief argument with the soldiers who come through the center of town on a boxcar resembles Gatewood's chagrin and threats at Dry Fork in *Stagecoach;* the resemblance undercuts the comic, knockabout air that Ford has provided for this entire sequence.

When the cowhands arrive, Wyatt is engrossed in the poker game and offers no resistance to their entry on horseback into the saloon. It is only after Joe becomes outraged at Earp's disbelief in what he is saying about the Indians that the lawman becomes serious. When the irate cowpoke draws, Wyatt easily wounds him in the foot; however, this erstwhile hero is now someone who shoots from ambush and worries about the hole in his coat, a figure far different from the moral leader of *My Darling Clementine*. The mayor's complaint that Joe's blood is messing up his floor forces Wyatt into operating in yet another parody of the earlier film. Since a wounded foot hardly seems life-threatening, Earp's ministrations to the cowboy seem comic. After the successful surgery, Joe's wound is appropriately dressed in a red bandanna, and he and his friends are kicked out of the bar. When Wyatt returns to the poker table, Blair is relieved because a cigar ash has not fallen; the sheriff criticizes Doc for not performing the operation and only then learns that Holliday is really a dentist.

The ensuing chase of the Indians turns into even more of a farce because of the abilities of the pursuers and because of Wyatt's avowed aim to head them in a direction away from that in which the Cheyennes were supposed to be approaching. Earp's use of the phrase "as a Christian gentleman," which echoes the burial of Trooper Smith in *She Wore a Yellow Ribbon*, again reinforces the revisionist emphasis of the entire section. The Dodge City sequence, however, is finally unsettling because no serious retribution falls on Joe. His wounded foot hardly represents an adequate punishment for his ruthless killing and scalping of the hungry Indian; by implication, the dominant ruling class of Dodge City is even more corrupt and hypocritical than those seen in the towns of *Stagecoach*. The sutler who raises his prices for drinks when Archer's column enters a fort would fit well in this revised Dodge City, a place that symbolizes the dominant, unthinking, white society of *Cheyenne Autumn*.

The flag raised at the opening of *Stagecoach*—when the riders tear in with their news of Geronimo—establishes the frontier setting as well as the importance of the army. The opening dialogue sequence in the telegraph office foreshadows the beginning of *Cheyenne Autumn*; however, in *Stagecoach* it is the information not received over the wire that sets up the conflict, whereas the news actually received in the later film motivates the Indians. There is poetic justice when Gatewood is caught by a telegraphed message to Lordsburg, since the very object about which he lied trips him up. Doc Boone's recovery of his shingle from his landlady's front porch and his storage of it on the stagecoach roof foreshadow the great weight attached to a similar object in *The Man Who Shot Liberty Valance*. Hank Plummer holds symbolic cards just before he hears of Ringo's arrival; after he wins with aces and eights, an anonymous remark about this being "the dead man's hand" and a lingering shot of the cards clearly foreshadow his death.

Although the Cheyennes cut the telegraph lines and leave a dead soldier at the foot of one pole, they are usually associated with more positive (i.e., tribal) objects. The sacred bundle, by which Tall Tree's authority is passed on, operates as a talisman, for its passage from Little Wolf to Dull Knife marks a central plot development. When the dying Tall Tree selects Little Wolf and not his own son-in-law to be war chief, Dull Knife's dismay quickly gives way to his sense of brotherhood with and responsibility to the new leader. When Little Wolf places the sacred object in Dull Knife's keeping after killing Dull Knife's son Red Shirt, the communal responsibility that attaches to this object again comes to the fore. Dull Knife cannot retaliate on his longtime blood brother because no man can be war chief and kill another Cheyenne; at the same time, Little Wolf's actions completely sever the ties between him and his people. By passing the bundle, Little Wolf chooses a lonely life while fore-stalling any feud between himself and Dull Knife.

The blackboards and slates in *Cheyenne Autumn* are even more obviously symbolic. Deborah's schoolroom, in which the idealistic Quaker girl contin-ues to pull the bell chord even though Little Wolf has ordered the Indian chil-dren not to attend, is where Archer first argues with her. The captain tries to convince Deborah that the Cheyennes are among the world's most militaris-tic peoples, but he fails to persuade her. Archer may be accurate, but Debo-rah operates out of an idealistic rather than a materialistic persuasion, and it is her faith that touches the captain so much that he writes out a proposal on her blackboard. After she goes with the Cheyennes, Deborah's reasons are set forth on the same board. While she blushingly erased what Archer had writ-ten earlier, she now casts her future so that it symbolically overlays Archer's romantic feelings.

During the journey Deborah continues to teach the Cheyenne children the rudiments of English; however, at one point, she needs to have the con-nection explained when one of her charges draws a buffalo and pronounces the Indian word for that animal. In essence, the well-meaning Miss Wright really knows little about the Cheyennes. She wants to indoctrinate them into white ways but is, at best, a sympathetic tourist whose approach to the Indi-ans is a shortsighted variation of the other attitudes expressed by white soci-ety toward the native Americans. The final sequence, in which Deborah remains with Archer as the Cheyenne girl goes to her own people, symbol-izes the superficiality that has always existed between the Indians and this admittedly well-meaning white woman.

The characters in *Stagecoach* and *Cheyenne Autumn* exhibit distinctive types, for some of them are unchanging while others almost miraculously grow. Buck, Curly, and Gatewood do not significantly alter but rather reveal their characters during the course of *Stagecoach*, while Braden and Wessels have similarly fixed personalities in *Cheyenne Autumn*. The "flat" characters in *Stage-coach* thus include one tainted and two good-hearted figures, whereas those in *Cheyenne Autumn* are both villains. The world of the earlier film offers redemp-tive possibilities, since its minor characters not only feel sympathy for Ringo and Dallas but also act to alter the future for these two. Gatewood's obvious self-centeredness also distinguishes Braden and Wessels, characters whose moral myopia brings greater harm to society than anything the banker-thief does. The grimmer reality in *Cheyenne Autumn* is that Braden and Wessels are in charge and that only death or rebellion can bring them to heel—a prospect that is further implied when Schurz is able to dissuade the colonel from attacking at Victory Cave only by appealing to more powerful forces (the courts). Gatewood's obnoxious personality can be held in check by those around him, but the two mad army officers cannot be controlled by their more rational subordinates.

Curly and Buck function as a comic chorus from Tonto to Lordsburg. Their dialogue frequently finds them at odds as the sheriff ponders facts and the stage driver prattles about his large Mexican family. Buck regrets that he mentioned that he had seen the Plummers in Lordsburg, since he realizes that this information has motivated Curly to come along and seek Ringo. Later, after they have picked up the Ringo Kid, the rotund driver urges Curly to let Ringo shoot it out with his enemies. Buck consistently gets checkmated by the sheriff during the group discussions at the waystations; he adds another ironic touch, similar to Doc's premature toast, when he sings about their safe arrival in Lordsburg just before the Apaches swoop down. The essential goodness of the stage driver is nicely caught in the wordless sympathetic expression he gives Ringo in Lordsburg and in the disingenuous way in which he greets the arrival of Lucy Mallory's baby. Buck, a man with several children, asks Peacock if he knew about Mrs. Mallory's condition — a question both comic and revelatory of genuine innocence.

Curly's personality, if more complicated, is also essentially fixed. The sheriff is devoted to social order, as seen in the ways he organizes and maintains the trip and in how he gradually emerges as a guardian for those weaker than himself. Thus, he argues that allowing Ringo to fight it out with the Plummers will only perpetuate the feud between the families. Curly is also more observant, for he is almost immediately bothered by the contradiction between Lieutenant Blanchard's news that the telegraph line has been destroyed and Gatewood's remark, after hailing the coach, that he has just received a message from Lordsburg. Curly's conspiracy with Doc Boone to send Ringo and Dallas away further marks him as a sentimentalist who chooses with his heart instead of his head. The sheriff's compassion is seen earlier when Buck apologizes for thinking that Curly wanted to catch Ringo only for the reward money. The lawman heatedly responds that he wanted to catch the Kid to save Ringo from being killed by the Plummers because Curly and Ringo's father had been good friends. This idealistic outburst culminates with Curly's aside that he could, however, use the five-hundred-dollar reward. His decision to let Ringo evade the law and take Dallas across the border shows Curly in his kindest, most paternal light.

The pompous Gatewood, who never attains any such stature, remains a hypocritical villain up to his final moment on screen. If the banker is seen in humorous circumstances, he is not the source of comedy in them. His insistence to the payroll messengers that their company should deposit its wages in his bank in advance establishes Gatewood's hypocrisy, for the couriers wisely note that such a procedure would be good business only for the banker — and Ford's camera then lingers briefly and tellingly on Gatewood. When his wife arrives with her demand for money to pay the butcher, this same close-up is intercut just before Gatewood absconds with the payroll. The shrewish wife contributes to his crime, for her remark that they are to dine with the ladies of the "Law and Order League" seems to represent an emotional last straw for the aged banker. Naturally, Gatewood smiles and insists that he will be there for the meal.

When next seen, the banker is clambering aboard the stagecoach and learning, to his chagrin, that Geronimo is on the loose. When Ringo comes aboard, Gatewood conspicuously moves his bag away from the protagonist, and he later reseats himself in the dining room at Dry Fork after Hatfield has persuaded Lucy to move away from the Kid and Dallas. Gatewood's arguments with Lieutenant Blanchard reflect his anxious need to get to Lordsburg, and once the coach has left Dry Fork without an escort, he prattles about his outrage that bank examiners were due to check his books and so admits that he has been a thief for some time. At Apache Wells, Gatewood badmouths the army because there is no escort column there, and Ringo silences him by saying that the cavalry has more than enough to do in the endangered territory.

At the birth scene, the aged banker is conspicuously absent, and his subsequent quarreling with Hatfield about allowing Lucy an additional day of rest only further underlines his self-preoccupation. On the morning after Doc has delivered "Little Coyote," Gatewood offers to join Boone in a drink. The physician steadfastly refuses and even goes so far as to throw away what he had already poured for himself. This comic bit, which is augmented when the liquor causes the fire to spurt up as Peacock stands next to it, marks the extreme distaste that Boone has for the banker. Gatewood's imbibing features elaborate facial gestures; using such histrionics to delineate villainy is, perhaps, a melodramatic excess, but it is perfectly consistent with Ford's perceptions and presentations of evil in his westerns.

Gatewood slips completely after Apache Wells, when he blurts out a remark about being caught in a "trap like this" after working so long to gain a nest egg; he reiterates his dismay at Lee's Ferry by asking, "Where's the army?" Like most of the others, he assumes an ironic confidence just before the Apache assault when he apologizes for his previous rudeness; equally characteristically, he cowers during the running battle with Geronimo's horse soldiers. Once in Lordsburg, Gatewood returns to character by urging that the local sheriff handcuff Ringo immediately; however, the lawman asks who the banker is and then informs Gatewood that he is under arrest for robbery. Our last view of Gatewood finds him struggling with the very handcuffs he had just suggested for the Kid and being led away by the sheriff and a gawking mob.

The martinet commanders of *Cheyenne Autumn* represent a kind of Peter Principle at work in Ford's cavalry. While the duplicity of Major Frazier was held in bounds because he never left Fort Grant in *Two Rode Together*, Braden and Wessels command in the field and affect the lives of those around them in the most immediate ways. Braden, Archer's first commander, is irritated because the congressional party has not arrived; thus, the major distrusts and dislikes the political brass, but his concern does not extend to the waiting Cheyennes. He can simply retire to his tent and wait for news; when a telegram announces there will be no visit, Braden is concerned only with the delay that he must experience in building barracks. He upbraids Deborah, who asks that he intercede for the Cheyennes, by stating that he can only carry out orders and that he has learned never to question his superiors. Once Archer has started in pursuit of the Cheyennes, Braden brings artillery to the ravine where the captain has encountered Indian resistance. The major is costumed like Colonel Thursday in *Fort Apache*, whereas Archer, in a buckskin jacket, resembles Brittles in *She Wore a Yellow Ribbon*. Braden immediately threatens Archer with a court-martial because of the way the captain has conducted the pursuit. The major then orders that his cannons start firing, and he wreaks havoc on the distant Indian column; however, such rashness gets him killed when the Cheyennes swoop down and drive off the cavalry's horses.

Captain Wessels is a more sinister figure, albeit one with the same blind allegiance to duty that marks Braden. At a dinner party at which he receives orders that the Cheyennes must be returned to their original reservation, Wessels parades his interest in the Native Americans by showing off his book collection. That the bulk of such works are in German suggests that Wessels's criticism of the inaccuracies of Fenimore Cooper's fictional Indians may simply be a case of the pot calling the kettle black. When the bedraggled Cheyennes enter Fort Robinson, Wessels is delighted because he sees their capture as ensuring his promotion. Wessels's emergence as a tyrant is rationalized somewhat by his drinking, which seems to represent the guilt he cannot voice; however, the commander of Fort Robinson is so overdrawn that he becomes an embarrassment. Wessels's inhumanity to the Cheyennes is finally counteracted by his removal from command by the post physician (Sean McClory) on the very night that the Indians break free. Wessels insults the Cheyennes during an earlier meeting in the warehouse, but all he can do is reciprocate the stubbornness shown by Dull Knife and Spanish Woman (Dolores Del Rio).

In his quarters, in a nightshirt and obviously drunk, Wessels sputters as the physician and the other officers remove him from command at a time that is already too late. After the fight between the Cheyennes and the post troopers, a stricken Wessels wanders among the fallen and is upbraided by Lieutenant Scott, who asks if orders have been followed sufficiently. Such invective makes a somewhat sympathetic figure out of the hateful martinet the plot has worked so hard to create. In a brief earlier scene, Archer criticizes a report forwarded by Wessels only to be told that it is never wise to question those in authority; as a result, the protagonist applies for leave. Wessels questions Archer's timing, but his bad manners obscure any of the practicality of such an inquiry. In many ways Wessels raises the same moral issues implicit in *Fort*

Apache; however, the cards are stacked too high against him, for he is condemned both for what he does and for what he cannot prevent. His apparent drunken madness as he walks out of the frame may represent poetic justice, but such melodramatic villainy fails to elicit the same degree of interest that attaches to Colonel Thursday.

Characters who change and grow more morally persuasive are less obvious in *Stagecoach*, where their alterations appear in brief actions rather than as extensively pondered matters. The socially despised figures in *Stagecoach* are the test for its more respectable characters, who respond with differing degrees of insight. Gatewood, naturally, never sees Ringo, Doc, or Dallas as worth his concern or attention. He has little to say to or about any of them, except to suspiciously eye the Kid and then ironically speak out against him in Lordsburg. Lucy Mallory tries to make amends with Dallas in that town, but her belated apology is cut short by the heroine; only the guilt in Mrs. Mallory's eyes suggests any real growth. It is, finally, Hatfield who moves away from the genteel priggishness he exhibits in the dining room at Dry Fork. The gambler rakes Doc Boone over the coals at Apache Wells when Lucy collapses; however, once the southern belle is out of danger, Hatfield praises the physician, and we never hear him criticizing Boone again. As a measure of his change, Hatfield starts to notice Gatewood's egocentric complaints and even sticks up for Ringo at one point when the banker speaks badly of him.

The whiskey drummer Peacock, though less of a snob, also changes during the trip; he becomes more openly a gentleman with Dallas and even urges her to visit him in "Kansas City, Kansas," when he is carried past her on a stretcher in Lordsburg. Peacock exhibits the same initial rudeness that Curly and Hatfield do toward Dallas; however, he redeems himself by including her (as she holds the baby) when he urges that "all" the ladies present should be blessed. Curly becomes polite to Dallas only after Ringo upbraids him at Dry Fork ("Ain't you going to ask the other lady?"), but Hatfield never shows any sort of softening toward Dallas, as seen when he offers water to Lucy in a silver cup and pointedly ignores Dallas. Curly's dislike of the gambler, a dislike apparent at Tonto, and Doc Boone's ironic use of the word "gentleman" when criticizing Hatfield for shooting a man in the back foreshadow the demented glee with which the ex–Confederate fights the Apaches. His desire to shoot Lucy rather than let her become a prisoner of the Indians (and suffer the proverbial "fate worse than death") represents Hatfield's chivalrous racism, and the irony of his timing suggests the futility of his outlook. Like the foolhardy charging Confederates at Newton Station in *The Horse Soldiers*, Hatfield has become an anachronism in the age in which he finds himself. Because he still wants to serve the snobbish Lucy Mallory and ignore the more compassionate Dallas, Hatfield's death represents poetic justice.

The characters who change in *Cheyenne Autumn* are military subordinates whose attitudes reflect directly on their superiors. The most obvious of these figures is Sergeant Wichowsky, who comes to hate what he has been ordered to do to the Cheyennes. The Polish noncom believes he and his outfit are mercenaries hired simply to punish those who do not agree with the dominant political order. Wichowsky sees an honor and a necessity in fighting Indians who are armed and can retaliate, but he sees none in chasing the Cheyennes, who are not eager to fight. His dismay reaches such proportions that he initially refuses to reenlist; however, the sight of his outfit moving out without him brings Wichowsky back into line as the "lifer" that he is. In Wichowsky's cavalry, there is no place where a good man can live an uncomplicated existence devoted to duty, as there was in Fort Stark at the end of *She Wore a Yellow Ribbon*; there is, instead, only the prospect of serving under competent but limited leaders, like Archer, who must take orders from even less competent men, like the colonel at Victory Cave. Dr. O'Carberry, the post physician at Fort Robinson, also exhibits a new attitude when he invokes his authority against Wessels, a decision he makes only after considerable pressure from Deborah about the freezing Cheyennes. The doctor, who initially claims to be dedicated only to "self-preservation," finally chooses compassion over obedience. O'Carberry also ceases being a drunk because of his wish that he were a better doctor when the wounded Indian girl is brought to him; later he appears exultant, like the sober Doc Boone, when called on in a medical crisis.

The most thoroughly changed character in *Cheyenne Autumn* is Lieutenant Scott, who goes from being a blind Indian hater to a supporter of the Cheyennes at Fort Robinson and a veritable voice of justice with Captain Wessels. Scott initially wants to gain revenge for his dead father, an officer whom Archer had known. The similarity between Scott's motivations and those of Ethan Edwards is striking; however, the younger man is forced to overcome his irrationality and to replace it with compassion. Scott initially acts like the foolhardy Thursday when confronted by the Cheyennes. When Archer's column reaches a bluff overlooking the Indians crossing a river that represents the boundary of their reservation, Scott is outraged by his commander's failure to attack and is checked only by the old army routine of putting such complaints in writing. Further along, when the cavalry again catches up to the Cheyennes and Archer tries to induce the Indians into attacking his force, Scott blatantly disobeys by leading a full-scale charge against the Cheyenne position. In essence, the young man has been assigned York's task at the end of *Fort Apache* but takes it on himself to play the part of Thursday instead; his defeat amid the burning prairie shrubbery places him clearly on the side of the latter.

The young man's survival enables him to see his folly, a perception that the more experienced enlisted men under his command possessed from the start of his ill-considered charge. Scott's wound, which forces him to stay behind in a hospital when Archer leaves, symbolizes the painful lesson the young man is internalizing, and his reappearance at his commander's camp in a snowstorm demonstrates his conversion. Archer even hails this change when he admits that the now-chastened Scott may actually become a good soldier. At Fort Robinson, after Archer has gone to Washington, Scott accompanies O'Carberry when the doctor relieves Wessels; and given the rapport that has developed between the lieutenant and a wounded Cheyenne girl, it is only natural that Scott should be the one to chastise Wessels after the battle in the stockade. If Scott's open defiance at this point suggests that he has grown to be a competent officer, it also presents a different picture of Ford's cavalry, for moral perceptions are now deemed superior to institutional obligations. It is difficult to imagine the junior officers of Ford's earlier films, voicing criticism of a superior officer, no matter what the provocation. Scott's moral growth again reveals the pessimistic world of *Cheyenne*.

Doc Boone is one of the most ornately written parts in all of Ford's westerns; although this may be because *Stagecoach* is the only one of these films scripted by Dudley Nichols, rhetoric is essential to the character. Boone functions as an authority whose judgments on men and society are nearly always right and whom others ask for advice because of his ostensible experience and wisdom. His gift for hyperbole is first seen when he accosts his erstwhile landlady by quoting Marlowe on Helen of Troy; indeed, the entire less-than-heroic side of Tonto society is brought out in such a reference, for Boone's juxtaposition of legend and heroic action with the shrew appropriately reduces the surroundings. Doc's rhetoric also emphasizes how he and Dallas are being victimized when he compares their walk down main street to a procession toward the guillotine. Inside the saloon, Doc charms a free drink from Jerry (Jack Pennick) only to spit half of it out when he learns that Peacock is a whiskey salesman. After Ringo's arrival, Doc insists that he once fixed the young man's broken arm, but he learns that it was the Kid's brother he helped and who has since been murdered.

At Dry Fork, where he enthusiastically chums around with Billy Pickett, Doc offers a typical rhetorical flourish to his decision about going on. After remarking that somewhere there may be "the right bullet or the wrong bottle for Josiah Boone," he insists that all he really wants is another drink. Boone thus emerges as the spokesman for merriment in life, a veritable Falstaff of the frontier who is recognized as such by the truly good people wherever he goes. In the stagecoach, after growing weary of listening to Gatewood's prattle about what the country needs, Doc urges that "fuddle" is what is truly missing. At Apache Wells, Boone abandons his drinking when Mrs. Mallory collapses, and he starts on a regimen of black coffee and vomiting. Hatfield can only rail at him while Curly and Ringo help Doc regain his sobriety. In characteristic fashion, after the baby has been born Boone accepts the others' congratulations and proceeds to get a drink; however, even his love of whiskey is tempered later when he throws away a full glass rather than take a drink with Gatewood.

When Dallas tells Doc that Ringo has proposed, he warns that the girl is going to be hurt worse than she ever has been before. His concern, of course, arises from the possibility that Ringo will die in Lordsburg or that the young man will reject Dallas once he discovers the truth about her past. Boone denies that he is an authority ("Who am I to tell you what's right or wrong?"), but then he sends Ringo into the kitchen to be with Dallas as the others, again, take up the question of whether to go on. On the final leg of the journey, in keeping with everyone else's euphoria, Doc ironically proposes a toast to a group whose company he is fairly certain he will never enjoy again. In Lordsburg Boone shows up in the saloon and asks for the bottle from which Hank and his brothers have been drinking, moments before Buck comes in to announce that Ringo will be in the streets to fight the Plummers. When Hank picks up a shotgun, Doc threatens him with a murder charge and, in so doing, demonstrates his courage. Hank sneers that he will deal with Boone after Ringo has been killed, and Doc comically begs the bartender never to let him stick his neck out again. In the final scene of *Stagecoach*, Doc is convinced that Dallas and Ringo need to be saved from the "blessings of civilization," and so he hurls stones at the buckboard's horses to give the young couple a running start toward their escape. Curly's inarticulate laughter and his offer of a drink accord with the matter-of-fact character he is. Doc also remains solidly in character with his comic admonition that he will have "just one," and so he brings *Stagecoach* to its appropriately unsentimental verbal ending.

The only benevolent authority figure in *Cheyenne Autumn* is Secretary of the Interior Schurz, who, significantly, lives in Washington, far from where his wisdom and compassion should be exercised. Schurz, like Doc Boone, is under attack by the society around him, for he must ward off would-be office seekers and social planners eager to profit from the Indian lands while fighting a political battle with the army over jurisdiction. His initial appearance, in which he chides a congressional delegation with remarks about "dollar patriots" eager to get rich off Indian misery, establishes Schurz's decency; at the same time, the contrast between the congressional committees that fail to arrive at the Cheyenne reservation and those who manage to lobby in the secretary's office makes an obvious point about political efficiency. Schurz's appeal to one of the senators (Denver Pyle) on the basis that they fought together at Gettysburg sets the stage for the secretary's later scene with the portrait of Lincoln; his argument to his former military comrade that the Cheyennes are similar to the slaves for whom they struggled in the Civil War makes a thematic point of *Cheyenne Autumn* overtly clear. Archer's appearance in Schurz's waiting room unsettles the officious aide (Carleton Young) who controls appointments. When the secretary emerges from his office, a horde of applicants forces Schurz to seek the privacy of a basement retreat to find out exactly what is happening at Fort Robinson. After he has sent Archer away, Schurz symbolically asks Lincoln's portrait, "Old friend, what would you do?"

The secretary's authority finally emerges at Victory Cave, where he all but unilaterally persuades both sides to stop fighting. Schurz simply overrides the pompous colonel in command and, despite Red Shirt's wild shot, proceeds into the Indian cave to negotiate with Little Wolf and Dull Knife. Schurz then symbolically offers cigars in place of the Indians' peace pipe, for which there is no tobacco; thus, the secretary brings *Cheyenne Autumn* to its first, and most obvious, dramatic ending. Schurz is the rare honest official who is willing to take responsibility for doing the right thing — a figure whom Archer and the other good characters have been seeking since the start of the film. It is a measure of Ford's increasing pessimism that reaching such an individual requires so much effort in *Cheyenne Autumn*: Archer's trip to Washington is at least as physically lengthy as the Cheyennes' trek to their homeland.

From her first appearance in *Stagecoach*, Lucy Mallory acts the "proper lady": standoffish with those she sees as social inferiors. The brief exchange between her and Buck in Tonto, with her insistence on tea and his on a place where she might get coffee, establishes Mrs. Mallory's "breeding"; her reception by friends, accompanied by Hatfield's doffing his hat, places her as a cavalry wife. Lucy's question about Hatfield ("Who was that gentleman?") further identifies her as someone who does not know the ways of the West and will have to learn them at some personal cost. Mrs. Mallory's determination to rejoin her husband is seen when she argues that Doc Boone can take care of any complications in her pregnancy; when she overcomes her initial distress at Dry Fork; and when she subsequently decides to go on in spite of the Indian threat. At Apache Wells, Lucy gets more bad news about her husband and, despite Dallas's attempt to be consolatory, caves in to the pressure and gives birth prematurely. At the end of their pursuit by Geronimo's force, Lucy hears the bugle call — demonstrating that she will, indeed, make a good cavalry wife. However, in Lordsburg she is quickly subsumed by the same social proprieties that enveloped her in Tonto. Lucy accepts Hatfield's chivalry as the normal order of things without ever showing any great concern for him; she takes his platonic affection as her natural right and so only slowly comes to appreciate the ways of the frontier world into which she has come. While Hatfield gradually recognizes the worth of Doc Boone, Lucy slowly comes to identify with Dallas. However, her efforts at rapprochement are checked when Dallas treats Lucy's faint overtures as too little, too late, and too easy inside the confines of Lordsburg.

As the heroine of *Stagecoach*, Dallas appears far more domestic than erotic, despite her ostensible profession. She clearly articulates the idea that civilized ostracism can be worse than uncivilized danger for someone, like herself, who is without power or influence. Her tears over being driven away from Tonto are ironic given the fact that such a good woman's being hounded out of town is clearly a comment more telling about that place than about her. Since Tonto combines moral zealotry, in its anxious matrons who assail the girl and Doc Boone, and a craving for sin, in its cowhands who ogle Dallas's ankle, staying there hardly represents a worthwhile goal for someone as special as the heroine. As Dallas puts it so nicely when Curly asks if anyone wants to leave the stagecoach in Tonto, there are "worse things than Apaches." While she elicits chivalrous and romantic sentiments from Ringo, Dallas's true worth is revealed by her devotion to Lucy and the baby. During the snowstorm, Dallas offers to have Mrs. Mallory rest against her, but she is naturally refused. As a nurse, Dallas not only stays up all night but also gladly undertakes further domestic chores in the morning when Doc Boone asks her to make coffee.

The heroine's brief account of surviving as an orphan and being on her own ("You gotta live") demonstrates Dallas's independence. No one has approached her decently for so long that Ringo's offer stuns her into realizing that she actually has fallen in love with him. Dallas reaches even greater heights when she argues with Ringo about his need for revenge. She pleads that she does not intend to throw her life away by waiting for a dead man — a prospect she sees for Ringo because of his feud with the Plummers. Momentarily in control, Dallas gets the protagonist to begin to ride off when Apache war smoke cuts short his attempted flight. The hero, who has gone only because Dallas has promised to join him at the first opportunity, cannot ignore the greater collective danger. In assuming custody of Lucy's baby, Dallas gradually transforms herself into a veritable Madonna. By the time she is relieved of the infant by a solicitously persistent nurse in Lordsburg, her devotion to "Little Coyote" has clearly proved her moral worth. Dallas, like Mary Kate in *The Quiet Man* after the burning of the monetary dowry, remains content to exist as a partner to the man she loves. Ringo's abiding faith, which does not question her past, serves as a sufficient reason for Doc and Curly to send the lovers away at the end.

As a Quaker, Deborah Wright emerges very quickly as the most idealistic figure in *Cheyenne Autumn*. Her compassion for the Indians causes her to appeal to or to cajole Braden, Archer, Wessels, and O'Carberry in the hope of improving the Cheyennes' lot. In her initial conversation with Archer, after their feelings have been established by his setting up a broken chair at the dinner table she has arranged for the congressional party, which never shows up, Deborah posits herself as the guardian of the future. She does not want to deal with the historical or social pasts that have made the Cheyennes into what they are but seeks instead to transform them, through education, into useful members of the dominant white society. Deborah's role as a teacher is constantly underlined by her emphases on words and language, while her tough idealism enables her to ignore Little Wolf's warning that she should go back instead of accompanying the Cheyennes. Her blackboard message to Archer and her lost diary, which Plumtree finds, keep them linked; while her caring for the little Cheyenne girl who is wounded by Braden's shelling shows

Deborah functioning as a nurse. The heroine's status among the Indians is further established when she argues about their appropriating one of her horses and when Little Wolf intercedes so that she can keep the animal in spite of tribal need.

Throughout her odyssey with the Cheyennes, Deborah is never assaulted or even flirted with. Unlike the violent, nightmare worlds we see in *The Searchers* and *Sergeant Rutledge,* where the threat of Indian "defilement" was either present or strongly suggested, *Cheyenne Autumn* clearly implies the Cheyennes' civilized conduct with a white woman. Indeed, Deborah fares better with the Indians than she would in a town like Dodge City. Ford's last western does not feature a love story, since Archer's feelings for Deborah are not dramatically reciprocated by the girl, who seemingly has more important things on her mind. Deborah's release of her wounded charge at the final Cheyenne camp symbolizes the loss that she has experienced; in effect, the well-meaning Quaker teacher cannot hope to become a permanent part of the Cheyenne community, which is returning to its ancestral ways, so she rides off with Archer in what is surely one of the most resigned romantic finales in any Hollywood film. Deborah finally realizes, in spelling out the word "home" for her little Cheyenne friend, that the youngster must be given up to the home for which she and her people have suffered and struggled. The Quaker heroine can only attempt to find a comparable place with Archer, and the juxtaposition of these lovers with Little Wolf and his wife riding into the sunset suggests that although the journey has ended for some, it remains an ongoing trek for others.

The Ringo Kid's heroic actions clearly stamp him as the protagonist of *Stagecoach.* In a bit of hoary plotting, he is out to revenge the deaths of his father and his brother after he has spent time in prison because of being framed by their killers. Ringo's appearance on the trail, with a saddle that he eventually jettisons at Lee's Ferry, emphasizes the Apache threat: arguing that he should keep his rifle, he mentions seeing a burning ranch house the night before. Inside the coach, during the quarrel between Doc and Hatfield over the former's cigar smoke, Ringo interjects to calm down the gambler by urging, "Doc don't mean no harm." His chivalry toward Dallas is first seen when he insists that she have a drink after Mrs. Mallory has been served; this behavior continues at Dry Fork where, after sitting next to her, he ironically takes the blame for their ostracism. On the ride through the snowstorm, Ringo and Dallas exchange glances and smiles to foreshadow their even more marked looks when the girl holds Lucy's baby.

Ringo's proposal in the courtyard further demonstrates the purity of his character, for he insists that he knows all he wants or needs to know about Dallas. His nobility is then extended when he abandons his escape attempt in the face of a greater danger ("Look at them hills!"). He emerges as the man of action during the Indian assault when he not only kills an Apache who has managed to get on the lead horses but also catches the loose reins of these animals just as the cavalry arrives. In Lordsburg, before he goes off to face the Plummers with the symbolic three bullets he has kept in his hat, Ringo makes sure that Dallas will get to his ranch. His reiteration of his feelings for Dallas ("We ain't never goin' to say good-bye") neatly foreshadows the ending of *Stagecoach*. Such essential goodness sparks a recognition in Doc and Curly, both of whom risk their lives and reputations to aid Ringo throughout the climactic moments in Lordsburg.

Archer is the protagonist of *Cheyenne Autumn* if only because of his dual function as performer and narrator. From his first moment on screen, he appears deeply divided by the ways in which the Cheyennes are treated and his duties as an officer. His argument with Deborah over the fighting prowess of the Cheyennes seemingly disguises his own compassion, which might well interfere with his official responsibilities. Archer's frequent scenes in tents and wearing a buckskin jacket link him to Captain Brittles and Colonel Yorke; however, his prowess as a fighting commander is consistently limited by colleagues' and subordinates' foolhardy actions, a problem that does not hinder the commanders in *She Wore a Yellow Ribbon* and *Rio Grande*. Archer knows what to do, but he is, finally, not capable of achieving a military success against the Cheyennes. His best plan is undone by Scott, an underling he has not been able to correct by example or advice. With the image of an impotent Archer railing against Scott's foolish charge, Ford offers us a different kind of western protagonist.[3] This captain must win his battles in offices after seeing his horses driven off (at the ravine) and then functioning as the commander of a retreat (in the wake of Scott's horrendous blunder) in the field. Archer can confront Wessels over a report and even insist on going to Washington, where he describes Fort Robinson as a place in which authority has "gone mad"; but his most heroic action consists of throwing down his gunbelt after Red Shirt has fired wildly at Secretary Schurz.

Archer thus emerges as a man of peace driven by a populist credo. When he discusses the plight of the Cheyennes with Schurz, the captain insists "the people wouldn't have liked" what he has seen at the Nebraska outpost. Archer thus embodies the notion that American democracy works if the public is truly informed about what is going on; however, considering the institutions that seemingly prevent their being so informed — military and civilian bureaucracies as well as newspapers — the protagonist's sentiments appear a bit shortsighted. Archer resembles Stoddard in *The Man Who Shot Liberty Valance* in being the representative of a newer type of civilization, one in which the arts of peace and coexistence must replace the older methods of direct confrontation. Archer's moral journey finally consists of his arriving at a point where defending the Cheyennes becomes more important than protecting his military career. Ringo could use older, western methods of direct action against offending individuals because there was still a faraway place to which he and

Dallas could flee to; Archer, by contrast, must come to terms with a world in which various divergent interests — politicians, the denizens of Dodge City, the army, and the Indians — must all be brokered.

The same necessity for a less confrontational style of leadership can be seen among the Cheyennes. The principal Indian characters must purge their society by exorcising its more warlike individuals and bringing its more conciliatory elements to the forefront. Tall Tree, who collapses under the sun at the opening of *Cheyenne Autumn* and then dies on the trail, represents the older authority that has guided the Cheyennes. The chief's burial on the prairie puts the burden squarely on the new leader, Little Wolf. Spanish Woman, Tall Tree's daughter, who provides verbal hints about what the Cheyennes are feeling throughout, performs the first of two burial rites when she decorates her father's funeral bier. Earlier, she greets the dawn with a symbolic lifting and spreading of earth in a familiar Indian gesture (Cochise in *Fort Apache*, Elena in *Two Rode Together*); and her insistence to Deborah that the Indian children will survive because "they are Cheyenne" places her at the center of the tribe's spiritual life. Her son, Red Shirt, resembles other rebellious and foolhardy braves (the other Red Shirt in *She Wore a Yellow Ribbon*, Running Wolf in *Two Rode Together*) by virtue of his costuming. His failure to learn caution or discretion (as seen in his premature firing on Plumtree and Smith at the ravine), his seduction of Little Wolf's youngest wife, and his shooting at Archer and Schurz at Victory Cave mark him as an anachronistic danger to Cheyenne society. Red Shirt's quick death at Little Wolf's hands symbolizes his foolish warrior bravado: he charges headlong and screaming before dismounting and is abruptly cut down by his more efficient adversary.

Little Wolf's ferocious dedication marks him as the leader needed for a crisis. His open challenge after waiting for the congressional committee ("The white man remembers nothing!") shows his courage; and his acceptance of the sacred bundle, which he takes to mean a dedication so severe that he must abstain from lovemaking, proves he is the man for the moment. Like Archer, Little Wolf must endure the shortcomings of subordinates and allies; he rectifies Red Shirt's premature firing by conducting a successful attack on the cavalry's horses, and he patiently endures Dull Knife's defection to Fort Robinson and forgives it with magnanimity. Little Wolf triumphs publicly by getting the Cheyennes to Victory Cave and by concluding, with Schurz, a treaty that grants them access to the land from which they came.

As a private individual, however, the war chief ironically fails because he cannot accept the traducing of his honor by Red Shirt and forces a decisive confrontation with the impetuous warrior. Little Wolf's success in their duel spells an end to his existence as a Cheyenne; he comes to resemble Tom Doniphon in *The Man Who Shot Liberty Valance* or Ethan Edwards in *The Searchers* by becoming a veritable outcast. Dull Knife's accession to power completes the transformation of Cheyenne society. The new chief shows that the new society has come under the care of a leader seemingly more able to cope with the compromised and compromising ways of modern times. Ford's final western thus ends on a highly resigned note by showing, yet again, the often painful losses that accompany any major social choice. Ultimately, the restructuring of communities can be achieved only by the sacrifices of individuals whose rewards are obscurity and loneliness.

Conclusion

John Ford's western films exhibit striking similarities in character types, thematic concerns, and plot motifs. These cohesive elements arose because Ford flourished in Hollywood during the heyday of the studio system and so was able to create a "stock company" of actors, writers, and technicians. Thus, he made the system work for him and, ultimately, exercised a greater degree of artistic control than did many a less independent or later director. The processes by which Ford and his screenwriters adapted and transformed literary sources into viable shooting scripts that are permeated with the director's thematic preoccupations, the consistent artistic style that various technical experts added to his films, and the recurrent and consciously varied casting patterns that the director employed all contribute to our sense of the continuous and coherent universe of Ford's westerns. Indeed, Ford's creative personality was so distinctive that his vision clearly imposed on and controlled these other contributors and collaborators.

His first and most easily discerned thematic motif centers around the U.S. cavalry. This military family supplies both protection and purpose to those who faithfully serve its larger institutional and social aims. Those who join its ranks must recognize their need for apprenticeship: young women learn to be "army" (to quote Nathan Brittles in *She Wore a Yellow Ribbon*) while young men learn to be soldiers. However, even though an individual may be asked to lay down his life in the performance of duty, he gains both a present and a permanent identity by embodying the group's purposes, mores, and etiquette. The individual must finally learn never to place personal goals or ambitions (the desire for glory) over the cavalry's more realistic and humane controlling aim (duty). *Fort Apache* and *Rio Grande* show how the ideal commander ultimately combines the professional and the human sides of cavalry life; *She Wore a Yellow Ribbon* and *Sergeant Rutledge* urge that individual soldiers derive their personal identities from the larger and all but mystical allegiance to which they have committed themselves in the cavalry.

Ford's second major motif is organized around male partnerships. The need for heroic action against the anticivilized elements that constantly

279

John Ford with legendary Hollywood costume designer Edith Head.

threaten or thwart the advance of urban civilization is, of course, a constant in western films, and male bonding is thus an almost inevitably prevalent feature within this genre. If Ford's heroic partners overcome the outlaws and so bring society's weaker members (whether found in town or on the trail) to safety in an acceptable fashion, their personal alliances do not always survive such successes. Only the simpler younger heroes of *Wagonmaster* ride together into a shared future; the protagonists of *Two Rode Together* survive, but they separate because they have come to realize the futility of what they have done as well as their own personal shortcomings. Death in action supplies a legendary patina for one of the principals in *My Darling Clementine* while the other is shown riding off to the hero's proverbial next quest. The natural phenomenon of death, operating over a span of decades, casts a final melancholy and pensive air over the far-less-happily paired protagonists at the center of *The Man Who Shot Liberty Valance.*

Journeys that force individuals to change through confrontations with both external and internal forces structure the third of Ford's leading motifs. Such symbolic treks are motivated by the need for restoration or escape; ironically, one of these purposes often creates the other as a result of what the characters experience while traveling. The fleeing outlaws of *Three Godfathers* are brought back into civilization by their own consciences and their desert encounter with the mother and child. The alienated protagonist of *The Searchers* finally succeeds in restoring a lost child only to realize that he himself can never be reassimilated into the civilized society to which he has returned. Whereas the lovers of *Stagecoach* manage to escape to the idyllic bliss of their own place outside the confines of society ("over the border"), the romantic pair in *Cheyenne Autumn* must resign themselves to lesser expectations as they begin their journey back to where their trek began.

In his masterful survey of western films, William Everson has argued that a limited number of plots recur repeatedly in the genre.[1] His list includes the pioneer wagon-train trek, the cattle drive, the building of a railroad, the taming of a sin town, the infiltration of an outlaw band by an undercover agent, the provocation of Indians, the escape from prison, the managing of a freight line, the range war between cattlemen and farmers, and the simple quest for revenge for a murdered relative (usually a father). Although many westerns combine these basic plot motivations, Ford's films are never controlled by such immediate concerns. *Wagonmaster* obviously represents a pioneers-on-the-move situation, just as *My Darling Clementine* draws on the sin-town motif; *Fort Apache* has the provoked Indians, *The Man Who Shot Liberty Valance* embodies a range war, and the hero in *Stagecoach* is out for revenge.

Yet in none of these films do we feel that this plot situation is more than a background condition against which Ford's characters can live their own lives and through which the director's own thematic concerns can be dramatized. Often Ford's films transcend or alter these basic plot motivations, as we can see in *My Darling Clementine,* whose sin town lacks any master criminal, and in *Fort Apache,* where the Indians are riled up by a martinet military commander rather than the usual gunrunners. Range wars and personal revenge figure in *The Man Who Shot Liberty Valance* and *Stagecoach,* but these conditions are nowhere near as engrossing for the characters in these films as they are for the casts in *Shane* and *Winchester '73.* Ford's films are populated with characters who are not nearly as limited as George Stevens's knightly gunfighter or Anthony Mann's obsessed Lin McAdam.

We can better understand Ford's capacity for characterization by comparing his films to those of Alfred Hitchcock. The master of a very different kind of movie making, in many ways Hitchcock is a more technically finished filmmaker, one whose visual economy is often stunning and whose handling of plots is far more adroit than Ford's. As a commentator on modern life and the twentieth century, Hitchcock often provides gripping images (his numerous symbolic shots of stairways), moments (the carousel struggle in *Strangers on a Train*), and even characters (Uncle Charlie in *Shadow of a Doubt*). However the very inexorability of what happens in Hitchcock's films reduces many of his characters to the level of puppets being manipulated by the master's expert handling. Very few viewers are apt to be overly concerned with what happens to, say, Roger Thornhill (Cary Grant in *North by Northwest*) once the film is over. His time of trial may lead to some modifications in his future life (although even this possibility might be questioned), but, finally, his character has been designed to fit a plot rather than drawn to explore human complexity.

We need only think of how Ethan Edwards is presented and developed in *The Searchers* to realize the difference between Ford and Hitchcock. Ethan is simply a more passionate and feeling character than Thornhill. He has a past that continues to impinge on him emotionally in the film's present; thus, Ethan, like all of his creator's characters, embodies a genuine sense of history as a lived experience. Much of our appreciation of the thematic depths of Ford's westerns ultimately derives from this aspect of his art; indeed, Ethan Edwards's personality keeps spilling out (both psychologically and visually) of the film in which he resides. This kind of character drawing, which we see again and again in Ford's westerns, will be dismaying to some viewers, but for others it sets his works apart. For Hitchcock, characters exist to serve a plot; for Ford, a plot exists to accent the characters.

Such an outlook underscores another of Ford's abiding strengths. He is an idealist and a sentimentalist when it comes to people and society. Even in his later westerns, when he sets out to revise earlier perceptions and calls into question so many of the values that colored his previous works, Ford emphasizes what has been lost rather than focusing on the grim realities that now dominate. Working in a genre that had nearly always lent itself to myth-making and idealization, Ford consistently strove to present a usable version of the American past. His westerns not only achieve that goal but do so in a critical and dialectical manner that makes them far more than entertainments meant to occupy us for their running lengths. Allan Bloom, in deploring the historicist ways in which we have come to view the U.S. Constitution and its framers, acutely touches on why westerns have become passé: "Finally, in curious harmony with the Southerners, the radicals in the civil rights movement succeeded in promoting a popular conviction that the Founding was, and the American principles are, racist. The bad conscience they promoted killed off the one continuing bit of popular culture that celebrated the national story — the Western."[2] Certainly no other film artist has managed to celebrate that story in more sophisticated or more challenging terms than John Ford did in his twelve sound westerns.

Notes

Introduction

1. The major commentators include Lindsay Anderson, Andrew Sarris, J. A. Place, and Tag Gallagher. For the titles of their works and those of others, see the bibliography.

2. For Nugent's remarks on Ford's training him for screenwriting, see Tag Gallagher, *John Ford: The Man and His Films* (Berkeley: U of Cal. Pr., 1986), 247.

Chapter 1

1. The most important history of the western is that written by William Everson; in addition, Jim Kitses, Kim Newman, Will Wright, Philip French, and Richard Slotkin provide worthwhile commentaries. See the bibliography.

2. The filmography in Tag Gallagher's *John Ford: The Man and His Films* (Berkeley: U of Cal. Pr., 1986), 501–46, details Ford's surviving and lost titles from the silent era.

3. The popularity of *Tombstone* (Hollywood Pictures, 1993) and the appearance of *Geronimo* (Columbia, 1993), as well as the production of *Wyatt Earp* (1994), suggest that the western is, perhaps, coming back.

Chapter 2

1. Peter Bogdanovich, *John Ford* (Berkeley: U of Cal. Pr., 1967, 1978), 108.

2. Tag Gallagher, *John Ford: The Man and His Films* (Berkeley: U of Cal. Pr., 1986), 22.

3. Frank N. Magill, ed., *Magill's Survey of Cinema: Silent Films*, vol. 3 (Englewood Cliffs: Salem Press, 1982), 1063.

4. *The Last Outlaw* (RKO, 1936) stars Harry Carey in a remake of Ford's original sound feature of 1919. The story resembles that of Rip Van Winkle in that an old convict (Carey) must deal with the modern world after he is released from prison. That he ultimately triumphs over modern gangsters by using antiquated ("western") ways is in keeping with the often conservative nature of Ford's westerns. According to

283

Gallagher (545), Ford briefly considered doing a sound remake of *The Last Outlaw* with Carey in 1943.

5. Gallagher, 32.

6. Andrew Sarris, *The American Cinema* (New York: Dutton, 1968), 44.

Chapter 3

1. Tag Gallagher, *John Ford: The Man and His Films* (Berkeley: U of Cal. Pr., 1986), 121–22.

2. Walter D. Edmonds, *Drums Along the Mohawk* (Boston: Little, Brown, 1936), 9.

3. Edmonds, 584.

Chapter 4

1. One exception is Lee Pfeiffer, *The John Wayne Scrapbook* (Secaucus: Citadel Press, 1989), 77–82.

2. Tag Gallagher, *John Ford: The Man and His Films* (Berkeley: U of Cal. Pr., 1986), 161.

3. David Buttolph enjoyed a lengthy Hollywood career at 20th Century–Fox and Warner Bros., although he also freelanced at other studios. Buttolph honed his skills as a "western music" specialist on such 20th Century–Fox films as *The Return of Frank James* (1940) and *Western Union* (1941). He worked with Ford on *Tobacco Road* (20th Century–Fox, 1941) as well as *The Horse Soldiers*, and he contributed to the score for *My Darling Clementine*. Buttolph's most famous melody is, undoubtedly, the main theme to the television series *Maverick*.

Chapter 5

1. Huston's screenplay for *The Maltese Falcon* (Warner Bros., 1941) contains only one notable line ("It's the stuff that dreams are made of") that does not appear in the original Dashiell Hammett novel.

2. The bank representative (Cliff Clark) in Ford's *Grapes of Wrath* (20th Century–Fox, 1940) is a more humane version of Gatewood set within the depression era.

3. James Warner Bellah, "Massacre," in Bill Prozini and Martin Greenberg, eds., *The Reel West* (New York: Doubleday and Company, 1984), 37.

4. Tag Gallagher, *John Ford: The Man and His Films* (Berkeley: U of Cal. Pr., 1986), 220.

5. James Warner Bellah, "War Party," *Saturday Evening Post* (June 19, 1948), 110.

6. Peter Kyne, *The Three Godfathers* (New York: Cosmopolitan Books, 1922 [1913]), 22.

7. Robert Lyons, ed., *My Darling Clementine* (New Brunswick: Rutgers UP, 1984), 3–19.

Chapter 6

1. Peter Bogdanovich, *John Ford* (Berkeley: U of Cal. Pr., 1967, 1978), 104.

Chapter 7

1. Peter Bogdanovich, *John Ford* (Berkeley: U of Cal. Pr., 1967, 1978), 74.
2. Tag Gallagher, *John Ford: The Man and His Films* (Berkeley: U of Cal. Pr., 1986), 257.

Chapter 8

1. *My Darling Clementine* has several technical glitches, which become apparent only after repeated viewings. Chihuahua appears in black stockings inside the saloon when she spies on Wyatt's cards and is then bare-legged when he throws her into the horse trough moments later; Jack Pennick mysteriously replaces the first coach driver on Doc's mad dash out of Tombstone; and Wyatt goes from being unlathered to completely lathered within a moment in the barbershop when Mr. Bon Ton is interrupted by the rampaging Indian Charlie.

Chapter 9

1. Lindsay Anderson, *About John Ford* (New York: McGraw-Hill, 1981), praises *Wagonmaster* (127–29) while dismissing *Two Rode Together* (171). Andrew Sarris, *The John Ford Movie Mystery* (Bloomington: Ind. U. Pr., 1975), finds much to admire in both films (162–66, 151–52).

Chapter 11

1. Tag Gallagher, *John Ford: The Man and His Films* (Berkeley: U of Cal. Pr., 1986), is extensive in praising *Seven Women* (436–50). John Baxter, *The Cinema of John Ford* (New York: A. S. Barnes, 1971), declares *Donovan's Reef* to be the director's "last important film" (172); Andrew Sarris, *The John Ford Movie Mystery* (Bloomington: Ind. U. Pr., 1975), also defends and praises this film (153–54).
2. Richard Hageman, W. Franke Harling, John Leipold, Leo Shuken, and Louis Gruenberg won the Oscar in 1939 for "Best Score."
3. J. A. Place, *The Western Films of John Ford* (Secaucus: Citadel Press, 1974), 236.

Conclusion

1. William Everson, *The Hollywood Western* (Secaucus: Citadel Press, 1992), 9–21.
2. Allan Bloom, *The Closing of the American Mind* (New York: Simon and Schuster, 1987), 56.

Bibliography

Anderson, Lindsay. *About John Ford.* New York: McGraw-Hill, 1981.

Anobile, Richard, ed. *Stagecoach.* New York: Avon, 1974.

Baxter, John. *The Cinema of John Ford.* New York: A. S. Barnes, 1971.

Bellah, James Warner. "Mission with No Record." *Saturday Evening Post.* (September 27, 1947).

_____. "War Party." *Saturday Evening Post.* (June 19, 1948).

Bloom, Allan. *The Closing of the American Mind.* New York: Simon and Schuster, 1987.

Bogdanovich, Peter. *John Ford.* Berkeley: University of California Press, 1967, 1978.

_____. *Pieces of Time.* New York: Arbor House, 1985.

Buscombe, Edward, ed. *The BFI Companion to the Western.* New York: Atheneum, 1988.

_____. *Stagecoach.* London: British Film Institute, 1992.

Calder, Jenni. *There Must Be a Lone Ranger.* New York: Taplinger Publishing Company, 1975.

Cook, Will. *Two Rode Together* (originally published as *Commanche Captives*). New York: Bantam Books, 1959.

Coursodon, Jean-Pierre (with Pierre Sauvage). *American Directors.* Volume I. New York: McGraw-Hill, 1983.

Davis, Ronald L. *John Ford: Hollywood's Old Master.* Norman: University of Oklahoma Press, 1995.

Edmonds, Walter D. *Drums Along the Mohawk.* Boston: Little, Brown and Company, 1936.

Everson, William. *The Hollywood Western.* Secaucus: Citadel Press, 1992.

Ford, Dan. *Pappy: The Life of John Ford.* Englewood Cliffs: Prentice-Hall, 1979.

French, Philip. *Westerns.* New York: Viking Press, 1973.

Gallagher, Tag. *John Ford: The Man and His Films.* Berkeley: University of California Press, 1986.

Garfield, Brian. *Western Films: A Complete Guide.* New York: Rawson Associates, 1982.

Gussow, Mel. *Don't Say Yes Until I Finish Talking.* New York: Pocket Books, 1972.

Hardy, Phil. *The Film Encyclopedia: The Western.* New York: William Morrow and Company, 1983.

Hitt, Jim. *The American West from Fiction* (1823–1976) *Into Film* (1909–1986). Jefferson, North Carolina: McFarland and Company, 1990.

Kitses, Jim. *Horizons West.* Bloomington: University of Indiana Press, 1969.

Kyne, Peter. *The Three Godfathers.* New York: Cosmopolitan Books, 1922 (1913).

Lake, Stuart. *Wyatt Earp: Frontier Marshal.* New York: Bantam Books, 1959 (1931).

LeMay, Alan. *The Searchers.* London: Collins, 1955.

Lyons, Robert, ed. *My Darling Clementine.* New Brunswick: Rutgers University Press, 1984.

McBride, Joseph, and Michael Wilmington. *John Ford.* New York: Da Capo, 1975.

Nachbar, Jack, ed. *Focus on the Western.* Englewood Cliffs: Prentice-Hall, 1974.

Newman, Kim. *Wild West Movies.* London: Bloomsbury, 1990.

Nugent, Frank S., and Patrick Ford. *Wagonmaster.* New York: Frederick Ungar Publishing, n.d.

Peary, Danny. *Cult Movies 2.* New York: Dell Publishing Company, 1983.

Pfeiffer, Lee. *The John Wayne Scrapbook.* Secaucus: Citadel Press, 1989.

Place, J. A. *The Non-Western Films of John Ford.* Secaucus: Citadel Press, 1979.

_____. *The Western Films of John Ford.* Secaucus: Citadel Press, 1974.

Proni, Bill, and Martin Greenberg, eds. *The Reel West.* New York: Doubleday and Company, 1984.

Ray, Robert D. *A Certain Tendency of the Hollywood Cinema, 1930–1980.* Princeton: Princeton University Press, 1985.

Reed, Joseph W. *Three American Originals: John Ford, William Faulkner, and Charles Ives.* Middletown, Conn.: Wesleyan University Press, 1984.

Sandoz, Mari. *Cheyenne Autumn.* New York: Avon Books, 1964 (1953).

Sarris, Andrew. *The American Cinema.* New York: Dutton, 1968.

_____. *The John Ford Movie Mystery.* Bloomington: Indiana University Press, 1975.

Schickel, Richard. *Schickel on Film.* New York: William Morrow and Company, 1989.

Sinclair, Andrew. *John Ford: A Biography.* New York: Dial Press, 1979.

Slotkin, Richard. *Gunfighter Nation.* New York: Atheneum, 1992.

Smith, Henry Nash. *Virgin Land.* New York: Vintage Books, 1950.

Stowell, Peter. *John Ford.* Boston: Twayne Publishers, 1986.

Tuska, John. *The American West in Film.* Lincoln: University of Nebraska Press, 1988.

Wheeler, David, ed. *No, But I Saw the Movie.* New York: Penguin Books, 1989.

Wright, Will. *Sixguns and Society.* Berkeley: University of California Press, 1975.

Filmography: Ford's Westerns

1917

THE TRAIL OF HATE (Universal). 2 reels. Writer: Ford. Cast: Ford (Lieutenant Jack Brewer), Duke Worne (Captain Dana Holden), Louise Granville (Madge).

THE SCRAPPER (Universal). 2 reels. Writer: Ford. Photo.: Ben Reynolds. Cast: Ford (Buck Logan), Louise Granville (Helen Dawson), Duke Worne (Jerry Martin), Jean Hathaway (Martha Hayes).

THE SOUL HERDER (Universal). 3 reels. Writer: George Hively. Photo.: Ben Reynolds. Cast: Harry Carey (Cheyenne Harry), Jean Hersholt (the Parson), Elizabeth Jones (Mary Ann), Vester Pegg (Topeka Jack), Hoot Gibson (Chuck Rafferty).

CHEYENNE'S PAL (Universal). 2 reels. Writer: Charles J. Wilson, Jr. Photo.: Friend Baker. Cast: Harry Carey (Cheyenne Harry), Vester Pegg, Hoot Gibson, Ed Jones.

STRAIGHT SHOOTING (Universal). 5 reels. Writer: George Hively. Photo.: George Scott. Cast: Harry Carey (Cheyenne Harry), Molly Malone (Joan Sims), Duke Lee (Thunder Flint), Vester Pegg (Placer Fremont), Hoot Gibson (Sam Turner).

THE SECRET MAN (Universal). 5 reels. Writer: George Hively. Photo.: Ben Reynolds. Cast: Harry Carey (Cheyenne Harry), Morris Foster (Harry Beaufort), Elizabeth Jones (his child), Steve Clemente (Pedro), Vester Pegg (Bill), Hoot Gibson (Chuck Fadden).

A MARKED MAN (Universal). 5 reels. Writer: George Hively from a story by Ford. Photo.: John W. Brown. Cast: Harry Carey (Cheyenne Harry), Molly Malone (Molly Young), Harry Rattenbury (her father), Vester Pegg (Kent), Hoot Gibson.

BUCKING BROADWAY (Universal). 5 reels. Writer: George Hively. Photo.: John W. Brown. Cast: Harry Carey (Cheyenne Harry), Molly Malone (Helen Clayton), L. M. Wells (Ben Clayton), Vester Pegg (Captain Thornton).

1918

THE PHANTOM RIDERS (Universal). 5 reels. Writer: George Hively, from a story by Henry McRae. Photo.: John W. Brown. Cast: Harry Carey (Cheyenne Harry), Molly Malone (Molly), Buck Connor (her father), Vester Pegg (outlaw leader).

WILD WOMEN (Universal). 5 reels.

Writer: George Hively. Photo.: John W. Brown. Cast: Harry Carey (Cheyenne Harry), Molly Malone (the Princess), Martha Maddox (the Queen), Vester Pegg, Ed Jones.

THIEVES' GOLD (Universal). 5 reels. Writer: George Hively from a story by Frederick Bechdolt. Photo.: John W. Brown. Cast: Harry Carey (Cheyenne Harry), Molly Malone (Alice Norris), L. M. Wells (Savage), Vester Pegg (Padden).

THE SCARLET DROP (Universal). 5 reels. Writer: George Hively from a story by Ford. Photo.: Ben Reynolds. Cast: Harry Carey (Kaintuck Cass), Molly Malone (Molly Calvert), Vester Pegg (Captain Marley Calvert).

HELL BENT (Universal). 5700' (approx. 63 min.). Writer: Ford; Harry Carey. Photo.: Ben Reynolds. Cast: Harry Carey (Cheyenne Harry), Neva Gerber (Bess Thurston), Duke Lee (Cimarron Bill), Vester Pegg (Jack Thurston), Joseph Harris (Beau, an outlaw).

A WOMAN'S FOOL (Universal). 60 minutes. Writer: George Hively from the novel *Lin McLean* by Owen Wister. Photo.: Ben Reynolds. Cast: Harry Carey (Lin McLean), Betty Schade (Katy), Roy Clark (Tommy Lusk), Molly Malone (Jessamine).

THREE MOUNTED MEN (Universal). 6 reels. Writer: Eugene B. Lewis. Photo.: John W. Brown. Cast: Harry Carey (Cheyenne Harry), Joe Harris (Buck Masters), Neva Gerber (Lola Masters).

1919

ROPED (Universal). 6 reels. Writer: Eugene B. Lewis. Photo.: John W. Brown. Cast: Harry Carey (Cheyenne Harry), Neva Gerber (Aileen Judson Brown), Molly McConnell (Mrs. Judson Brown), J. Farrell MacDonald (butler).

THE FIGHTING BROTHERS (Universal). 2 reels. Writer: George Hively from a story by George C. Hull. Photo.: John W. Brown. Cast: Pete Morrison (Sheriff Pete Larkin), Hoot Gibson (Lonnie Larkin), Yvette Mitchell (Conchita), Jack Woods (Ben Crawley), Duke Lee (Slim).

A FIGHT FOR LOVE (Universal). 6 reels. Writer: Eugene B. Lewis. Photo.: John W. Brown. Cast: Harry Carey (Cheyenne Harry), Joe Harris (Black Michael), Neva Gerber (Kate McDougall), Mark Fenton (her father), J. Farrell MacDonald (priest), Chief Big Tree (Swift Deer).

BY INDIAN POST (Universal). 2 reels. Writer: H. Tipton Steck from a story by William Wallace Cook. Cast: Pete Morrison (Jode McWilliams), Duke Lee (Pa Owens), Madga Lane (Peg Owens), Ed Jones (Stumpy), Hoot Gibson (Chub).

THE RUSTLERS (Universal). 2 reels. Writer: George Hively. Photo.: John W. Brown. Cast: Pete Morrison (Ben Clayburn), Helen Gibson (Nell Wyndham), Jack Woods (Sheriff Buck Farley), Hoot Gibson (deputy).

BARE FISTS (Universal). 5,500' (approx. 61 min.). Writer: Eugene B. Lewis from a story by Bernard McConville. Photo.: John W. Brown. Cast: Harry Carey (Cheyenne Harry), Molly McConnell (his mother), Joseph Girard (his father), Howard Enstedt (his brother Bud), Betty Schade (Conchita), Vester Pegg (Lopez), Joe Harris (Boone Travis).

GUN LAW (Universal). 2 reels. Writer: H. Tipton Steck. Photo.: John W. Brown. Cast: Pete Morrison (Dick Allen), Hoot Gibson (Bart Stevens), Helen Gibson (Letty), Jack Woods (Cayuse Yates), Ed Jones.

THE GUN PACKER (Universal). 2 reels. Writer: Karl R. Coolidge from a story by Ford and Harry Carey. Photo.: John W. Brown. Cast: Ed Jones (Sandy McLoughlin), Pete Morrison ("Pearl

Handle" Wiley), Madga Lane (Rose McLoughlin), Jack Woods (Pecos Smith), Hoot Gibson (outlaw leader).

RIDERS OF VENGEANCE (Universal). 6 reels. Writer: Ford; Harry Carey. Photo.: John W. Brown. Cast: Harry Carey (Cheyenne Harry), Seena Owen (the girl), Joe Harris (Sheriff Gale Thurman), J. Farrell MacDonald (Buell), Jennie Lee (Harry's mother), Vester Pegg.

THE LAST OUTLAW (Universal). 2 reels. Writer: H. Tipton Steck from a story by Evelyne Murray Campbell. Photo.: John W. Brown. Cast: Ed Jones (Bud Coburn), Richard Cumming (Sheriff Brownlo), Lucille Hutton (Idaleen Coburn).

THE OUTCASTS OF POKER FLAT (Universal). 6 reels. Writer: H. Tipton Steck from Bret Harte stories. Photo.: John W. Brown. Cast: Harry Carey (Square Shootin' Lanyon/John Oakhurst), Cullen Landis (Billy Lanyon/ Tommy Oakhurst), Gloria Hope (Ruth Watson/Sophy), J. Farrell MacDonald, Joe Harris, Duke Lee, Vester Pegg.

THE AGE OF THE SADDLE (Universal). 6 reels. Writer: George Hively from a story by B. J. Jackson. Photo.: John W. Brown. Cast: Harry Carey (Cheyenne Harry), Joe Harris (Sheriff Hildebrand), Duke Lee (Sheriff Faulkner), Peggy Pearce (Madeline Faulkner), Vester Pegg, Ed Jones, Andy Devine.

THE RIDER OF THE LAW (Universal). 5 reels. Writer: H. Tipton Steck from a story by G. P. Lancaster. Photo.: John W. Brown. Cast: Harry Carey (Jim Kyneton), Gloria Hope (Betty), Vester Pegg (Nick Kyneton), Joe Harris, Jack Woods, Duke Lee.

A GUN FIGHTIN' GENTLEMAN (Universal). 5 reels. Writer: Hal Hoadley from a story by Ford and Harry Carey. Photo.: John W. Brown. Cast: Harry Carey (Cheyenne Harry), J. Barney Sherry (John Merritt), Kathleen O'Con-

nor (Helen Merritt), Duke Lee, Joe Harris.

MARKED MEN (Universal). 5 reels. Writer: H. Tipton Steck from Peter B. Kyne's *The Three Godfathers*. Photo.: John W. Brown. Ed.: Frank Lawrence; Frank Atkinson. Cast: Harry Carey (Cheyenne Harry), J. Farrell MacDonald (Tom McGraw), Joe Harris (Tom Gibbons), Charles Lemoyne (Sheriff Peter Cushing).

1920

JUST PALS (Fox). 5 reels. Writer: Paul Schofield from a story by John McDermott. Photo.: George Schneiderman. Cast: Buck Jones (Bim), Helen Ferguson (Mary Bruce), George E. Stone (Bill), Duke Lee (Sheriff).

THE WALLOP (Universal). 4,539° Writer: George C. Hull from a story by Eugene Manlove Rhodes. Photo.: Harry C. Fowler. Cast: Harry Carey (John Wesley Pringle), Joe Harris (Barela), Charles Lemoyne (Matt Lisner), J. Farrell MacDonald (Neuces River), Noble Johnson (Espinol).

DESPERATE TRAILS (Universal). 4,973°. Writer: Elliott J. Clawson from a story by Courtney Riley Cooper. Photo.: Harry C. Fowler; Robert DeGrasse. Cast: Harry Carey (Bert Carson), Irene Rich (Mrs. Walker), George E. Stone (Danny Boy).

ACTION (Universal). 4,590° Writer: Harvey Gates from a story by J. Allen Dunn. Photo.: John W. Brown. Cast: Hoot Gibson (Sandy Brooke), Francis Ford (Soda Water Manning), J. Farrell MacDonald (Mormon Peters), Ed Jones.

SURE FIRE (Universal). 4,481° Writer: George C. Hull from a story by Eugene Manlove Rhodes. Photo.: Virgil G. Miller. Cast: Hoot Gibson (Jeff Bransford), Molly Malone (Marian Hoffman), Reeves "Breezy" Eason, Jr. (Sonny).

1923

THREE JUMPS AHEAD (Fox). 4,854ʼ Writer: Ford. Photo.: Daniel B. Clark. Cast: Tom Mix (Steve Clancy), Alma Bennett (Annie Darrell), Virginia True Boardman (Mrs. Darrell), Francis Ford (Virgil Clancy).

NORTH OF HUDSON BAY (Fox). 4,973ʼ Writer: Jules Furthman. Photo.: Daniel B. Clark. Cast: Tom Mix (Michael Dane), Kathleen Kay (Estelle MacDonald), Jennie Lee (her mother), Frank Campeau (Cameron MacDonald), Eugene Pallette (Peter Dane).

1924

THE IRON HORSE (Fox). 11,335ʼ (approx. 125 minutes) Writer: Charles Kenyon from a story by Kenyon and John Russell. Photo.: George Schneiderman; Burnett Guffey. Music: Erno Rapee. Cast: George O'Brien (Davy Brandon), Madge Bellamy (Miriam Marsh), Francis Powers (Sergeant Slattery), J. Farrell MacDonald (Corporal Casey), James Welch (Private Schultz), Fred Kohler (Deroux), Cyril Chadwick (Peter Jesson).

1926

THREE BAD MEN (Fox). 8,710ʼ (approx. 97 minutes). Writer: Ford and John Stone from the novel Over the Border by Herman Whitaker. Photo.: George Schneiderman. Cast: George O'Brien (Dan O'Malley), Olive Borden (Lee Carlton), J. Farrell MacDonald (Mike Costigan), Tom Santschi (Bull Stanley), Frank Campeau (Spade Allen), Louis Tellegen (Sheriff Layne Hunter), Vester Pegg.

1939

DRUMS ALONG THE MOHAWK (20th Century–Fox). Technicolor; 103 minutes. Prod.: Darryl Zanuck; Raymond Griffith. Writers: Lamar Trotti; Sonya Levien; (uncredited) William Faulkner. Source: Drums Along the Mohawk (novel) by Walter Edmonds (1936). Photo.: Bert Glennon; Ray Rennahan. Art Dir.: Richard Day; Mark Lee Kirk. Music: Alfred Newman. Ed.: Robert Simpson. Cast: Claudette Colbert (Lana Borst Martin), Henry Fonda (Gil Martin), Edna May Oliver (Mrs. McKlennar), Eddie Collins (Christian Reall), John Carradine (Caldwell), Doris Bowdon (Mary Reall Weaver), Jessie Ralph (Mrs. Weaver), Robert Lowery (John Weaver), Arthur Shields (Reverend Rosenkrantz), Roger Imhof (General Herkimer), Francis Ford (Joe Boleo), Ward Bond (Adam Hartmann), Russell Simpson (Dr. Petry), Chief Big Tree (Blue Back), Spencer Charters (Fisk, an innkeeper), Jack Pennick (drill sergeant).

STAGECOACH (Walter Wanger–United Artists). B & W, 97 minutes. Prod.: Walter Wanger. Writer: Dudley Nichols. Source: "Stage to Lordsburg" (short story) by Ernest Haycox (1937). Photo.: Bert Glennon. Art Dir.: Alexander Toluboff (credited); actually Wiard Ihnen, the set decorator on the film. Music: Richard Hageman; W. Franke Harling; John Leipold; Leo Shuken; Louis Gruenberg (arrangers-adapters of American folk tunes of the 1880s). Ed.: Otho Lovering; Dorothy Spencer; Walter Reynolds. Cast: John Wayne (the Ringo Kid, Henry Ringo), Claire Trevor (Dallas), John Carradine (Hatfield), Thomas Mitchell (Dr. Josiah Boone), Andy Devine (Buck, the stage driver), Donald Meek (Samuel Peacock), Louise Platt (Lucy Mallory), George Bancroft (Sheriff Curly Wilcox), Berton Churchill (Henry Gatewood), Tim Holt (Lieutenant Blanchard), Tom Tyler (Hank Plummer), Joseph Rickson (Luke Plummer), Vester Pegg (Ike Plummer), Chris Pin Martin (Chris, stationmaster at Apache Wells), Elvira Rios (Yakima,

Chris's Indian wife), Francis Ford (Billy Pickett, stationmaster at Dry Fork), Marga Daighton (Mrs. Pickett), Yakima Canutt (stuntman; double for Wayne), Chief Big Tree (Indian messenger at opening), Jack Pennick (Jerry, the barman in Tonto), Leroy Mason (deputy in Tonto), Brenda Fowler (Mrs. Gatewood), Nora Cecil (Dr. Boone's housekeeper), Duke Lee (Sheriff of Lordsburg).

1946

MY DARLING CLEMENTINE (20th Century–Fox). B & W, 97 minutes. Prod.: Samuel G. Engel. Writers: Engel; Winston Miller. Source: *Wyatt Earp, Frontier Marshal* (biography) by Stuart Lake (1931). Photo.: Joseph P. McDonald; Fred Sersen (Spec. Eff.). Art Dir.: James Basevi; Lyle Wheeler. Music: Cyril Mockridge. Ed.: Dorothy Spencer; Darryl Zanuck (uncredited). Cast: Henry Fonda (Wyatt Earp), Linda Darnell (Chihuahua), Victor Mature (Dr. John Holliday), Walter Brennan (Pa Clanton), Tim Holt (Virgil Earp), Ward Bond (Morgan Earp), Cathy Downs (Clementine Carter), Alan Mowbray (Granville Thorndyke), John Ireland (Billy Clanton), Grant Withers (Ike Clanton), Roy Roberts (Mayor "Jess" [?] of Tombstone), Jane Darwell (brothel madam), Russell Simpson (John Simpson), Francis Ford (Dad, attendant on Thorndyke and Earp), J. Farrell MacDonald (Mac, the bartender), Don Garner (James Earp), Ben Hall (Mr. Bon Ton, the barber), Arthur Walsh (hotel clerk), Jack Pennick (stage driver), Mickey Simpson (Sam Clanton), Fred Libby (Phinn Clanton), Harry Woods (first sheriff in Tombstone), Charles Stevens (Indian Charlie), Earle Fox (tinhorn gambler), Don Barclay (opera house owner), Mae Marsh (woman in wagon with John Simpson).

1948

FORT APACHE (Argosy-RKO). B & W, 127 minutes. Prod.: Ford; Merian C. Cooper. Writer: Frank S. Nugent. Source: "Massacre" (short story) by James Warner Bellah (1947). Photo.: Archie Stout; William Clothier (2nd Unit). Art Dir.: James Basevi. Music: Richard Hageman. Ed.: Jack Murray. Cast: Henry Fonda (Lieutenant Colonel Owen Thursday), John Wayne (Captain Kirby York), Shirley Temple (Philadelphia Thursday), John Agar (Lieutenant Michael O'Rourke), Ward Bond (Sergeant Major O'Rourke), George O'Brien (Captain Sam Collingwood), Victor McLaglen (Sergeant Mulcahy), Pedro Armendariz (Sergeant Beaufort), Anna Lee (Mrs. Collingwood), Irene Rich (Mrs. O'Rourke), Guy Kibbee (Dr. Wilkens), Grant Withers (Silas Meacham), Miguel Inclan (Cochise), Jack Pennick (Sergeant Shattuck), Mae Marsh (Mrs. Gates), Dick Foran (Sergeant Quincannon), Frank Ferguson (newsman at final conference), Movita Castenada (Guadalupe), Hank Worden (southern recruit), Mary Gordon (Ma, at opening waystation), Cliff Clark (stage driver), Francis Ford (shotgun rider).

THREE GODFATHERS (Argosy-MGM). Technicolor, 106 minutes. Prod.: Ford; Merian C. Cooper. Writers: Frank S. Nugent; Laurence Stallings. Source: *The Three Godfathers* (novel) by Peter B. Kyne (1913). Photo.: Winton Hoch; Charles P. Boyle (2nd Unit). Art Dir.: James Basevi. Music: Richard Hageman. Ed.: Jack Murray. Cast: John Wayne (Robert Hightower), Pedro Armendariz (Pete/Pedro Fuerte), Harry Carey, Jr. (The Abilene Kid/William Kearney), Ward Bond (Sheriff Pearly "Buck" Sweet), Mildred Natwick (the mother; niece to Sweet), Charles Halton

(Mr. Latham, the banker), Jane Darwell (Miss Florie), Mae Marsh (Mrs. Sweet), Guy Kibbee (judge), Dorothy Ford (Ruby Latham), Ben Johnson; Fred Libby; Michael Dugan; Hank Worden (deputies), Jack Pennick (Luke, train conductor), Ruth Clifford (woman in bar in New Jerusalem), Francis Ford (drunk in bar at New Jerusalem).

1949

SHE WORE A YELLOW RIBBON

(Argosy-RKO). Technicolor, 103 minutes. Prod.: Ford; Merian C. Cooper; Lowell Farrell (Assoc.). Writers: Frank S. Nugent; Laurence Stallings. Source: "War Party" (short story) by James Warner Bellah (1948). Photo.: Winton Hoch; Charles Boyle (2nd Unit). Art Dir.: James Basevi. Music: Richard Hageman. Ed.: Jack Murray; Barbara Ford (Asst.). Cast: John Wayne (Captain Nathan Brittles), Joanne Dru (Olivia Dandridge), John Agar (Lieutenant Flint Cohill), Ben Johnson (Sergeant Tyree), Harry Carey, Jr. (Lieutenant Pennell), Victor McLaglen (Sergeant Quincannon), Mildred Natwick (Mrs. Abbey Allshard), George O'Brien (Major Mack Allshard), Arthur Shields (Dr. O'Laughlin), Francis Ford (Irish barman), Harry Woods (Karl Rynders, the sutler), Chief Big Tree (Pony-That-Walks), Noble Johnson (Red Shirt), Cliff Lyons (Trooper Cliff, in first scene), Tom Tyler (Corporal Quayne), Michael Dugan (Sergeant Hockbauer), Mickey Simpson (Wagner, the blacksmith), Fred Libby (Corporal Krumrein), Rudy Bowman (Private Smith).

1950

RIO GRANDE (Argosy-Republic). B
& W, 105 minutes. Prod.: Ford; Merian C. Cooper. Writer: James Kevin McGuinness. Source: "Mission with No Record" (short story) by James Warner Bellah (1949).

Photo.: Bert Glennon; Archie Stout (2nd Unit). Art Dir.: Frank Hotaling. Music: Victor Young; songs by Stan Jones, Dale Evans, Tex Owens. Ed.: Jack Murray; Barbara Ford (Asst. Ed.). Cast: John Wayne (Lieutenant Colonel Kirby Yorke), Maureen O'Hara (Kathleen Yorke), Ben Johnson (Trooper Tyree), Claude Jarman, Jr. (Trooper Jeff Yorke), Harry Carey, Jr. (Trooper Sandy Boone), Victor McLaglen (Sergeant Quincannon), J. Carroll Naish (General Philip Sheridan), Chill Wills (Dr. Wilkins), Grant Withers (sheriff), Peter Ortiz (Captain St. Jacques), Steve Pendelton (Captain Prescott), Karolyn Grimes (Margaret Mary Bell), Fred Kennedy (Trooper Heinze), Ken Curtis (lead singer, Sons of the Pioneers), Shug Fisher (stuttering bugler).

WAGONMASTER (Argosy-RKO).
B & W, 86 minutes. Prod.: Ford; Merian C. Cooper; Lowell Farrell (Assoc.). Writers: Frank S. Nugent; Patrick Ford; Ford (uncredited). Source: Original screenplay. Photo.: Bert Glennon; Archie Stout (2nd Unit). Art Dir.: James Basevi. Music: Richard Hageman; songs by Stan Jones. Ed.: Jack Murray; Barbara Ford (Asst.). Cast: Ben Johnson (Travis Blue), Harry Carey, Jr. (Sandy Owens), Joanne Dru (Denver), Ward Bond (Elder Wiggs), Charles Kemper (Uncle Shiloh Clegg), Alan Mowbray (Dr. A. Locksley Hall), Jane Darwell (Sister Ledyard), Ruth Clifford (Fleuretty Phyffe), Russell Simpson (Elder Perkins), Kathleen O'Malley (Prudence Perkins), James Arness (Floyd Clegg), Fred Libby (Reese Clegg), Hank Worden (Luke Clegg), Mickey Simpson (Jesse Clegg), Francis Ford (Mr. Peachtree), Cliff Lyons (sheriff of Crystal City), Don Summers (Sam Jenkins), Movita Castenada (Navajo woman who is attacked).

1956

THE SEARCHERS (Warner Bros.).
Technicolor, 119 minutes. Prod.: Merian

C. Cooper; C. V. Whitney; Patrick Ford (Assoc.). Writer: Frank S. Nugent. Source: *The Searchers* (novel) by Alan LeMay (1954). Photo.: Winton Hoch; Alfred Gilks (2nd Unit). Art Dir.: Frank Hotaling; James Basevi. Music: Max Steiner; song by Stan Jones. Ed.: Jack Murray. Cast: John Wayne (Ethan Edwards), Jeffrey Hunter (Martin Pauley), Vera Miles (Laurie Jorgenson), Ward Bond (Reverend/Captain Samuel Clayton), Natalie Wood (Debbie Edwards as an adult), John Qualen (Lars Jorgenson), Olive Carey (Mrs. Jorgenson), Henry Brandon (Chief Scar), Harry Carey, Jr. (Brad Jorgenson), Antonio Moreno (Emilio Figueroa, the Mexican trader), Hank Worden (Mose Harper), Lana Wood (Debbie Edwards as a child), Walter Coy (Aaron Edwards), Pippa Scott (Lucy Edwards), Dorothy Jordan (Martha Edwards), Patrick Wayne (Lieutenant Greenhill), Beulah Archuletta (Look), Peter Mamokos (Futterman), Bill Steele (Nesby), Ruth Clifford (mad woman at fort), Mae Marsh (woman at fort), Billy Cartledge (Edwards's son).

1959

THE HORSE SOLDIERS (United Artists). Technicolor, 119 minutes. Prod.: John Lee Mahin and Martin Rackin. Writers: Mahin and Rackin. Source: *The Horse Soldiers* (novel) by Harold Sinclair (1954). Photo.: William Clothier. Art Dir.: Frank Hotaling. Music: David Buttolph; "I Left My Love" by Stan Jones. Ed.: Jack Murray. Cast: John Wayne (Colonel John Marlowe), William Holden (Major Hank Kendall), Constance Towers (Hannah Hunter), Althea Gibson (Lukey), Willis Bouchey (Colonel Philip Secord), Carleton Young (Colonel Jonathan Miles), Judson Pratt (Sergeant Major Kirby), Bing Russell (Dunker), Hoot Gibson (Trooper), Anna Lee (Mrs.

Buford), Russell Simpson (Sheriff Henry Goodboy), Stan Jones (General Grant), Richard Cutting (General Sherman), Basil Ruysdael (commandant, Jefferson Military Academy), Ken Curtis (Wilkie), O. Z. Whitehead (Hoppy Hopkins), Denver Pyle (Jagger Jo), Strother Martin (Virgil), Hank Worden (Deacon), Jack Pennick (Sergeant Major Mitchell), Charles Seel (bartender at Newton Station).

1960

SERGEANT RUTLEDGE (Warner Bros.). Technicolor, 111 minutes. Prod.: Patrick Ford; Willis Goldbeck. Writers: Goldbeck; James Warner Bellah. Source: Original Screenplay. Photo.: Bert Glennon. Art Dir.: Eddie Imazu. Music: Howard Jackson; song by Mack David and Jerry Livingston. Ed.: Jack Murray. Cast: Woody Strode (Sergeant Braxton Rutledge), Jeffrey Hunter (Lieutenant Tom Cantrell), Constance Towers (Mary Beecher), Billie Burke (Cordelia Fosgate), Willis Bouchey (Colonel Otis Fosgate), Juano Hernandez (Sergeant Matthew Luke Skidmore), Carleton Young (Captain Shattuck), Judson Pratt (Lieutenant Mulqueen), Fred Libby (Chandler Hubble), Toby Richards (Lucy Dabney), Jan Styne (Chris Hubble), Charles Seel (Dr. Eckner), Jack Pennick (sergeant and court bailiff), Hank Worden (Laredo, the impatient cowman on the train), Shug Fisher (Mr. Owens, the train conductor).

1961

TWO RODE TOGETHER (Columbia). Technicolor, 109 minutes. Prod.: Stan Sheptner. Writer: Frank S. Nugent. Source: *Commanche Captives* (novel) by Will Cook (1958). Photo.: Charles Lawton. Art Dir.: Robert Peterson. Music: George Duning. Ed.: Jack Murray. Cast: James Stewart (Sheriff Guthrie McCabe),

Richard Widmark (Lieutenant Jim Gary), Shirley Jones (Marty Purcell), Linda Cristal (Elena de la Madriaga), Andy Devine (Sergeant Posey), John McIntire (Major Frazier), Paul Birch (Edward Purcell), Willis Bouchey (Henry J. Wringle), Henry Brandon (Quana Parker), Harry Carey, Jr. (Ortho Clegg), Ken Curtis (Greeley Clegg), Olive Carey (Mrs. Frazier), Chet Douglas (Ward Corby), Annelle Hayes (Belle Aragon), David Kent (Running Wolf), Jeanette Nolan (Mrs. McCandless), John Qualen (Ole Knudsen), Ford Rainey (Henry Clegg), Woody Strode (Stone Calf), Cliff Lyons (William McCandless), Mae Marsh (Hannah Clegg).

1962

THE MAN WHO SHOT LIBERTY VALANCE (Paramount). B & W, 122 minutes. Prod.: Willis Goldbeck. Writers: Goldbeck; James Warner Bellah. Source: "The Man Who Shot Liberty Valance" (short story) by Dorothy Johnson (1951). Photo.: William Clothier. Art Dir.: Hal Pereira; Eddie Imazu. Music: Cyril Mockridge; theme from *Young Mr. Lincoln* by Alfred Newman. Ed.: Otho Lovering. Cast: James Stewart (Ransom Stoddard), John Wayne (Tom Doniphon), Vera Miles (Hallie Stoddard), Lee Marvin (Liberty Valance), Edmond O'Brien (Dutton Peabody), Andy Devine (Link Appleyard), Ken Murray (Dr. Willoughby), John Carradine (Major Starbuckle), Jeanette Nolan (Nora Ericson), John Qualen (Lars Ericson), Lee Van Cleef (Reese), Strother Martin (Floyd), Jack Pennick (bartender), Willis Bouchey (train conductor), Carleton Young (newspaper editor), Woody Strode (Pompey), Denver Pyle (Amos Carruthers), O. Z. Whitehead (Ben Carruthers), Robert F. Simon (Handy Strong), Paul Birch (mayor of modern-day Shinbone), Joseph Hoover (under-

taker), Anna Lee (stage passenger threatened by Valance), Charles Seel (president of the election council), Shug Fisher (stuttering cowboy).

HOW THE WEST WAS WON (MGM). Technicolor; 162 minutes. (Ford directed "The Civil War"—25 minutes, 13 seconds). Prod.: Bernard Smith. Writer: James R. Webb. Source: Original Screenplay. Photo.: William Daniels; Milton Krasner; Charles Lang, Jr.; Joseph La Shelle. Art Dir.: George W. Davis; William Ferrari; Addison Hehr. Music: Alfred Newman; Ken Darby. Ed.: Harold F. Kress. Cast: George Peppard (Zeb Rawlings), Carroll Baker (Eve Prescott Rawlings), Russ Tamblyn (Confederate deserter), Claude Johnson (Jeremiah Rawlings), Andy Devine (Corporal Peterson), James Stewart (Linus Rawlings), Willis Bouchey (doctor), Harry Morgan (General Grant), John Wayne (General Sherman), Raymond Massey (Abraham Lincoln), Spencer Tracy (narrator).

1964

CHEYENNE AUTUMN (Warner Bros.). Technicolor; 159 minutes. Prod.: Bernard Smith. Writers: James R. Webb; Patrick Ford (uncredited). Source: *Cheyenne Autumn* (novel) by Mari Sandoz (1953). Photo.: William Clothier. Art Dir.: Richard Day. Music: Alex North. Ed.: Otho Lovering. Cast: Richard Widmark (Captain Thomas Archer), Carroll Baker (Deborah Wright), James Stewart (Wyatt Earp), Edward G. Robinson (Secretary Carl Schurz), Karl Malden (Captain Wessels), Sal Mineo (Red Shirt), Dolores Del Rio (Spanish Woman), Ricardo Montalban (Little Wolf), Gilbert Roland (Dull Knife), Arthur Kennedy (Doc Holliday), Patrick Wayne (Lieutenant Scott), Elizabeth Allen (Guinivere Plantagenet), John Carradine (Major Jeff Blair), Victor

Jory (Tall Tree), Mike Mazurki (Sergeant Stanislaw Wichowsky), George O'Brien (Major Braden), Sean McClory (Dr. O'Carberry), Judson Pratt (mayor of Dodge City), Ken Curtis (Joe), Harry Carey, Jr. (Trooper Smith), Ben Johnson (Trooper Plumtree), Willis Bouchey (colonel at Victory Cave), Carleton Young (aide to Schurz), Denver Pyle (U.S. senator in Schurz's office), Bing Russell (telegraph operator), Charles Seel (sympathetic newspaper editor).

Index

Action 19, 291
Agar, John 22, 50, 63, 82, 103, 121
The Age of the Saddle 18, 291
Aldrich, Robert 9
Alger, Horatio 51
Allen, Elizabeth 24, 257, 263
Altman, Robert 9
Andersonville (prison) 40
Apache 12
Archuletta, Beulah 29
Argosy (production company) 64, 187
Armendariz, Pedro 19, 72, 83, 218
Arness, James 185
Arrowhead 98
Arrowsmith 28, 29, 30
"Assembly" (bugle call) 53
August, Joseph 29
Autry, Gene 5, 21

The Badlanders 12
Baker, Carroll 36, 55, 79, 251
Bancroft, George 59, 250
Barclay, Don 159
Bare Fists 18, 290
The Baron of Arizona 12
"The Battle Hymn of the Republic"
  140, 258
Baxter, Warner 19, 22
"Beautiful Dreamer" 93
Bellah, James Warner 56, 58, 59, 61,
  66
Bellamy, Madge 19
Bend of the River 13
The Big Country 9
The Big Sky 10
The Big Trail 5
Billy the Kid (1930) 10

Birch, Paul 163, 189
Birth of a Nation 47
The Black Watch 56
Bloom, Allan 282
Boccherini, Luigi 190
Boetticher, Budd 7, 12–13
Boley, May 25
Bond, Ward 22, 25, 26, 34, 35, 42, 44,
  53, 63, 71, 74, 83, 152, 189, 216, 224
"The Bonnie Blue Flag" 54, 227
Boone, Richard 13
Borden, Olive 20
Born Reckless 56
Bouchey, Willis 36, 38, 43, 48, 78, 121,
  163, 191, 261
Bowdon, Doris 26
Bowman, Rudy 27, 122
Brady, Alice 26
Brando, Marlon 7, 44
Brandon, Henry 43, 97, 190, 219
The Bravados 11, 18
Brennan, Walter 21, 81, 151
Brigham Young 11
"Bringing in the Sheeves" 225
Broken Arrow 11
Bronson, Charles 15
Brooks, Ted 17
Brown, Harry Joe 12
Brown, Tom 22
Buchanan Rides Alone 12, 13
Bucking Broadway 18, 289
Buffalo Bill 11, 97
Burke, Billie 121
"Bury Me Not on the Lone Prairie"
  140
Butch Cassidy and the Sundance Kid 7
Buttolph, David 53–54
By Indian Post 18, 290

Cain, Christopher 9
The Caine Mutiny (novel) 83
Campeau, Frank 20
"Camptown Races" 257
"Captain Buffalo" 140
Cardinale, Claudia 15
Carey, Harry 5, 16, 17, 18, 19, 21, 172, 225
Carey, Harry, Jr. 19, 24, 26, 53, 55, 65, 67, 72, 78, 79, 85, 121, 138, 186, 189, 218, 219, 260
Carey, Olive 205, 227
Carradine, John 15, 32, 60, 152, 250, 263
Carson City 11
Castenada, Movita 102
Cecil, Nora 261
Chadwick, Cyril 20
"Charge" (bugle call) 53
Cheyenne 11
Cheyenne Autumn 1, 3, 4, 20, 23, 29, 37, 43, 55, 56, 59, 61, 79, 80, 97, 116, 118, 187, 196, 197, 210, 219, 249–278, 281, 296–297
Cheyenne Autumn (novel) 78–80
Cheyenne's Pal 16, 289
Chief Big Tree 23, 32, 66, 126
"Chuckawalla Swing" 187
Churchill, Berton 61, 250
Cimarron (1930) 5
Cimarron (1960) 13
Cimino, Michael 9
Clark, Cliff 102
Clifford, Ruth 189
Clift, Montgomery 10
Cobb, Lee J. 14
Colbert, Claudette 31, 44
Collins, Eddie 35
Colman, Ronald 28
Colorado Territory 11
Columbia (studio) 22
Comanche Captives (novel) 56, 76–78
Comanche Station 12
Command Decision 83
Cook, Will 56, 76
Cooper, Gary 14
Cooper, James Fenimore 268
Coroner Creek 7
Costner, Kevin 9
The Covered Wagon 5, 19
Cowboy 11

The Cowboys 9
Coy, Walter 73, 222
Cristal, Linda 76, 186
Cromwell, Richard 26
Cruze, James 5, 19
Curtis, Ken 51, 78, 98, 189, 254
Curtiz, Michael 7, 10
Cutting, Richard 40

Daighton, Marga 250
Dailey, Dan 24
Dances with Wolves 9
Dark Command 11
Darnell, Linda 81, 149
Darwell, Jane 156, 189, 231
Daves, Delmer 11
David, Mack 140
Decision at Sundown 12, 13
Dehner, John 14
Del Rio, Dolores 268
DeMille, Cecil B. 5
Desperate Trails 19, 291
Destry Rides Again 7, 18
de Toth, Andre 11
Devil's Doorway 13
Devine, Andy 36, 59, 70, 150, 202, 254
"Dixie" 47, 54, 68, 94, 101, 116, 140
Dodge City 7, 10
Donovan's Reef 24, 25, 26, 27, 29, 56, 249, 263
Douglas, Chet 76, 192
Douglas, Kirk 7
Downs, Cathy 44, 81, 149
Dru, Joanne 24, 43, 50, 65, 103, 186
Drum Beat 12
Drums Along the Mohawk 4, 31–36, 44, 46, 221, 292
Duel in the Sun 7, 10
Dugan, Michael 65, 124
Duning, George 186
Duryea, Dan 13
Dwan, Alan 80

Eagle-Lion (production company) 73
Eastwood, Clint 14, 15, 35
Edmonds, Walter 31
El Dorado 10
Eldridge, Florence 28

Engel, Samuel 80
Everson, William 281

The Fall of the Roman Empire 250
The Far Country 13
Faulkner, William 32
Ferguson, Frank 100
A Fight for Love 18, 290
The Fighting Brothers 18, 290
"The First Kiss" 149
Fisher, Shug 86, 171
A Fistful of Dollars 14
Five Card Stud 11
Fix, Paul 126
Fleming, Victor 5
Fonda, Henry 15, 22, 44, 47, 55, 62,
   83, 87, 149, 162
For a Few Dollars More 14
Foran, Dick 83
Ford, Dorothy 44, 71, 221
Ford, Francis 5, 16, 20, 30, 32, 35, 102,
   123, 160, 245, 250
Ford, Glenn 7
Ford, John: arrival in Hollywood 16;
   attitude toward musical score 10; the
   cavalry 279; character emphasis 282;
   creative partnership with Harry
   Carey 16–19; historical "impression-
   ism" 138; on historical realities in
   film 39–40; the journey motif 281;
   male partnerships 279–281; portrayals of Indians 258–259; retirement 9;
   revenge as a plot motif 13; screenwriting advice 3; silent films 16;
   "stock company" 279; technical and
   narrative continuities 22–37
Ford, Wallace 28
Fort Apache 3, 4, 14, 20, 21, 22, 23, 24,
   28, 29, 30, 40, 44, 50, 51, 52, 55, 56,
   61, 64, 65, 66, 67, 68, 71, 79, 82–117,
   119, 121, 124, 128, 130, 133, 135, 141,
   143, 145, 146, 171, 191, 197, 206, 226,
   243, 258, 260, 268, 270, 277, 279,
   281, 293
Forty Guns 12
Foster, Preston 12
Foster, Stephen 256
Four for Texas 12
Fowler, Brenda 22, 261
Fox (studio) 20

From Hell to Texas 11
From Here to Eternity (novel) 83
Frontier Marshal 56, 80, 81
The Fugitive (1947) 28, 56, 72
Fuller, Samuel 12
The Furies 13

Gable, Clark 23
Garden of Evil 11
Gardner, Ava 24
Garner, Don 26, 149
"Garry Owen" 140, 219
"Geniveve" 94
Giant 10
Gibson, Althea 41
Gibson, Hoot 5, 17, 19
"The Girl I Left Behind Me" 93, 134,
   139
Glennon, Bert 34
Goldbeck, Willis 56
"Golden Slippers" 93
Gone with the Wind 47, 52
The Good, the Bad and the Ugly 15
"Goodbye Old Paint" 225
"Goodnight Ladies" 93
Gordon, Mary 111
Grant, Cary 282
The Grapes of Wrath 3, 25, 26, 27, 28,
   29, 30, 31, 49
Grapewin, Charlie 27
Gray, Zane 11
The Great Train Robbery (1903) 5
Grierson's Raid (1863) 40, 44, 52
Griffith, D.W. 5
Grimes, Karolyn 95
A Gun Fightin' Gentleman 18, 291
Gun Law 18, 290
The Gun Packer 18, 290
Gunfight at the O.K. Corral 12, 80
The Gunfighter 11

Hadley, Reed 12
Hageman, Richard 91, 139
Hall, Ben 159
Hall, Jon 24
The Hallelujah Trail 12
Halton, Charles 28, 230
Hamlet (play) 159, 167, 178–179
Hang 'Em High 15

Harris, Joe 18, 19
Hart, W.S. 12
Harte, Bret 19
Hathaway, Henry 9, 11, 36
Hawks, Howard 10
Haycox, Ernest 56
Hayes, Annelle 76, 191
Hayes, Helen 28
Hays Office (Motion Picture Producers and Distributors of America) 32, 57, 60
Heaven's Gate 9
Heflin, Van 35
Heggen, Thomas 83
Hell Bent 18, 290
Hellman, Sam 56, 80
Henry, O. 69, 70
Hepburn, Katharine 30
Hernandez, Juano 123
Heston, Charlton 14
High Lonesome 73
High Noon 7, 11
High Plains Drifter 15
Hill, Walter 9
Hitchcock, Alfred 281–282
Holden, William 7, 39, 61
Holt, Tim 59, 152, 260
"Home on the Range" 150
Hoover, Joseph 175
The Horse Soldiers 4, 19, 26, 27, 28, 37, 38–55, 61, 118, 122, 125, 197, 210, 269, 295
Hour of the Gun 12
How Green Was My Valley 24, 25, 30, 31
How the West Was Won 4, 35, 36–37, 296
Hughes, Howard 7
Hunter, Jeffrey 24, 35, 73, 118, 219
The Hurricane 24, 27, 28, 56, 61, 64
Huston, John 10, 59, 73

"I Dream of Jeannie" 256
"I Left My Love" 53
I Shot Jesse James 12
Imhof, Roger 33
In Old Arizona 5
Ince, Thomas 5
Inclan, Miguel 23, 93
The Indian Fighter 11

The Informer 25, 28, 29, 30, 56, 72
Ireland, John 12, 81, 149
The Iron Horse 5, 19–20, 21, 292

Jarman, Claude, Jr. 26, 42, 67, 86
Jesse James 7, 11
Johnny Guitar 7, 12
Johnson, Ben 35, 53, 55, 65, 67, 79, 86, 97, 122, 186, 259
Johnson, Dorothy 19, 56, 69
Johnson, Nobel 66, 126
Jones, Buck 5, 19, 21
Jones, Ed 18
Jones, James 83
Jones, Shirley 76, 189
Jones, Stan 40, 53, 186, 226
Jordan, Dorothy 44, 221
Jory, Victor 97, 225
Jubal 12
Judge Priest 22, 24, 26, 27, 28, 29, 30, 31, 37, 56
Just Pals 19, 291

Karloff, Boris 22
Kasdan, Lawrence 9
Kass, Judith 17
"Kathleen" 93, 114, 115
Kazan, Elia 7
Kemper, Charles 22, 185
Kennedy, Arthur 13, 14, 257, 263
Kennedy, Fred 85
Kent, David 190
Kerrigan, J.M. 25
Kibbee, Guy 63, 73, 99, 231
King, Henry 7, 11, 18
Kohler, Fred 20
Kohler, Fred, Jr. 26
Kyne, Peter B. 18, 21, 56, 71, 216

Ladd, Alan 10, 35
Laemmle, Carl 5, 16
Lake, Stuart 56, 80
Lancaster, Burt 7
Lang, Fritz 10
Lang, June 30
The Last Frontier (a.k.a. *Savage Wilderness*) 13
The Last Hurrah 24, 25, 26, 27, 37, 56

The Last Outlaw 18, 291
The Last Sunset 12
The Last Train from Gun Hill 12
Lean, David 10
Lee, Anna 42, 44, 63, 87, 172, 186
The Left-Handed Gun 7
LeMay, Alan 10, 56, 73, 216
Leone, Sergio 7, 14–15
Levien, Sonya 32
Libby, Fred 121, 185
The Life and Times of Judge Roy Bean 10
Little Big Man 9
Livingston, Jerry 140
London, Julie 14
The Long Riders 9
The Long Voyage Home 25, 27, 29, 56
The Lost Patrol 22, 25, 26, 27, 29, 30, 56
Louise, Anita 22
Lowery, Robert 32
Lyons, Cliff 189, 194, 219

McCabe and Mrs. Miller 9
McClintock! 7
McClory, Sean 61, 268
McCrea, Joel 14
MacDonald, J. Farrell 18, 19, 20, 156
McDonald, Joseph 151
McDowall, Roddy 31
"MacGuffin" 167
McGuinness, James Kevin 56
McIntyre, John 14, 194
McKinney, Bill 15
McLaglen, Victor 20, 23, 25, 27, 28, 51, 59, 65, 67, 83, 85, 98, 123
McNally, Stephen 13
The Magnificent Seven 12
Mahin, John Lee 40, 44
Mailer, Norman 83
Major Dundee 14
Malden, Karl 79, 119, 259
Malone, Molly 17
Mamokos, Peter 228
The Man from Colorado 7
The Man from Laramie 13
The Man from the Alamo 12
Man of the West 14
The Man Who Shot Liberty Valance 3, 4, 18, 21, 26, 27, 28, 29, 31, 40, 55, 56, 70, 71, 79, 147–184, 187, 234, 242,

247, 251, 262, 264, 276, 277, 281, 296
"The Man Who Shot Liberty Valance" (story) 19, 56, 58, 61, 64, 69–71
Man Without a Star 10
Mann, Anthony 7, 9, 13–14, 78, 187, 250, 281
March, Fredric 30
A Marked Man 18, 289
Marked Men 21, 71, 291
Marlowe, Christopher 271
Marsh, Mae 204, 228
Marshall, George 7, 18, 36
Martin, Strother 41, 70, 152, 165
Marvin, Lee 21, 26, 69, 150
Mary of Scotland 28, 29, 30, 56
Mason, Leroy 49, 261
"Massacre" 56, 61–64
Massey, Raymond 10, 24, 37
Mature, Victor 55, 61, 145
Maynard, Ken 5
Mazurki, Mike 43, 79, 261
Meek, Donald 60, 250
Men Without Women 56
Mendelssohn, Felix 226
MGM (studio) 22, 71
Miles, Vera 25, 75, 150, 219
Miller, Winston 56, 80
Mineo, Sal 80, 249
"Mission with No Name" 56, 66–68
The Missouri Breaks 9
Mister Roberts (novel) 83
Mitchell, Thomas 20, 25, 60, 61, 250
Mitchum, Robert 7
Mix, Tom 5, 19, 21
Mockridge, Cyril 150
Mogambo 11, 23, 24, 27, 29
Montalban, Ricardo 80, 97, 249
Montgomery, Robert 28
Monument Valley 118, 136, 137, 168, 187, 216, 253
Moore, Pauline 30
Moreno, Antonio 222
Morgan, Harry 36, 51
Morricone, Ennio 15
Morrison, Pete 18
Mowbray, Alan 81, 159, 186
Murray, Ken 61, 164
"My Country, 'Tis of Thee" 34
My Darling Clementine 4, 13, 20, 21, 24, 25, 26, 27, 29, 30, 36, 37, 44, 46,

55, 56, 59, 61, 62, 70, 71, 80, 81, 87,
100, 122, 147–184, 185, 186, 189, 196,
202, 207, 221, 226, 230, 234, 256,
262, 263, 280, 281, 293
My Fair Lady 249

Naish, J. Carroll 68, 87
The Naked and the Dead (novel) 83
The Naked Spur 13
Natwick, Mildred 23, 65, 119, 218
Nelson, Ralph 9
Newman, Alfred 33–34, 36–37, 150
Nichols, Dudley 13, 56, 271
Nolan, Jeanette 22, 70, 77, 155, 191
North, Alex 253, 257
North by Northwest 282
North of Hudson Bay 19, 292
"Now I Lay Me Down to Sleep" 221
Nugent, Frank 3, 56

"O Come All Ye Faithful" 225
"O My Darling Clementine" 149
O'Brien, Edmond 29, 61, 70, 152
O'Brien, George 19, 20, 21, 23, 44, 63,
85, 119, 141, 259
O'Hara, Maureen 27, 35, 42, 44, 67,
82, 116
Oliver, Edna May 32
O'Malley, Kathleen 187
Once Upon a Time in the West 14
One Eyed Jacks 7
Ortiz, Peter 95, 103
"Our Father" (prayer) 244
The Outcasts of Poker Flat 19, 291
The Outlaw 7
The Outlaw Josey Wales 15
The Ox-Bow Incident 11

Pale Rider 15, 35
Pat Garrett and Billy the Kid 14
Peck, Gregory 11
Peckinpah, Sam 7, 9, 14, 15
Pegg, Vester 17
Pendelton, Steve 103
Penn, Arthur 7, 9
Pennick, Jack 35, 47, 71, 83, 125, 165,
237, 271
Peppard, George 36

The Peter Principle 267
Peters, Jean 44
The Phantom Riders 18, 289
Pilgrimage 56
Pin Martin, Chris 250
The Plainsman (1936) 5, 92
Platt, Louise 60, 250
The Plough and the Stars 56
Porter, Edwin S. 5
Pratt, Judson 20, 42, 134, 263
The Prisoner of Shark Island 19, 22, 23,
29, 30, 37, 54
The Professionals 7
Pursued 7, 11
Pyle, Denver 41, 272

Qualen, John 30, 44, 70, 78, 152, 191,
219
The Quiet Man 3, 35, 44, 52, 56, 186
Quillan, Eddie 26

Rackin, Martin 40, 44
Rainey, Ford 191
Rancho Notorious 10
Ranown (production company) 13
Rapee, Erno 20
Ray, Nicholas 7, 12
Rebel Without a Cause 12
"Recall" (bugle) 53
Red River 10
Reed, Donna 27
Remington, Frederic 253
Rennahan, Ray 34
Republic (studio) 11
The Return of Frank James 10
Rich, Irene 23, 44, 63
Richards, Toby 121
Ride Lonesome 12
Ride the High Country 14
The Rider of the Law 19, 291
Riders of Vengeance 18, 291
Rio Bravo 10
Rio Grande 4, 24, 26, 27, 29, 35, 36,
42, 43, 47, 50, 51, 52, 54, 55, 56, 61,
66, 68, 82–117, 119, 128, 134, 146, 171,
183, 186, 197, 214, 220, 223, 256,
258, 260, 276, 279, 294
Rio Lobo 10
Rios, Elvira 258

The Rising of the Moon 56
Ritter, Tex 5
RKO (studio) 22, 187
Robards, Jason, Jr. 15
Robinson, Edward G. 29, 79, 258
Rogers, Roy 21
Roland, Gilbert 97, 256
Romero, Cesar 23, 80
Roped 18, 290
Ruggles, Wesley 5
Run of the Arrow 12
Russell, Bing 45, 260
The Rustlers 18, 290
Ruysdael, Basil 41
Ryan, Robert 13
Rydell, Mark 9

Sandoz, Mari 56, 78
Santa Fe Trail 10
Santschi, Tom 20
Sarris, Andrew 21
Saskatchewan 11
The Scarlet Drop 18, 290
Schaeffer, Jack 70
Scott, Pippa 138, 219
Scott, Randolph 7, 10, 11, 12, 13, 14, 80
The Scrapper 16, 289
The Searchers 4, 10, 13, 14, 17, 21, 24, 25, 26, 27, 28, 30, 31, 35, 36, 42, 43, 44, 47, 51, 53, 55, 56, 60, 64, 68, 71, 76, 114, 118, 122, 134, 138, 149, 171, 183, 185, 186, 191, 194, 210, 216–248, 251, 253, 255, 258, 275, 277, 281, 282, 294–295
The Searchers (novel) 73–76
Seas Beneath 56
The Secret Man 18, 289
Seel, Charles 127, 262
Selznick, David O. 10
Sergeant Rutledge 3, 4, 22, 26, 30, 31, 50, 52, 54, 61, 103, 118–146, 169, 180, 186, 234, 253, 256, 275, 279, 295
Sergeants Three 12
Seven Men from Now 12
Seven Women 11, 249
Shadow of a Doubt 282
Shakespeare, William 1
"Shall We Gather at the River" 149, 186, 225, 226, 256

Shane 10, 35, 70, 71, 281
She Wore a Yellow Ribbon 4, 14, 20, 23, 24, 25, 26, 27, 28, 29, 30, 31, 35, 37, 38, 41, 43, 50, 51, 52, 54, 56, 57, 59, 60, 61, 62, 64, 66, 67, 68, 98, 103, 118–146, 158, 171, 189, 190, 219, 222, 223, 224, 226, 234, 251, 253, 255, 256, 258, 259, 260, 264, 268, 270, 276, 277, 279, 294
Shields, Arthur 31, 128
The Shootist 9
Siegel, Don 9
"Silent Night" 225
Silver River 11
Silverado 9
Simon, Robert F. 70, 163
Simpson, Mickey 124, 185
Simpson, Russell 28, 41, 81, 160, 189
Sinclair, Harold 38, 41, 44–45
"Skip to My Loo" 227
Smith, C. Aubrey 23
Soldier Blue 9, 98
The Soul Herder 16, 289
"Stage to Lordsburg" 56, 59–61
Stagecoach 3, 4, 5, 7, 13, 17, 20, 22, 27, 29, 39, 55, 56, 59, 62, 63, 80, 153, 164, 191, 192, 195, 202, 223, 224, 230, 234, 249–278, 287, 292
Stallings, Laurence 57
Steamboat Round the Bend 56
Steele, Bill 240
Steele, Bob 5
Steiner, Max 226–227
Stevens, Charlie 25, 159
Stevens, George 10, 281
Stewart, James 13, 14, 36, 43, 55, 69, 76, 149, 186, 257
Straight Shooting 16–18, 20, 289
The Stranger Wore a Gun 11
Strangers on a Train 282
Strauss, Johann, Jr. 186
"The Streets of Laredo" 225
Strode, Woody 54, 70, 77, 118, 150, 187
Stuart, Gloria 22
Sturges, John 12
Styne, Jan 126
Summers, Don 26, 200
The Sun Shines Bright 27, 57
Sure Fire 19, 291

The Tall T 12, 13
Tamblyn, Russ 36
"Taps" (bugle) 140
Tellegen, Louis 20
Temple, Shirley 22, 23, 44, 64, 82
"Ten Thousand Cattle" 149
"There's No Place Like Home" 94
They Died with Their Boots On 11, 92
They Were Expendable 24, 25, 26, 27, 28, 29, 30, 64
Thieves' Gold 18, 290
Three Bad Men 5, 20–21, 292
Three Godfathers (1936) 71
Three Godfathers (1948) 3, 4, 5, 19, 21, 26, 27, 28, 30, 31, 44, 50, 55, 56, 57, 71, 122, 158, 185, 216–248, 281, 293
Three Godfathers (novel) 18, 21, 71–73
Three Jumps Ahead 19, 292
Three Mounted Men 18, 290
3:10 to Yuma 11
The Tin Star 13
Tiomkin, Dimitri 10
Tolstoy, Count Leo 71
Towers, Constance 27, 39, 125
Tracy, Spencer 24, 37
The Trail of Hate 16, 289
Trevor, Claire 60, 249
Trotti, Lamar 32
True Grit 11
The True Story of Jesse James 12
Twelve O'Clock High 83
20th Century–Fox (studio) 11, 22, 151
Two Mules for Sister Sara 15
Two Rode Together 3, 4, 13, 14, 22, 23, 24, 28, 30, 43, 52, 55, 56, 59, 76, 185–215, 219, 222, 243, 247, 251, 263, 267, 277, 280, 295–296
Tyler, Tom 35, 61, 118, 124, 255

Ulzana's Raid 12
Unforgiven 15
The Unforgiven 10, 73
Union Pacific 5
United Artists (studio) 73
Universal (studio) 11, 12, 16, 19
Uris, Leon 80

Van Cleef, Lee 70, 152, 165
Vera Cruz 12
Vernon, John 15
Vicksburg (battle) 41
Vidor, King 10
Virginia City 10, 47
The Virginian (1929) 5
Viva, Zapata! 7, 44

Wagner, Richard 236
Wagonmaster 4, 22, 26, 29, 30, 53, 55, 73, 177, 185–215, 220, 243, 251, 255, 256, 280, 281, 294
The Wallop 19, 291
Walsh, Arthur 159
Walsh, Raoul 5, 7, 9, 11
War and Peace (novel) 71
"War Party" 56, 64–66
Warden, Jack 25
Warner Bros. (studio) 10, 11, 249
Wayne, John 5, 7, 9, 10, 18, 23, 24, 25, 26, 27, 28, 30, 35, 37, 38, 42, 44, 51, 55, 59, 63, 64, 65, 67, 70, 71, 74, 82, 83, 97, 118, 143, 150, 216, 219, 249, 253
Wayne, Patrick 74, 219, 260
Weaver, Marjorie 30
Webb, James R. 56
Wee Willie Winkie 23, 24, 26, 27, 28, 29, 30
Wellman, William 11
Westbound 12, 13
Western Union 10
The Westerner 9
Whalen, Michael 30
What Price Glory 24, 26, 29, 30
"When Johnny Comes Marching Home" 37, 54
Whitehead, O. Z. 47
Widmark, Richard 14, 23, 43, 55, 76, 79, 186, 251
The Wild Bunch 14
Wild Women 18, 289
Wills, Chill 68, 86
Winchester '73 13, 281
Withers, Grant 62, 68, 85, 86, 100, 151
A Woman's Fool 18, 290
Wood, Lana 43, 219
Wood, Natalie 25, 219
Woods, Harry 100, 126, 179

Worden, Hank 10, 51, 71, 74, 98, 128, 185, 222, 225
Wouk, Herman 83
Wyatt Earp: Frontier Marshal (biography) 56, 80–81
Wyler, William 9

"Yankee Doodle" 34
"Yellow Ribbon" 139

"Yellow Rose of Texas" 226
Young, Carleton 30, 41, 52, 121, 125, 154, 272
Young Guns 9
Young Mr. Lincoln 25, 26, 28, 29, 30, 37, 54, 64, 87, 102, 125, 150

Zinnemann, Fred 7

Historical Impressions 138
" realities in film 39, 40
the journey motif 281
Male partnerships 279–281
portrayals of Indians 258–259
revenge motif 13;